Communications in Computer and Information Science 2769

Rationale

The CCIS series is devoted to the publication of proceedings of computer science conferences. Its aim is to efficiently disseminate original research results in informatics in printed and electronic form. While the focus is on publication of peer-reviewed full papers presenting mature work, inclusion of reviewed short papers reporting on work in progress is welcome, too. Besides globally relevant meetings with internationally representative program committees guaranteeing a strict peer-reviewing and paper selection process, conferences run by societies or of high regional or national relevance are also considered for publication.

Topics

The topical scope of CCIS spans the entire spectrum of informatics ranging from foundational topics in the theory of computing to information and communications science and technology and a broad variety of interdisciplinary application fields.

Information for Volume Editors and Authors

Publication in CCIS is free of charge. No royalties are paid, however, we offer registered conference participants temporary free access to the online version of the conference proceedings on SpringerLink (http://link.springer.com) by means of an http referrer from the conference website and/or a number of complimentary printed copies, as specified in the official acceptance email of the event.

CCIS proceedings can be published in time for distribution at conferences or as post-proceedings, and delivered in the form of printed books and/or electronically as USBs and/or e-content licenses for accessing proceedings at SpringerLink. Furthermore, CCIS proceedings are included in the CCIS electronic book series hosted in the SpringerLink digital library at http://link.springer.com/bookseries/7899. Conferences publishing in CCIS are allowed to use our online conference service (Meteor) for managing the whole proceedings lifecycle (from submission and reviewing to preparing for publication) free of charge.

Publication process

The language of publication is exclusively English. Authors publishing in CCIS have to sign the Springer CCIS copyright transfer form, however, they are free to use their material published in CCIS for substantially changed, more elaborate subsequent publications elsewhere. For the preparation of the camera-ready papers/files, authors have to strictly adhere to the Springer CCIS Authors' Instructions and are strongly encouraged to use the CCIS LaTeX style files or templates.

Abstracting/Indexing

CCIS is abstracted/indexed in DBLP, Google Scholar, EI-Compendex, Mathematical Reviews, SCImago, Scopus. CCIS volumes are also submitted for the inclusion in ISI Proceedings.

How to start

To start the evaluation of your proposal for inclusion in the CCIS series, please send an e-mail to ccis@springer.com

Byungjoon Kim
Editor

Frontiers of Computer Vision

31st International Workshop, IW-FCV 2025
Seoul, South Korea, February 10–12, 2025
Revised Selected Papers

Editor
Byungjoon Kim
Korea AI Certification
Seongnam, Korea (Republic of)

ISSN 1865-0929 ISSN 1865-0937 (electronic)
Communications in Computer and Information Science
ISBN 978-981-95-4577-3 ISBN 978-981-95-4578-0 (eBook)
https://doi.org/10.1007/978-981-95-4578-0

This Springer imprint is published by the registered company Springer Nature Singapore Pte Ltd.
The registered company address is: 152 Beach Road, #21-01/04 Gateway East, Singapore 189721, Singapore

Preface

This volume contains the proceedings of the 31st International Workshop on Frontiers of Computer Vision (IW-FCV 2025), held in Seoul, South Korea, on February 10–12, 2025. IW-FCV was initiated over three decades ago to foster academic collaboration among researchers in computer vision and artificial intelligence, particularly between South Korea and Japan. Over the years, it has evolved into an important international forum for presenting innovative research and applications in computer vision and related areas.

A total of 59 submissions were received for IW-FCV 2025. Following a single-blind peer review process, in which each paper received at least two independent reviews, 29 papers were initially accepted. After the final editorial process, 23 papers were included in this CCIS volume, consisting of 18 full papers and 5 short papers. No invited papers were included in this volume.

The papers included in this volume cover a wide range of timely and important topics, including video analysis, multimodal and cross-modal learning, robotic vision systems, digital content creation for cultural heritage, medical imaging applications, and recent advances in deep learning and image processing technologies.

We sincerely thank all members of the Organizing Committee and Program Committee, as well as the reviewers, authors, and participants, for their valuable contributions to IW-FCV 2025. We also express our gratitude to Springer Nature for publishing these proceedings in the Communications in Computer and Information Science (CCIS) series.

We hope that this volume will serve as a valuable resource and inspiration for researchers and practitioners in the field of computer vision.

May 2025

Byungjoon Kim
Yongduek Seo

Organization

General Chairs

Yongduek Seo	Sogang University, South Korea
Hiroyuki Ukida	Tokushima University, Japan

Program Chairs

Choonsung Shin	Chonnam National University, South Korea
Go Irie	Tokyo University of Science, Japan

Publication Chair

Byungjoon Kim	Korea AI Certification & Sogang University, South Korea

Technical Program Committee

Akinori Hidaka	Tokyo Denki University, Japan
Atsushi Shimada	Kyushu University, Japan
Chansoo Lee	Youngnam University, South Korea
Eiichiro Momma	Nihon University, Japan
Gou Koutaki	Kumamoto University, Japan
Hideo Saito	Keio University, Japan
Hidehiro Ohki	Oita University, Japan
Hiroaki Aizawa	Hiroshima University, Japan
Hirooki Aoki	Chitose University, Japan
Hironobu Fujiyoshi	Chubu University, Japan
Hiroshi Tanaka	Fujitsu Limited, Japan
Hitoshi Habe	Kindai University, Japan
Hyun-Deok Kang	UNIST, South Korea
In Kyu Park	Inha University, South Korea
Inseop Na	Chonnam National University, South Korea
Jae-Ho Lee	Electronics and Telecommunications Research Institute, South Korea

Jaeil Kim	Kyungpook National University, South Korea
Ji-Yun Cheon	Seoul Media Institute of Technology, South Korea
Keiji Yanai	University of Electro-Communications, Japan
Kazuaki Nakamura	Tokyo University of Science, Japan
Kenji Terada	Tokushima University, Japan
Kengo Terasawa	Future University Hakodate, Japan
Kyoung Ho Choi	Mokpo National University, South Korea
Kuryong Kwon	Pukyong National University, South Korea
Maiya Hori	Kyushu University, Japan
Manabu Hashimoto	Chukyo University, Japan
Masashi Nishiyama	Tottori University, Japan
Masashi Toda	Kumamoto University, Japan
Min-Jeong Oh	Chungang University, South Korea
Minoru Mori	Kanagawa Institute of Technology, Japan
Minsu Cho	Pohang University of Science and Technology, South Korea
Moon-Ho Jeon	Kwangwoon University, South Korea
Naoshi Kaneko	Tokyo Denki University, Japan
Namho Hur	Electronics and Telecommunications Research Institute, South Korea
Rui Ishiyama	NEC Corporation, Japan
Seiya Ito	National Institute of Information and Communications Technology, Japan
Soo Hyung Kim	Chonnam National University, South Korea
Soon Ki Jung	Kyungpook National University, South Korea
Soon-Yong Park	Kyungpook National University, South Korea
Shuichi Akizuki	Chukyo University, Japan
Suk Hwan Lee	Tong Myong University, South Korea
Takayoshi Yamashita	Chubu University, Japan
Takahiro Okabe	Okayama University, Japan
Takashi Shibata	NEC Corporation, Japan
Takayuki Fujiwara	Hokkaido Information University, Japan
Toru Tamaki	Nagoya Institute of Technology, Japan
Tsubasa Minematsu	Kyushu University, Japan
Wonjun Kim	Konkuk University, South Korea
Wataru Ohyama	Tokyo Denki University, Japan
Yoshinori Kuno	Saitama University, Japan
Youngho Lee	Mokpo National University, South Korea
Yuji Oyamada	Tottori University, Japan
Yusuke Kameda	Sophia University, Japan

Steering Committee

Jong-Il Park	Hanyang University, South Korea
Junichiro Hayashi	Kagawa University, Japan
Kazuhiko Sumi	Aoyama Gakuin University, Japan
Kanghyun Jo	University of Ulsan, South Korea
Kiryong Kwon	Pukyong National University, South Korea
Kunihito Kato	Gifu University, Japan
Makoto Niwakawa	Meidensha Corporation, Japan
Soon Ki Jung	Kyungpook National University, South Korea
Yoshimitu Aoki	Keio University, Japan

Advisory Committee

Chilwoo Lee	Chonnam National University, South Korea
Hiroyasu Koshimizu	Chukyo University/YYC-Solution, Japan
Kazuhiko Yamamoto	Gifu University, Japan
Rin-ichiro Taniguchi	Kyusyu University, Japan
Takio Kurita	Hiroshima University, Japan
Weon-Geun Oh	Electronics and Telecommunications Research Institute, South Korea

Contents

Extracting Temporal Features Robust to Headwear Variation from Video Sequences of Body Sway for Person Identification

Takuya Kamitani(✉), Haruki Nakayama, and Masashi Nishiyama

Tottori University, Tottori 680-0945, Japan
{takuya.kamitani,nishiya}@tottori-u.ac.jp

Abstract. Person identification can be performed using temporal features extracted from video sequences of body sway captured by an overhead camera. We propose a method for extracting such temporal features in a manner that is robust to headwear variation. When people are wearing headwear, such as a cap or helmet, their head shapes observed by the camera change significantly according to the type of headwear. Existing methods for person identification cannot achieve high accuracy in the presence of headwear variation because the features used by existing methods are strongly affected by the changes in head shapes. To extract temporal features that are not influenced by headwear variation, we measure the time-series signals representing body sway by estimating the center positions from head shapes. Moreover, we propose a learning-based low-pass filter to remove the components that are uninformative from the frequency components of the time-series signals, while retaining the informative components. Experimental results show that our temporal features significantly enhance the accuracy of person identification in the presence of headwear variation, compared with the use of existing features.

Keywords: Person identification · Headwear variation · Body sway · Temporal feature extraction · Learning-based low-pass filter

1 Introduction

Person identification is a technique for determining whether the same people appear in video sequences captured by cameras installed at different locations [1, 11, 12]. Person identification is often used to monitor people entering and exiting specific areas, such as factories and event venues. To identify people accurately, it is important to select cues that represent personal identities. In recent years, body sway has attracted attention as a suitable cue for person identification. Body sway refers to the subtle swaying movement of the entire body of a person while standing. By using body sway, it is possible to accurately identify people who are waiting for traffic lights to change or elevators to arrive.

B. Kim (Ed.): IW-FCV 2025, CCIS 2769, pp. 1–15, 2026.
https://doi.org/10.1007/978-981-95-4578-0_1

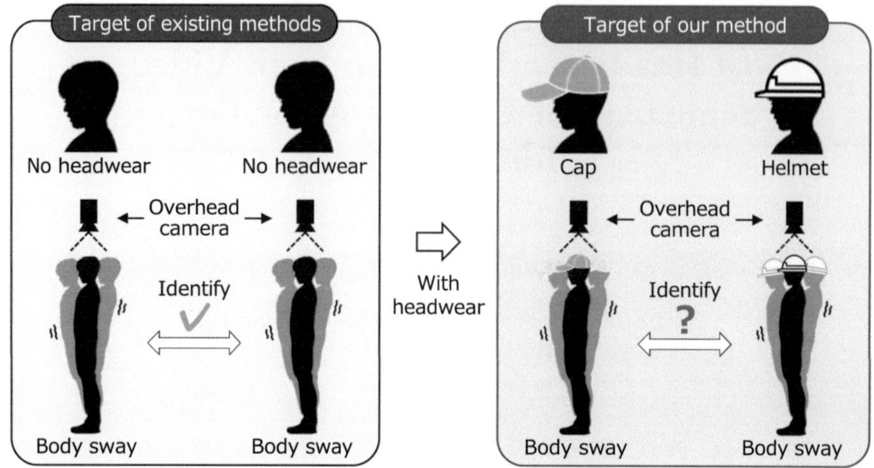

Fig. 1. Target of our method. Our method is intended to identify people with headwear in video sequences of body sway.

Several existing methods [5,6] have been proposed to identify people by their body sway from video sequences captured by an overhead camera. These existing methods determine whether two video sequences show the same person by extracting spatiotemporal features of head shape and head movement that uniquely identify each person. Existing methods have the constraint that people must not be wearing any headwear, as shown in Fig. 1. However, people sometimes do wear headwear that is suitable and appropriate for the situation. For example, factory workers may wear caps or helmets while working on production lines, and participants in costume events may wear long-hair wigs or Afro wigs to dress up.

When people are wearing headwear, their head shapes observed by an overhead camera change according to the type of headwear worn. Figure 2 shows examples of the head shapes of the same person without headwear and with a cap, a helmet, a long-hair wig, and an Afro wig. The figure compares the head shapes with and without headwear. The head shape with a cap is similar to an ellipse because of the hat brim. In addition, the head shape with a helmet is similar to a circle, and the shape with a long-hair wig or an Afro wig is similar to that of the wig itself. In summary, the head shape varies according to the type of headwear worn.

Problems arise if existing methods [5,6] are used directly to identify people with various types of headwear. The spatiotemporal features used by these existing methods capture personal identity by the spatial representation of shape and the temporal representation of movement. The spatial shape representation focuses on the head shape itself, whereas the temporal movement representation focuses on the slight movement of the head shape. Because both the spatial shape representation and the temporal movement representation rely on the head

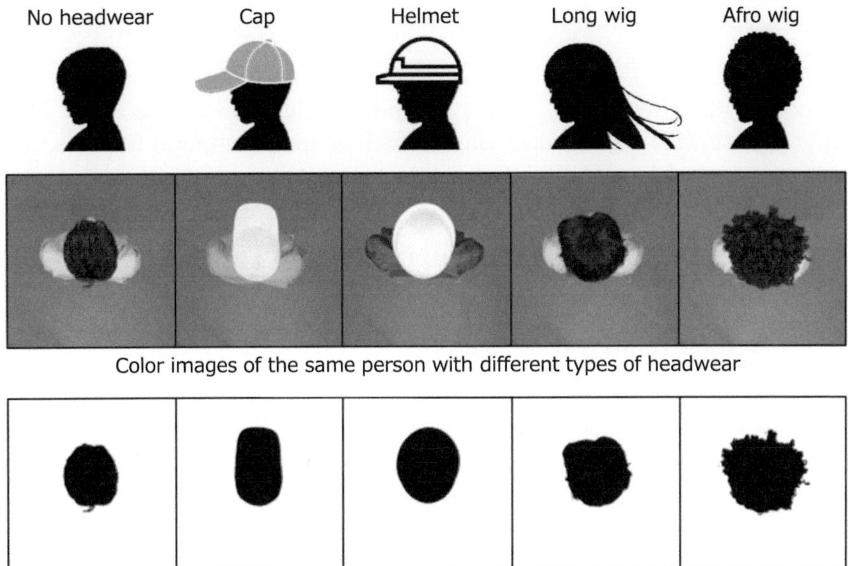

Fig. 2. Examples of variation in headwear types. Color images were acquired by an overhead camera, showing the same person wearing different types of headwear. Silhouette images, representing the head shape of the person with each type of headwear, were estimated from the color images. (Color figure online)

shape, the spatiotemporal features vary when the head shape varies. Therefore, person identification becomes less accurate if the existing spatiotemporal features are used to identify people wearing various types of headwear.

In this paper, we propose a method for extracting temporal features that are robust to headwear variation, in person identification using body sway, by avoiding representations that rely on head shape. We measure the time-series signals of the center positions estimated by spatially averaging the pixel coordinates of each head shape from a video sequence captured by an overhead camera. To enhance the accuracy of person identification, we then extract temporal features with only the low-frequency components of the time-series signal, using a newly designed learning-based low-pass filter.

Our contributions are summarized as follows.

- We clarify the existence of informative components and uninformative components contained in temporal features (Sect. 2.4).
- We present a learning-based low-pass filter that removes the uninformative components and retains the informative components to extract temporal features that are robust to headwear variation (Sect. 3.1).
- Using an original dataset of video sequences of people with no headwear and with four different types of headwear, we demonstrate significantly enhanced

accuracy of person identification in the presence of headwear variation, compared with existing methods (Sects. 3.2 and 3.4).

The experimental results show that the person identification accuracy of our temporal features is higher than that of existing spatiotemporal features in the presence of headwear variation.

2 Influence of Headwear Variation on Temporal Features Extracted from a Video Sequence of Body Sway

2.1 Design of Temporal Features

As noted in Sect. 1, the spatiotemporal features of existing methods [5,6] are strongly affected by head shape variation because these features have representations that rely on the head shape. Using these representations, it is hard to capture personal identity in the presence of headwear variation. Therefore, we consider extracting temporal features that focus only on the head movement, ignoring the head shape. To obtain such features, we improve the procedure for temporal feature extraction used by the existing methods. Specifically, we estimate the center positions of the head shape by averaging, and measure the time-series signals of head movement.

Figure 3 shows the procedure for temporal feature extraction that improves on that of existing methods [5,6]. First, in step P1, we acquire a color video sequence using an overhead camera and estimate a silhouette sequence of the head shape from it. We apply the deep image matting technique [10] to perform this silhouette estimation. Second, in step P2, we estimate the center positions of the head shapes in the silhouette sequence. Specifically, in each silhouette frame, we calculate the center position as a two-dimensional vector by spatially averaging the pixel coordinates of the head shape. We then set the origin to the average of the center positions. Third, in step P3, we measure two time-series signals by treating each component of the two-dimensional vectors separately in the left–right and front–back directions. Fourth, in step P4, we estimate power spectral densities [9] from each time-series signal using the Fourier transform. Finally, we extract temporal features by combining these power spectral densities into one. In this paper, we refer to this feature extraction procedure as the improved existing method. Despite our improvements, we found that this method achieved only small improvements in person identification accuracy in the presence of headwear variation. In the following sections, we experimentally investigate why the accuracy improvements were small when the improved existing method was used.

2.2 Evaluation Dataset

We created an original dataset to evaluate person identification accuracy in the presence of headwear variation. We acquired color video sequences of the body

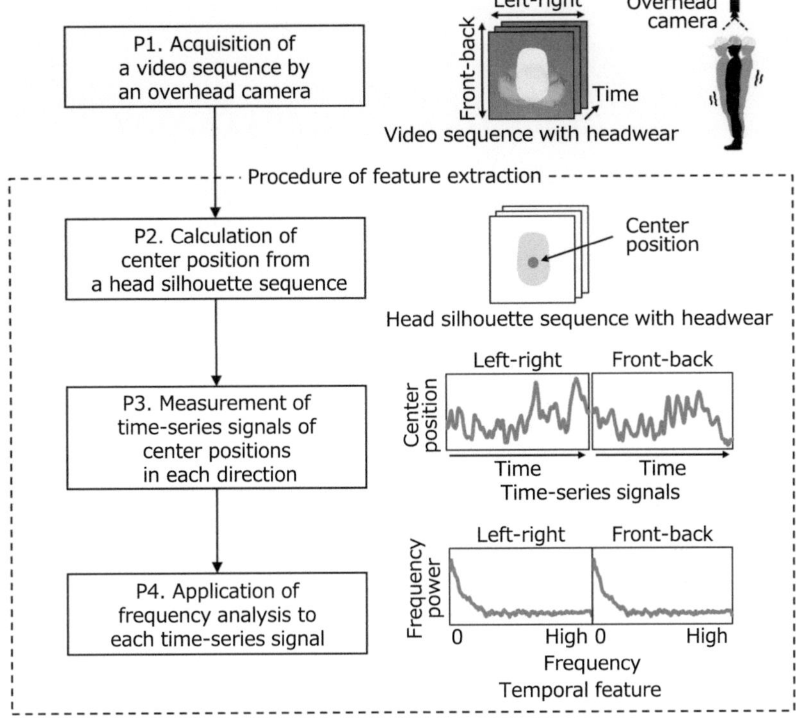

Fig. 3. Procedure used by the improved existing method of Sect. 2.1 for extracting temporal features from a video sequence of body sway by estimating center positions from head shapes.

sway of participants with no headwear and with the following four different types of headwear.

No Headwear: Participants had no headwear, representing a situation in which people are commuters. There were no restrictions on the hairstyle of each participant. Figures 4(a) and 5(a) show examples of participants with no headwear observed from above and from the side, respectively.

Cap: Participants wore yellow caps with brims, representing a situation in which people work on a production line of small consumer goods. We instructed all participants to wear these caps so that the brims were in the same direction as their faces. Figures 4(b) and 5(b) show examples of participants wearing caps observed from above and from the side.

Helmet: Participants wore white helmets with short brims, representing a situation in which people are employed in a large industrial factory. We instructed all participants to wear these helmets so that the short brims were in the same direction as their faces. Figures 4(c) and 5(c) show examples of participants wearing helmets observed from above and from the side.

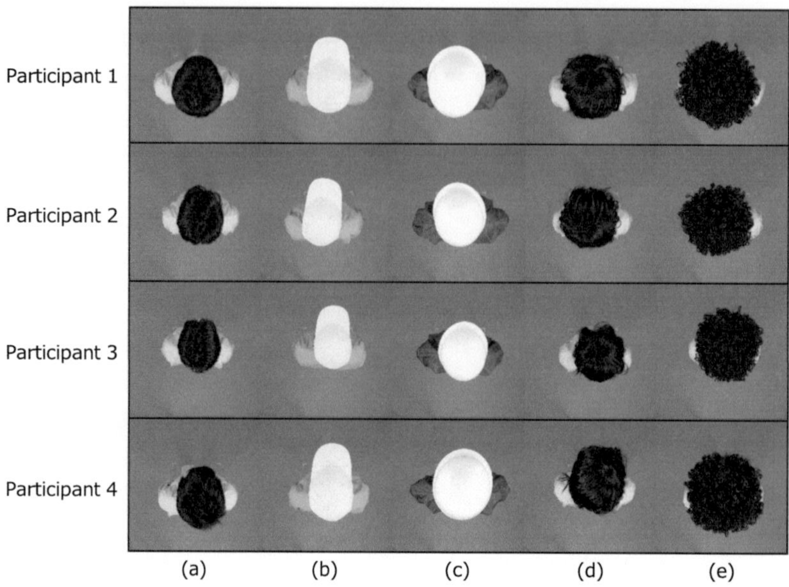

Fig. 4. Examples of color images of participants when wearing different types of headwear. The participants were observed from an overhead camera. The images in each row show the same person and those in each column depict the same type of headwear. Columns (a), (b), (c), (d), and (e) show images with no headwear, a cap, a helmet, a long wig, and an Afro wig, respectively. (Color figure online)

Long Wig: Participants wore long wigs, representing a situation in which people appear on a theatre stage. We instructed all participants to wear these wigs so that the long-hair parts of the wigs remained behind their heads. Figures 4(d) and 5(d) show examples of participants wearing long wigs observed from above and from the side.

Afro Wig: Participants wore Afro wigs, representing a situation in which people attend a costume event. We instructed all participants to wear these wigs in an arbitrary direction. Figures 4(e) and 5(e) show examples of participants wearing Afro wigs observed from above and from the side.

We observed 50 participants with mean age of 22.0 (standard deviation 1.9) years. Figure 6 shows the environment in which the body sway of the participants was observed. Participants were instructed to maintain an upright posture and focus on the designated marker during observation. An overhead camera was set at a height of 2.4 m above the floor. A mark was placed on the floor under the overhead camera and participants were instructed to stand on it. The camera resolution was set to 1920×1080 pixels and the sampling rate 30 Hz. Each participant was observed twice for each type of headwear, and each participant's headwear was replaced in a random order. Hence, the total number of observations per participant was ten. The length of each observation was 120 s.

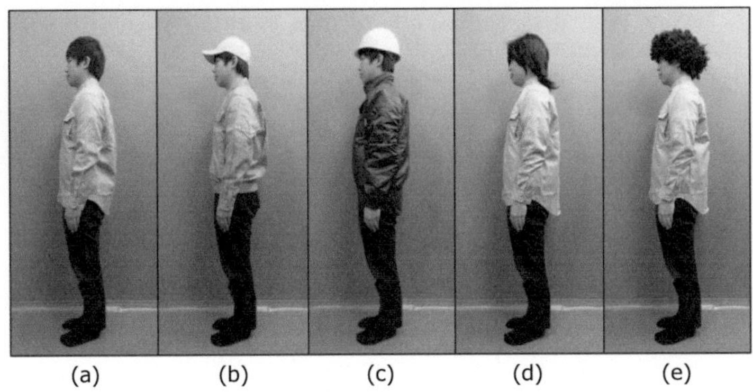

Fig. 5. Examples of color images of a participant wearing different types of headwear. The participant was observed by a side-view camera. (Color figure online)

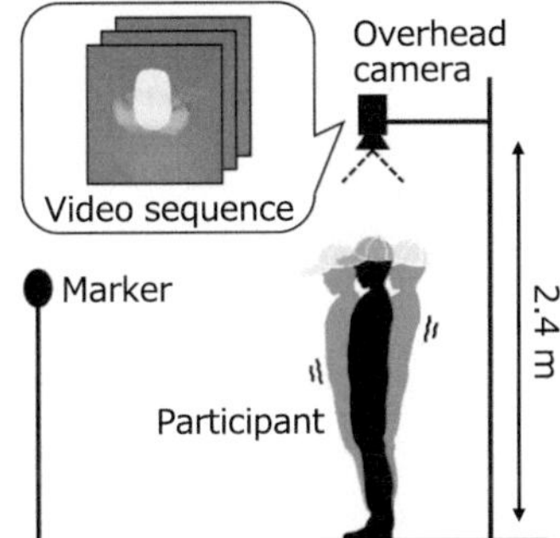

Fig. 6. Experimental setting for capturing a video sequence using an overhead camera.

2.3 Accuracy of Person Identification Using Temporal Features of Improved Existing Method

We evaluated the accuracy of person identification in the presence of headwear variation. The purpose of this experiment was to confirm that the accuracy enhancement was slight even if we used the temporal features of the improved existing method, as noted in Sect. 2.1. The person identification task performed in this experiment was a search for the person appearing in a query video sequence among preregistered galleries of video sequences. We selected one of the five types of headwear for the query and a different type for the gallery in each trial of person identification. Hence, there were ${}_5\mathrm{P}_2 = 20$ permutations of headwear types for person identification. We applied the nearest neighbor algorithm with Euclidean distance for identifying people by using temporal features of the improved existing method. The number of participants for person identification was 50. We used the n-th matching rate and the normalized area under the curve (nAUC) of the cumulative match characteristics to evaluate the accuracy of person identification. The n-th matching rate is the probability that the

Table 1. Comparison of the accuracy (%) of person identification using the existing methods [5,6] and the improved existing method (Sect. 2.1).

Method	N = 1	N = 5	N = 10	N = 15	NAUC
Existing methods [5,6]	3.7	14.2	26.4	36.2	56.2
Improved existing method (Sect. 2.1)	5.2	18.8	31.3	43.3	59.7

person appearing in a query also appears in one of the top n galleries when the galleries are ranked in order of similarity (to the query). A larger value of the n-th matching rate indicates better accuracy. The nAUC is the area under the curve plotting the n-th rank (on the horizontal axis) against the n-th matching rate (on the vertical axis). A larger value of nAUC indicates better accuracy.

Table 1 shows the n-th matching rates and nAUC of the improved existing method and of the existing methods. From the experimental results, we confirmed that the improved existing method is only a slight enhancement of the existing methods. In the next section, we investigate the reason for this and explore the possibility of a more significant enhancement of the person identification accuracy.

2.4 Influence of Headwear Variation on Temporal Features

In this section, we investigate why the improved existing method could not enhance the accuracy of person identification. We assume the reason to be that its temporal features contain components that are uninformative for person identification in the presence of headwear variation. When these uninformative components are present, even if the query and gallery show the same person, the distance between the temporal features of the query and those of the gallery may be large. Furthermore, if the query and gallery show different people, the distance between the temporal features of the query and those of the gallery may be small. Consequently, we believe that these uninformative components may lead to incorrect identification.

To investigate the existence of uninformative components contained in the temporal features of the improved existing method, we calculated the within-person and between-person distances from the temporal features. The within-person distance was calculated when the query and gallery showed the same person. Conversely, the between-person distance was calculated when the query and gallery showed different people. To obtain these distances, we subtracted the frequency powers of the temporal features of the query from those of the temporal features of the gallery, squared the differences, and summed them for all frequency powers. We believe that the frequency bands in which the within-person and between-person distances are similar contain uninformative components that cause errors in person identification.

Figure 7 shows the within-person and between-person distances in temporal features of the improved existing method. The figure shows that the within-person and between-person distances are similar for frequencies greater than

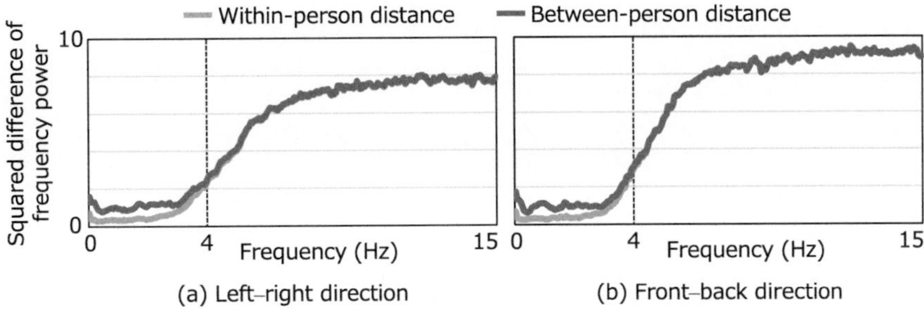

Fig. 7. Within-person and between-person distances in temporal features of the improved existing method. The orange and purple curves plot the within-person and between-person distances, respectively. (a) Left–right direction. (b) Front–back direction. (Color figure online)

4.0 Hz (the high-frequency band) in both the left–right (a) and front–back (b) directions. Conversely, the within-person and between-person distances are different for frequencies less than 4.0 Hz (the low-frequency band). These results suggest that the temporal feature components in the high-frequency band are uninformative and should be removed to enhance the person identification accuracy in the presence of headwear variation. Conversely, the temporal feature components in the low-frequency band are informative and should be retained. In the next section, we describe how to extract temporal feature components only in the low-frequency band and remove those in the high-frequency band.

3 Temporal Features of the Proposed Method

3.1 Design of a Learning-Based Low-Pass Filter

To enhance the accuracy of person identification in the presence of headwear variation, we need to extract temporal feature components in the low-frequency band, as explained in Sect. 2.4. To achieve this, we propose a learning-based low-pass filter that determines the range of the low-frequency band containing only components that are informative for person identification. To design this low-pass filter, we need to select a suitable threshold. The threshold is a parameter that determines the range of the low-frequency band. We consider selecting this threshold automatically, according to the distances between temporal features. The ideal threshold should decrease the within-person distance and increase the between-person distance. The proposed method uses a separation metric [7] to automatically find such a threshold. The separation metric should have a high value if the within-person distances are small and the between-person distances are large. We use this method to select thresholds separately in the left-right and front-back directions of body sway.

To obtain a threshold that is robust to headwear variation, we prepare a training dataset of temporal features of people wearing multiple types of headwear. The separation metric chosen is the ratio of the between-person distance to the within-person distance. We calculate the values of the separation metric by searching frequencies of temporal features at fixed intervals in the training dataset from zero to the maximum obtainable frequency. We then select the threshold that maximizes the value of the separation metric.

The proposed method is intended to perform person identification in a manner that is robust to headwear variation by extracting temporal features with a learning-based low-pass filter. Figure 8 shows the procedure used by the proposed method. The steps from P1 to P4 are the same as in Fig. 3. Step P5 of the proposed method uses a learning-based low-pass filter to extract the frequency powers of the low-frequency band only.

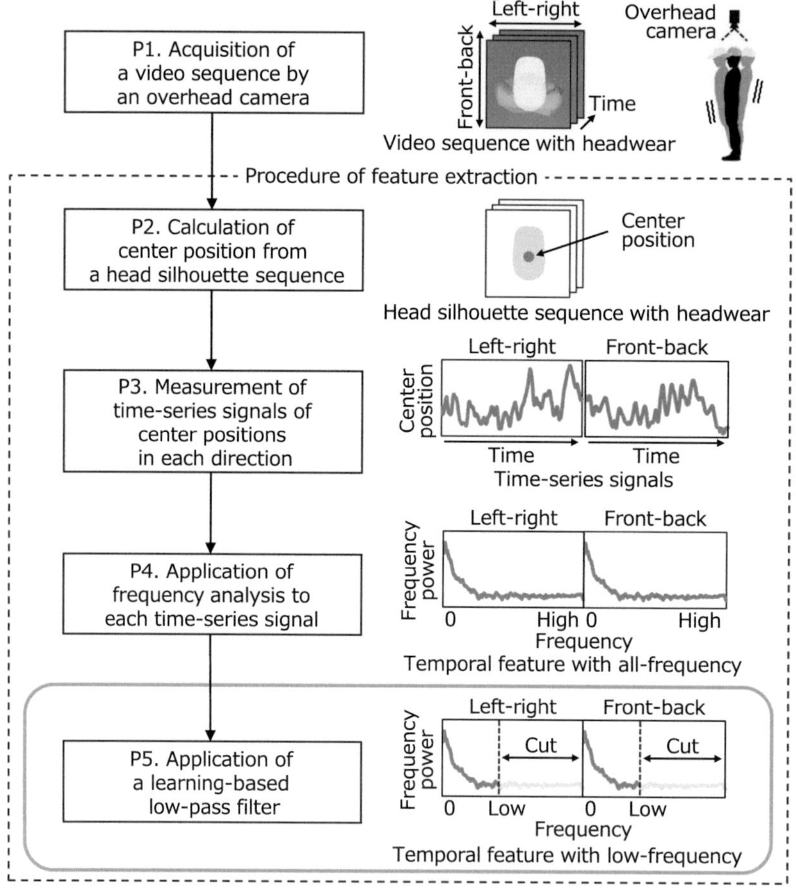

Fig. 8. Procedure used by the proposed method with a learning-based low-pass filter for extracting temporal features in the low-frequency band from a video sequence of body sway.

3.2 Accuracy of Person Identification Using Temporal Features of the Proposed Method

We investigated whether temporal features of the proposed method with a learning-based low-pass filter could enhance the accuracy of person identification in the presence of headwear variation. We created two sets (training set and evaluation set) of video sequences from the 50 participants described in Sect. 2.2. The training set contained ten randomly selected participants and the evaluation set contained the remaining 40 participants. The training set always included the five types of headwear described in Sect. 2.2. For each training set, we searched for the optimal threshold of the low-pass filter in 0.05-Hz increments. We repeated each trial, in which ten participants were randomly selected as the training set, five times and calculated the accuracy of person identification for each trial. We set the threshold of the low-pass filter to a constant value for each evaluation set. The other experimental conditions were the same as those described in Sect. 2.3. We again used the n-th matching rate and nAUC to evaluate the accuracy of person identification.

Table 2 shows the n-th matching rate and nAUC of person identification using temporal features of the proposed method and the improved existing method. The proposed method and the improved existing method were described in Sects. 3.1 and 2.1, respectively. The results show that the temporal features of the proposed method are superior to those of the improved existing method with respect to person identification accuracy. Therefore, we believe that the proposed method can enhance the accuracy of person identification in the presence of headwear variation.

Table 2. Comparison of the accuracy (%) of person identification using our proposed method (Sect. 3.1) and the improved existing method (Sect. 2.1).

Method	N = 1	N = 5	N = 10	N = 15	NAUC
Proposed method (Sect. 3.1)	**44.2**	**78.6**	**89.2**	**94.2**	**92.1**
Improved existing method (Sect. 2.1)	6.3	21.9	38.1	51.0	60.1

3.3 Comparison with the Use of Temporal Features in the High-Frequency Band

In the previous section, we demonstrated that the proposed method could enhance the accuracy of person identification by extracting temporal features from only the low-frequency band, using a learning-based low-pass filter. In this section, we discuss the accuracy achieved when temporal features are extracted from the high-frequency band. We compared temporal features extracted from the low-frequency band with those extracted from the high-frequency band and those obtained without filtering. The other experimental conditions were the same as those described in Sect. 3.2.

Table 3 shows the n-th matching rate and nAUC of person identification using temporal features extracted from the low-frequency band, the high-frequency band, and without filtering. The results indicate that the use of temporal features from only the low-frequency band enhances the accuracy of person identification compared with the use of features from only the high-frequency band or without filtering. Therefore, we believe that using only a low-frequency band is beneficial for temporal feature extraction for identifying people accurately from body sway in the presence of headwear variation.

Table 3. Comparison of the accuracy (%) of person identification using temporal features extracted from the low-frequency band, the high-frequency band, and without filtering.

Frequency band	N = 1	N = 5	N = 10	N = 15	NAUC
Low-frequency band (proposed)	**44.2**	**78.6**	**89.2**	**94.2**	**92.1**
High-frequency band	4.5	17.1	31.5	44.6	55.6
Without filtering (low+high frequencies)	6.3	21.9	38.1	51.0	60.1

3.4 Comparison with Features of Existing Methods Based on Human Movement

The proposed method extracts temporal features from body sway, which is a type of human movement. Existing methods have been proposed that extract features from human movement other than body sway, for example, gait recognition [4] and action recognition [2,3,8]. Because the features extracted by these existing methods are based on human movement, they may achieve high accuracy in person identification when head shape varies because of headwear variation. To test this hypothesis, we evaluated the person identification accuracy achieved by the use of features extracted with GEI [4], DI [3], C3D [8], and TimeSformer [2]. It should be noted that we used convolutional neural networks to reduce the dimensionality of GEI and DI features and extracted only factors that are significant for enhancing the accuracy of person identification. We applied the nearest neighbor algorithm when identifying people using each feature, in the same manner as in Sect. 3.2. The experimental conditions other than the feature extraction methods were the same as those described in Sect. 3.2. The details of the feature extraction of existing methods are as follows.

Gait Energy Image (GEI) [4]**:** We extracted features by using GEI and ResNet101. We created 15 GEIs by randomly cutting out 15 short video sequences of length 8.5 s from the silhouette sequence described in Sect. 2.1 and averaging the short video sequence as a single image. To enhance the person identification accuracy, we used a pretrained ResNet101 model with ImageNet-1k and

Table 4. Comparison of the accuracy (%) of person identification using the proposed method, the existing method using gait recognition [4], and the existing methods using action recognition [2,3,8].

Method	N = 1	N = 5	N = 10	N = 15	NAUC
Proposed	**44.2**	**78.6**	**89.2**	**94.2**	**92.1**
GEI [4]	8.0	30.2	53.3	69.9	72.4
DI [3]	15.8	45.9	67.5	81.4	80.4
C3D [8]	16.2	47.8	68.1	79.7	79.8
TimeSformer [2]	10.1	33.4	52.1	64.7	70.1

fine-tuned it with 1500 GEIs created from the training set described in Sect. 3.2. Finally, we obtained feature maps by inputting the GEIs into ResNet101.

Dynamic Image (DI) [3]**:** We extracted features by using DI and ResNet101. We created 15 DIs by randomly cutting out 15 short video sequences from a color video sequence, in the same manner as described above for GEI, and applying RankSVM to each short video sequence. To enhance the person identification accuracy, we used a pretrained ResNet101 model with ImageNet-1k and fine-tuned it with 1500 DIs from the training set. Finally, we obtained feature maps by inputting the DIs into ResNet101.

C3D [8]**:** We extracted features by using C3D. We acquired 15 short video sequences in the same manner as described above for DI. We selected 16 frames from each short video sequence at equal intervals to reduce memory usage. We then trained the C3D model with 1500 short video sequences created from the training set. Finally, we obtained feature maps by inputting the short video sequences into C3D.

TimeSformer [2]**:** We extracted features by using TimeSformer. We acquired 15 short video sequences in the same manner as described above for DI. We selected eight frames from each short video sequence at equal intervals to reduce memory usage. We then used a pretrained TimeSformer model with Kinetics-400 and fine-tuned it with 1500 short video sequences created from the training set. We used divided space-time attention as a self-attention scheme. Finally, we obtained feature maps by inputting the short video sequences into TimeSformer.

Table 4 shows the n-th matching rate and nAUC of person identification using the features of our method of Sect. 3.1 and the existing methods [2–4,8] that are based on human movement. The results indicate that the features of the proposed method are superior to those of the existing methods with respect to person identification accuracy. This experiment provided further confirmation that the proposed method can enhance the accuracy of person identification in the presence of headwear variation.

4 Conclusions

In this paper, we proposed a method of extracting temporal features that are robust to headwear variation for person identification using a video sequence of body sway observed by an overhead camera. When people wear headwear, their head shapes in a video sequence become different even though they have the same identity. To alleviate the influence of head shape changes caused by headwear variation, we measured time-series signals by estimating center positions from each person's head shapes. Furthermore, we discovered that frequency powers of the time-series signal in the low-frequency band contained components that were more informative for person identification in the presence of headwear variation. Therefore, we designed a learning-based low-pass filter using separation metrics to automatically extract the frequency powers in the low-frequency band from the time-series signal. The experimental results show that the proposed method using the learning-based low-pass filter can extract temporal features that are informative for person identification in the presence of headwear variation. Moreover, we confirmed that the proposed method achieves significantly higher accuracy of person identification than existing methods that were designed for extracting features from human movement.

In future work, we will further enhance the accuracy of person identification in the presence of headwear variation by examining the underlying mechanism of body sway. Furthermore, we plan to identify people wearing other types of headwear.

Acknowledgments. We thank Professor Yoshio Iwai for his valuable advice and suggestions during this research.

References

1. Bedagkar-Gala, A., Shah, S.K.: A survey of approaches and trends in person re-identification. Image Vis. Comput. **32**(4), 270–286 (2014)
2. Bertasius, G., Wang, H., Torresani, L.: Is space-time attention all you need for video understanding? In: Proceedings of the International Conference on Machine Learning (2021)
3. Bilen, H., Fernando, B., Gavves, E., Vedaldi, A.: Action recognition with dynamic image networks. IEEE Trans. Pattern Anal. Mach. Intell. **40**, 2799–2813 (2017)
4. Han, J., Bhanu, B.: Individual recognition using gait energy image. IEEE Trans. Pattern Anal. Mach. Intell. **28**(2), 316–322 (2006)
5. Kamitani, T., Yamaguchi, Y., Nishiyama, M., Iwai, Y.: Identifying people using body sway in case of self-occlusion. In: Proceedings of International Workshop on Frontiers of Computer Vision, pp. 1–13 (2020)
6. Kamitani, T., Yoshimura, H., Nishiyama, M., Iwai, Y.: Temporal and spatial analysis of local body sway movements for the identification of people. IEICE Trans. Inf. Syst. **102**(1), 165–174 (2019)
7. Otsu, N.: A threshold selection method from gray-level histograms. IEEE Trans. Syst. Man Cybern. **9**(1), 62–66 (1979)

8. Tran, D., Bourdev, L., Fergus, R., Torresani, L., Paluri, M.: Learning spatiotemporal features with 3D convolutional networks. In: Proceedings of the IEEE International Conference on Computer Vision, pp. 4489–4497 (2015)
9. Welch, P.: The use of fast Fourier transform for the estimation of power spectra: a method based on time averaging over short, modified periodograms. IEEE Trans. Audio Electroacoust. **15**(2), 70–73 (1967)
10. Xu, N., Price, B., Cohen, S., Huang, T.: Deep image matting. In: Proceedings of the IEEE Conference on Computer Vision and Pattern Recognition, pp. 2970–2979 (2017)
11. Zheng, L., Shen, L., Tian, L., Wang, S., Wang, J., Tian, Q.: Scalable person re-identification: a benchmark. In: Proceedings of the IEEE International Conference on Computer Vision, pp. 1116–1124 (2015)
12. Zheng, L., Zhang, H., Sun, S., Chandraker, M., Yang, Y., Tian, Q.: Person re-identification in the wild. In: Proceedings of the IEEE Conference on Computer Vision and Pattern Recognition, pp. 1367–1376 (2017)

Multi-Group Vision Semantic Centroid for Semantic Segmentation

Jialei Chen[1(✉)], Daisuke Deguchi[1], Chenkai Zhang[1], Zhenzhen Quan[1,2], Seigo Ito[1], and Hiroshi Murase[1]

[1] Nagoya University, Nagoya 464-8601, Japan
{chen.jialei.s6,zhang.chenkai.d4, quan.zhenzhen.g7}@s.mail.nagoya-u.ac.jp, {ddeguchi, murase}@nagoya-u.jp, iseigo@vislab.is.i.nagoya-u.ac.jp

[2] Shandong University, Qingdao 266237, Shandong, China

Abstract. Multi-media processing has achieved great success based on semantic segmentation. Semantic segmentation can be viewed as pixel clustering based on semantic prototypes. However, existing methods focus more on consistent semantics while ignoring the consistency in vision, making this task challenging. Motivated by the success of discrete visual representation learning, we propose Multi-group Visual Semantic Centroid (MVSC) to better cluster the pixels while maintaining consistent semantics of the dense features for any image encoder. Specifically, we randomly initialize multiple groups of prototypes as multi-groups in visual space. The visual features are also randomly split into the same groups and forced to be aligned with the corresponding prototypes. Then these visual prototypes are projected into the semantic space and supervised by the same classifier as the dense features. Compared with existing methods, MVSC further considers the visual space and thus facilitates the task. Experimental results on COCO-Stuff show great improvements compared with previous methods.

Keyword: Category centroid · Representation learning · Semantic segmentation

1 Introduction

For multi-media processing, semantic segmentation improves the user experience by enhancing the content understanding in many aspects, *e.g.*, AR/VR scenarios. Different from the image classification task that recognizes the category of the whole image [19, 24], semantic segmentation aims to classify each pixel into its right category [5, 6, 22]. Since FCN [22] treats semantic segmentation as a pixel level classification, semantic segmentation has entered into a new era.

Before the wide use of transformer [26], researchers try to enlarge the receptive field, *e.g.*, DeepLab series [6, 7], deformable convolution [11], and fuse the multi-scale information, *e.g.*, FCN [22], PSPNet [32] to improve the segmentation performance. After the great success of ViT [13], designing transformer structures fitting for segmentation became popular, *e.g.*, Segformer [30], SETR [33].

B. Kim (Ed.): IW-FCV 2025, CCIS 2769, pp. 16–29, 2026.
https://doi.org/10.1007/978-981-95-4578-0_2

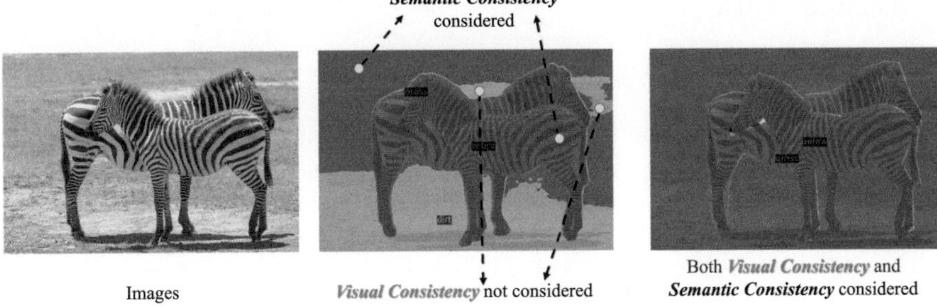

Fig. 1. Visual consistency and semantical consistency. Visual consistency indicates that the pixels belonging to the same object should belong to the same category. While the semantical consistency demonstrates that the pixels belonging to the same category should be segmented correctly. Existing methods pay much attention to the semantical consistency (the top caption in the middle image) while ignoring the visual consistency (the bottom caption in the middle image). Our methods consider both semantical and visual consistency.

When we revisit the semantic segmentation, we find that this task can be decoupled into two aspects: semantic consistency and visual consistency as shown in Fig. 1. Semantic consistency demonstrates that each pixel should be correctly classified, while visual consistency demonstrates that the pixels of one object should belong to the same category. Though remarkable, existing methods devoted all their efforts to maintaining semantical consistency, while ignoring visual consistency, leading to sub-optimal performance.

Motivated by the success of discrete visual representation learning [14, 25], we propose Multi-group Visual Semantic Centroid (MVSC) to consider both visual and semantical consistency for any image encoder. Specifically, we first randomly initialize a group of vectors that contains the same number as the categories in the dataset, acting as the prototypes for each category in the vision space. Then the visual features from the feature extractor are also randomly separated into G groups as different groups and aligned with the corresponding visual category prototypes. Finally, the visual category prototypes are mapped to the semantic space and supervised by pixel-level annotations with the same classifier as the dense representation. To further model the visual diversity, we expand the Visual Semantic Centroid to Multi-group Visual Semantic Centroid by expanding one group of centroids to multiple groups.

Different from the existing methods that devote all the efforts to semantical consistency, our methods further consider visual consistency. Experimental results on COCO-Stuff [2] dataset show great performance improvement compared with previous methods in mIoU.

In summary, our contributions can be listed as follows:

1) We propose MVSC to entangle the vision and semantics.
2) We propose a novel way to optimize the MVSC.
3) Experimental results show great improvements on COCO-Stuff.

2 Related Work

2.1 CNN-Based Semantic Segmentation

As one of the most significant tasks in computer vision, semantic segmentation aims to classify each pixel into its right category. Based on this idea, FCN [22], as the first fully convolutional network for semantic segmentation, inspires the following researchers. For example, DeepLab series [6, 7] enlarges the receptive field to further improve the performance. Deformable convolution [11] and Non-local network [28] further expand the receptive fields by breaking the fixed geometric structures of CNN modules. There are also some methods that utilize the multiscale features to enhance the representation ability, especially for the small and the boundary of different categories. For example, FCN [22] and SegNet [1] add the features of different scales from the encoder while recovering the size of the output features. Though remarkable, existing CNN-based segmentation methods fail to consider visual consistency leading to sub-optimal performance.

2.2 Transformer-Based Semantic Segmentation

Since the great success of the self-attention mechanism in natural language processing [26], more and more research endeavors try to transfer the success from language to vision. ViT [13] as one of the representative works proves the potential of transformer in computer vision. Since then, transformers are applied to many downstream tasks [3, 8, 9, 21]. For semantic segmentation, transformer based methods can be grouped into two categories: backbone design and sparse prediction. Backbone design methods try to design the backbone that fits the semantic segmentation, *e.g.*, Segformer [30], SETR [33]. Sparse prediction methods, *e.g.*, maskformer [9] and mask2former [8], leverage the property of the transformer decoder where a group of trainable queries is first initialized. During training, these queries are matched with the ground truth through bipartite matching, and the classification and mask prediction are decoupled. However, the queries are data-agnostic which leads to sub-optimal performance.

3 Method

3.1 Preliminaries and Method Overview

Visual and semantical consistency in semantic segmentation. Given a dataset $\mathrm{D} = \{\mathbf{X}_i, \mathbf{Y}_i\}_{i=0}^{M}$ where $\mathrm{X}_i \in \mathrm{R}^{H\times W}$ is the images, $\mathrm{Y}_i \in$ is the corresponding pixel-level annotation, i is the index of the image, and M indicates the size of the dataset. During training, $\underset{D\times H\times W}{\mathbf{X}}$ is first fed into an image encoder to obtain the pixel-level representation R where D indicates the channel numbers. Finally, R is fed into a trainable classifier W_c for prediction.

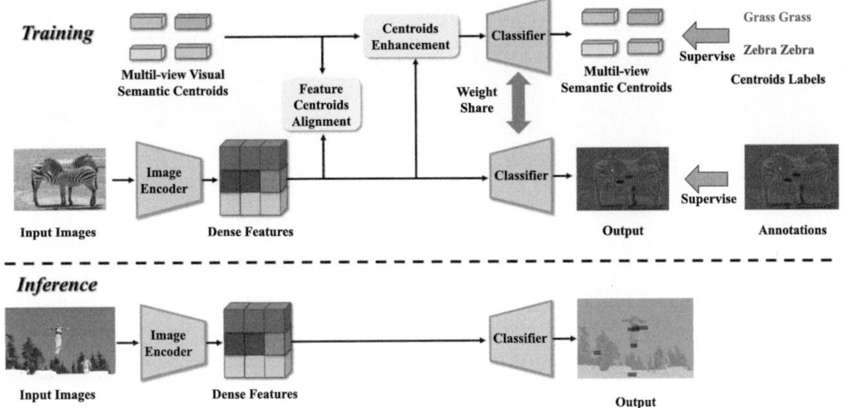

Fig. 2. The overview of the proposed methods. During training, We first initialize multi groups of vectors as the vision semantic centroids as multi-groups. Then, the image is fed into an image encoder to obtain the dense features. The dense features and the centroids are then aligned through the feature centroid alignment and centroid enhancement. Finally, the features and the centroids are put into the same classifier and supervised by the corresponding labels.

A very natural observation is that a baby does not know any category information about the world, but the baby can tell which objects belong to the same category. We call this property visual consistency. Then, an adult can teach the child what category this object belongs to and be agnostic about the environment. We call this property semantical consistency. Though many works try to improve the segmentation performance in many ways, *e.g.*, designing powerful backbones [17, 30, 33], enlarging the receptive fields [6, 11] or utilizing multi-scale features [1, 22, 29], they still achieve sub-optimal performance due to the mere focus on semantic consistency and the ignorance on visual consistency. Similar works are maskformer and mask2former, however, the queries are data-agnostic, and our method is not.

Method overview. The overall structure is shown in Fig. 2. To consider the visual consistency, we propose Multi-group Visual Semantic Centroids (MVSC). First, we randomly initialize G groups of vectors as the category centroid as multi-groups in visual space, and each group contains the same number of categories in a dataset. Then, to ensure visual consistency, the visual features are aligned with the centroids through Feature Centroid Alignment. Next, inspired by the great success of discrete representation in image generation [14, 25], we enhance the MVSC by the centroid enhancement. Finally, the MVSC and the visual features are projected to the semantic space by the same classifier and supervised by the corresponding category and pixel-level annotations. We will introduce the details in the following sections (Fig. 3).

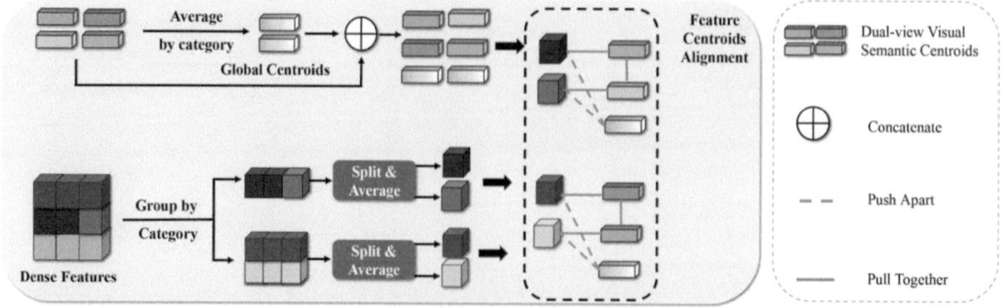

Fig. 3. The overview of Multi-group Visual Semantic Centroids (MVSC). Multiple groups of category centroids are first averaged within the same category across different groups to obtain global centroids. Next, the features are divided into the same groups as the category centroids and averaged based on their ground-truth labels. Finally, contrastive learning is applied to pull centroids from the same group closer together while pushing centroids from different groups further apart.

3.2 Feature Centroid Alignment

Before the training procedure, we randomly initialize G groups of vectors $\mathrm{V}_1,\mathrm{V}_2...\mathrm{V}_g$ as the centroids of each category in vision space where $\mathrm{V}_1,\mathrm{V}_2,...\mathrm{V}_g \in \mathrm{R}^{C\times D}$ and C indicates the number of categories. Given one mini-batch of input $X_b^{B\times H\times W}$ where B is the size of the mini-batch and the corresponding annotations Y_b, suppose there are N unique categories in X_b. First, based on Y_b, we group the visual features R_b by the categories to obtain a set C. Each element in C is:

$$\mathrm{C} = \{\mathrm{R}_n\}\text{where } \mathrm{R}_n = \mathrm{R}_b \cdot 1(\mathrm{Y}_b = n) \tag{1}$$

where $n \in N$ indicates the nth category in Y_b. Then the R_n is randomly split into the same groups and the elements in each group are averaged to obtain the centers of each group $\mathrm{R}_{n1},\mathrm{R}_{n2}...\mathrm{R}_{ng}$.

For each group of centroids, we also average them to obtain the global centroid $\mathrm{V}_G \in \mathrm{R}^{C\times D}$. The Feature Centroid Alignment can be represented as:

$$\mathcal{L}_{fca}(R,V) = \sum_{i}^{N} \frac{r_i^T \cdot v_i}{r_i^T \cdot v_i + \sum_{j\neq i}^{N} r_i^T \cdot v_{j'}}, \tag{2}$$

where $v^{'} \in \mathrm{V}_G$ indicates the global centroid of a specific category. Besides, to further enhance the visual consistency, we further pull close the centroids belonging to the same category. Specifically, we randomly separate the centroids except the global centroid into two groups. Then we reduce the cosine similarity of the two groups:

$$\mathrm{L}_{cos}(V_1, V_2) = 1 - cos(V_1, V_2), \tag{3}$$

3.3 Centroid Enhancement

Though Feature Centroids Alignement improves the visual consistency, the Visual Semantic Centroids are still data-agnostic, leading to sub-optimal visual consistency.

In this section, we propose a simple but effective Centroid Enhancement to solve this problem inspired by the great success of discrete representation in image generation [14, 25].

Specifically, after obtaining R_n, we pick the centroids $R^{'}$ whose labels appear in Y_b. Then we update the $V^{'}$ as:

$$V' = V + R - SG(R) \tag{4}$$

where SG indicates the stop gradient operation. Then, the augmented centroids are fed into the classifier and supervised by the corresponding category labels.

Discussions on Centroid Enhancement. Though simple, we want to discuss the reasons why this operation works. The first reason is that this operation to implicitly extracts the region-level information. Even if the value of the centroid does not change, the gradient of the visual features that are assigned to the centroid is copied. The copied gradient helps the image encoder learn the region-level information. The second reason is that the copied gradient helps the upgrade of the vision semantic centroids. To make the analysis easier, we ignore the gradient of L_{fca}. Without the copied gradient, the gradient for the visual semantic centroids is $\partial L/\partial W_c$ where L indicates the total loss. With the copied gradient the new gradient for the visual semantic centroid is $\partial L/\partial W_c \cdot (1 + \partial W_c/\partial E)$. Note that $\partial W_c/\partial E$ indicates the scale of how the encoder increases. Therefore, the visual semantic centroids can update at the same scale as the encoder and avoid the encoder's collapse to meaningless centroids.

3.4 Training Objectives and Inference

During training, the total loss functions are listed as follows:

$$L = \lambda_f \cdot L_{fca} + \lambda_c \cdot L_{cos} + L_{ce} + \lambda_v \cdot L_v \tag{5}$$

where λ_c, λ_f and λ_v are hyperparamters to control the scale of the corresponding loss. During Inference, as shown in Fig. 2 (bottom), only the image encoder and the classifier is needed for the final output.

4 Experiments

4.1 Experiment Setup

Dataset and Implementation Details. We conducted experiments on the COCO-Stuff dataset [2] where 9K images are used for training and 1K images are used for evaluating the final performance. For the categories, this dataset contains 80 object categories, *e.g.*, person, car, and 91 stuff categories, *e.g.*, grass, wall. For semantic segmentation, all the 171 categories are used.

Table 1. Comparison with State-of-the-Art Methods on COCO-Stuff Dataset where the highest performance is highlighted in bold.

Publication	Method	Backbone	mIoU	Gain
CVPR15	FCN [22]	RN101 [19]	33.0	+10.6
CVPR19	SVCNet [12]	RN101 [19]	39.6	+4.0
ECCV18	DANet [15]	RN101 [19]	39.7	+3.9
ICCV19	SpyGR [20]	RN101 [19]	39.9	+3.7
ICCV19	ACNet [16]	RN101 [19]	40.1	+3.5
ECCV20	OCR [31]	HRNetV2 [27]	40.5	+3.1
NeurIPS21	MaskFormer [9]	RN101 [19]	39.8	+3.8
TPAMI21	HRNet [27]	HRNetV2 [27]	38.7	+4.9
CVPR22	ProtoSeg [35]	Swin-B [21]	42.4	+1.2
CVPR22	ProtoSeg [35]	MiT-B4 [30]	43.3	+0.3
CACML24	CM [4]	MiT-B4 [30]	43.2	+0.4
NeurIPS21	SegFormer [30] SegFormer+Ours	MiT-B4 [30]	42.9 43.6	+0.7

We use MMsegmentation [10] as the base to complete our algorithm. For each experiment in one dataset, we follow the default settings. Specifically, for COCO-Stuff, all the backbones are first pre-trained on ImageNet1K [23] and the decode head initialized by He initialization [18]. We rescale the short scale of the image to train crop size while keeping the aspect ratio unchanged. Random scale jittering with a factor in [0.5, 2], random horizontal flipping, random cropping, and random color jittering are applied as the data augmentation. The optimizer is AdamW. The learning rate is scheduled following the polynomial annealing policy. In addition, the batch size is 16 and the crop size is 512 × 512 pixels. 80K iterations are needed to obtain the best performance. τ is set to 0.07. λ_f is set as 0.1 and λ_c is set as 1, and λ_v is set as 0.05 in training.

For simplicity, we do not apply any test-time data augmentation. Our model is implemented in PyTorch and trained on 8 V100 GPUs with 32 GB memory per card. Testing is conducted on the same machine. We report each model's mean intersection over the union (mIoU) score.

4.2 Comparison with State-of-the-Art

We conduct experiments on the COCO-Stuff dataset to compare the performance with other methods as shown in Table 1. From the table, we observe that traditional methods like FCN and SVCNet, which utilize the ResNet-101 backbone, achieve mIoUs of 33.0% and 39.6%, respectively. More recent methods, such as MaskFormer and ProtoSeg, demonstrate improvements, with mIoUs of 39.8 and 43.3%. Notably, SegFormer, which uses the MiT-B4 backbone, achieves a strong performance with a mIoU of 42.9%. First, we compare the performance with the baseline method Segformer [30]. For Segformer-B4, they achieve 42.9% mIoU. After adding our proposed methods, the performance boosts up to 43.6%, which is a 0.7% improvement, indicating our effectiveness.

Table 2. Ablation on the CE where 'CE' indicates the centroid enhancement.

$\mathcal{L}_{cfa}$	$\mathcal{L}_{cos}$	$\mathcal{L}_{v}$	CE	mIoU	mAcc
✓	✓	✓	✓	**32.6**	**44.0**
-	✓	✓	✓	31.4	41.8
✓	-	✓	✓	32.2	43.0
✓	✓	-	✓	32.3	43.3
✓	✓	✓	-	32.1	42.8
-	-	-	-	30.9	41.1

Table 3. Ablation on the group of prototypes.

Group Num	Backbone	mIoU	mAcc
1	Segformer-B0	32.2 32.0	43.1 43.4
2		32.6	44.0
4			
8		32.3	43.8

Compared with other SOTA methods, *e.g.*, ProtoSeg [35], under the same backbone, *i.e.*, Segformer-B4, our method can still be 0.3% higher than them. When we compare one of the latest methods, *i.e.*, CM [4], we can achieve 0.4% higher mIoU than them. In summary, Our approach achieves the highest mIoU score of 43.6%. This demonstrates the superiority of our method compared to both classical and modern segmentation techniques.

Visualization of Predictions. We further visualize the prediction of our model as shown in Fig. 6. We can find that our method has very similar results with the ground truth label indicating the effectiveness of our method.

4.3 Ablation Study

To evaluate whether each proposed method can work as expected, we conduct ablation experiments on all the parts of the proposed methods. Note that for the ablation studies, to further indicate the generalization of our method, the dataset we use is ADE20K dataset [34] which is comprised of 150 categories to be segmented. For this dataset, 20K images are used for training and 2K images for evaluation. The model we use is Segformer-B0 and trains 20K iterations. λ is set as 0.05 and γ is set as 0.1 during training (Table 2).

First, we conducted a comprehensive evaluation of the effectiveness of each component in our model, with the results detailed in Table 3. The baseline model, which serves as our point of comparison, does not incorporate any of the proposed enhancements and achieves a baseline performance of 30.9% mIoU and 41.1% mAcc. This serves as a foundational reference for understanding the impact of each subsequent modification.

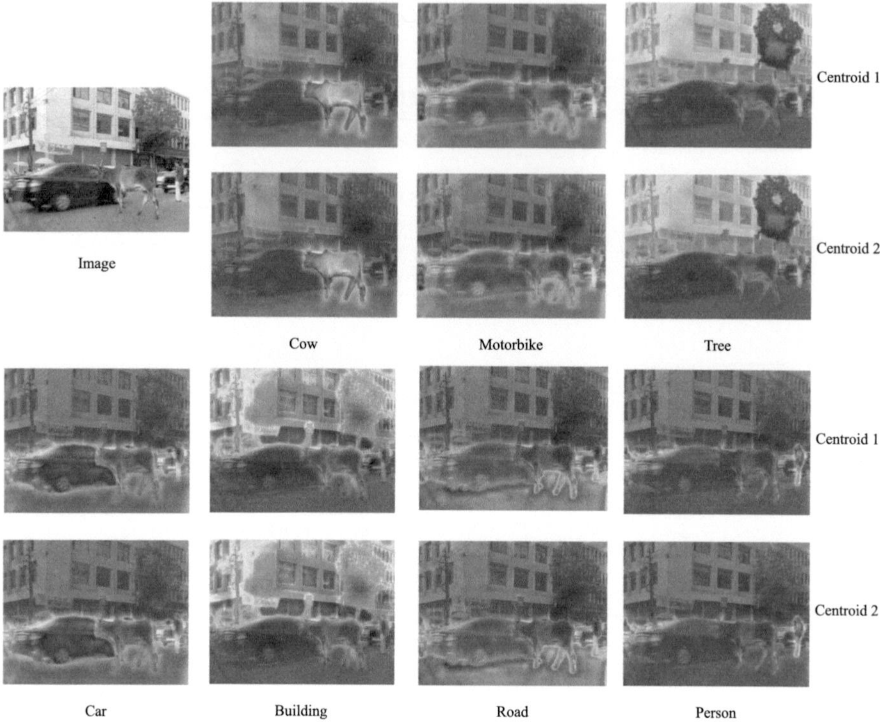

Fig. 4. Visualization of centroid heatmap in complex scenes where the red color indicates that the pixel is similar to the centroid and the blue color indicates the opposite.

As illustrated in the table, when all the proposed methods are integrated, our model achieves its peak performance, with mIoU rising to 32.6% and mAcc to 44.0% (first row). This demonstrates the synergistic effect of combining our techniques, yielding substantial improvements in both segmentation accuracy and mean accuracy. To better understand the contribution of each individual component, we systematically ablated them one by one. First, we removed the centroid-feature alignment mechanism, which led to a noticeable decrease in performance, with mIoU dropping to 31.4% and mAcc to 42.4% (second row). This indicates the critical role that clustering plays in organizing and refining the visual space, ensuring that similar features are grouped effectively, which directly enhances segmentation performance. Next, we evaluated the impact of the centroid-pulling mechanism, specifically the loss function L_{cos}, which is designed to ensure the compactness of centroids in the feature space. When this component was ablated, the model's performance suffered a significant reduction, with mIoU decreasing by 0.4% and mAcc by 1.0%. This substantial drop underscores the importance of maintaining tight, well-defined clusters in the feature space, which is crucial for accurate and consistent segmentation. Following this, we examined the effect of removing the projection back to the semantic space, represented by L_v. The absence of this component led to a decline in performance, with mIoU falling to 32.2% and mAcc to 43.3%. This result highlights the necessity of semantic consistency, as projecting features back to the semantic space ensures that the learned features remain aligned with the semantic labels, thereby preserving the interpretability and accuracy of the segmentation output. Lastly, we considered the effect of removing the centroid enhancement technique. Without this enhancement, the model's performance further declined, with mIoU reduced to 32.1% and mAcc to 42.8%. This demonstrates the value added by the centroid enhancement process, which strengthens the representation of feature centroids and thus contributes to the overall robustness and precision of the segmentation model. Collectively, these ablation studies provide strong evidence for the effectiveness of each proposed method. The consistent improvements across various metrics, when these methods are applied, affirm their importance in achieving superior segmentation performance. Each component plays a vital role in refining the model's ability to accurately segment and classify objects within complex visual scenes, leading to SOTA results.

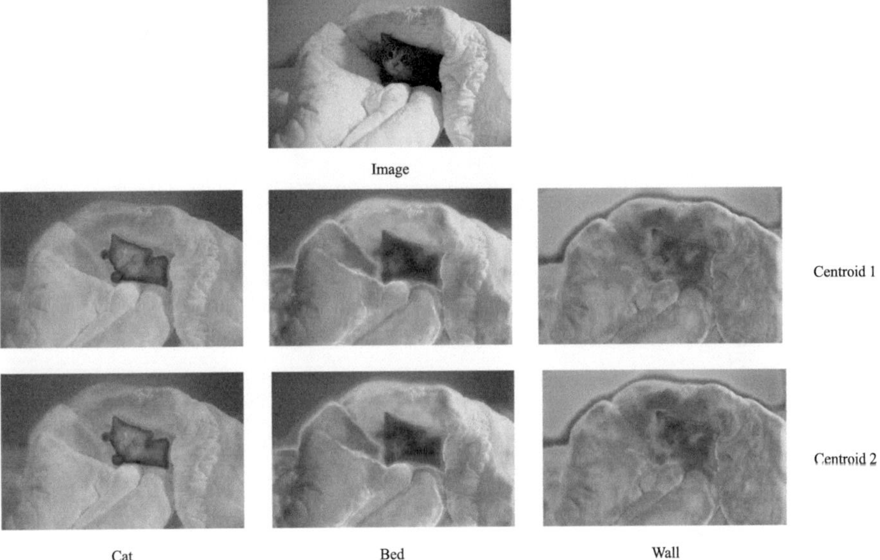

Fig. 5. Visualization of centroid heatmap in simple scenes where the red color indicates that the pixel is similar to the centroid and the blue color indicates the opposite.

Next, we conduct experiments on the group number of prototypes, and the results are shown in Table 3. As can be seen from this table, when the group number is set as 4, the model can reach its best mIoU and mAcc performance to 32.6% and 44.0%. Note that when multi-group strategy is not used, *i.e.*, the group is set as 1, the performance drops to 32.2% for mIoU and 43.1% to mAcc indicating the effectiveness of multi-group strategies.

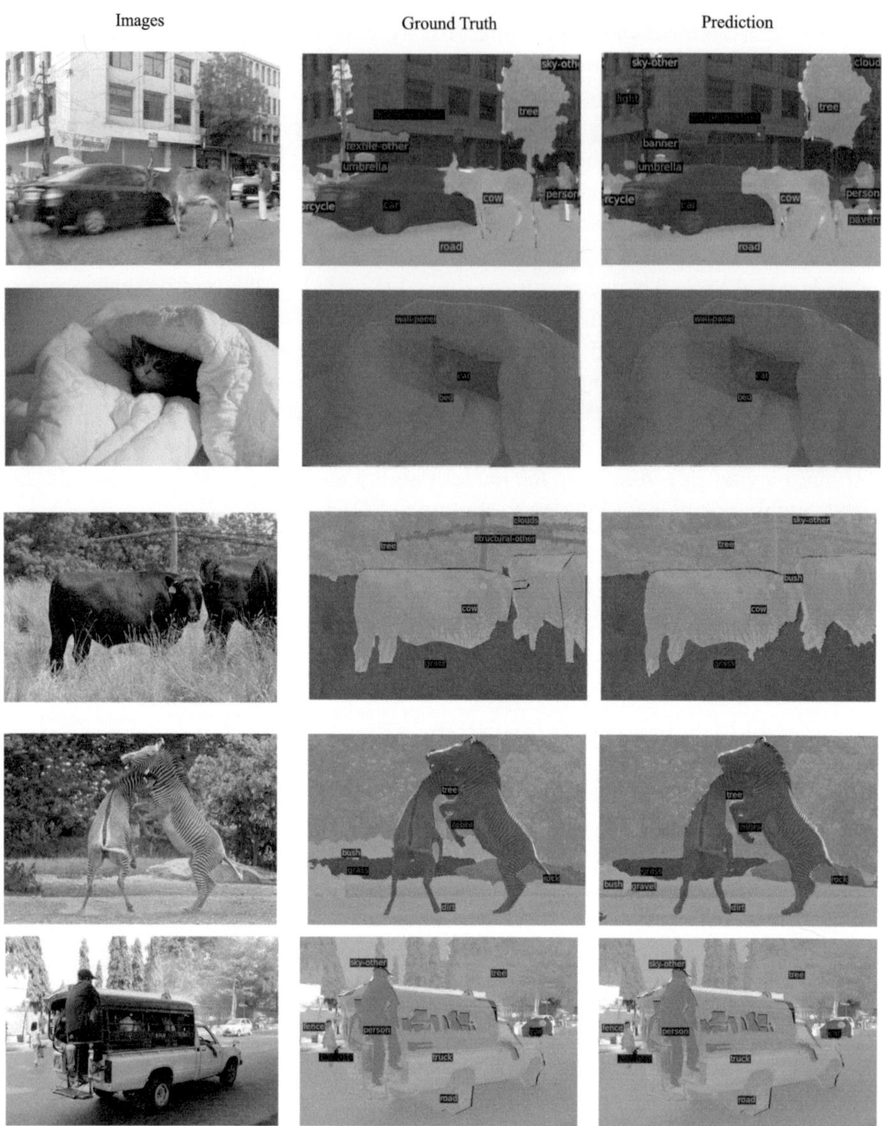

Fig. 6. Visualization of the prediction.

4.4 Qualitative Results

Visualization of centroid heatmap where the red color indicates that the pixel is similar to the centroid and the blue color indicates the opposite. First, we visualize the centroid to validate if the features are clusters in the visual space. We randomly choose two images as the visualization sample. Next, we compute the cosine similarity between the dense features and the centroid by group and visualize it. The results are shown in Fig. 4 and Fig. 5. We randomly choose two of the four prototypes to visualize. From Fig. 4, we can find that no matter the large objects, *e.g.*, buildings and roads, or small objects, *e.g.*, person and motorbike, the visual features are all very compact with the centroids. In Fig. 5, even the categories with similar appearance, *i.e.*, wall and bed, the visual features can be grouped into the right category, indicating the effectiveness of our methods. Visualization of Predictions. Finally, we visualize the predictions of our model as shown in Fig. 6. First, we give the prediction of the images in Fig. 4 and 5. As can be seen from the figure, the corresponding objects can be segmented correctly. Besides, we give another 4 images and all of them can achieve satisfying results.

5 Conclusion

In this paper, we presented a Multi-group Visual Semantic Centroid (MVSC) method, aimed at improving semantic segmentation performance for any image encoder. MVSC is motivated by the consideration that semantic segmentation should consider both visual consistency and semantic consistency. To achieve these two consistencies, we propose Feature Centroid Alignment and Centroids Enhancement to optimize the MVSC. Feature Centroid Alignement clusters the dense features in the visual space and Centroids Enhancement helps the centroids be updated at the same scale as the image encoder. Through extensive experiments and comparative analysis with state-of-the-art methods, our approach demonstrated superior performance, achieving a new benchmark mIoU of 43.6. This result not only surpasses the original SegFormer model by a significant margin of +0.7 mIoU but also outperforms other leading segmentation models. Future work could explore the application to additional segmentation tasks, further solidifying its role in next-generation computer vision systems.

Acknowledgment. This work was supported by the annual project funding of the Smart State Governance Laboratory, Shandong University, and JSPS KAKENHI Grant Number 23K28164 and 24H00733, and JST CREST Grant Number JPMJCR22D1. All the computations of this paper are carried out on the supercomputer "Flow" at the Information Technology Center, Nagoya University.

References

1. Badrinarayanan, V., Kendall, A., Cipolla, R.: Segnet: a deep convolutional encoder-decoder architecture for image segmentation. IEEE Trans. Pattern Anal. Mach. Intell. **39**(12), 2481–2495 (2017)
2. Caesar, H., Uijlings, J., Ferrari, V.: Coco-stuff: thing and stuff classes in context. In: Proceedings of the IEEE Conference on Computer Vision and Pattern Recognition, pp. 1209–1218 (2018)
3. Carion, N., et al.: Endto-end object detection with transformers. In: European Conference on Computer Vision, pp. 213–229. Springer (2020)
4. Chen, J., Deguchi, D., Zhang, C., Murase, H.: Centroid module for shaping feature space in semantic segmentation. In: Proceedings of the 2024 3rd Asia Conference on Algorithms, Computing and Machine Learning. CACML '24, New York, NY, USA, pp. 71–75. Association for Computing Machinery (2024). https://doi.org/10.1145/3654823.3654837

5. Chen, J., Deguchi, D., Zhang, C., Zheng, X., Murase, H.: Frozen is better than learning: a new design of prototype-based classifier for semantic segmentation. Pattern Recogn. **152**, 110431 (2024)
6. Chen, L.C., Papandreou, G., Kokkinos, I., Murphy, K., Yuille, A.L.: Deeplab: semantic image segmentation with deep convolutional nets, atrous convolution, and fully connected crfs. IEEE Trans. Pattern Anal. Mach. Intell. **40**(4), 834–848 (2017)
7. Chen, L.C., Zhu, Y., Papandreou, G., Schroff, F., Adam, H.: Encoder-decoder with atrous separable convolution for semantic image segmentation. In: Proceedings of the European Conference on Computer Vision (ECCV), pp. 801–818 (2018)
8. Cheng, B., Misra, I., Schwing, A.G., Kirillov, A., Girdhar, R.: Masked-attention mask transformer for universal image segmentation. In: Proceedings of the IEEE/CVF Conference on Computer Vision and Pattern Recognition, pp. 1290–1299 (2022)
9. Cheng, B., Schwing, A., Kirillov, A.: Per-pixel classification is not all you need for semantic segmentation. Adv. Neural. Inf. Process. Syst. **34**, 17864–17875 (2021)
10. Contributors, M.: Mmsegmentation: openmmlab semantic segmentation toolbox and benchmark (2020)
11. Dai, J., et al.: Deformable convolutional networks. In: Proceedings of the IEEE International Conference on Computer Vision, pp. 764–773 (2017)
12. Ding, H., Jiang, X., Shuai, B., Liu, A.Q., Wang, G.: Semantic correlation promoted shape-variant context for segmentation. In: Proceedings of the IEEE/CVF Conference on Computer Vision and Pattern Recognition, pp. 8885–8894 (2019)
13. Dosovitskiy, A., et al.: An image is worth 16x16 words: transformers for image recognition at scale. arXiv preprint arXiv:2010.11929 (2020)
14. Esser, P., Rombach, R., Ommer, B.: Taming transformers for high-resolution image synthesis. In: Proceedings of the IEEE/CVF Conference on Computer Vision and Pattern Recognition, pp. 12873–12883 (2021)
15. Fu, J., et al.: Dual attention network for scene segmentation. In: Proceedings of the IEEE/CVF Conference on Computer Vision and Pattern Recognition, pp. 3146–3154 (2019)
16. Fu, J., et al.: Adaptive context network for scene parsing. In: Proceedings of the IEEE/CVF International Conference on Computer Vision, pp. 6748–6757 (2019)
17. Guo, M.H., Lu, C.Z., Hou, Q., Liu, Z., Cheng, M.M., Hu, S.M.: Segnext: rethinking convolutional attention design for semantic segmentation. Adv. Neural. Inf. Process. Syst. **35**, 1140–1156 (2022)
18. He, K., Zhang, X., Ren, S., Sun, J.: Delving deep into rectifiers: surpassing humanlevel performance on imagenet classification. In: Proceedings of the IEEE International Conference on Computer Vision, pp. 1026–1034 (2015)
19. He, K., Zhang, X., Ren, S., Sun, J.: Deep residual learning for image recognition. In: Proceedings of the IEEE Conference on Computer Vision and Pattern Recognition, pp. 770–778 (2016)
20. Li, X., Yang, Y., Zhao, Q., Shen, T., Lin, Z., Liu, H.: Spatial pyramid based graph reasoning for semantic segmentation. In: Proceedings of the IEEE/CVF Conference on Computer Vision and Pattern Recognition, pp. 8950–8959 (2020)
21. Liu, Z., et al.: Swin transformer: hierarchical vision transformer using shifted windows. In: Proceedings of the IEEE/CVF International Conference on Computer Vision, pp. 10012–10022 (2021)
22. Long, J., Shelhamer, E., Darrell, T.: Fully convolutional networks for semantic segmentation. In: Proceedings of the IEEE Conference on Computer Vision and Pattern Recognition, pp. 3431–3440 (2015)
23. Russakovsky, O., et al.: Imagenet large scale visual recognition challenge. Int. J. Comput. Vision **115**, 211–252 (2015)

24. Szegedy, C., et al.: Going deeper with convolutions. In: Proceedings of the IEEE Conference on Computer Vision and Pattern Recognition, pp. 1–9 (2015)
25. Van Den Oord, A., Vinyals, O., et al.: Neural discrete representation learning. In: Advances in Neural Information Processing Systems, vol. 30 (2017)
26. Vaswani, A., et al.: Attention is all you need. In: Advances in Neural Information Processing Systems, vol. 30 (2017)
27. Wang, J., et al.: Deep high-resolution representation learning for visual recognition. IEEE Trans. Pattern Anal. Mach. Intell. **43**(10), 3349–3364 (2020)
28. Wang, X., Girshick, R., Gupta, A., He, K.: Non-local neural networks. In: Proceedings of the IEEE Conference on Computer Vision and Pattern Recognition, pp. 7794–7803 (2018)
29. Xiao, T., Liu, Y., Zhou, B., Jiang, Y., Sun, J.: Unified perceptual parsing for scene understanding. In: Proceedings of the European Conference on Computer Vision (ECCV), pp. 418–434 (2018)
30. Xie, E., Wang, W., Yu, Z., Anandkumar, A., Alvarez, J.M., Luo, P.: Segformer: simple and efficient design for semantic segmentation with transformers. In: Advances in Neural Information Processing Systems, vol. 34 (2021)
31. Yuan, Y., Chen, X., Wang, J.: Object-contextual representations for semantic segmentation. In: Computer Vision–ECCV 2020: 16th European Conference, Glasgow, UK, August 23–28, 2020, Proceedings, Part VI 16. pp. 173–190. Springer (2020). https://doi.org/10.1007/978-3-030-01228-1_26
32. Zhao, H., Shi, J., Qi, X., Wang, X., Jia, J.: Pyramid scene parsing network. In: Proceedings of the IEEE Conference on Computer Vision and Pattern Recognition, pp. 2881–2890 (2017)
33. Zheng, S., et al.: Rethinking semantic segmentation from a sequence-to-sequence perspective with transformers. In: Proceedings of the IEEE/CVF Conference on Computer Vision and Pattern Recognition, pp. 6881–6890 (2021)
34. Zhou, B., Zhao, H., Puig, X., Fidler, S., Barriuso, A., Torralba, A.: Scene parsing through ade20k dataset. In: Proceedings of the IEEE Conference on Computer Vision and Pattern Recognition, pp. 633–641 (2017)
35. Zhou, T., Wang, W., Konukoglu, E., Van Gool, L.: Rethinking semantic segmentation: a prototype view. In: Proceedings of the IEEE/CVF Conference on Computer Vision and Pattern Recognition, pp. 2582–2593 (2022)

A Cross-Modal Knowledge Distillation Approach for RGB-to-Infrared Video Action Recognition

Zhenzhen Quan[1,2], Daisuke Deguchi[2], Jialei Chen[2], Chenkai Zhang[2], Yujun Li[1(✉)], Seigo Ito[2], and Hiroshi Murase[2]

[1] Shandong University, Qingdao 266237, Shandong, China
quan.zhenzhen.g7@s.mail.nagoya-u.ac.jp, liyujun@sdu.edu.cn
[2] Nagoya University, Nagoya 464-8601, Japan
{ddeguchi,murase}@nagoya-u.jp, {chen.jialei.s6, zhang.chenkai.d4}@s.mail.nagoya-u.ac.jp, iseigo@vislab.is.i.nagoya-u.ac.jp

Abstract. In the domain of human action recognition (HAR), infrared data has emerged as a pivotal sensing technology in robotic applications due to its robust performance under low-light or rapidly changing lighting conditions. However, HAR methods that depend exclusively on infrared data fall short due to the lack of color and texture features. Combining other modal data, such as RGB modality, can alleviate this problem. In this paper, we introduce a cross-modal knowledge distillation approach that achieves knowledge transfer by using a teacher network with RGB data input to guide the recognition of an infrared data student network. The RGB data is exclusively utilized during the training phase. To make full use of RGB information, firstly, we construct a multi-scale graph cross-attention module between different convolutional layers of the teacher and student networks to reduce the modality difference between infrared data and RGB data modalities. Secondly, we employ a decoupled knowledge distillation module (DKD) to focus on more dark knowledge, i.e., knowledge related to similar behaviors, thereby enhancing the network's robustness. We prove the effectiveness of the proposed approach on two datasets, i.e., NTU RGB+D and PKU-MMD datasets, providing strong support for the intelligent behavior of robots in various environments.

Keyword: Human action recognition · RGB videos · Infrared videos

1 Introduction

As robotics technology rapidly progresses, human action recognition (HAR) systems are being increasingly adopted in areas such as security monitoring, medical care, and human-computer interaction [4, 9, 10]. By recognizing and understanding human actions, robots can carry out tasks with enhanced intelligence and autonomy. However, traditional HAR systems predominantly depend on RGB data, which offers rich visual

B. Kim (Ed.): IW-FCV 2025, CCIS 2769, pp. 30–42, 2026.
https://doi.org/10.1007/978-981-95-4578-0_3

information under optimal lighting conditions. Yet, their performance deteriorates significantly in low-light or rapidly changing lighting environments, thereby restricting the system's range of applications. Infrared data, i.e., near infrared data, serves as an excellent alternative or supplement since it relies on thermal radiation information and is unaffected by visible light conditions. This allows it to operate reliably across a wide range of lighting environments.

However, HAR methods that depend exclusively on infrared data also have limitations. In scenarios where color and texture features are essential, infrared images sometimes fail to accurately analyze actions due to their absence of these features. Furthermore, the acquired infrared images frequently suffer from coarse resolution due to the intrinsic noise interference of the infrared image receiver. In contrast, RGB data provides clear textures and high-quality images, addressing the shortcomings of infrared images in human action recognition. By combining RGB and infrared data, the complementary information from both modalities can guide infrared action recognition and enhance the performance.

Therefore, we raise a cross-modal knowledge distillation approach that utilizes a teacher-student network to transfer cross-modal knowledge from an RGB data teacher network to an infrared data network. Notably, the RGB data is involved solely during the training phase. To make RGB data better guide infrared data recognition, firstly, we construct a multi-scale graph cross-attention module (MGCAM) in different intermediate convolutional layers to reduce the modality difference between infrared data and RGB data modalities and obtain the fused information between heterogeneous data. Then, we employ a decoupled knowledge distillation module (DKD) to obtain the output layer information of the teacher and student networks according to its relevance to the target, focusing on more dark knowledge and improving the network's generalization capabilities.

The primary contributions of this work are as follows:

1) We construct a multi-scale graph cross-attention module across various intermediate convolutional layers to learn similar features from different modalities.
2) We construct teacher and student networks and use decoupled knowledge distillation to transfer complementary information from the RGB modality.
3) We showcase the efficacy and viability of our approach via experimental validation on both the NTU RGB+D and PKU-MMD datasets.

The structure of this paper is outlined as follows: Section II provides a review of related work. Section III introduces the raised approach. Section IV details datasets, experimental setup, and results. Lastly, Section V concludes the paper.

2 Related Work

2.1 Action Recognition based on RGB and Infrared Data

In recent years, there has been a growing interest among researchers in the field of HAR, largely driven by advancements in deep learning. Extensive research has been conducted not only in HAR based on RGB data [1, 12, 25, 26] but also in infrared human action recognition [11, 14]. Nie et al. [16] introduced an innovative 3D ConvNet featuring a deep architecture and residual structure to enhance the classification performance of infrared videos. Meng et al. [3] utilized convolutional neural networks to develop a framework for analyzing human behavior around parked aircraft. Additionally, there are also some studies based on both RGB and infrared data. Zhu et al. [29] explored a feature mapping method for the same action from the visual spectrum to the infrared range. Hilsenbeck et al. [7] recorded infrared and visible spectra through Hough forest and constructed a multispectral behavioral dataset. Sun et al. [22] proposed a robust feature matching strategy utilizing feature matching and multi-object tracking in complex, non-flat environments of infrared-RGB videos. Piao et al. [19] introduced the use of convolutional neural networks (CNNs) to create weight maps expressing the significance of individual pixels, which are then used for weighted fusion in action analysis. Quan et al. [20] employed attention relation matching and activation domain consistency constraints to minimize the modality differences between RGB and infrared data. Unlike the aforementioned methods, we consider constructing graph cross-view attention map to learn similar features across different modalities.

2.2 Knowledge Distillation

Knowledge distillation has received widespread attention due to its ability to transfer knowledge from larger networks to smaller ones [8]. Park et al. [17] considered both distance and angular losses to reduce the differences between different data structures. Tung et al. [24] focused solely on student networks learning the representational space information of teacher networks rather than the representational information. Touvron et al. [23] created distillation tokens leveraging the transformer architecture to enable knowledge distillation. Zhao et al. [28] decomposed the knowledge distillation loss based on its relevance to the target and introduced a decoupled knowledge distillation method. Gou et al. [5] examined the cross-channel features of different samples as well as the various channels of a single sample. Guo et al. [6] highlighted the significance of class attention transfer in enhancing the performance of convolutional networks. Unlike previous knowledge distillation methods, we raise MGCAM across various feature layers to transfer informations and DKD to focus on more dark knowledge.

3 Methodology

3.1 Overview

The schematic of our raised approach is depicted in Fig. 1. In our approach, the teacher network (TN) takes RGB video as input, whereas the student network (SN) takes infrared video as input. And the TN is involved solely during the training phase, while only the SN is utilized during the testing phase. To make full use of RGB information, we construct the MGCAM to merge features from the intermediate layer of both networks, allowing the integration of different modalities at the intermediate layers. Moreover, we leverage the DKD module to extract both positive and negative information from the TN, effectively guiding the SN in action analysis.

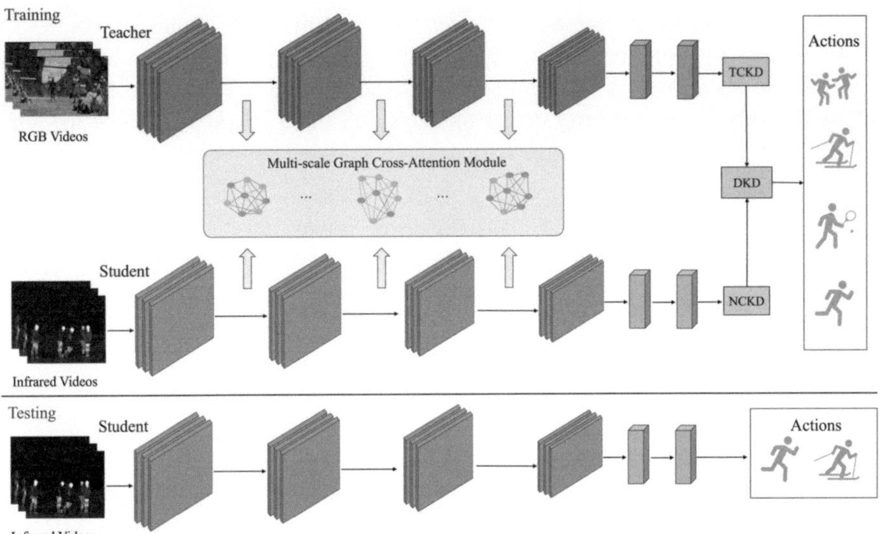

Fig. 1. The framework of the raised approach. Where TCKD, NCKD, and DKD denote target class knowledge distillation, non-target class knowledge distillation, and decoupled knowledge distillation. Notably, during the testing stage, only the student network is utilized.

3.2 Multi-scale Graph Cross-Attention Module

To reduce the discrepancies between the modalities of RGB data and infrared data, we consider the information fusion between feature layers of different scales from both modalities. Therefore, we raise MGCAM, as shown in Fig. 2. By constructing graph structures of different modal features, we utilize graph-based information to perform cross-view attention calculations, thus capturing the intermodal information.

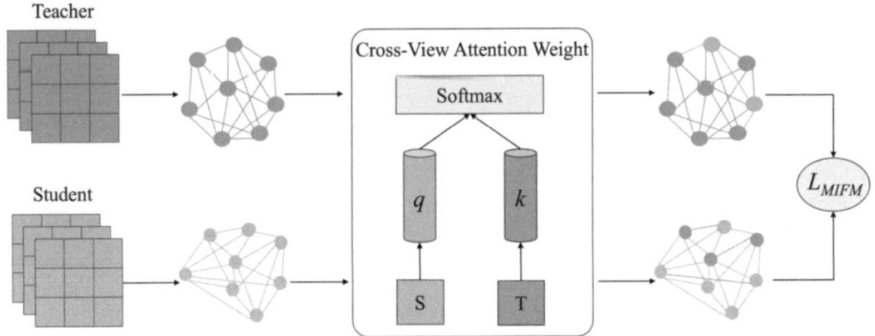

Fig. 2. The design of the multi-scale graph cross-attention module.

We assume that the i th feature layer of the SN is $F_i^S \in \mathbb{R}^{b \times c \times h \times w}$, where b denotes the batch size, c represents the channel dimension, and h, w are the height and width of the spatial dimension. The feature layer j of the TN is $F_j^T \in \mathbb{R}^{b \times c \times h \times w}$. Inspired by

[15], we construct graphs representing the feature F_i^S from the ith feature layer of the SN and the feature F_j^T from the jth feature layer of the TN. The features extracted from the feature layers are viewed as vertices in a graph, where the connections between features obtained by Gaussian similarity define the edges of the graph. We calculate the edge weights $E_{ij} \in \mathbb{R}^{b\times b}$ between feature data through gaussian similarity:

$$E_{ij} = \exp\left(-\frac{\|F_i^S - F_i^S\|}{2}\right). \tag{1}$$

And then we get the graph matrix $Q \in \mathbb{R}^{b\times b}$ through graph Laplacian normalization [2].

$$Q = D^{-\frac{1}{2}} E_{ij} D^{-\frac{1}{2}}, \tag{2}$$

$D \in \mathbb{R}^{b\times b}$ is a diagonal matrix, with each diagonal element (n, n) representing the sum of the corresponding row n in the edge weight matrix.

Then, we use the graph matrices of SN and TN to calculate cross-view attention weights A_{ij}^S, which capture the similarity between diverse forms of knowledge:

$$A_{ij}^S = soft\max\left(\frac{Q_i^S \left(Q_j^T\right)^T}{\sqrt{d}}\right), \tag{3}$$

where Q_i^S represents the graph matrix of the i-th feature layer of the SN, and Q_j^T represents the graph matrix of the j-th feature layer of the TN. Q_i^S and Q_j^T are obtained by Eq. (2).

The fused feature map $W_j^T \in \mathbb{R}^{b\times c\times h\times w}$ for the j-th feature layer of the TN is obtained by combining the feature activation map A_j with the cross-view attention weight A_{ij}^S using a linear operation.

$$W_j^T = A_{ij}^S A_j. \tag{4}$$

Similarly, we can get the fused feature map $W_i^S \in \mathbb{R}^{b\times c\times h\times w}$ for the i-th feature layer of the SN is:

$$W_j^T = A_{ij}^S A_j. \tag{5}$$

We calculate the mean square error (MSE) loss between the fused feature maps of the SN and those of the TN. This loss helps in learning the knowledge of the middle layers:

$$L_{MGCAM} = \frac{1}{k}\left(\sum_{i,j=1}^{k} \left\| \frac{W_j^T}{\left\|W_j^T\right\|_2} - \frac{W_i^S}{\|W_i^S\|_2} \right\|_2^2\right), \tag{6}$$

where $\|\cdot\|_2^2$ is the MSE calculation, and k is the number of the feature layers for graph cross-attention computation. To obtain more fusion information of multi scale features from RGB modality and infrared modality, we incorporate graph cross-attention computation into each residual block of both the TN and SN.

3.3 Decoupled Knowledge Distillation Module

During the distillation process, some information is relevant to the target, while some is not. Therefore, the distillation loss can also be decomposed in terms of its relevance to the target [28]:

$$L_{DKD} = \alpha_T L_{TCKD} + \alpha_N L_{NCKD}, \tag{7}$$

where α_T, α_N represent distinct hyperparameters. L_{TCKD} refers to target class knowledge distillation, while L_{NCKD} is non-target class knowledge distillation.

$$L_{TCKD} = KL\left(p^T \middle\| p^S\right), \tag{8}$$

$$L_{NCKD} = KL\left(\hat{p}^T \middle\| \hat{p}^S\right), \tag{9}$$

where $p = \left[p_m, p_{\setminus m}\right] \in \mathbb{R}^{1\times 2}$ denotes the binary probability p_m of the target class and the binary probabilities $p_{\setminus m}$ of all other non-target classes. $\hat{p} = \left[\hat{p}_1, \cdots, \hat{p}_{m-1}, \hat{p}_{m+1}, \cdots, \hat{p}_C\right] \in \mathbb{R}^{1\times(C-1)}$ is independently modeling the probabilities between non-target classes without considering the m-th class. After de coupling, the knowledge distillation loss can obtain more dark knowledge from nontarget classes by L_{NCKD}.

The total loss for training the SN comprises both the decoupled knowledge distillation loss and the cross-entropy loss L_{CE} between the SN's output and the ground truth label. The complete loss function is:

$$L = L_{CE} + \alpha L_{DKD} + \beta L_{MGCAM}, \tag{10}$$

The steps of the raised approach are shown in Alg. 1.

Algorithm 1

INPUT: Action categories, teacher network, student network, the cross-entropy loss L_{CE}, $L^T{}_{CE}$ the decoubled knowledge distillation loss L_{DKD}, the multi-scale graph cross-attention loss L_{MGCAM}, learning rate, total iterations and hyperparameters a, β, a_T, a_N

OUTPUT: Student network

INITIALIZE: Learning rate, total iterations and hyperparmeters a, β, a_T, a_N

PRETRAIN TEACHER NETWORK:

for $i \leftarrow 0$ **to** total iterations **do**

train the teacher network with L^T_{CE}

update: The teacher network parameters

end for

TRAIN STUDENT NETWORK:

for $j \leftarrow 0$ **to** total iterations **do**

train the student network based on $L = L_{CE} + aL_{DKD} + \beta L_{MGCAM}$

update: The student network parameters

end for

4 Experiments

4.1 Datasets

1) The NTU RGB + D dataset [21] comprises various data types, such as RGB, skeleton, depth map, and infrared data. It encompasses a total of 60 action classes and contains over 56,000 videos. In this paper, we select ten daily-life related categories (drop, throw, stand up, pick up, clap, brush teeth, drink, wash hair, sit, and eat) to evaluate our approach, as shown in Fig. 3.
2) The PKU-MMD dataset [13] contains data modalities such as RGB, infrared data, depth, and 3D joint. It consists of 51 action categories and includes over 1,000 lengthy videos. For our evaluation, we focus on all RGB and infrared data categories, assessing our approach's effectiveness using the mean average precision (mAP) across cross-view and cross-subject settings.

4.2 Experimental Setup

The teacher network employs ResNet50 as its backbone, whereas the student network uses ResNet18 as its backbone. For both datasets, the segment is 8. The batch size of the pretrained teacher network is 16, while that of the student network is set to 8. For the NTU RGB+D dataset, the learning rate is 0.001, the hyperparameters $\alpha, \beta, \alpha_T, \alpha_N$ values are {0.1,1,0.7,0.35} and the number of epoch is 80. Similarly, for the PKU-MMD dataset, the learning rate is 0.001, the values of the hyperparameters $\{\alpha, \beta, \alpha_T, \alpha_N\}$ are {0.01,1,0.7,0.35} and the number of epoch is 120. All experimental procedures are carried out using the PyTorch framework on a single NVIDIA RTX 3090 GPU.

4.3 Comparison with Existing Methods

To assess the performance of our raised approach, we benchmark it against state- of-the-art approaches such as TSN [25], TSTDDs [14], ST [8], AT [27], SP [24], CC [18], RKD [17], CCSKD [5] on the NTU RGB+D and PKU-MMD datasets.

As illustrated in Table 1 and 2, our approach outperforms existing methods on both datasets. Our approach achieves an accuracy of 80.86% on the NTU RGB+D dataset, 4.62% higher than CCSKD [5] method. On the PKU-MMD dataset, our approach achieves mean Average Precision (mAP) scores of 0.588 and 0.586 for the cross-view and cross-subject strategies, respectively. These findings suggest that our approach, by combining the MGCAM with the DKD, successfully mitigates the modality discrepancies and utilizes valuable knowledge from various teacher network feature layers to enhance the performance.

Moreover, we showcase the confusion matrix generated from the NTU RGB+D dataset, depicted in Fig. 4. According to Fig. 4, the recognition performance for the 10 selected actions from the NTU RGB+D dataset notably improves with the aid of RGB data. Actions like 'pick up', 'throw', and 'drink' show significantly enhanced recognition performance. However, the action 'stand up' shows relatively lower recognition rate. Among these, actions like 'pick up' and 'throw', known for their extensive motion ranges, exhibit distinct characteristics that aid in their identification. Unfortunately, there is a

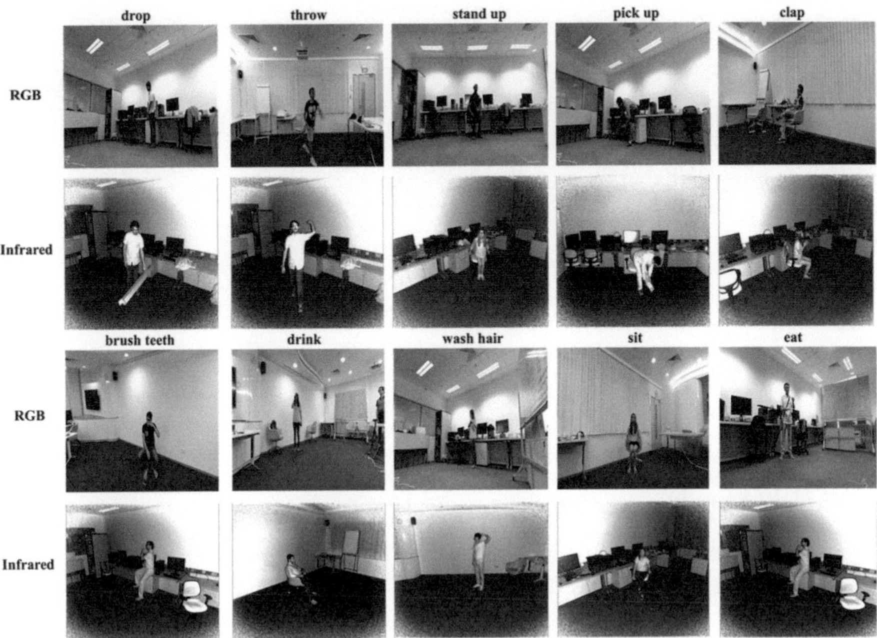

Fig. 3. The examples of NTU RGB + D dataset.

Table 1. The results of the raised approach and the existing methods on the NTU RGB + D dataset.

Method	Teacher	Student	Teacher Input	Student Input	Accuracy (%)
TSTDDs [14]	-	-		IR Videos	72.36
ST [8]	ResNet50	ResNet18	RGB Videos	IR Videos	74.69
AT [27]	ResNet50	ResNet18	RGB Videos	IR Videos	74.58
SP [24]	ResNet50	ResNet18	RGB Videos	IR Videos	76.03
CC [18]	ResNet50	ResNet18	RGB Videos	IR Videos	75.21
RKD [17]	ResNet50	ResNet18	RGB Videos	IR Videos	74.38
CCSKD [5]	ResNet50	ResNet18	RGB Videos	IR Videos	76.24
Ours	ResNet50	ResNet18	RGB Videos	IR Videos	**80.86**

22% probability of misclassification, where 'sit' is erroneously categorized as 'stand up'. This confusion arises because these two actions are opposites and have a similar intermediate phase, leading to ambiguity.

Table 2. The results of the raised approach and the existing methods on the PKU- MMD dataset.

Method	Teacher Input	Student Input	Cross-View	Cross-Subject
TSN [25]	-	IR Videos	0.539	0.567
ST [8]	RGB Videos	IR Videos	0.554	0.574
AT [27]	RGB Videos	IR Videos	0.562	0.584
SP [24]	RGB Videos	IR Videos	0.582	0.570
CC [18]	RGB Videos	IR Videos	0.580	0.567
RKD [17]	RGB Videos	IR Videos	0.579	0.578
CCSKD [5]	RGB Videos	IR Videos	0.556	0.565
Ours	RGB Videos	IR Videos	**0.588**	**0.586**

4.4 Ablation Study

To evaluate the contributions of the MGCAM and DKD in our approach, we constructed 3 variations based on our raised approach: 1) Student network baseline: The student network is used exclusively, with training and testing conducted using only infrared data, shown in the 2nd line of Table 3 and Table 4. 2) Ours (w/o MGCAM): Our raised approach without the multi-scale graph cross-attention module, shown in the 3rd line of Table 3 and Table 4. 3) Ours (w/o DKD): Our raised approach without the decoupled knowledge distillation module, shown in the 4th line of Table 3 and Table 4.

As depicted in Table 3 and Table 4, the MGCAM and DKD modules play crucial roles in our approach's performance. From the data presented in the 2nd and 3rd rows of Table 3 and Table 4, it is evident that MGCAM plays a crucial role. This indicates that bridging the modality gap between infrared data and RGB data is crucial. Additionally, both Ours (w/o MGCAM) and Ours (w/o DKD) achieve better performance than the student network baseline. This demonstrates that the MGCAM and DKD are helpful for information fusion of different modalities and extraction of complementary knowledge to enhance infrared data analysis.

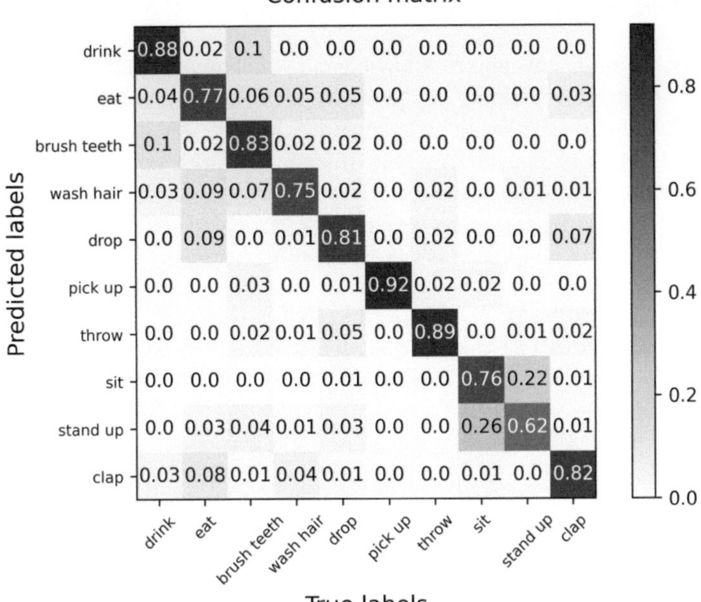

Fig. 4. The confuse matrix of NTU RGB + D dataset.

Table 3. The results on the NTU RGB + D dataset. w/o stands for without.

MGCAM	DKD	Teacher Input	Student Input	Accuracy (%)
–	–	–	IR Videos	71.20
–	✓	RGB Videos	IR Videos	78.60
✓	–	RGB Videos	IR Videos	80.04
✓	✓	RGB Videos	IR Videos	**80.86**

Table 4. The results on the PKU-MMD dataset. w/o stands for without, CV stands Cross-View and CS stands for Cross-Subject.

MGCAM	DKD	Teacher Input	Student Input	CV	CS
–	–	–	IR Videos	0.539	0.567
–	✓	RGB Videos	IR Videos	0.557	0.571
✓	–	RGB Videos	IR Videos	0.575	0.574
✓	✓	RGB Videos	IR Videos	**0.588**	**0.585**

5 Conclusion

In this paper, we raise a decoupled knowledge distillation approach using graph cross-attention. To reduce the modality gap between infrared data and RGB data modalities, we construct a multi-scale graph cross-attention module that operates across various convolutional layers of both teacher and student networks, enabling the learning of analogous features across modalities. Additionally, to enhance the network's robustness by leveraging more dark knowledge, we employ a decoupled knowledge distillation loss. The effectiveness of our approach is validated on two datasets.

Acknowledgement. This work was supported by JSPS KAKENHI Grant Number 23K28164 and 24H00733, and JST CREST Grant Number JPMJCR22D1. We employed the NTU RGB+D Action Recognition Dataset, which was developed by the ROSE Lab at Nanyang Technological University in Singapore.

References

1. Chen, T., Yu, H., Yang, Z., Li, Z., Sun, W., Chen, C.: OST: refining text knowledge with optimal spatio-temporal descriptor for general video recognition. In: Proceedings of the IEEE/CVF Conference on Computer Vision and Pattern Recognition, pp. 18888–18898 (2024). https://doi.org/10.48550/arXiv.2312.00096
2. Chung, F.R.: Spectral graph theory, vol. 92. American Mathematical Soc. (1997)
3. Ding, M., Ding, Y., Wei, L., Xu, Y., Cao, Y.: Individual surveillance around parked aircraft at nighttime: thermal infrared vision-based human action recognition. IEEE Trans. Syst. Man Cybern. Syst. **53**(2), 1084–1094 (2022). https://doi.org/10.1109/TSMC.2022.3192017
4. Frank, A.E., Kubota, A., Riek, L.D.: Wearable activity recognition for robust human-robot teaming in safety-critical environments via hybrid neural networks. In: Proceedings of the 2019 IEEE/RSJ International Conference on Intelligent Robots and Systems (IROS), pp. 449–454. IEEE (2019). https://doi.org/10.1109/IROS40897.2019.8968615
5. Gou, J., Xiong, X., Yu, B., Zhan, Y., Yi, Z.: Channel correlation-based selective knowledge distillation. IEEE Trans. Cogn. Dev. Syst. (2022). https://doi.org/10.1109/TCDS.2022.3232569
6. Guo, Z., Yan, H., Li, H., Lin, X.: Class attention transfer based knowledge distillation. In: Proceedings of the IEEE/CVF Conference on Computer Vision and Pattern Recognition, pp. 11868–11877 (2023). https://doi.org/10.48550/arXiv.2304.12777
7. Hilsenbeck, B., Münch, D., Grosselfinger, A.K., Hübner, W., Arens, M.: Action recognition in the longwave infrared and the visible spectrum using hough forests. In: 2016 IEEE International Symposium on Multimedia (ISM), pp. 329–332. IEEE (2016). https://doi.org/10.1109/ISM.2016.0072
8. Hinton, G., Vinyals, O., Dean, J.: Distilling the knowledge in a neural network. arXiv preprint arXiv:1503.02531 (2015). http://arxiv.org/abs/1503.02531
9. Iqbal, T., Rack, S., Riek, L.D.: Movement coordination in human–robot teams: a dynamical systems approach. IEEE Trans. Robot. **32**(4), 909–919 (2016). https://doi.org/10.1109/TRO.2016.2570240
10. Iqbal, T., Riek, L.D.: Coordination dynamics in multihuman multirobot teams. IEEE Robot. Autom. Lett. **2**(3), 1712–1717 (2017). https://doi.org/10.1109/LRA.2017.2673864

11. Jiang, Z., Rozgic, V., Adali, S.: Learning spatiotemporal features for infrared action recognition with 3d convolutional neural networks. 2017. arXiv preprint arXiv:1705.06709 (2017). http://arxiv.org/abs/1705.06709
12. Li, Y., Ji, B., Shi, X., Zhang, J., Kang, B., Wang, L.: Tea: temporal excitation and aggregation for action recognition. In: Proceedings of the IEEE/CVF Conference on Computer Vision and Pattern Recognition. pp. 909–918 (2020). https://doi.org/10.48550/arXiv.2004.01398
13. Liu, C., Hu, Y., Li, Y., Song, S., Liu, J.: PKU-MMD: a large scale benchmark for continuous multi-modal human action understanding. arXiv preprint arXiv:1703.07475 (2017). http://arxiv.org/abs/1703.07475
14. Liu, Y., Lu, Z., Li, J., Yang, T., Yao, C.: Global temporal representation based CNNs for infrared action recognition. IEEE Signal Process. Lett. **25**(6), 848–852 (2018). https://doi.org/10.1109/LSP.2018.2823910
15. Nie, F., Xu, D., Tsang, I.W.H., Zhang, C.: Flexible manifold embedding: a framework for semi-supervised and unsupervised dimension reduction. IEEE Trans. Image Process. **19**(7), 1921–1932 (2010). https://doi.org/10.1109/TIP.2010.2044958
16. Nie, J., Yan, L., Wang, X., Chen, J.: A novel 3d convolutional neural network for action recognition in infrared videos. In: 2021 4th International Conference on Information Communication and Signal Processing (ICICSP). pp. 420–424. IEEE (2021). https://doi.org/10.1109/ICICSP54369.2021.9611896
17. Park, W., Kim, D., Lu, Y., Cho, M.: Relational knowledge distillation. In: Proceedings of the IEEE/CVF Conference on Computer Vision and Pattern Recognition, pp. 3967–3976 (2019). https://doi.org/10.48550/arXiv.1904.05068
18. Peng, B., et al.: Correlation congruence for knowledge distillation. In: Proceedings of the IEEE/CVF International Conference on Computer Vision, pp. 5007–5016 (2019)
19. Piao, J., Chen, Y., Shin, H.: A new deep learning based multi-spectral image fusion method. Entropy **21**(6), 570 (2019). https://doi.org/10.3390/e21060570
20. Quan, Z., Chen, Q., Li, Y., Liu, Z., Cui, Y.: Arctic: a knowledge distillation approach via attention-based relation matching and activation region constraint for RGB-to-infrared videos action recognition. Comput. Vis. and Image Und. **237**, 103853 (2023). https://doi.org/10.1016/j.cviu.2023.103853
21. Shahroudy, A., Liu, J., Ng, T.T., Wang, G.: Ntu rgb+ d: a large scale dataset for 3D human activity analysis. In: Proceedings of the IEEE Conference on Computer Vision and Pattern Recognition, pp. 1010–1019 (2016)
22. Sun, X., Xu, T., Zhang, J., Zhao, Z., Li, Y.: An automatic multi-target independent analysis framework for non-planar infrared-visible registration. Sensors **17**(8), 1696 (2017). https://doi.org/10.3390/s17081696
23. Touvron, H., Cord, M., Douze, M., Massa, F., Sablayrolles, A., Jégou, H.: Training data-efficient image transformers & distillation through attention. In: International Conference on Machine Learning, pp. 10347–10357. PMLR (2021)
24. Tung, F., Mori, G.: Similarity-preserving knowledge distillation. In: Proceedings of the IEEE/CVF International Conference on Computer Vision, pp. 1365–1374 (2019)
25. Wang, L., et al.: Temporal segment networks: towards good practices for deep action recognition. In: European Conference on Computer Vision. pp. 20–36. Springer (2016)
26. Wu, W., Sun, Z., Ouyang, W.: Revisiting classifier: transferring vision- language models for video recognition. In: Proceedings of the AAAI Conference on Artificial Intelligence, vol. 37, pp. 2847–2855 (2023). https://doi.org/10.1609/aaai.v37i3.25386
27. Zagoruyko, S., Komodakis, N.: Paying more attention to attention: improving the performance of convolutional neural networks via attention transfer. In: Proceedings of the International Conference on Learning Representations, pp. 1–13 (2017). https://doi.org/10.48550/arXiv.1612.03928

28. Zhao, B., Cui, Q., Song, R., Qiu, Y., Liang, J.: Decoupled knowledge distillation. In: Proceedings of the IEEE/CVF Conference on Computer Vision and Pattern Recognition, pp. 11953–11962 (2022). https://doi.org/10.48550/arXiv.2203.08679
29. Zhu, Y., Guo, G.: A study on visible to infrared action recognition. IEEE Signal Process. Lett. **20**(9), 897–900 (2013). https://doi.org/10.1109/LSP.2013.2272920

Automating Wood Grain Sensory Evaluation via Image Feature Fusion Approach Using Vision-Language Models

Haruto Yoshida[1(✉)], Kunihito Kato[1], Dan Sasai[2], Yasuo Shiozawa[2], Kazunori Terada[1], and Yoshikazu Hayashi[1]

[1] Gifu University, 1-1 Yanagito, Gifu City, Gifu 501-1193, Japan
yoshida@cv.info.gifu-u.ac.jp

[2] Yamaha Corporation, 10-1 Nakazawa-cho, Chuo-ku, Hamamatsu City, Shizuoka 430-8650, Japan

Abstract. This research addresses the automation of wood grain sensory evaluation and judgment rationale generation using a small dataset. Wood grain sensory evaluation involves assessing sensory elements such as color and pattern, which leads to significant variations in evaluator judgments. This challenge complicates the establishment of consistent evaluations, standardization of evaluations, and evaluator training. To address this issue, we construct a dataset using data collected from an expert wood grain evaluator and fine-tune a Vision-Language Model (VLM) to automate wood grain sensory evaluation and generate judgment rationales. However, existing VLMs are found to have insufficient capabilities in extracting local image features, which is crucial for this type of evaluation. To improve local feature extraction capabilities, we modify the architecture of the existing VLM. Specifically, we integrate features from the intermediate layers of a CLIP ViT-based model with those from a Convolutional Neural Network (CNN), creating a model that can capture both local and global image characteristics. By fine-tuning this model, we aim to enhance the accuracy of wood grain sensory evaluation and rationale generation.

Keywords: Vision-Language Model · Sensory Evaluation · Explainability

1 Introduction

Sensory evaluation is a quality assessment method that utilizes the five human senses: vision, hearing, smell, taste, and touch. In wood grain sensory evaluation, evaluations are performed based on sensory attributes such as color and pattern. Consequently, variations in quality judgment results among evaluators have been identified as a critical challenge. This issue complicates the establishment of consistent evaluations, standardized evaluations, and evaluator training. To address this challenge, there is a growing need for automated sensory evaluation technologies capable of providing wood grain quality judgment results along with their corresponding rationales.

B. Kim (Ed.): IW-FCV 2025, CCIS 2769, pp. 43–55, 2026.
https://doi.org/10.1007/978-981-95-4578-0_4

In this research, we aim to automate wood grain sensory evaluation and generate rationales using Vision-Language Models (VLMs). VLMs represent a rapidly evolving research field that has demonstrated high performance across a wide range of Vision-Language tasks by leveraging their extensive pre-trained knowledge. As these models are progressively advancing in research domains dealing with sensory values such as human preferences and emotional values [1, 2], we anticipate that by fine-tuning a VLM using data collected from expert evaluators, we can realize the automation of wood grain sensory evaluation and generate rationales. Conventional methods for handling sensory values primarily involve quantifying them as numerical values [3]. However, these methods require data collection through multiple rounds of subjective evaluation experiments, resulting in significant human and time costs. Additionally, because these methods convert the abstract concept of sensory values into numerical values, interpreting the model outputs can be challenging. To address these issues, utilizing VLMs to express sensory values in natural language offers a more human-like and intuitive approach, enabling outputs that are easier to interpret.

However, existing VLMs may not be fully suitable for wood grain sensory evaluation due to limitations in image feature extraction capabilities. Wood grain sensory evaluation depends on specific criteria such as the presence or absence of "stripes" (individual lines), their color intensity, the presence of "layers" (collections of fine lines), and "material color contrast". This requires both local and global feature extraction. In contrast, contemporary VLMs, predominantly based on CLIP ViT, tend to extract global features and lack robust local feature extraction capabilities, rendering them potentially unsuitable for wood grain sensory evaluation. CLIP ViT refers to a Vision Transformer (ViT) [5] trained through Contrastive Language-Image Pretraining (CLIP) [4].

Therefore, this research focuses on enhancing local feature extraction capabilities and improving image feature extraction for wood grain sensory evaluation by modifying existing VLM architectures. Specifically, we will improve local feature extraction by utilizing features obtained from the intermediate layers of a CLIP ViT-based model and features from a Convolutional Neural Network (CNN). While features from the final layer of CLIP ViT-based models tend to capture global characteristics, features from intermediate layers are effective in capturing local details [6]. Previous work, such as ViP-LLaVA [7], has demonstrated the benefits of utilizing intermediate layer features to enhance local feature extraction. Furthermore, CNNs are known for their ability to extract local features [8]. By integrating these features, we expect to extract the image features necessary for wood grain sensory evaluation, potentially improving the accuracy of automating wood grain sensory evaluation and rationale generation. Building on this, we modify the architecture of existing VLM to emphasize local feature extraction and fine-tune the modified model using a dataset collected from expert evaluators, aiming to automate wood grain sensory evaluation and generate rationales.

Our experiments demonstrated that integrating intermediate features from CLIP ViT-based models with CNN features significantly improved both quality judgment accuracy and rationale generation.

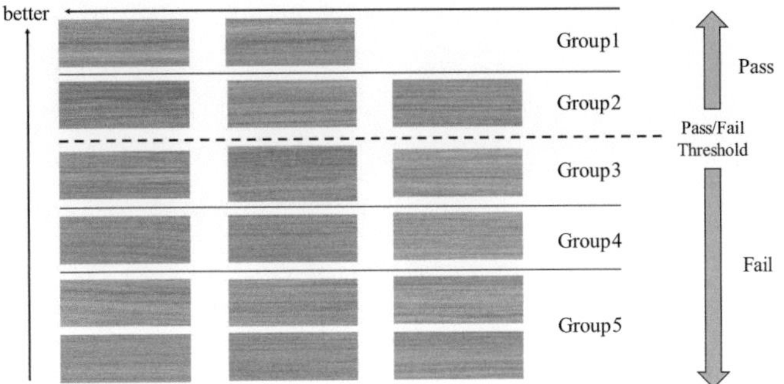

Fig. 1. Images divided into five groups by the evaluator during the criteria collection phase. Group 1 represents the highest quality, and Group 5 the lowest. Within each group, images are arranged from left to right in descending order of quality, with those on the left being of higher quality.

2 Related Work

2.1 Research on Handling Sensory Values Using VLMs

Recent research on VLMs has actively explored human preferences and sensory values. For instance, reference [1] investigated Image Aesthetic Assessment (IAA) by utilizing user comments to naturally express human opinions and preferences about image beauty. Existing IAA methods relied on labeled scores, which simplified visual aesthetic perception, but by incorporating comprehensive user comments, they addressed this limitation. Reference [2] focused on understanding artistic images using VLMs. By training VLMs with artistic images and text, they enabled the linguistic expression of emotions that artistic images evoke in humans.

Building on these studies, employing VLMs to handle human preferences and sensory values allows for linguistic expression of human sensibilities, resulting in outputs that are closer to human expression and more interpretable. In our research, we aim to apply VLMs to wood grain sensory evaluation to express evaluators' sensory perceptions and evaluation criteria and generate easily interpretable judgment rationales.

2.2 Enhancing Local Feature Extraction Capabilities in VLMs

Contemporary VLM research often employs CLIP ViT-based models without considering the image encoder's characteristics. However, when using features from the final layer, CLIP ViT-based models may have insufficient local feature extraction capabilities, potentially limiting performance in tasks requiring fine-grained feature capture like line detection.

While features from CLIP ViT-based models' final layer tend to capture global characteristics, using intermediate layer features can enhance local feature extraction capabilities. ViP-LLaVA addressed this by utilizing features from intermediate layers (6th, 15th, 18th, 21st, and 24th layers) instead of the final layer, effectively handling local features that CLIP ViT-based models struggle with. As a VLM capable of processing arbitrary visual prompts, ViP-LLaVA captured both local and global features through these intermediate layers, enabling effective visual prompt recognition.

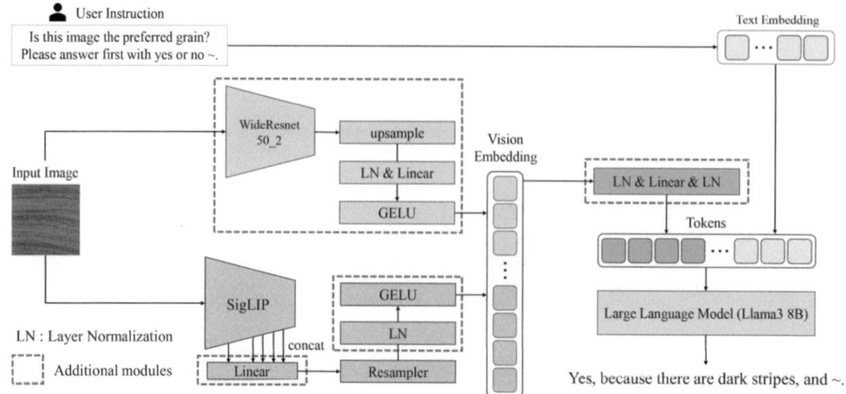

Fig. 2. Overall architecture of the modified model

Furthermore, integrating features from a CLIP ViT-based model and other models can help capture a broader range of features. Reference [9] successfully integrated features from CLIP ViT's intermediate layers with those from DINO V2's [10] intermediate layers using a novel method. This approach leveraged both local and global features, achieving performance improvements across various Vision-Language tasks.

Informed by these insights, our research aims to enhance local feature extraction and improve wood grain sensory evaluation accuracy by integrating features from a CLIP ViT-based model's intermediate layers with features from a CNN, which are known for capturing local features.

3 Method

3.1 Dataset Construction

Before collecting quality judgment results and their rationales from the evaluators for inclusion in the dataset, we first elicit the evaluation criteria from them, who hold them as tacit knowledge. Evaluators only judge whether wood grain patterns are pass or fail during routine evaluations and may not be accustomed to verbalizing the rationale behind their decisions. Therefore, by identifying factors related to sensory evaluation in advance, it becomes easier for evaluators to verbalize their reasoning during the subsequent data collection phase.

In the process of collecting evaluation criteria, we present 30 images side by side and ask the evaluators to arrange them into five groups, ranked from best quality to lowest quality. We then identify the group representing the threshold for acceptable quality and ask the evaluators to describe the criteria for this threshold by comparing images from different groups. When collecting quality judgment results and their rationales, we first ask the evaluators to provide a quality judgment result for each image and then elicit the rationale behind their decisions. During this process, the images are arranged and presented in the same five groups as they were divided during the criteria collection phase, allowing evaluators to refer to the criteria as needed, as shown in Fig. 1. After collecting quality judgment results and rationales for all images, we re-confirm the data to address any discrepancies in quality judgment results or inconsistencies in the rationale descriptions that may arise during the process.

Using the collected quality judgment results and rationales, we create standardized statements. To enable quantitative evaluation of the results generated by the VLM, the target statements are standardized into the format: "Yes/No, because ~." This structure allows for quantitative evaluation of quality judgment results based on the presence of "Yes" or "No" in the generated statements.

3.2 Model Architecture Improvements

Overview of Model Improvements. In this research, we use MiniCPM Llama3-V 2.5[11] as the base model. MiniCPM-Llama3-V 2.5 is a model with performance comparable to GPT-4V-1106, Gemini Pro, and Claude3 in benchmark evaluations. It employs SigLIP SoViT-400 m/14 (SigLIP) [12] as the image encoder and Llama3 [13] as the Large Language Model (LLM). SigLIP is a derivative model of CLIP ViT. By integrating features obtained from the intermediate layers of SigLIP and those obtained from a CNN, the model's ability to extract local features is enhanced. However, the features from the intermediate layers of SigLIP and the CNN have different dimensions and characteristics, making direct integration challenging. To address this, we introduce additional modules to transform each feature into a form that can be effectively integrated. The overall architecture of the modified model is shown in Fig. 2. In Fig. 2, "Additional modules" represent the newly added modules. After applying these methods, we fine-tune the model using the dataset constructed in Sect. 3.1 to perform sensory evaluation and generate rationales for wood grain images. Some of the additional modules do not have pretrained weights. Therefore, during fine-tuning, modules without pretrained weights are trained from scratch.

SigLIP Intermediate Features. We extract features from the intermediate layers (6, 15, 18, 21, 24) of SigLIP and treat the combined features as the output of SigLIP. The selection of these intermediate layers follows the approach used in ViP-LLaVA. In the MiniCPM-Llama3-V 2.5 model architecture, the features obtained from SigLIP are input to the Resampler. The Resampler consists of Linear, Layer Normalization [14], and Multi-head Cross Attention layers, and its role is to adjust feature dimensions and effectively integrate the visual features with language features. However, due to the extraction of features from multiple intermediate layers of SigLIP, the resulting feature dimensions do not match the corresponding input dimensions of the Resampler. Therefore, we introduce an additional Linear layer to adjust the features obtained from the intermediate layers to match the input dimensions of the Resampler. The combined features from multiple intermediate layers of SigLIP are input into this Linear layer to adjust the feature dimensions before passing them to the Resampler. Next, to facilitate integration with the features obtained from the CNN, we introduce Layer Normalization and GELU [15], which adjust the features obtained from the Resampler for easier integration. This allows effective integration with the features from the CNN while utilizing the pretrained Resampler. Since all the modules added in this section do not have pretrained weights, they are trained from scratch during fine-tuning.

You are trying to tell if a candidate set of captions is describing the same image as a reference set of captions, focusing on the elements 'stripe', 'material color contrast', and 'layers'.
Please note that each of these elements represents a completely different characteristic and should be evaluated separately without conflating them.
Candidate set:
{candidate_statements}
Reference set:
{target_statements}
On a precise scale from 0 to 100, how likely is it that the candidate set is describing the same image as the reference set based on the specified elements, considering the evaluation of differences in number and degree, and treating each element as a completely separate characteristic? (JSON format, with a key "score", value between 0 and 100, and a key "reason" with a string value.)

Fig. 3. The prompt used for evaluation with GPT-4o. It is an improved version of the prompt used in CLAIR. The text in blue indicates the sentences added in this research.

CNN Features. In this research, we adopt WideResnet50_2 [16] as the CNN and extract features from Layer4. The extracted features need to be integrated with those obtained from SigLIP. Thus, we introduce additional modules to ensure effective integration. First, we perform upsampling using bicubic interpolation to adjust the featuredimensions. Bicubic interpolation calculates new values using a weighted average of 16 neighboring pixels and is widely used in the field of image processing for high-quality interpolation. In this research, we apply bicubic interpolation spatially to the features obtained from WideResnet50_2 to adjust their dimensions. Next, we add Layer Normalization, Linear, and GELU. We apply Layer Normalization to normalize the features and use Linear and GELU layers to adjust the feature dimensions, preparing them for effective integration with the intermediate features of SigLIP. While Batch Normalization [17] is commonly used as a normalization technique in CNNs, Layer Normalization is mainly used in Transformer-based models, including CLIP ViT. SigLIP also uses Layer Normalization for feature normalization. Thus, we employ Layer Normalization to ensure effective integration with SigLIP features. For the modules added in this section, we use the WideResnet50_2 model pretrained on ImageNet. However, the other added modules do not have pretrained weights, so they are trained from scratch during fine-tuning.

Fusion of SigLIP Intermediate Features and CNN Features. After adjusting the features obtained from the SigLIP intermediate layers and WideResnet50_2 using the previously described methods, we integrate these features and input them, along with the language features, into the LLM to output the quality judgment result and rationale for the input image. However, integrating the features from SigLIP and WideResnet50_2 leads to discrepancies with the input feature dimensions corresponding to the LLM. Thus, we introduce a feature dimension adjustment module. Specifically, we add Layer Normalization, Linear, and Layer Normalization. After integrating the features obtained from SigLIP and WideResnet50_2, we utilize Layer Normalization to enhance the uniformity of the integrated features, then input them into a Linear layer to adjust the feature dimensions. Finally, we apply Layer Normalization again and feed the features, alongside the language features, into Llama3 8B. This process enables effective integration of the features obtained from the SigLIP intermediate layers and WideResnet50_2, allowing the model to generate quality judgment results and rationales. The modules added in this section do not have pretrained weights. Thus, they are trained from scratch during fine-tuning.

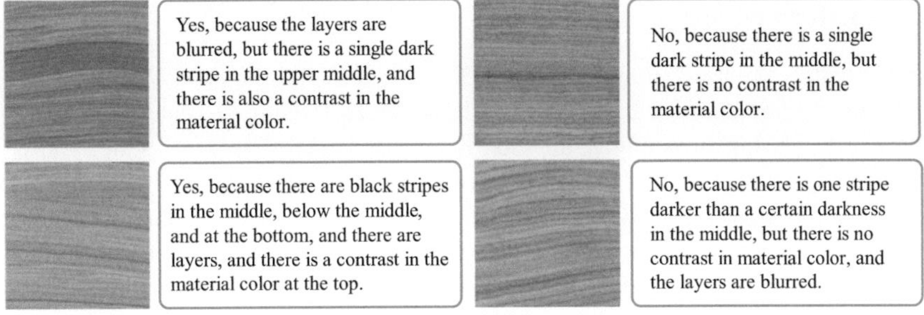

Fig. 4. Examples of data included in the constructed dataset

3.3 Evaluation Method

As evaluation metrics, we use the accuracy of "Yes" and "No" in the model's output, as well as BLEU1 [18], ROUGE-L [19], Sentence BERT similarity [20], and ChatGPT-based evaluation for comparing the target sentences (excluding "Yes" and "No") with the model's output sentences. For the ChatGPT-based evaluation, we follow the approach used in CLAIR [21] to evaluate the model's output. In CLAIR, as shown in Fig. 3, the text in black represents the prompts used to ask ChatGPT to rate how similar the model's output sentence and the target sentence are in terms of referring to the same image, on a scale from 0 to 100. This enables a more human-like evaluation compared to BLEU1, ROUGE-L, and Sentence BERT similarity. However, ChatGPT has not been trained on specialized terms such as "stripe" or "layer," which are commonly used in wood grain sensory evaluation. As a result, it may confuse these terms and produce inappropriate evaluations. Therefore, we modify the prompt provided to ChatGPT, as shown in Fig. 3. In the revised prompt, we include instructions to evaluate without confusing key features like "stripe" or "layer" and to focus on the number and degree of these features. This modification aims to provide an evaluation that is more specialized for wood grain sensory evaluation.

4 Experiments

4.1 Dataset Construction

We elicited evaluation criteria from a single expert evaluator by presenting 30 wood grain images. The evaluation criteria included the presence, color, and intensity of features such as "stripe", "material color contrast", and "layer". Subsequently, we collected quality judgment results and rationales for 130 wood grain images, with 65 images classified as good and 65 as defective. The ground truth sentences followed the format "Yes/No, because ~.", beginning with the quality judgment result (Yes/No) followed by the rationale. Examples of data included in the constructed dataset are shown in Fig. 4.

4.2 Experimental Setup

In this research, we used MiniCPM-Llama3-V 2.5 as the base model. We modified the model structure as described in Sect. 3 and fine-tuned it using the dataset constructed in Sect. 4.1. During fine-tuning, all modules were set to a trainable state, and their parameters were updated.

The dataset included ten semantically equivalent but differently phrased sentences paired with each image. During training, one of these sentences was randomly selected and used as the target for calculating the loss between the target sentence and the model's output. The input question was phrased to first ask for a binary quality judgment and then request an explanation of the rationale, such as, "Is this image the preferred grain? Please answer first with yes or no and then give the reason for your decision." Similarly, ten semantically equivalent but differently phrased versions of the input question were prepared, and one was randomly selected during training.

For evaluation, the model's output sentences were divided into the quality judgment result (Yes/No) and the rationale (the portion after "because"). Using the metrics described in Sect. 3.3, we evaluated the accuracy of the evaluation and the rationale generation. ChatGPT-based evaluation employed GPT-4o (2024–11-22). Additionally, we adopted four-fold cross-validation, using the mean and standard deviation of the four validation runs to report performance for each evaluation metric.

The optimization method was AdamW [22], with a learning rate of 1e-6 and a batch size of 64. Fine-tuning was conducted using eight NVIDIA RTX A6000 GPUs (48GB each).

4.3 Comparative Experiments

To verify the effectiveness of the SigLIP intermediate features and CNN features in automating wood grain sensory evaluation, we conducted experiments in which each feature was used individually without integration.

For the SigLIP intermediate features, we adjusted the feature dimensions obtained from the SigLIP intermediate layers using an additional Linear layer, and then input these features into the Resampler. The features obtained from the Resampler, along with the language features, were then fed into Llama3 8B to generate the quality judgment result and rationale. In Sect. 3, we added Layer Normalization and GELU to effectively integrate SigLIP intermediate features with CNN features, and also added Layer Normalization, Linear, and Layer Normalization to enhance the uniformity of the integrated features. However, when using the SigLIP intermediate features individually, these additional modules are not necessary and are therefore omitted.

Similarly, for the CNN features, integration with the SigLIP intermediate features is not required. Thus, the features obtained from Layer4 of WideResnet50_2 were adjusted by performing upsampling using bicubic interpolation and further adjusted using Linear and GELU. These adjusted features, along with the language features, were then fed into Llama3 8B to generate the quality judgment result and rationale. Among the processes described in Sect. 3.2, Layer Normalization after upsampling was not performed. Likewise, the Layer Normalization, Linear, and Layer Normalization added just before integrating with the language features were also omitted, similar to the case with SigLIP intermediate features.

Table 1. Results for the test data. "Baseline" refers to the results obtained by fine-tuning the base model of this research, MiniCPM-Llama3-V 2.5. "SigLIP-IF" represents the results when the model architecture is modified to extract features from intermediate layers of SigLIP. "CNN" indicates the results when the model architecture is modified to extract features from WideResNet50_2. "Ours" refers to the results obtained by modifying the model architecture as shown in Fig. 2.

Model	Accuracy↑	BLEU1↑	ROUGE-L↑	Sentence BERT↑	GPT 4o↑
Baseline	0.746 ± 0.080	0.356 ± 0.021	0.363 ± 0.014	0.788 ± 0.016	0.519 ± 0.021
SigLIP-IF	$\mathbf{0.792 \pm 0.041}$	0.373 ± 0.008	0.388 ± 0.028	0.799 ± 0.009	0.516 ± 0.054
CNN	0.753 ± 0.095	0.350 ± 0.012	0.385 ± 0.008	0.791 ± 0.013	0.491 ± 0.045
Ours	0.776 ± 0.070	$\mathbf{0.424 \pm 0.026}$	$\mathbf{0.448 \pm 0.014}$	$\mathbf{0.810 \pm 0.015}$	$\mathbf{0.524 \pm 0.022}$

4.4 Results and Discussion

Quantitative Evaluation. Table 1 shows the results for the test data. Table 1 includes the accuracy of quality judgment (Yes/No) and the results of BLEU1, ROUGE-L, Sentence BERT similarity, and GPT-4o evaluations for the rationale generation under each model.

From the "Baseline" results in Table 1, we confirmed that constructing a dataset from quality judgment results and rationales collected from an expert evaluator and fine-tuning the model allowed accurate prediction of quality judgments with an accuracy of 0.746. Without fine-tuning, the model outputs "Yes" for all test data, demonstrating that even with a small dataset of 130 images, fine-tuning effectively improved the model's performance.

Comparing "Baseline" and "SigLIP-IF," we observed improved accuracy, BLEU1, ROUGE-L, and Sentence BERT similarity when using SigLIP intermediate features. For evaluation, accuracy significantly improved by 0.046 compared to "Baseline," suggesting that the features obtained from SigLIP intermediate layers captured the necessary image features for wood grain sensory evaluation. Moreover, rationale generation also showed improvements in metrics other than GPT-4o evaluation. This improvement can be attributed to the intermediate features effectively capturing the necessary image characteristics for wood grain sensory evaluation. Additionally, the enhanced accuracy in the quality judgment likely contributed to the subsequent improvement in rationale generation accuracy. Recent text generation models, including MiniCPM-Llama3-V 2.5, generate sentences by predicting the next word based on the preceding context. In this research, "Yes/No" is output first, followed by the rationale. Thus, incorrect predictions in the quality judgment often led to incorrect rationales. Conversely, when the quality judgment was correct, the rationale also tended to be correct. Therefore, improving the accuracy of quality judgments contributed to better rationale generation. When using CNN features, no significant improvement was observed in accuracy, ROUGE-L, or

Sentence BERT similarity compared to “Baseline,” and GPT-4o evaluation showed a significant decline. This result may be due to the difficulty in training the additional modules. When using CNN features, all processing steps, from feature extraction by WideResnet50_2 to integration with language features, relied on additional modules introduced during fine-tuning. Modifying all image feature extraction processes in a model pre-trained on large-scale data and training it on a small dataset of approximately 100 images is challenging. Considering the challenge and improvements compared to “Baseline,” CNN features likely capture image features required for wood grain sensory evaluation better than SigLIP alone.

Table 2. Examples of the model’s output on test data. The correct sentence, the result using the baseline model MiniCPM-Llama3-V 2.5 (Baseline), and the result using the modified model as shown in Fig. 2 (Ours) are presented. Red text indicates incorrect responses, while blue text represents correct responses.

	Yes, because there is one dark stripe in the middle, there are layers, and there is also a contrast in the material color.		No, because there is a contrast in material color in the middle, but there are no stripes darker than a certain darkness, and no layers.		Yes, because there are no dark stripes, but there is a uniform contrast in material color throughout.
Baseline	Yes, because material color contrast is missing, yet two dark stripes are in the middle, with one more above the bottom, creating uniform blur.	**Baseline**	No, because the middle hosts a single black stripe, with material color contrast lacking elsewhere.	**Baseline**	Yes, because there are no layers, but the middle has two dark stripes, and above, there is a contrast in material color.
Ours	Yes, because there is one dark stripe in the middle and there is a contrast in the material color.	**Ours**	No, because there is a contrast in material color, but there are no stripes and no layers.	**Ours**	Yes, because the middle lower part hosts stripes darker than brown, with material color contrast present.

In “Ours,” all evaluation metrics improved compared to “Baseline.” This confirms the effectiveness of integrating SigLIP intermediate features and CNN features for automating wood grain sensory evaluation. Notably, BLEU1 and ROUGE-L, which evaluate word overlap between the model’s output and target sentences, showed significant improvements. This suggests enhanced ability to accurately capture the features of the target wood grain images. Furthermore, improvements in Sentence BERT similarity and GPT-4o evaluations indicate that the generated rationales were semantically closer to the target sentences. These results demonstrate that integrating SigLIP intermediate features and CNN features effectively captured both local and global features, leading to improved performance.

The quantitative evaluations for each model show that SigLIP intermediate features and CNN features capture the local features required for wood grain sensory evaluation. Furthermore, integrating these features allowed broader feature capture, resulting in improved accuracy. Thus, the proposed method in this research provides an effective feature extraction approach for automating wood grain sensory evaluation.

Qualitative Evaluation. Table 2 shows examples of the model’s outputs on the test data. From Table 2, we can confirm that both “Baseline” and “Ours” are capable of generating rationale for judgments using terms commonly employed by an expert evaluator in sensory evaluations, such as "stripe." This demonstrates the effectiveness of fine-tuning the VLM using the dataset constructed in this research, even for qualitative evaluations.

Furthermore, as observed in the first and second examples from the left in Table 2, "Ours" captures the features required for evaluation from the wood grain images more accurately than "Baseline" and outputs them as part of the rationale. In wood grain sensory evaluation, judgments are primarily based on the presence and intensity of "stripe," the existence of "material color contrast," the presence of "layer," and an overall evaluation of whether the entire wood grain exhibits sufficient contrast. Among these, the most critical factor, "stripe," is categorized by the evaluator based on their subjective perception into groups such as "black stripe," "dark stripe," "stripe that is darker than brown but lighter than dark," and "brown stripe," ranked from best to worst. These groupings are based on subtle color differences that vary among evaluators. Therefore, it is challenging for a model to learn such nuanced criteria. In the output examples from "Baseline," the model fails to accurately recognize "stripe," leading to incorrect counts of "stripe" and irrelevant outputs related to "stripe." Similarly, "Baseline" struggles to accurately capture "material color contrast" and "layers." In contrast, "Ours" accurately identifies the number and color of "stripe" and outputs them as part of the rationale. Additionally, it tends to provide precise outputs regarding "material color contrast" and "layer." These results suggest that the proposed method, which integrates SigLIP intermediate features with CNN features, improves the model's ability to extract local features and accurately identify the characteristics required for wood grain sensory evaluation.

However, as shown in the third example in Table 2, generating accurate rationale remains challenging for certain input images. For instance, when dark and thick "stripe" are present, accurate rationale generation becomes difficult. While dark lines are generally classified as "stripe," if the lines are too thick, they are not identified as "stripe" but are instead considered part of the wood's natural color. In the third example, "Ours" outputs that there is a stripe with a color intermediate between dark and brown, but in reality, this represents the natural color of the wood and should be described as "material color contrast." Such data patterns are scarce within the dataset, making it difficult for the model to learn them effectively.

5 Conclusion

In this research, we constructed a dataset comprising quality judgments and rationales provided by an expert evaluator for wood grain images. We fine-tuned a VLM with this dataset to automate wood grain sensory evaluation and generate judgment rationales. To enhance local feature extraction, we modified the VLM by integrating intermediate features from SigLIP, a CLIP ViT-based model, with features from WideResnet50_2, a CNN. Experimental results demonstrated that integrating these features improved both the accuracy of quality judgment and rationale generation. Qualitative evaluations showed that the proposed method effectively captured key features such as "stripe" and "material color contrast," demonstrating its suitability for wood grain sensory evaluation.

Future work will focus on improving accuracy through data augmentation to address errors caused by rare data patterns. While expanding the dataset through additional expert evaluations is one solution, it is impractical due to the burden on evaluators. Instead, data augmentation techniques can be employed to artificially increase sample diversity, provided they align with evaluator criteria to maintain dataset consistency. Additionally, validating the effectiveness of CLAIR's modified prompts and GPT-4o as evaluation metrics remains an open challenge. While these prompts were adapted for wood grain sensory evaluation, their reliability and alignment with human evaluations need further verification. Establishing this correlation will ensure these metrics can be confidently applied in future studies.

Acknowledgments. This research was conducted with the support of data provided by Yamaha Fine Technologies Co., Ltd., as well as the cooperation of evaluators in completing the surveys. Additionally, part of this research was supported by JSPS KAKENHI Grant Number JP23K11283.

References

1. Ke, J., Ye, K., Yu, J., Wu, Y., Milanfar, P., Yang, F.: VILA: learning image aesthetics from user comments with vision-language pretraining. arXiv:2303.14302 (2023)
2. Yuan, Z., He, Y., Wang, K., Ye, Y., Sun, L.: ArtGPT-4: towards artistic-understanding large vision language models with enhanced adapter. arXiv:2305.07490 (2023)
3. Tobitani, K., Matsumoto, T., Tani, Y., Fujii, H., Nagata, N.: Modeling of the relation between impression and physical characteristics on representation of skin surface quality. In: The Institute of Image Information and Television Engineers, vol. 71, no. 11, pp. 259–268 (2017)
4. Radford, A., et al.: Learning transferable visual models from natural. arXiv:2103.00020 (2021)
5. Dosovitskiy, A., et al.: An Image is Worth 16x16 Words: transformers for Image recognition at scale. arXiv:2010.11929 (2020)
6. Li, Y., Li, Z., Zeng, Q., Hou, Q., Cheng, M.M.: Cascade-CLIP: cascaded vision language embeddings alignment for zero-shot semantic segmentation. arXiv:2406.00670 (2024)
7. Cai, M., et al.: ViP-LLaVA: making large multimodal models understand arbitrary visual prompts. arXiv:2312.00784 (2023)
8. Geirhos, R., Rubisch, P., Michaelis, C., Bethge, M., Wichmann, F.A., Brendel, W.: ImageNet-trained CNNs are biased towards texture; increasing shape bias improves accuracy and robustness. arXiv:1811.12231,(2018)
9. Jiang, D., et al.: From CLIP to DINO: visual encoders shout in multi-modal large language models. arXiv:2310.08825 (2023)
10. Oquab, M., et al.: Dinov2: learning robust visual features without supervision. arXiv:2304.07193 (2023)
11. Yao, Y., et al.: MiniCPM-V: a GPT-4V level MLLM on your phone. arXiv:2408.01800 (2024)
12. Zhai, X., Mustafa, B., Kolesnikov, A., Beyer, L.: Sigmoid loss for language image pre-training. arXiv:2303.15343 (2023)
13. Dubey, A., et al.: (434 additional authors not shown).: the Llama 3 herd of models. arXiv:2407.21783 (2024)
14. Ba, J.L., Kiros, J.R., Hinton, G.E.: Layer normalization. arXiv:1607.06450 (2016)
15. Hendrycks, D., Gimpel, K.: Gaussian Error Linear Units (GELUs). arXiv:1606.08415 (2016)
16. Zagoruyko, S., Komodakis, N.: Wide residual networks. arXiv:1605.07146 (2016)
17. Ioffe, S., Szegedy, C.: Batch normalization: accelerating deep network training by reducing internal covariate shift. arXiv:1502.03167 (2015)

18. Papineni, K., Roukos, S., Ward, T., Zhu, W.J.: Bleu: a method for automatic evaluation of machine translation. In: Proceedings of the 40th Annual Meeting of the Association for Computational Linguistics (ACL), pp. 311–318 (2002)
19. Lin, C.-Y.: Rouge: a package for automatic evaluation of summaries. In: Text Summarization Branches Out, pp. 74–81 (2004)
20. Reimers, N., Gurevych, I.: Sentence-BERT: sentence embeddings using Siamese BERT-networks. arXiv:1908.10084 (2019)
21. Chan, D., Petryk, S., Gonzalez, J., Darrell, T., Canny, J.: CLAIR: evaluating image captions with large language models. arXiv:2310.12971 (2023)
22. Loshchilov, I., Hutter, F.: Decoupled weight decay regularization. arXiv:1711.05101 (2017)

Behavior Analysis of Grokking with Flooding

Hiroto Ito and Minoru Mori(✉)

Kanagawa Institute of Technology, Atsugi-Shi, Kanagawa 243-0292, Japan
mmori@ic.kanagawa-it.ac.jp

Abstract. In deep learning, a phenomenon has recently been reported, in which the generalization performance is rapidly improved by learning a model until losses become almost zero during learning, and by continuing learning for a further large number of epochs after over-fitting. This is known as "Grokking". In addition, "Flooding" is a method to improve recognition accuracies by learning a model to control that its loss becomes non-zero during a learning process. In this paper, we report on the effect of applying Flooding in a situation where Grokking occurs during learning a model, using a controlled environment with specific datasets, deep learning models, and hyper-parameters. In the evaluation experiments, we have confirmed that the application of Flooding sometimes improves recognition accuracies even in situations where Grokking occurs.

Keywords: Deep neural network · Over-fitting · Grokking · Flooding

1 Introduction

Deep Neural Networks (DNNs) have seen significant advances in recent years, being utilized in various fields including image recognition and natural language processing. Despite their strength in generalization, one common issue in DNNs, similar to other machine learning models, is over-fitting, where the model fits the training data too closely during training, resulting in poor performance on unseen data. A multitude of regularization techniques have been proposed to alleviate this issue. Among these are L1 regularization [1] and L2 regularization [2], which modify the loss function to prevent over-fitting. Additionally, regularization methods such as Dropout [3] and Batch Normalization [4], are often applied within DNN layers. One recent work on regularization is Flooding [5], which differs from traditional techniques in that it modifies the training process to ensure that losses remain slightly non-zero, thus preventing over-fitting via a longer training process. The double-descent phenomenon has also been observed when training models using Flooding [6]. Another recent work on over-fitting is Grokking [7]. Grokking is a phenomenon in which generalization performance improves rapidly by continuing learning for very long steps after training losses become almost zero and over-fitting has occurred. Liu et al. [8] have described learning as a process unfolding in the order of initialization, over-fitting, and representation learning. Then Grokking is considered to be a phase transition from over-fitting to representation learning. Furthermore, Liu et al. [9] and Humayun et al. [10] have shown that Grokking occurs across multiple

B. Kim (Ed.): IW-FCV 2025, CCIS 2769, pp. 56–67, 2026.
https://doi.org/10.1007/978-981-95-4578-0_5

datasets and DNN architectures. When comparing these two studies, these perspectives are seemingly contradictory. While Flooding aims to prevent zero losses during training, Grokking involves allowing training losses to drop and keep zero on longer epochs. Our study focuses on the effects of applying Flooding in situations where Grokking occurs. Specifically, we first explore the conditions under which Grokking occurs by tuning several parameters. Next, we examine the impact on recognition accuracy when incorporating Flooding under Grokking-prone conditions.

2 Related Works

This section describes two research topics, Flooding and Grokking, on over-fitting in deep learning.

2.1 Flooding

Over-fitting is a common problem in machine learning that affects the ability of a model to generalize to new data. To address this issue, various regularization techniques have been proposed. In the field of DNNs, some popular methods include Dropout [3] and batch normalization [4], which are described in Sect. 1. Other techniques include Early stopping [11] and Data augmentation [12, 13]. On the loss functions, techniques such as L1 and L2 regularization [1, 2] are often used. Flooding, a novel approach proposed by Ishida et al. [5], offers an alternative strategy. Whereas conventional methods aim to minimize the difference between the model's outputs and correct labels during training, Flooding introduces a "flood level" that is slightly above zero and trains a model to keep the loss not zero but close to the flood level. By doing so, Flooding ensures that the model is trained for a longer period without over-fitting the training data, ultimately enhancing its generalization performance. This technique helps to prevent over-fitting by reducing the model's complexity and encouraging it to learn more robust and generalizable features. Figure 1 depicts a relation among training loss, test loss, and epoch number with/without Flooding. Specifically, the process is as follows: Let $flood$ be the flood level and let $loss_{org}$ be a loss between the output of the model and correct label of training data. Then, a loss corrected by Flooding, $loss_{flood}$, is calculated by the following equation,

$$\mathrm{loss}_{flood} = \left|\mathrm{loss}_{org} - flood\right| + flood. \tag{1}$$

From Eq. 1, when $loss_{org}$ is greater than the flood level, the value of $loss_{flood}$ remains unchanged. On the other hand, when $loss_{org}$ is below the flood level, the $loss_{flood}$ is computed as the difference between flood level and the loss of the model plus the flood level. This procedure always pushes $loss_{flood}$ above the flood level $flood$. Updating weight parameters of the model using $loss_{flood}$ instead of $loss_{org}$ prevents the model from over-fitting. However, setting an appropriate value of the flood level, $flood$, is difficult, and the flood level must be determined experimentally as a hyper-parameter.

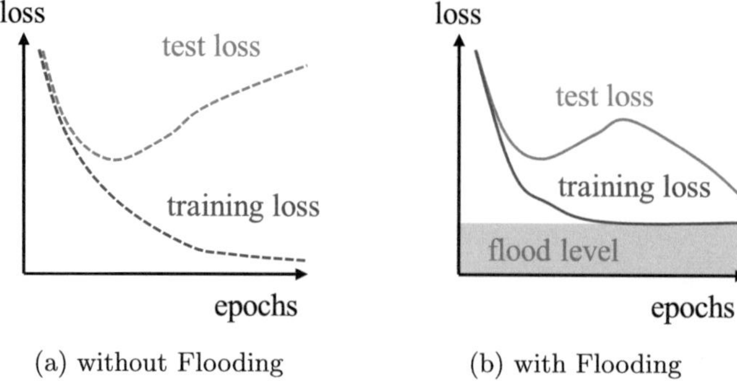

Fig. 1. Overview of over-fitting with/without Flooding.

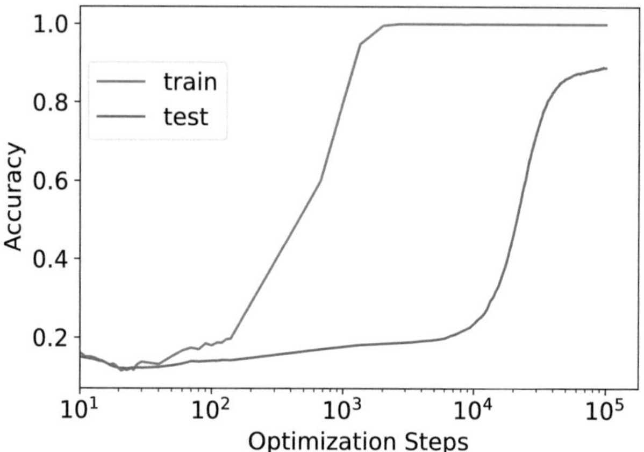

Fig. 2. Grokking. The red line shows training accuracy and the green line shows test accuracy. The training accuracy becomes 100% after 10^3 epochs. The test accuracy becomes 90% over after 10^5 epochs. This gap is regarded as "Grokking".

2.2 Grokking

Power et al. [7] have recently reported a novel phenomenon in the training of DNNs where the model's generalization performance can rapidly improve after over-fitting, provided that the training is continued for a significantly larger number of steps. They have termed this phenomenon "Grokking". Their study has also shown that the smaller the training dataset, the longer it takes for the model to reach generalization through Grokking. Figure 2 illustrates trends in training and test accuracies during Grokking. Furthermore, Liu et al. [8] have described that the learning process occurs in three stages: initialization, over-fitting, and representation learning. Grokking can be seen as a transition from over-fitting to representation learning, where the model has sufficiently learned a robust and generalizable representation of the data. It is believed that the generalization performance after Grokking is higher because the model has reached a global minimum after sufficient representation learning. On the contrary, when the training dataset is smaller, more epochs are required to reach a global minimum since more parameter updates are needed. Initially, the learning target was simple mathematical formulas solved through learning algorithms. However, after the report by Power et al. [7], similar phenomena have been observed in learning tasks such as time-series data including language and image recognition [8–10]. These findings suggest that Grokking may be a more general phenomenon applicable to various learning tasks.

3 Validation of Combination of Flooding and Grokking

This section provides the validation procedures on the combination of Flooding and Grokking. First, we describe conditions that induce the occurrence of Grokking. Next, we explain the detailed procedure of our evaluation.

3.1 Conditions for Grokking Occurrence

In their study, Liu et al. [9] investigated the conditions under which over-fitting and Grokking occur using the MNIST dataset [14]. In a preliminary analysis, they examined how many training steps were required to achieve a test recognition rate of over 60% when the number of training data was reduced. In both of their and our papers, the number of training data is referred to as the "training points." Their results revealed that unless the number of training steps surpassed 10^4, the test recognition rate did not exceed 60% when the number of training points was less than 3,000. On the basis of these results, this paper will perform experiments using MNIST as the experimental data and reduce the number of training points to less than 3,000.

In order to induce Grokking, Liu et al. [9] also multiplied the initialized DNN weight parameters by a factor called the initialization scale to further examine the effect of weight initialization on the difficulty of training. Figure 3 displays recognition rates of the training and test data of MNIST against the initialization scale, which represents the value multiplied to all the weights and biases in the DNN model. Here, the reason for multiplying each weight parameter by the initialization scale is to make the learning more difficult and facilitate over-fitting. The training data consists of only 1,000 samples. The horizontal axis represents the number of learning steps. The vertical axis shows the recognition rate. The red plot line indicates the results of the training data, while the green line represents the results for the test data. As depicted on the right bar, darker colors indicate a larger initialization scale. Based on Fig. 3, higher initialization scales result in more Grokking. These results suggest that larger weights and biases tend to lead to over-fitting of the training data. This can be regarded as equivalent to L1 and L2 regularization, where weights are controlled by restricting their magnitude through repeated penalizations. In this case, however, there is no penalization but rather a direct relationship between the initialization scale and the degree of over-fitting. These results indicate that the model requires a larger number of parameter updates through back-propagation to reach the appropriate level or norm for generalization, similar to the observations in the L1 and L2 regularization methods. We introduce the same initialization scale in this paper to induce Grokking.

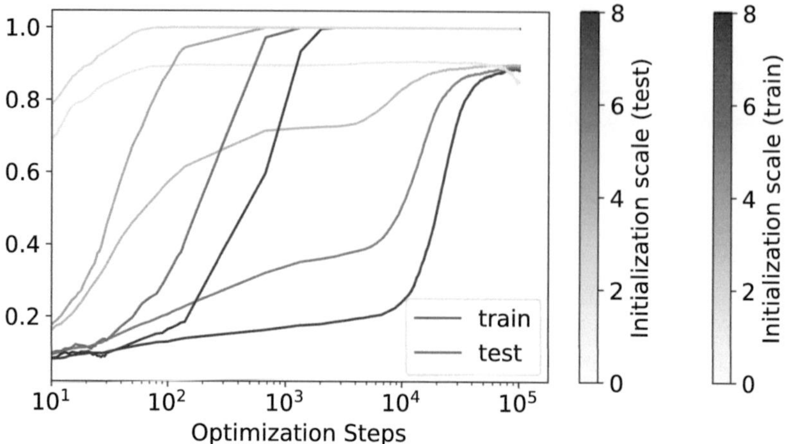

Fig. 3. Relationship between recognition accuracies and initialization scales in training using 1,000 samples of MNIST [9]. Each parameter in a model is multiplies by the initialization scale before training a model.

3.2 Validation Procedures

On the basis of certain results discussed in Sect. 3.1, we employ the following procedure to evaluate the effectiveness of Grokking and Flooding:

Firstly, we identify suitable training points and initialization scales that will be used to induce over-fitting and Grokking in the evaluation experiments. We train models without applying a Flooding technique and examine their recognition rates by plotting the data as in Fig. 4. In Fig. 4, the red plot line represents the recognition rate of the training data, the green line indicates the recognition rate of the test data, and the purple line plots the norm of the weights included in the model, respectively. The first vertical axis on the left side and the second vertical one on the right side indicate the recognition rate and the weight norm, respectively. The horizontal axis represents the number of learning steps, which are expressed on a log scale. On the basis of results in Fig. 4, we determine at which number of training steps over-fitting occurs and at which step the recognition rate increases suddenly during generalization. We then examine the difference between these step numbers to determine whether Grokking occurs. Secondly, after confirming the conditions for the occurrence or non-occurrence of Grokking, we investigate the effects of the Flooding technique. We train models using the Flooding technique with the same parameters as when Grokking occurs without Flooding. We confirm the effectiveness of Flooding by comparing the two results obtained with and without the Flooding technique. Here, as described in Sect. 2.1, it is required to determine the appropriate flood level experimentally. In this paper, we performed multiple experiments with different flood levels and used the flood level that resulted in the best recognition accuracy for the experiments in Sect. 4.

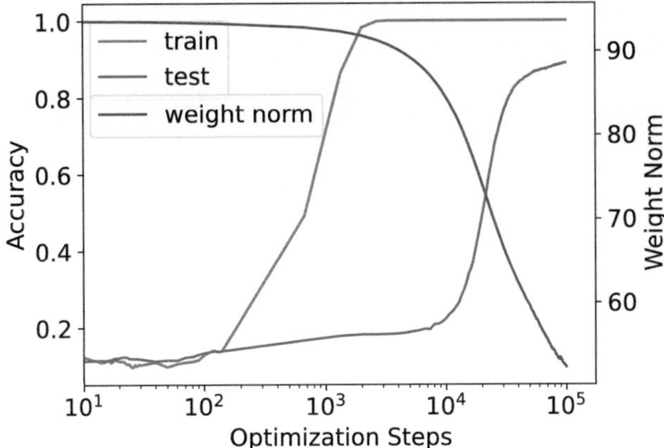

Fig. 4. Relationship among recognition rates for training data and test data and weight norm of parameters in the model.

4 Evaluation Experiments

This section reports experimental setup and results for validating the effect when combining Flooding and Grokking in learning DNN models.

4.1 Experimental Setup

The experimental setup in this paper is based on the experimental one conducted in [9]. The experimental dataset is MNIST [14]. For train points as the number of training data, we selected 1,000, 2,000, and 3,000 from 60,000 samples of training data. The number of test data is 10,000. We used a simple and small FCN-based model as DNN models; That consists of 3 Fully-connected layers. The input layer has 784 units as an input vector from an image of MNIST data. The hidden layers have 200 units. The output layer has 10 units as the number of classes. The reason for using such a small and simple DNN model is to make it easier to induce Grokking. Figure 5 depicts a structure of a DNN model used in our experiments. The activation function is ReLU [15]. AdamW [16] is used as the optimizer. The loss function is not cross entropy, that is often used, but mean squared error (MSE). MSE is calculated as differences between logits of the model and one-hot vectors as correct labels of training data. As parameter values of the initialization scale, 2.0, 4.0, 6.0, and 8.0 are used for increasing each weight in the model.

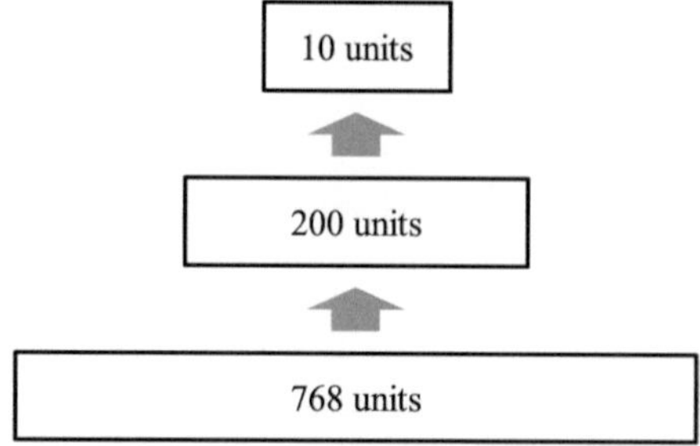

Fig. 5. DNN model used in our experiments.

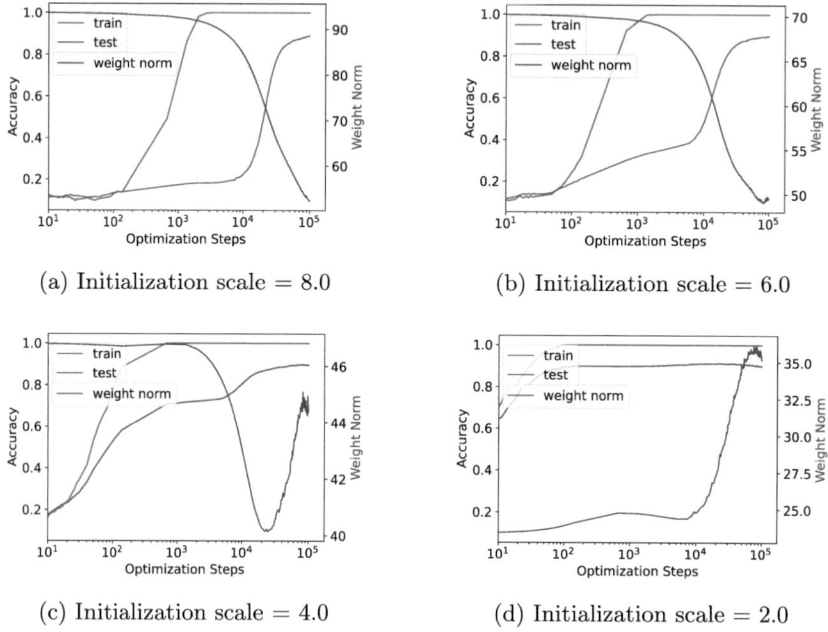

Fig. 6. Recognition accuracies for train and test data and weights norm using 1,000 train points on several initialization scales.

4.2 Confirmation of Grokking Occurrence Conditions

First, in order to check whether or not Grokking occurs, we trained DNN models shown in Fig. 5 using the experimental settings described in Sect. 4.1. Then, we plotted the obtained results for various different train point quantities and initialization scales in Fig. 6, Fig. 7, and Fig. 8. The first vertical axis in each graph expresses the recognition accuracies, the second vertical axis represents the weight norm, and the horizontal axis of each graph indicates the learning steps using a log scale. In each graph, the red plot line represents the recognition rate of the training data, the green line indicates the recognition rate of the test data, and the purple line plots the norm of the weights included in the model. The plots exhibit the same format as in Fig. 4. Within the plots, Grokking refers to a phenomenon in which the over-fitting and generalization are separate events, but determining a clear standard as to how far apart that should be considered Grokking can be difficult. For instance, deciding whether the result with 3,000 train points and an initialization scale of 8.0 or 6.0 fits the criterion of Grokking can be ambiguous. In this paper, we consider as Grokking if it is accompanied by a phenomenon in which norm of parameters in the model becomes rapidly smaller during generalization. Therefore, results such as those in the previous example are considered as Grokking. By comparing the graphs in Fig. 6, Fig. 7, and Fig. 8, it can be observed that there is a greater likelihood for Grokking to occur when the training data quantity is small, and the initialization scale is large. That is to say, Grokking is more likely to occur when the conditions of learning are not easy, and these results conform to those in prior studies. The final test data recognition rates, averaged over three models trained with different seeds for each condition, are tabulated in Table 1. Bold text indicates conditions in which Grokking occurred as indicated in Fig. 6, Fig. 7, and Fig. 8.

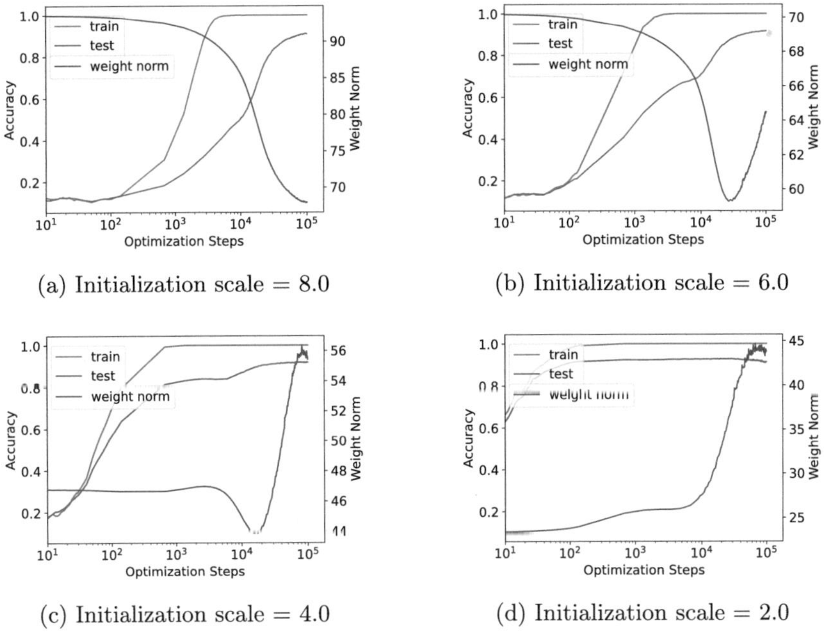

(a) Initialization scale = 8.0

(b) Initialization scale = 6.0

(c) Initialization scale = 4.0

(d) Initialization scale = 2.0

Fig. 7. Recognition results using 2,000 train points on several initialization scales on several initialization scales.

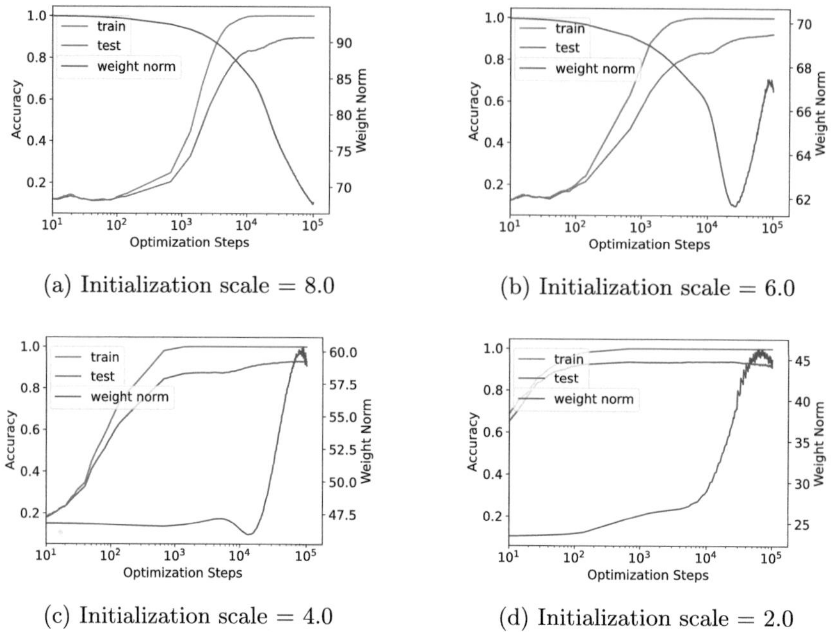

Fig. 8. Recognition results using 3,000 train points on several initialization scales on several initialization scales.

Table 1. Recognition accuracies without Flooding on several train points and initialization scale.

Train points	Initialization scale			
	8.0	6.0	4.0	2.0
1,000	**0.8890**	**0.8972**	0.8994	0.8615
2,000	**0.9082**	**0.9153**	0.9209	0.9147
3,000	**0.8983**	**0.9221**	0.9328	0.9213

4.3 Results with Flooding

Next, we evaluated the effect of applying a Flooding technique to the Grokking under the conditions for Grokking occurrence verified in Sect. 4.2. Flood levels in the experiments ranged from 0.000001, 0.000005, 0.00001, 0.00005, 0.0001, 0.0005, and 0.001. Table 2 shows the recognition results for all flood levels after applying Flooding to Grokking. Underlined entries indicate better results in relation to those without Flooding in Table 1. Bold text designates the best recognition for each initialization scale. Table 3 summarizes the optimum results for each initialization scale expressed in bold in Table 2. Each value in parentheses in each cell of Table 3 is the difference in recognition accuracy before and after applying Flooding. Table 2 and Table 3 show that, under the condition of a large initialization scale where Grokking is likely to occur, a positive effect is obtained at a certain large value of the flood level in Flooding, which is not an error level. On the other hand, when the initialization scale is small and Grokking is difficult to occur, there is almost no positive effect of Flooding even if the flood level is extremely small. In other words, even in situations where generalization is not easy and grokking occurs, which requires a large number of learning steps, further improvement of generalization ability can be achieved by Flooding if the flood level can be set appropriately. On the other hand, in situations where learning is easy, generalization is possible when learning occurs in a large number of learning steps, so the increase in error due to the setting of the flood level by Flooding is an obstacle to generalization, and conversely, is thought to lead to performance degradation.

Table 2. Recognition accuracies with Flooding at each parameter.

Train points	Init. Scale	Flood level						
		1*E*–6	5*E*–6	1*E*–5	5*E*–5	1*E*–4	5*E*–4	1*E*–3
1,000	8.0	0.8890	0.8879	0.8878	0.8922	**0.8935**	0.8723	0.8642
	6.0	0.8968	0.8951	**0.8974**	0.8946	0.8906	0.8715	0.8748
	4.0	0.8974	0.8967	**0.8982**	0.8893	0.8785	0.8606	0.8572
	2.0	0.8597	**0.8645**	0.8497	0.8070	0.8005	0.7988	0.8198
2,000	8.0	0.9082	0.9074	0.9081	0.9142	**0.9209**	0.9160	0.9129
	6.0	0.9153	0.9158	0.9152	0.9196	**0.9227**	0.9193	0.9133
	4.0	**0.9218**	0.9202	0.9191	0.9204	0.9174	0.9111	0.9036
	2.0	**0.9089**	0.9054	0.9042	0.8914	0.8839	0.909	0.931
3,000	8.0	0.8983	0.8978	0.8985	0.9005	0.9042	0.9052	**0.9089**
	6.0	0.9220	09226	0.9211	**0.9256**	0.9240	0.9201	0.9199
	4.0	0.9328	0.9323	0.9319	**0.9352**	0.9313	0.9235	0.9183
	2.0	**0.9198**	0.9111	0.9071	0.9092	0.9086	0.9110	0.9105

Table 3. Recognition accuracies with Flooding and differences between results with/without Flooding.

Train points	Initialization scale			
	8.0	6.0	4.0	2.0
1,000	**0.8935** (+0.0037)	**0.8974** (+0.0002)	0.8982 (–0.0012)	0.8645 (+0.0030)
2,000	**0.9209** (+0.0127)	**0.9227** (+0.0074)	0.9218 (+0.0009)	0.9089 (–0.0058)
3,000	**0.9098** (+0.0116)	**0.9256** (+0.0036)	0.9352 (+0.0019)	0.9198 (–0.0016)

4.4 Discussions

We examine the training transitions when the recognition accuracy is improved by applying Flooding. Figure 9 displays the recognition rates and parameter norm when Flooding is applied at an initialization scale of 8.0, where Grokking occurs, and for 1,000 and 2,000 training points, respectively. Although the Flooding application does not significantly change the overall trend of recognition rate variation, it causes the parameter norm to fall faster as the accuracy increases, which in turn accelerates the onset of generalization. These differences in the training transition may have contributed to improved generalization performance. Whether or not Flooding simultaneously serves to accelerate learning on top of improving generalization capabilities requires a closer examination.

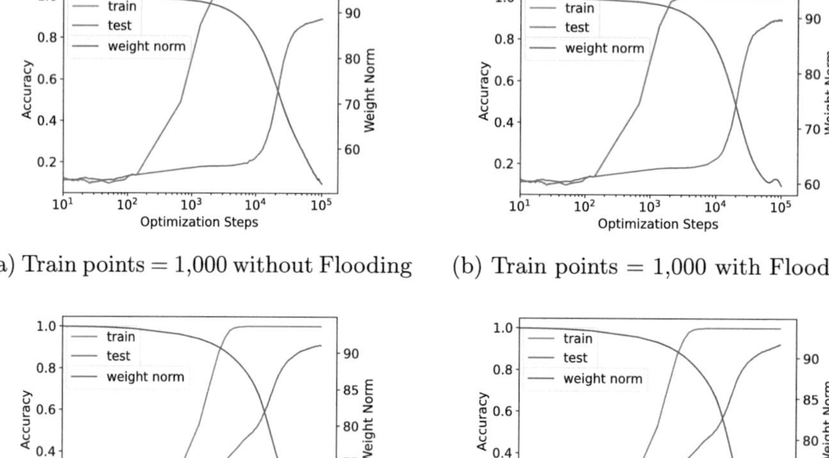

(a) Train points = 1,000 without Flooding (b) Train points = 1,000 with Flooding

(c) Train points = 2,000 with Flooding (d) Train points = 2,000 with Flooding

Fig. 9. Comparison of results using initialization scale = 8.0 without/with Flooding.

5 Conclusion

In this paper, we examined the effect of applying Flooding, a method to suppress over-fitting, to Grokking, a situation in which rapid generalization occurs by continuing learning for a long time even after over-fitting in DNNs. Our purpose here is to identify the advantages and disadvantages of Flooding towards the causes of Grokking. We analyzed these conditions by manipulating two parameters: training points, which refer to the number of training data, and initialization scale, which is the value multiplied by the weight bias. We investigated the conditions under which Grokking occurred and verified the change in recognition accuracy when Flooding was applied to each condition. The results of the validation experiments using small-scale DNNs indicate that the introduction of Flooding improves generalization performance in situations where over-fitting occurs and a certain degree of Grokking occurs. This indicates that the continuation of learning with a long number of steps is not necessarily the only factor that determines generalization. However, the application of Flooding may have a negative impact in cases where there are many learning steps and Grokking does not occur.

Future work includes validating the effect of Flooding on Grokking that occurs in larger models and on Grokking with different datasets.

References

1. Tibshirani, R.: Regression shrinkage and selection via the lasso. J. Roy. Stat. Soc. Ser. B (Methodological) **58**(1), 267–288 (1996)
2. Hoerl, A.E., Kennard, R.W.: Ridge regression: biased estimation for nonorthogonal problems. Technometrics **42**(1), 80–86 (2000)
3. Srivastava, N., Hinton, G., Krizhevsky, A., Sutskever, I., Salakhutdinov, R.: Dropout: a simple way to prevent neural networks from overfitting. J. Mach. Learn. Res. **15**(56), 1929–1958 (2014)
4. Ioffe, S., Szegedy, C.: Batch normalization: accelerating deep network training by reducing internal covariate shift. In: Proceedings of 32nd International Conference on Machine Learning, pp. 448–456 (2015)
5. Ishida, T., Yamane, I., Sakai, T., Niu, G., Sugiyama, M.: Do we need zero training loss after achieving zero training error? In: Proceedings of 37th International Conference on Machine Learning, pp. 4604–4614 (2020)
6. Nakkiran, P., Kaplun, G., Bansal, Y., Yang, T., Barak, B., Sutskever, I.: Deep double descent: where bigger models and more data hurt. J. Stat. Mech: Theory Exp. **2021**(12), 124003 (2021)
7. Power, A., Burda, Y., Edwards, H., Babuschkin, I., Misra, V.: Grokking: generalization beyond overfitting on small algorithmic datasets. In: Proceedings of International Conference on Learning Representation Workshop (2021)
8. Liu, Z., Kitouni, O., Nolte, N., Michaud, E.J., Tegmark, M., Williams, M.: Towards understanding grokking: an effective theory of representation learning. In: Proceedings of 36th Annual Conference on Neural Information Processing Systems (2022)
9. Liu, Z., Michaud, E.J., Tegmark, M.: Omnigrok: Grokking beyond algorithmic data. In: Proceedings of International Conference on Learning Representation (2023)
10. Humayun, A.I., Balestriero, R., Baraniuk, R.: Deep networks always Grok and here is why. In: Proceedings of International Conference on Learning Representation Workshop (2024)
11. Yao, Y., Rosasco, L., Caponnetto, A.: On early stopping in gradient descent learning. Constr. Approx. **26**(4), 289–315 (2007)
12. Shorten, C., Khoshgoftaar, T.M.: A survey on image data augmentation for deep learning. J. Big Data **6**(60) (2019)
13. Mumuni, A., Mumuni, F.: Data augmentation: a comprehensive survey of modern approaches. Array **16**, 100258 (2022)
14. LeCun, Y., Bottou, L., Bengio, Y., P. Haffner, P.: Gradient-based learning applied to document recognition. Proc. IEEE. **86**(11), 2278–2324 (1998)
15. Glorot, X., Bordes, A., Bengio, Y.: Deep sparse rectifier neural networks. In: Proceedings of International Conference on Artificial Intelligence and Statistics **15**, 315–323 (2011)
16. Loshchilov, I., Hutter, F.: Decoupled weight decay regularization. In: Proceedings of International Conference on Learning Representation (2019)

A Pseudo Optical-Axis-Matching Projector-Camera System by Using Intermediate Viewpoint Image Generation

Wataru Fujii[1(✉)], Chun Xie[2], and Itaru Kitahara[2]

[1] Master's Program in Intelligent and Mechanical Interaction Systems, University of Tsukuba, 1-1-1 Tennoudai, Tsukuba 305-8573, Ibaraki, Japan
fujii.wataru@image.iit.tsukuba.ac.jp

[2] Center for Computational Sciences, University of Tsukuba, 1-1-1 Tennoudai, Tsukuba 305-8577, Ibaraki, Japan
{xiechun,kitahara}@ccs.tsukuba.ac.jp

Abstract. Projection mapping is a technology that enables the display of visual content onto 3D objects using projectors. To dynamically change the projected content in response to varying real-world conditions, a projector-camera system is typically required, which combines a projector for displaying visual contents with a camera for capturing the target environment. However, estimating the geometric relationship between the projector and camera is a complex and time-consuming process, yet it is essential for accurately overlaying projection images onto real-world objects. To address this issue, a method involving the alignment of the optical axes of the projector and camera using a half-mirror has been proposed, which simplifies the alignment of their coordinate systems. However, this approach significantly reduces the intensity of the projected light, as half of the light is blocked. This research proposes a technique to pseudo-align the position and orientation of the projector and camera. Our method involves capturing two images using two cameras and synthesizing a novel viewpoint image at the optical center of the projector. This approach enables accurate projection onto 3D objects without the need for projector-camera calibration and avoids light loss during the process.

Keywords: Projection mapping · Novel viewpoint image generation · Optical axis matching

1 Introduction

Projection mapping is a technology that enables the projection of visual content onto 3D objects using projectors. By manipulating the projected content, it becomes possible to alter the color, pattern, and texture of objects [1–3]. With advancements in high-brightness projectors, image processing technologies, and projection mapping accuracy, this technique is gaining widespread societal adoption [4, 5]. Projection mapping is particularly prominent in illumination displays and light shows at events hosted in tourist attractions, attracting significant attention from visitors [6, 7]. Furthermore, it is being applied in fields such as behavioral support for children with developmental disabilities [8, 9].

B. Kim (Ed.): IW-FCV 2025, CCIS 2769, pp. 68–82, 2026.
https://doi.org/10.1007/978-981-95-4578-0_6

To dynamically change the projected content in response to real-world conditions, a projector-camera system is required. This system, often referred to as a pro-cam system, integrates a projector for image display and a camera for capturing the target environment. Applications of this system include projection mapping onto moving objects or objects with unknown position, orientation, and shape. In such scenarios, deriving the geometric relationship between the projector and camera through calibration is critical. A widely used calibration method is the coded pattern projection technique [10], which involves projecting striped images, known as gray code patterns, from the projector. The camera captures these projected images to establish pixel correspondence between the projector and the camera. However, this process is both time-intensive and unsuitable for dynamic environments, such as when objects are in motion. As a result, it poses significant challenges for real-time projection mapping applications.

An alternative approach, illustrated in Fig. 1, determines pixel correspondence between projected and captured images by aligning the optical axes of the projector and camera [11–13]. This method also establishes the geometric relationship between the two devices. Because it is physically challenging to perfectly align the optical centers of the projector and camera, techniques employing half-mirrors or beam splitters have been proposed [14]. Nevertheless, these approaches result in reduced brightness and diminished image quality due to the device's structural limitations.

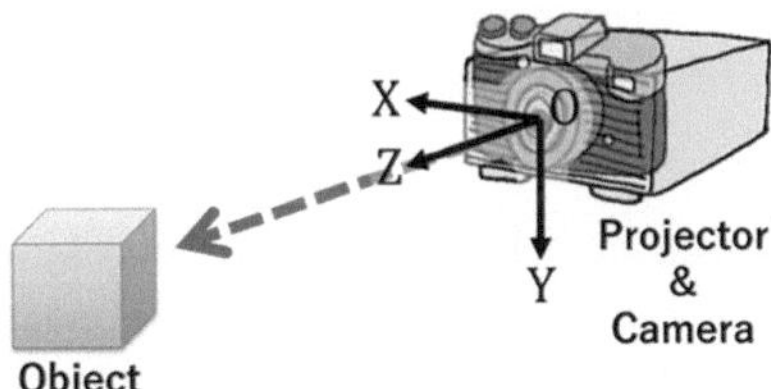

Fig. 1. Projector and camera aligned with the optical axes and coordinate system. The red dotted line represents the optical axis.

This research proposes a novel method to pseudo-align the optical axes of the projector and camera using intermediate viewpoint image generation, as shown in Fig. 2. The proposed method captures images using two cameras positioned on both sides of the projector and synthesizes an image as viewed from the optical center of the projector. This approach enables pseudo-alignment of the projector and cameras through computational processing, contrasting with previous methods that relied on physical adjustments to achieve optical-axis alignment.

The contributions of this research are as follows:

1. By generating an image from the optical center of the projector, the method enables accurate projection even when the 3D position or shape of the object is unknown, provided its 2D position on the projection plane is known.
2. The brightness of the projected image is higher compared to physical approaches, as 100% of the projector's light reaches the projection surface.
3. The integration of the projector and cameras into a single device enhances portability and ease of use.

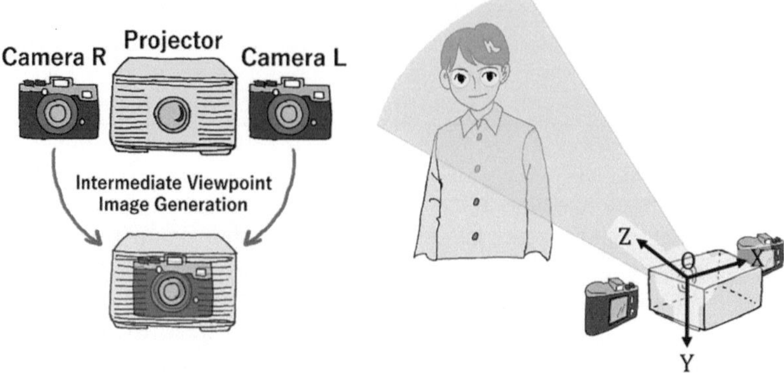

Fig. 2. Overview of the proposed method and application scenarios. The image observed at the optical center of the projector is generated using intermediate viewpoint image generation based on images captured by two cameras placed on both sides of the projector. Suppose image recognition processing can be performed on the generated image in real-time. In that case, it is possible to automatically detect the eyes of a person and suppress light illumination to that area, as shown in the figure on the right.

2 Related Works

2.1 Utilization of Projection Mapping

Projection mapping has been incorporated as a learning aid for children on the autism spectrum. Leme *et al.* have designed a new device that combines a projector and camera into one [9]. The integrated device requires little time for setup and can be easily transported to another room. It can also be used without problems by the average therapist who does not have expertise in programming. This research proposes a concept called panda masking. It detects the head of a person present in the projector's projection area and projects light after applying a masking process to suppress light illumination to that area. This process prevents the strong projection light of the projector from hitting the participant's eyes directly. Our method can be used to realize panda masking because it is possible to generate appropriate projected content based on the 2D information in the image observed from the optical center of the projector, even when the 3D positional orientation or shape of the target object is unknown.

2.2 Physical Optical Axis Matching Method

A common approach to align the optical axes of a projector and a camera involves modifying the optical path using physical devices. Fujii *et al.* demonstrated optical axis alignment for projector-camera systems by utilizing a beamsplitter [14]. A beamsplitter is an optical component that divides incoming light into two parts at a predetermined ratio, reflecting one part and transmitting the other. In their setup, a beamsplitter was positioned at a 45-degree angle between the projector and the projection target. The projection light from the projector passed through the beamsplitter to reach the projection surface, while the light reflected from the projection target was redirected at a right angle by the beamsplitter into the camera. This configuration successfully aligned the optical axes of the projector and camera within the section between the beamsplitter and the projection target, despite the devices being located in different physical positions.

However, two significant issues arise with this method. First, as the projection light passes through the beamsplitter, a portion is reflected, reducing the amount of light that reaches the projection surface. This results in insufficient brightness for the projected image. Second, to minimize the reduction in projected light, a beamsplitter with a higher transmission ratio can be used. However, this trade-off reduces the reflection ratio, thereby decreasing the amount of light entering the camera. Consequently, the camera's ability to capture optical information about the environment is compromised.

To address these limitations, this research employs a pseudo-optical-axis matching method based on computational processing, rather than relying on physical optical axis alignment. By avoiding light loss, this approach is expected to enhance both the brightness of the projected image and the accuracy of the captured image.

3 Optical-Axis-Matching by Intermediate Viewpoint Image Generation

In this section, we propose a method for pseudo-aligning the optical axes of the projector and camera through intermediate viewpoint image generation. The process flow of the proposed method is illustrated in Fig. 3, where a projector-camera system comprising one projector and two cameras is constructed. The optical axes of the projector and cameras are pseudo-aligned to facilitate accurate image projection.

3.1 Projector and Camera Positioning

Considcration of Placement Methods in Horizontal and Vertical Directions

The placement of the two cameras, both horizontally and vertically, is a critical design factor that affects the accuracy of novel viewpoint image generation. This research focuses on estimating the depth information of objects by matching feature points captured by the two cameras. To determine the optimal configuration, we analyzed horizontal and vertical camera placements.

Horizontal placement, where cameras are aligned from left to right, is an intuitive choice as it mirrors the human visual system. The human eyes are horizontally aligned, and depth perception is primarily based on horizontal disparity [15, 16]. This natural alignment is well-suited to existing visual data processing algorithms, offering compatibility and efficiency by leveraging established technologies and libraries.

In contrast, vertical placement aligns the cameras up and down, resulting in disparity along the height axis. This configuration deviates from natural visual intuition, potentially requiring customized processing algorithms and additional corrections. These adjustments could increase system complexity.

The accuracy of depth estimation is influenced by the degree of disparity, which depends on the baseline length between the cameras and their relative position to the observed object. In horizontal placement, objects are typically distributed across a broad horizontal plane, providing sufficient disparity for depth estimation. This setup enables effective utilization of the baseline length, which is advantageous for achieving high accuracy in depth estimation.

Conversely, in vertical placement, disparity occurs along the height axis. However, the height variation of objects in most observation scenes is generally less pronounced than width variation. Consequently, the disparity obtained from vertical placement is limited, leading to reduced accuracy in depth estimation [17].

Based on these considerations, we adopted a horizontal placement for the cameras to maximize depth estimation accuracy and minimize system complexity.

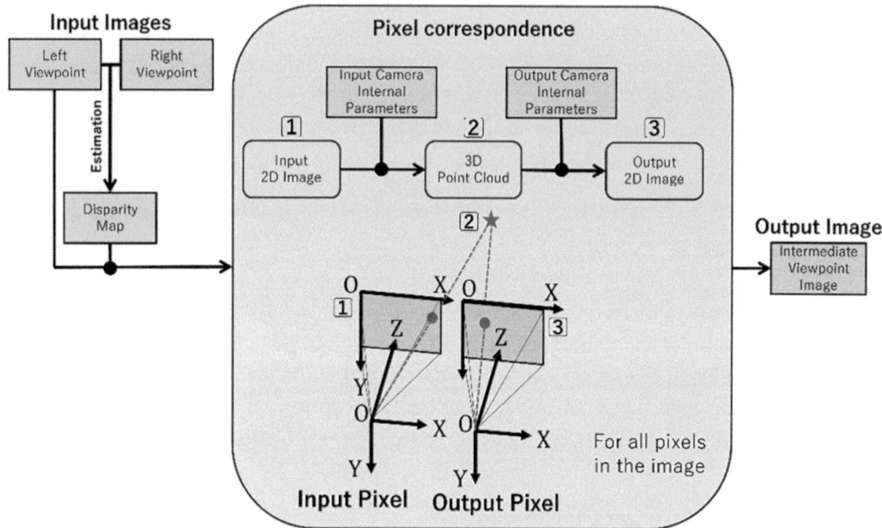

Fig. 3. Processing flow of the proposed method. A disparity image is obtained from the images captured by each camera. The intermediate viewpoint image is generated using the two captured images, the disparity image, the internal parameters of each camera, and the external parameters of camera R with respect to camera L as input. This image corresponds to the image observed at the optical center of the projector.

Depth Placement Considerations

Furthermore, to properly generate an image observed at the optical center of the projector, it is important to design the depth placement considering the relationship between the focal lengths of the projector and the camera.

The focal length of the projector is f_p, and the focal length of the camera is f_c. The following discussion is divided into three patterns according to the relationship between the focal lengths of the projector and camera.

$$f_p < f_c$$

This is the case when the focal length of the projector is shorter than the focal length of the camera. To align the optical center to a straight line, the camera must be placed in front of the projector, as shown in Fig. 4a.

$$f_p = f_c$$

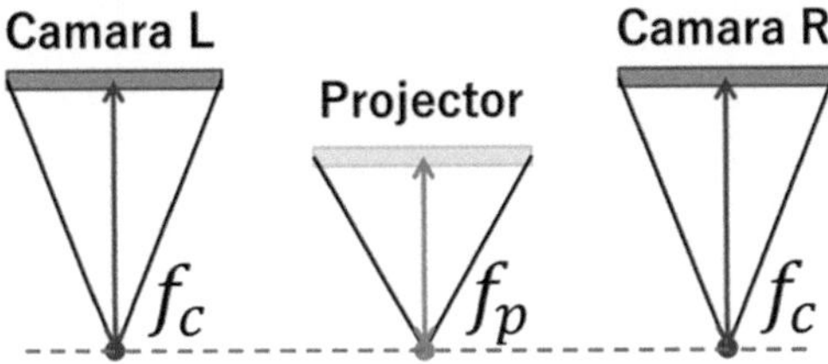

Fig. 4a. Projector-camera relationship for "$f_p < f_c$" case. The camera must be placed in front of the projector.

This is the case when the focal length of the projector is equal to the focal length of the camera. To align the optical center to a straight line, the depths of the camera and projector must be aligned, as shown in Fig. 4b.

$$f_p > f_c$$

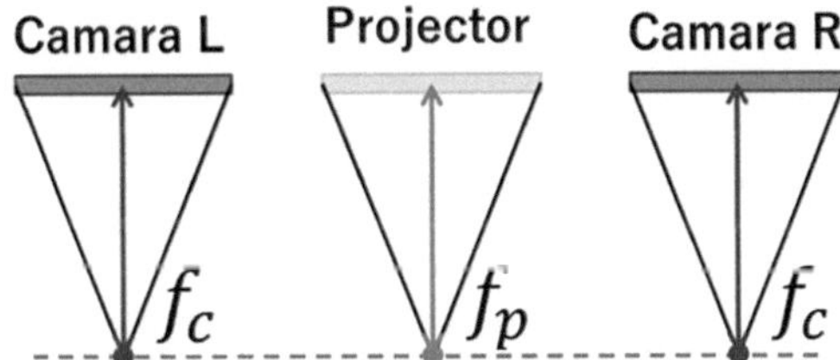

Fig. 4b. Projector-camera relationship when "$f_p = f_c$". The camera must be placed at the same depth as the projector.

This is the case when the focal length of the projector is longer than the focal length of the camera. To align the optical center to a straight line, the camera must be placed behind the projector, as shown in Fig. 4c.

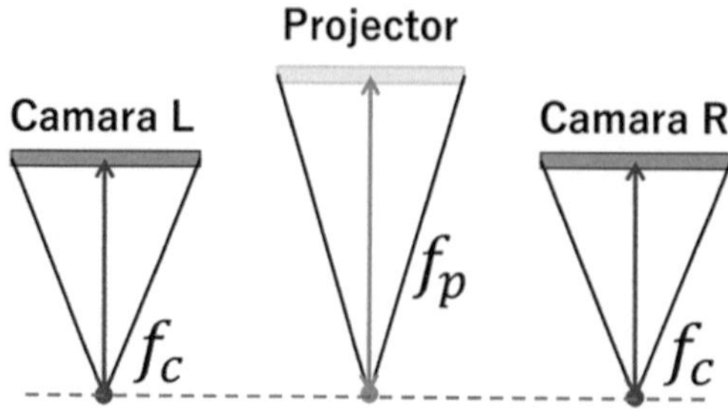

Fig. 4c. Projector-camera relationship when "$f_p > f_c$". The camera must be placed behind the projector.

3.2 Camera Calibration

Zhang's method [18] is employed to estimate the intrinsic and extrinsic parameters of the two cameras. The calibration process, illustrated in Fig. 5, involves synchronously capturing approximately 30 images of a checkerboard, which is slightly repositioned for each capture to ensure it appears in both camera views.

- **Intrinsic parameters** include details such as the camera's focal length, optical center, and lens distortion characteristics.
- **Extrinsic parameters** describe the relative positional and orientational relationship of the second camera as viewed from the reference camera.

Once these parameters are obtained through calibration, the device can be freely moved and used in various locations, provided the relative positional and orientational relationship between the cameras and the projector remains unchanged. This eliminates the need for recalibration at the projection site.

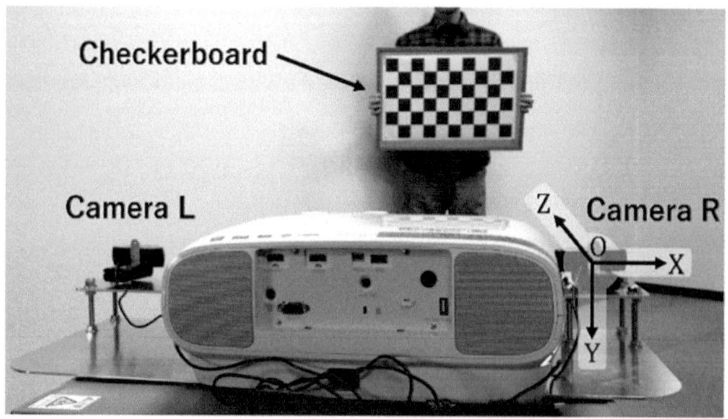

Fig. 5. Camera calibration using a checkerboard.

Intermediate image generation refers to synthesizing an image from a virtual camera positioned midpoint between the two input images. To achieve this, the parameters of the virtual camera are derived from the following matrices:

K Matrix (3 × 3): Represents the camera's intrinsic parameters. The **K** matrix for the virtual camera is assumed to be the same as that of the first input camera, as any differences between cameras using the same model are negligible and do not significantly affect parameter estimation.

R Matrix (3 × 3): Represents the camera's rotation in the world coordinate system. The **R** matrix is derived as follows:

- The **R** matrix represents the degree of rotation around the x-, y-, and z-axes, calculated as the product of three rotation matrices.
- It is first decomposed to extract rotation angles in Euler notation for each axis.
- The average of the rotation angles for the two input cameras is computed for each axis.
- Finally, the **R** matrix is reconstructed based on these averaged rotation angles.

T Matrix (3 × 1): Represents the camera's position in the world coordinate system. The **T** matrix values for the x-, y-, and z-axes are divided by 2 to calculate the midpoint between the two input cameras as viewed from one camera.

By combining these matrices, the virtual camera's parameters are accurately determined, enabling the generation of an intermediate viewpoint image that facilitates effective projection.

3.3 Intermediate Viewpoint Image Generation

Using images from two viewpoints as input, the image observed at the optical center of the projector is generated using intermediate viewpoint image generation. This allows the projector and camera positions to be matched in a pseudo-realistic manner. The target object is detected in the intermediate viewpoint image generated in the above process, and projection mapping is performed on the object. Even if the 3D position of the object in the world coordinate system is unknown, it can be projected as long as the 2D position in the image observed at the optical center of the projector is known.

4 Construction of Projector-Camera System

The constructed projector-camera system is shown in Fig. 6. Two cameras were installed on the left and right sides of the projector. Camera R is located on the right side and Camera L is located on the left side when facing the projection direction from the position of the back of the projector. Camera L and Camera R were positioned equidistant from the optical center of the projector. The projector was an EPSON EH-TW7100, and the camera was a Sony DSC-RX0. To prevent the projector and camera from being misaligned, they were fixed with bolts and nuts using aluminum plates. The height of the camera's shooting lens and the height of the optical center of the projector were adjusted to be equal. The installation angle was adjusted so that the optical axes of the projector and the camera were parallel. This was done to minimize the amount of correction for parallelization in the parallax image generation process at a later stage.

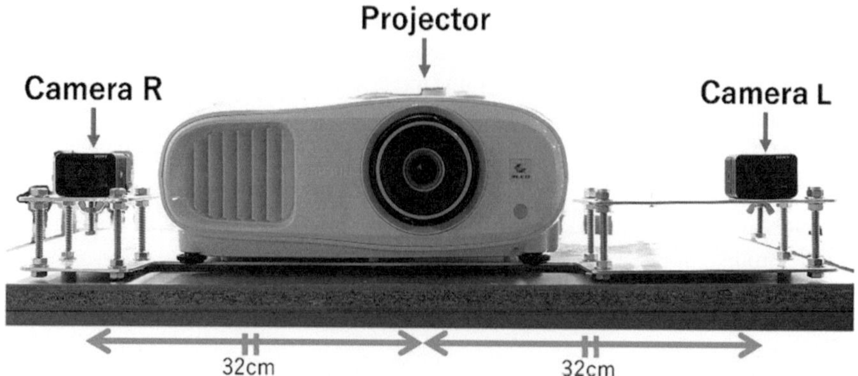

Fig. 6. Appearance of a projector-camera system consisting of a projector and two cameras. Camera R is located on the right side, and Camera L is located on the left side when facing the projection direction of the projector.

5 Optical Axis Matching by the Intermediate Viewpoint Image Generation

Camera L and Camera R capture the scene to be projected with the optical axes of the cameras aligned so that they are parallel to the optical axis of the projector. The HITNet (Hierarchical Iterative Tile Refinement Network for Real-time Stereo Matching) [19], which realizes highly accurate stereo matching processing between two input images without learning additional scene-specific features, is applied to the captured images to generate disparity images. Based on the two captured images and the estimated disparity image, the system reconstructs the view that would be observed at the optical center of the projector. Since the distance from the optical center of the projector to the lens of each camera is equal and the optical axes of the projector and each camera are fixed to be parallel, the intermediate viewpoint image of Camera L and Camera R and the image observed at the optical center of the projector are identical. The input images captured by Camera L and Camera R are shown in Fig. 7a and Fig. 7b, respectively. The disparity image generated by HITNet is shown in Fig. 8, and the image from the projector's optical center viewpoint is shown in Fig. 9. Furthermore, Fig. 10 shows the results of applying a median filter (kernel size 3×3) to Fig. 9. Finally, the results of filling in the missing areas using Telea's algorithm [20] are shown in Fig. 11.

As a comparison, a method using monocular depth estimation is also presented. To generate the intermediate viewpoint image, monocular depth estimation was performed using MiDaS (Mixing Datasets for Zero-shot Cross-dataset Transfer) [21]. This model is a monocular depth estimation model trained on several types of datasets and requires only one RGB image input to estimate the depth without the need for fine-tuning. The depth image generated by MiDaS using the image captured by camera L (Fig. 7a) as input is shown in Fig. 12, while the image observed at the optical center of the projector is shown in Fig. 13.

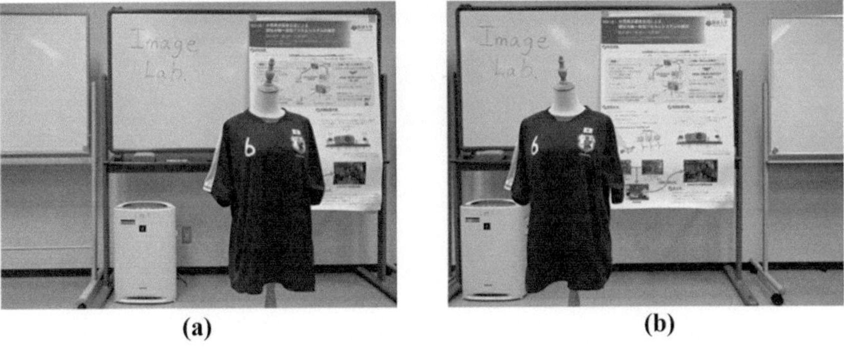

Fig. 7. **a.** An image captured by Camera L. **b.** An image captured by Camera R.

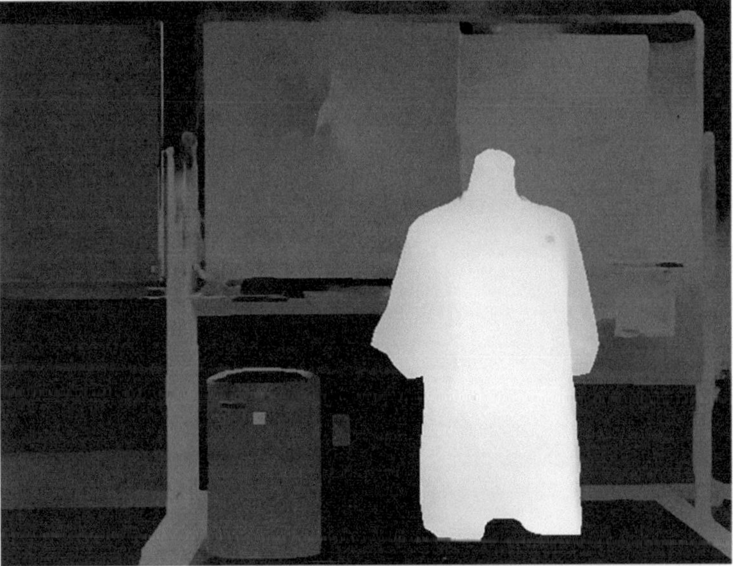

Fig. 8. A disparity image generated by HITNet. The image is displayed using the Magma color map, with black indicating a point with a smaller disparity at a farther distance and white indicating a point with a larger disparity at a closer distance.

Fig. 9. A projector-optical-center-view image generated from a captured image and the disparity image.

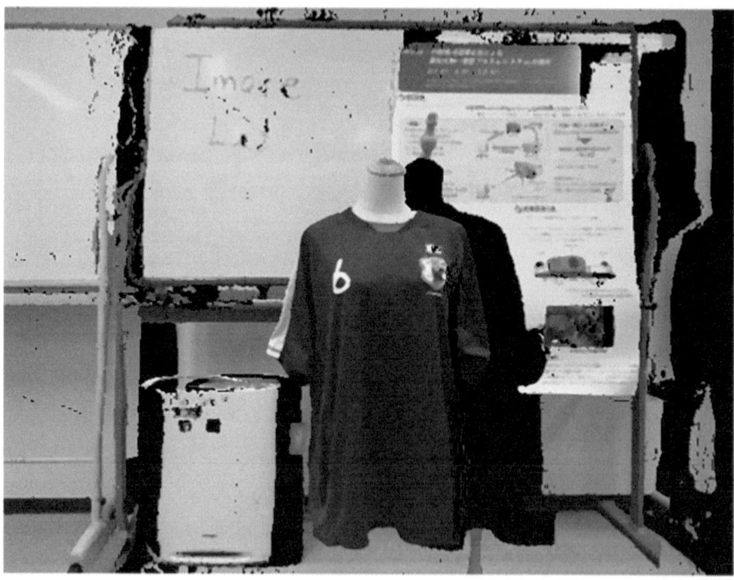

Fig. 10. A projector-optical-center-view with median filter applied to Fig. 9.

Fig. 11. A projector-optical-center-view with inpainting process applied to Fig. 10.

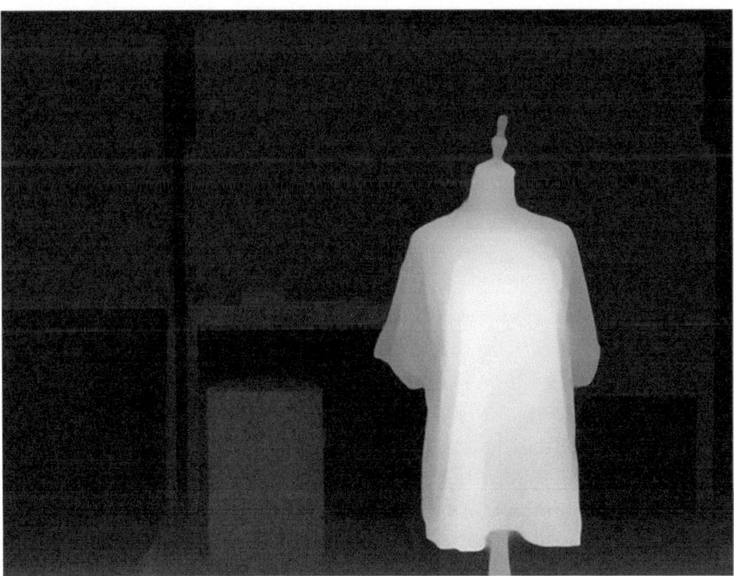

Fig. 12. A depth image generated by MiDaS, which is displayed using the inferno color map, with black indicating a point at a farther distance and white indicating a point at a closer distance.

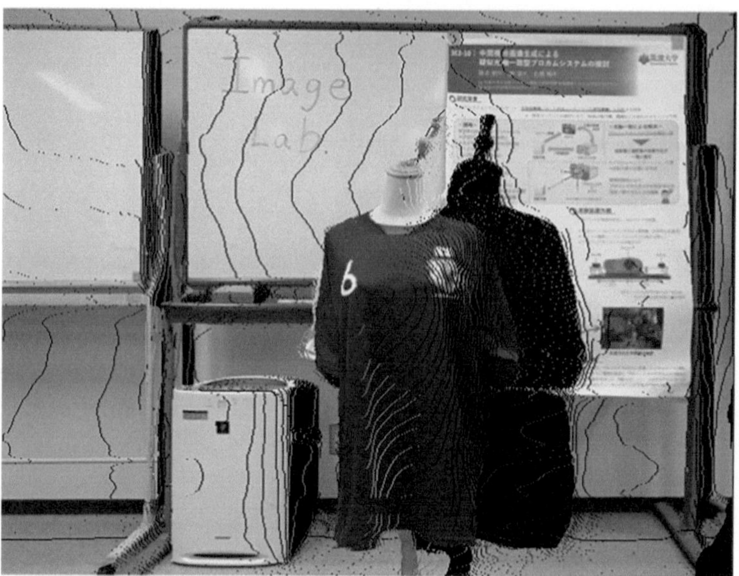

Fig. 13. A projector-optical-center-view generated from a captured image and the MiDaS depth image.

Figure 11 shows that the observed position of each object in the image changes appropriately as the viewpoint moves. Figure 13 shows that the amount of object movement is not appropriate when monocular depth estimation is used. This is because the depth estimation is not accurate due to the lack of information compared to the case using the two left and right viewpoint images.

On the other hand, there is still room for improvement in the quality of the generated images. In particular, the missing parts of the image are noticeable in the (foreground) area with a large disparity. Since image quality strongly depends on the accuracy of disparity image estimation, relatively good results are obtained when disparity image estimation accuracy is high, but overall image quality gets worse when estimation accuracy is low. In regions where texture is insufficient, similar patterns are repeated, or only one camera can observe from one of the cameras due to occlusion, stereo matching fails, and accurate disparity estimation is not possible.

Our method, an intermediate viewpoint image is generated using the left-view image and the disparity map corresponding to the left-view field of view. It is considered that missing areas could be reduced if a right-view image could be used. However, it is difficult to ensure consistency of disparity information between the left and right disparity maps in the HITNet algorithm currently employed. Therefore, effective integration of information from both viewpoints could not be achieved. Future work is needed to improve disparity estimation methods and strategies to fully leverage and appropriately integrate disparity information from both the left and right views.

Furthermore, replacing the Telea's algorithm inpainting method used in this research with a deep learning-based approach could improve image quality. On the other hand, there are concerns that it would be dependent on prior learning cases and that the processing time would be longer.

A quantitative evaluation was not conducted at this time. For example, consider a situation where a new third camera is placed at the midpoint between the two existing cameras after removing the projector. In this setup, we can evaluate quantitatively the accuracy of the intermediate viewpoint image by comparing it with the ground-truth image captured by the newly placed camera. Metrics such as PSNR (Peak Signal-to-Noise Ratio) and SSIM (Structural Similarity Index) could be utilized for this evaluation.

6 Conclusions

This research proposes a method to pseudo-align the optical axes of the projector and camera using intermediate viewpoint image generation. Our method used HITNet to estimate disparity based on images taken by two cameras placed on both sides of the projector and generated images observed at the optical center of the projector. We confirmed the possibility that the optical axes of the projector and the camera could be pseudo-aligned using the proposed method. In the future, we will improve the accuracy of the generated images. It is also planned to quantitatively evaluate the accuracy of these images. Then, we will apply an object detection algorithm to the generated images and conduct experiments in which light is actually projected from the projector.

This research received partial funding from the JSPS Grant-in-Aid for Scientific Research (Grant Number 23H00024).

References

1. Raskar, R., Welch, G., Low, K.L., Bandyopadhyay, D.: Shader lamps: Animating real objects with image-based illumination. Rendering Techniques, 2001, 12th (2001)
2. Miyashita, L., Watanabe, Y., Ishikawa, M.: Midas projection: Markerless and modelless dynamic projection mapping for material representation. ACM Trans. Graphics (TOG) **37**(6), 1–12 (2018)
3. Bermano, A.H., Billeter, M., Iwai, D., Grundhöfer, A.: Makeup lamps: live augmentation of human faces via projection. In: Computer Graphics Forum (2017)
4. Bimber, O., Emmerling, A., Klemmer, T.: Embedded entertainment with smart projectors. In: ACM SIGGRAPH 2005 Courses, pp. 8-es (2005)
5. Daisuke IWAI, Projection mapping technologies: a review of current trends and future directions. Proc. Jpn. Acad. Ser. B **100**(3), 234–251 (2024). Released on J-STAGE March 11 2024
6. Mine, M.R., Van Baar, J., Grundhofer, A., Rose, D., Yang, B.: Projection-based augmented reality in disney theme parks. Computer **45**(7), 32–40 (2012)
7. Tokyo Metropolitan Government. https://tokyoprojectionmappingproject.jp/en/. Accessed 13 Dec 2024
8. Takahashi, I., Oki, M., Bourreau, B., Kitahara, I., Suzuki, K.: FUTUREGYM: a gymnasium with interactive floor projection for children with special needs. Int. J. Child-Computer Interact. **15**, 37–47 (2018)
9. Leme, B., Oki, M., Suzuki, K.: A portable interactive projection device to provide visual support for children with special needs. In: IECON 2021–47th Annual Conference of the IEEE Industrial Electronics Society. IEEE (2021)

10. Geng, J.: Structured-light 3D surface imaging: a tutorial. Adv. Opt. Photon. **3**(2), 128–160 (2011)
11. Yamamoto, K., Iwai, D., Tani, I., Sato, K.: A monocular projector-camera system using modular architecture. IEEE Trans. Visual Comput. Graphics **29**(12), 5586–5592 (2022)
12. Amano, T., Komura, K., Sasabuchi, T., Nakano, S., Yamashita, S.: Appearance control for human material perception manipulation. In: Proceedings of the IEEE 21st International Conference on Pattern Recognition, pp. 13–16 (2012)
13. Punpongsanon, P., Iwai, D., Sato, K.: Projection-based visualization of tangential deformation of nonrigid surface by deformation estimation using infrared texture. Virtual Reality **19**(1), 45–56 (2015)
14. Fujii, K., Grossberg, M.D., Nayar, S.K.: A projector-camera system with real-time photometric adaptation for dynamic environments. In: 2005 IEEE Computer Society Conference on Computer Vision and Pattern Recognition (CVPR'05), vol. 1, pp. 814–821. IEEE (2005)
15. Howard, I.P., Rogers, B.J.: Depth perception. Stevens' handbook of experimental psychology. Sensation Percept. **1**, 77–120 (2002)
16. Read, J.: Early computational processing in binocular vision and depth perception. Prog. Biophys. Mol. Biol. **87**(1), 77–108 (2005)
17. Vienne, C., Plantier, J., Neveu, P., Priot, A.E.: The role of vertical disparity in distance and depth perception as revealed by different stereo-camera configurations. i-Perception **7**(6), 2041669516681308 (2016)
18. Zhang, Z.: A flexible new technique for camera calibration. IEEE Trans. Pattern Anal. Mach. Intell. **22**(11), 1330–1334 (2000)
19. Tankovich, V., Hane, C., Zhang, Y., Kowdle, A., Fanello, S., Bouaziz, S.: Hitnet: Hierarchical iterative tile refinement network for real-time stereo matching. In: Proceedings of the IEEE/CVF Conference on Computer Vision and Pattern Recognition, pp. 14362–14372 (2021)
20. Telea, A.: An image inpainting technique based on the fast marching method. J. Graphics Tools **9**(1), 23–34 (2004)
21. Ranftl, R., Lasinger, K., Hafner, D., Schindler, K., Koltun, V.: Towards robust monocular depth estimation: mixing datasets for zero-shot cross-dataset transfer. IEEE Trans. Pattern Anal. Mach. Intell. **44**(3), 1623–1637 (2020)

Multi-view Images Acquisition for Digital Content Creation of Cultural Heritage

Keita Kano[1](✉), Chun Xie[2], and Itaru Kitahara[2]

[1] Master's Program in Intelligent and Mechanical Interaction Systems, University of Tsukuba, 1-1-1 Tennoudai, Tsukuba 305-8573, Ibaraki, Japan
kanou.keita@image.iit.tsukuba.ac.jp

[2] Center for Computational Sciences, University of Tsukuba, 1-1-1 Tennoudai, Tsukuba 305-8577, Ibaraki, Japan
{xiechun,kitahara}@ccs.tsukuba.ac.jp

Abstract. The digitization of cultural heritage artworks and crafts has become a critical strategy for their preservation, actively promoted by governments worldwide. One approach to this digitization is the generation of free-viewpoint images. These images, created through scene reconstruction based on multi-view image acquisition, not only enable detailed reproduction of intricately shaped crafts but also allow interpolation of unknown viewpoints, offering broad potential applications in fields such as education, tourism, and research. However, securing specialized personnel to manage the processes leading up to multi-view image acquisition remains a significant challenge. This research focuses on developing optimized environments for multi-view image acquisition by leveraging neural network-based methods. By defining environmental settings, such as camera arrangements, as known configurations, it becomes possible to easily acquire the necessary multi-view images without requiring specialized knowledge. By evaluating the reconstructed images, we propose shooting environments suitable for multi-view image acquisition, aiming to support the creation of digital content and enhance its utility.

Keywords: Cultural Heritage · Multi-Viewpoint Imaging · Camera Layout · Digital Archives

1 Introduction

Cultural heritage embodies the identity of a nation and chronicles its historical journey [1]. Preserving these invaluable resources is crucial, as it is difficult to fully recover the damage. Traditional conservation methods face challenges due to factors like misplacement or deterioration over time. Therefore, exploring sustainable preservation methods that align with contemporary needs is essential. Digitization and public display of cultural assets, particularly artworks and crafts, have emerged as effective strategies to preserve and present them engagingly [2].

Digital archiving enables preservation, exhibition, and observation free from physical constraints, ensuring accessible information regardless of time or location. Given

B. Kim (Ed.): IW-FCV 2025, CCIS 2769, pp. 83–99, 2026.
https://doi.org/10.1007/978-981-95-4578-0_7

the challenges faced by cultural heritage, including preservation methods and exhibition to the general public, we focused on generating digital archives of visual content. This approach allows for non-degrading preservation and easy access, enabling anyone to view the content effortlessly. Furthermore, instead of relying on traditional fixed-viewpoint photographs, the use of free-viewpoint generation technology, which creates scenes based on multi-view data of the target object, allows for highly flexible and interactive content. Technological advancements, such as geometric algorithms and neural network-based 3D reconstruction techniques, hold immense potential.

Based on these considerations, we decided to adopt free-viewpoint generation technology. Particularly in the digitization of cultural heritage, free-viewpoint generation techniques utilizing neural networks are considered effective due to their broad expressive capabilities.

These challenges stem from the shortage of personnel with specialized knowledge required for multi-view image acquisition. This research focuses on optimizing camera arrangements for multi-view image acquisition. Since the quality of the input images significantly affects the reconstructed free-viewpoint images, quantifying the imaging environment is essential. By defining known configurations for camera placements and other environmental settings, even individuals without specialized expertise can perform the required image acquisition more easily. This paper aims to identify optimal imaging settings, including lighting and camera positions, for multi-view image acquisition through systematic image evaluation.

2 Related Works

Free-viewpoint generation methods enable the generation of images from arbitrary viewpoints as desired by the user. By leveraging this capability for interpolating between images, these methods have garnered attention for potential applications in various scenarios in recent years. Additionally, optimizing the environment can enable further improvements in accuracy.

2.1 3D Reconstruction Techniques Using Geometric Algorithms

One of the representative methods is photogrammetry, which automates processes such as Structure from Motion (SfM) [3,4] for estimating the external and internal parameters of a camera, and Multi View Stereo (MVS) [5] for reconstructing dense 3D shapes of scenes. Photogrammetry involves capturing an object from various angles to measure its dimensions, position, and shape non-invasively using multi-view images, and utilizing this data to generate a 3D model.

Combining photogrammetry with digital archiving has enabled initiatives like the 3D modeling of exhibition artifacts. Ito *et al.* [6] used photogrammetry software such as 3DF Zephyr Lite (3D Flow Inc.) [7] and RealityCapture (Epic Games Inc.) [8] to conduct surveys and generate CG models. The generated 3D models can be exported in various formats, making them compatible with multiple platforms. Cameras used for image capture included DSLR cameras, compact digital cameras, smartphone cameras, and cameras mounted on drones. While the process generally produced high-resolution reconstructions, areas with glossy surfaces exhibited significant defects. Additionally, some areas are incomplete due to insufficient photographic data.

2.2 3D Reconstruction Using Neural Networks

Another 3D reconstruction method called Neural Radiance Fields (NeRF), proposed by Ben Mildenhall *et al.* [9], has gained significant attention. NeRF trains a neural network to take a 5D vector comprising the position of a point in 3D space (x,y,z) and the viewing direction (θ,ϕ) as input and outputs the corresponding color (R,G,B) and density σ. The density parameter represents the transmission of light. Using volume rendering [10] based on the positions and viewing directions defined by camera rays, NeRF enables the generation of images corresponding to specific viewpoints, including complex shapes. The generated free-viewpoint images allow for seamless viewing even as the perspective changes, with new images continuously created according to the viewpoint while maintaining a sense of depth and realism. However, NeRF faces several issues, such as blurring in close-range renderings and aliasing artifacts in distant renderings.

To address the issues, an improved method known as Mip-NeRF (A Multiscale Representation for Anti-Aliasing Neural Radiance Fields) [11] has been proposed. Unlike conventional NeRF, which represents space as a single point, Mip-NeRF employs a multiscale representation that considers the spatial extent of a pixel and treats the input as a cone. This approach incorporates anti-aliasing during the volume rendering process, enabling the generation of smooth and realistic free-viewpoint images, even at high resolutions. Mip-NeRF successfully resolves the issues of blurred renderings at close distances and aliasing at far distances, which are challenges faced by NeRF. While maintaining the computational efficiency of NeRF, Mip-NeRF achieves higher accuracy, producing smoother and visually more precise images. When photographing cultural artifacts on display, there may be limited flexibility in adjusting the shooting distance. Therefore, the stability of Mip NeRF's accuracy across varying distances is considered highly beneficial.

Figure 1 shows a comparison of free-viewpoint generation results for glossy objects using Metashape [12], a photogrammetry software, and Mip-NeRF. It can be observed that Mip-NeRF is able to represent features that Metashape fails to capture. Cultural artifacts often include items with glossy surfaces or features that depend on the viewing angle, making Mip-NeRF more suitable for digitization.

Fig. 1. Free-viewpoint generation of objects with view-dependent colors such as specular and structural colors: Comparison results between Metashape and Mip-NeRF

2.3 Improvement of Sensing Quality Through Camera Network Configuration

In reconstruction, the quality of the input image set contributes to the output results, making environmental setup a crucial factor for achieving high-precision restoration.

Zhang *et al.* [13] conducted research aimed at optimizing sensing quality in camera networks and proposed a novel evaluation metric that considers camera viewpoints and distortion correction. Based on this metric, they optimized parameters such as camera positions, viewpoints, focal lengths, and distortion correction, thereby improving target coverage and position estimation accuracy. Notably, the proposed method demonstrated superior performance through simulations and experiments, showing reduced errors compared to conventional methods.

From these findings, it was concluded that accuracy improvement can also be expected in this research by optimizing environmental configurations.

3 Multi-view Images Acquisition

This research focuses on input multi-view images for the digitization of cultural heritage. Mip-NeRF is considered due to its ability to handle view-dependent colors such as specular and structural colors, offering a broader range of expressive possibilities compared to photogrammetry software.

For multi-view image acquisition, efficiency can be achieved by quantifying the range of shooting distances based on the number of required images, camera arrangements, and focal lengths necessary for accurate reconstruction of the target object. Since cultural heritage artifacts are often unique exhibits where close-range photography may not be feasible, it is desirable to establish a flexible range of shooting distances. Figure 2 illustrates the conditions based on the parameters of the shooting configuration.

The optimal shooting configuration for capturing is defined as follows:

- Full directional coverage of the target object.

  (Factors: camera layout and number of cameras).
- Flexibility in shooting distance from the subject.

  (Factors: shooting distance and focal length).
- Appropriate levels of brightness and contrast in images.

  (Factors: lighting arrangement and camera exposure settings).

4 Multi-view Images Acquisition Using Computer Graphics

In the case of training with Mip-NeRF, the quality of multi-view images and the accuracy of camera parameters significantly contribute to the precision of the results. When using real-world images, accurate camera parameters may not be obtainable if camera calibration is challenging, making it difficult to verify the impact of different shooting environments. To address this issue, an environment is constructed using open-source free 3DCG software. The advantages include not only the accuracy of camera calibration but also the ease of configuring arbitrary lighting and camera arrangements.

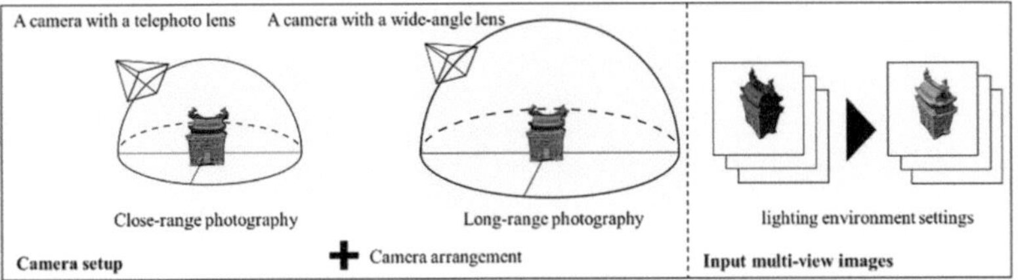

Fig. 2. A shooting configuration based on parameters: When capturing the subject so that the area visible to the camera is equally framed, the shooting distance differs between telephoto and wide-angle lenses. The input images set should preserve the details of the subject.

4.1 Camera Arrangement

This section focuses on the environmental configuration of camera arrangements. When acquiring multi-view images, random camera placement may result in insufficient coverage of certain areas of the target object and a lack of reproducibility. To address this issue, four types of camera arrangements, as shown in Fig. 4: (a) random, (b) grid arrangement, (c) circular arrangement, and (d) Fibonacci hemisphere arrangement [14]. As illustrated in Fig. 3, the cameras are positioned on the upper of a sphere with a radius r, maintaining a consistent distance from the target object. Additionally, the cameras are oriented to face the center of the target object.

The grid arrangement is a method in which cameras are evenly distributed on the surface of a sphere by systematically dividing the longitude.

The circular arrangement involves placing cameras in circular patterns at 30° and 60° latitude on a hemisphere. This configuration provides the advantage of obtaining shape information more easily due to its relatively systematic viewpoint placement.

The Fibonacci hemisphere arrangement uses a point placement algorithm based on the golden angle $\alpha \cong 137.5°$, derived from the Fibonacci sequence, to evenly distribute points on the surface of the upper hemisphere. The camera height is spaced linearly along z-coordinate. The azimuthal angle θ_i for each camera position is calculated as shown in Eq. (1):

$$\theta_i = i \bullet \alpha mod'2\pi\# \quad (1)$$

where, i represents the index of the camera position (0, 1, 2,…, $N - 1$). This method ensures that each camera is positioned uniformly over a hemisphere.

In a CG environment, a common feature of multi-view image acquisition is that all cameras are oriented toward the center and arranged on a hemisphere with a radius of r. On the other hand, the difference lies in the method of camera arrangement.

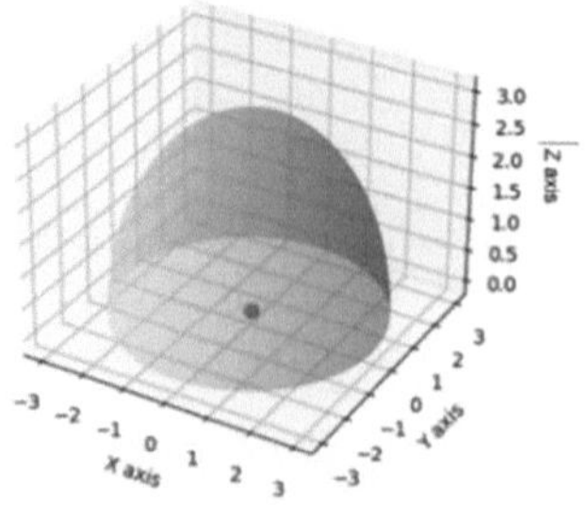

Fig. 3. Cameras are arranged on the upper hemisphere of a sphere with radius r. The red dot indicates the target object.

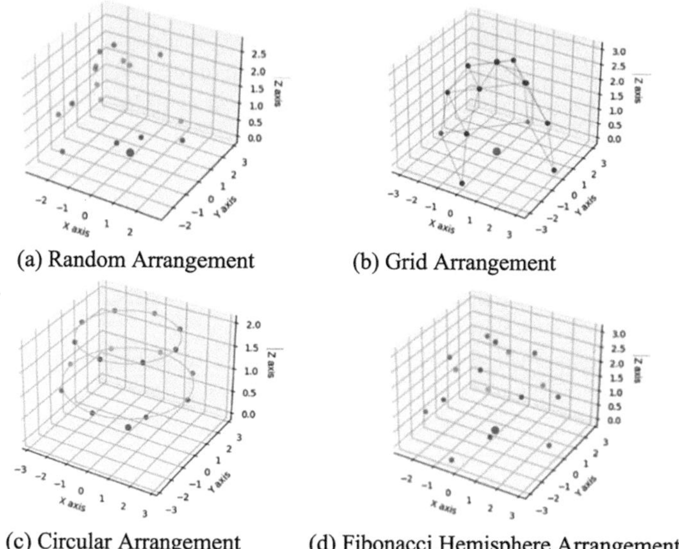

(a) Random Arrangement (b) Grid Arrangement

(c) Circular Arrangement (d) Fibonacci Hemisphere Arrangement

Fig. 4. Four types of camera arrangements. Each figure represents the case with 16 cameras. The red dot indicates the target object, and the blue dots represent the camera positions.

4.2 Lighting Control Based on Histograms

The brightness of input images have to be appropriately adjusted to prevent information loss across the entire image. For example, when an image suffers from overexposure (white clipping), it becomes difficult to distinguish which areas are brighter within the overexposed regions, resulting in a loss of information. Similarly, underexposure (black clipping) causes details in dark areas to be lost. To address this issue, this research aims to enhance the quality of input images by controlling their brightness through both light source placement and camera exposure adjustment.

First, the overall brightness of the image is controlled through camera exposure adjustments. This is achieved using a luminance histogram to ensure that the brightness of the image is appropriately distributed. The luminance histogram represents the distribution of brightness in the HSV color space and provides a direct evaluation of how bright or dark the entire image is. If the histogram skews significantly to the right, overexposure is present; if it skews to the left, underexposure occurs. Exposure settings are adjusted to ensure the histogram is centered, thereby avoiding such extremes.

Next, the local brightness balance within the image is refined by positioning light sources ("Light") appropriately. Specifically, evaluations are conducted on the front, back, and top surfaces of the target object, and the positions of the light sources are adjusted to achieve evenly distributed brightness. The suitability of the light source placement is assessed using an RGB histogram, which visualizes whether specific color components are uniformly distributed or concentrated within certain ranges. During this process, care is taken to avoid brightness imbalances in specific colors or regions.

Figure 5(a) and (b) illustrate the brightness comparisons using histograms.

By combining these methods, a set of input images with minimized brightness and color bias is obtained. Ultimately, the appropriate exposure adjustments and light source placements ensure a balanced brightness distribution across the target object and minimize information loss throughout the image.

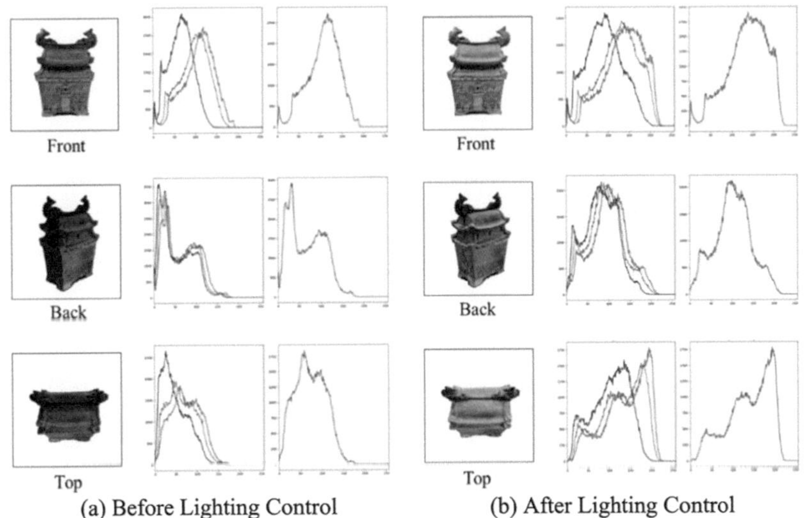

Fig. 5. Visualization of brightness and darkness using histograms. From left to right: original image, RGB histogram, and luminance histogram.

5 Focal Length and Field of View Settings

5.1 Focal Length of Camera Lenses

When artworks or crafts are displayed in narrow spaces, it can be difficult to step back and capture them from a distance. On the other hand, there are cases where barriers make it challenging to get closer to the subject. In such situations, it becomes necessary to adjust the focal length of the camera lens to photograph the subject. This requires a discussion on the relationship between focal length, shooting distance, and field of view.

The focal length of a camera lens refers to the distance from the lens to the image sensor when the lens is focused. Lenses with shorter focal lengths have a wider field of view, capturing a broader area. Conversely, lenses with longer focal lengths have a narrower field of view, resulting in a larger and more focused appearance of the subject. Generally, lenses with a wide field of view are called wide-angle lenses, while those with a narrow field of view are referred to as telephoto lenses.

For multi-view image acquisition in the CG environment, lenses with focal lengths ranging from 20 mm to 100 mm are used.

5.2 Normalization of Target Object Area in Images

Using the field of view (FoV) calculation formulas (2) and (3), the camera's angle of view is adjusted to ensure the entire target object fits within the frame [15]. This allows the proportion of the object in the image to remain consistent regardless of the focal length (f). Figure 6 illustrates a schematic diagram of the relationship between focal length and field of view.

Given that the size of the reconstructed model is 1.0 m in width, 1.5 m in depth, and 2.0 m in height, the vertical FoV (θ) is calculated. Additionally, the camera in the CG environment is configured with a full-frame image sensor measuring 36 mm horizontally and 24 mm vertically.

$$Vertical\theta = 2 \bullet \tan^{-1}\left(\frac{\frac{\text{Image Sensor Size}}{2}}{f}\right)\# \tag{2}$$

$$\tan\left(\frac{\theta}{2}\right) = \frac{\frac{ObjectHeight}{2}}{ShootingDistance}\# \tag{3}$$

The shooting distance in equation (3) corresponds to the radius setting in the CG environment. Figure 7 illustrates the appearance of images for various focal lengths under this configuration.

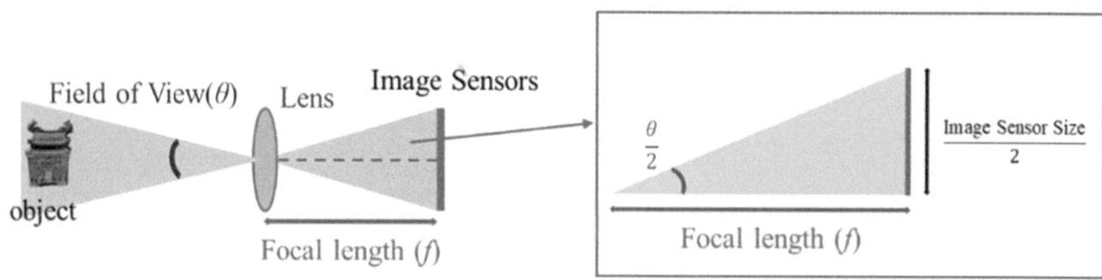

Fig. 6. Schematic diagram of focal length and field of view. A value of 24 mm is used for the calculation of the vertical field of view, corresponding to a full-frame image sensor.

Fig. 7. Appearance of images at different focal lengths. The area of the target object remains consistent.

6 Experiment

The shooting environment was created using Blender 3.6 [16], an open-source 3D CG software. The target object used in the experiment is a model with unique and complex shapes characteristic of cultural artifacts, measuring 1.0 m in width, 1.5 m in depth, and 2.0 m in height. By adjusting the camera parameters, the method can also accommodate objects of other sizes. Therefore, the insights gained from this experiment are considered applicable to other common cultural artifacts. As a reconstruction method, Mip-NeRF[11], which enables the reconstruction of complex shapes, is used. Multi-view images were captured using four different camera arrangements, with an image resolution of 800 pixels $\times$ 800 pixels, and divided into training, testing, and validation folders in a ratio of 7:2:1.

The experiment is conducted using an RTX 3090 GPU, where Mip-NeRF is trained for 100,000 steps to ensure convergence.

6.1 Evaluation Metrics for Novel View Images

The evaluation is conducted on 100 novel view images. As shown in Fig. 8, the evaluation is performed on both the entire image and only the target object excluding the background.

The evaluation metrics includes PSNR (Peak Signal-to-Noise Ratio), which measures image quality, and SSIM (Structural Similarity Index Measure) [17] and LPIPS (Learned Perceptual Image Patch Similarity) [18], which are perceptually oriented metrics.

PSNR is calculated based on the ratio of the maximum pixel value to noise.

SSIM measures the structural similarity between images, evaluating pixel values and contrast changes. It ranges from -1 to 1, with values closer to 1 indicating greater similarity between the two images.

LPIPS evaluates perceptual similarity using features extracted by a pre-trained convolutional neural network (CNN). The values range from 0 to 1, with smaller values indicating higher similarity. AlexNet is used as the CNN for this evaluation.

Additionally, the standard deviation (SD) for each evaluation metric is calculated.

(a) Entire Image

(b) Target object only

Fig. 8. Evaluation regions for novel view images. The hatched area in (b) is excluded from the evaluation.

6.2 Quantitative Evaluation

6.2.1 Evaluation Results Based on Camera Arrangements

Image evaluations are conducted with the focal length fixed at 60 mm across four different camera arrangements. The shooting distance is adjusted to ensure that the target object occupied the same proportion of the image area. The results for 16 cameras are shown in Table 1, and the results for 64 cameras are presented in Table 2. The highest accuracy in the table is highlighted in blue, and the second highest is highlighted in light blue.

From the results in Table 1, the Fibonacci hemisphere arrangement showed the best values with low variance. This is likely because this arrangement allows the cameras to evenly cover the target object without sparse areas. Additionally, comparing Tables 1 and 2, it is confirmed that a higher number of images improves accuracy and reduces variance. This is likely because denser camera coverage results in better rendering of the target object.

Table 1. Image evaluation results for each of the four camera arrangements with 16 cameras. The upper rows show the results for the entire image, while the lower rows show the results for the target object only.

Camera Placement	PSNR↑	SSIM↑	LPIPS↓	SD PSNR	SD SSIM	SD LPIPS
Random	18.8423	0.8625	0.2125	2.0395	0.0213	0.0274
Grid	21.4932	0.9043	0.0984	0.3572	0.0153	0.0113
Ring-shaped	19.0877	0.9128	0.1145	2.1242	0.0157	0.0286
Fibonacci Hemisphere	21.7969	0.9206	0.1033	0.6567	0.0106	0.0234
Random	20.2502	0.5971	0.2787	1.4750	0.0543	0.0238
Grid	21.4484	0.6844	0.1893	1.1042	0.0499	0.0209
Ring-shaped	23.4416	0.7759	0.1545	0.5716	0.0248	0.0122
Fibonacci Hemisphere	23.3645	0.7622	0.1622	0.4073	0.0216	0.0151

Table 2. Image evaluation results for each of the four camera arrangements with 64 cameras. The upper rows show the results for the entire image, while the lower rows show the results for the target object only.

Camera Placement	PSNR↑	SSIM↑	LPIPS↓	SD PSNR	SD SSIM	SD LPIPS
Random	22.2438	0.9311	0.0857	0.3387	0.0060	0.0107
Grid	22.3485	0.9361	0.0775	0.4160	0.0056	0.0096
Ring-shaped	21.1374	0.9260	0.1021	0.6650	0.0088	0.0232
Fibonacci Hemisphere	22.7364	0.9396	0.0737	0.4283	0.0049	0.0085
Random	23.6692	0.7837	0.1556	0.3024	0.0236	0.0084
Grid	23.6449	0.8018	0.1473	0.3193	0.0122	0.0125
Ring-shaped	23.8046	0.8153	0.1408	0.2721	0.0106	0.0116
Fibonacci Hemisphere	23.6989	0.7902	0.1535	0.2803	0.0128	0.0115

6.2.2 Evaluation Results Based on Variable Focal Lengths.

Tables 3, 4, 5, and 6 present the results of image evaluation conducted for each camera arrangement. In this evaluation, focal lengths ranging from 20 mm to 100 mm are used, and the shooting distances are adjusted to ensure that the target object's area occupied the same proportion in the images.

The result shows that focal lengths around 50 mm, generally considered standard lenses, demonstrated good performance. When using wide-angle lenses, projection distortion causes shape variations across viewpoints, making it difficult to learn a consistent shape and resulting in poor rendering. On the other hand, with telephoto lenses, the compression effect reduces the sense of depth, which likely contributed to the lower evaluation scores.

6.2.3 Image Evaluation Metrics and Target Object Area Ratio

Figure 9 shows the graph of image evaluation results based on the target object's area ratio relative to the shooting distance when the focal length is set to 50 mm. Additionally, Fig. 10 presents the area ratio and evaluation results for focal lengths ranging from 20 mm to 100 mm, with the field of view set to capture the entire target object.

Table 3. Evaluation results of novel view images obtained from 16 randomly captured multi-view images. Due to the irregular arrangement, there is a possibility that the camera positions are uneven. As a result, the variance is high.

Focal length [mm]	Distance [m]	PSNR↑	SSIM↑	LPIPS↓	SD PSNR	SD SSIM	SD LPIPS
20	1.7	10.6631	0.7867	0.3975	0.8518	0.0407	0.0659
35	2.9	26.8133	0.9112	0.0715	2.2165	0.0345	0.0237
50	4.2	26.3893	0.9249	0.0835	2.4184	0.0175	0.0203
60	5.0	18.8423	0.8625	0.2125	2.0395	0.0213	0.0274
70	5.8	23.9662	0.9021	0.0964	1.4517	0.0299	0.0176
85	7.1	10.3533	0.6146	0.5767	0.9008	0.0342	0.0406
100	8.4	9.5982	0.6719	0.5891	0.9442	0.0318	0.0432
20	1.7	5.0141	0.2801	0.5431	0.9887	0.0320	0.0281
35	2.9	21.0488	0.6466	0.1979	2.2577	0.1302	0.0553
50	4.2	22.5519	0.7260	0.1749	0.8879	0.0555	0.0186
60	5.0	20.2502	0.5971	0.2787	1.4750	0.0543	0.0238
70	5.8	21.0336	0.6502	0.1812	1.7767	0.1125	0.0342
85	7.1	8.4360	0.2111	0.4270	0.8489	0.0185	0.0254
100	8.4	5.1251	0.2700	0.5204	0.9459	0.0432	0.0444

The graphs represent results from capturing 16 multi-view images following the Fibonacci hemisphere configuration, but similar distributions are observed across all camera arrangements. These findings indicate that shooting distance and focal length are critical components for accurate rendering.

Table 4. Evaluation results of novel view images obtained from 16 multi-view images captured using the grid arrangement. Due to the difficulty of capturing all directions with 16 shots, the variance is high. Additionally, it has the lowest maximum accuracy value among the four types of arrangements.

Focal length [mm]	Distance [m]	PSNR↑	SSIM↑	LPIPS↓	SD PSNR	SD SSIM	SD LPIPS
20	1.7	10.6589	0.7907	0.3816	0.8299	0.0213	0.0398
35	2.9	25.4767	0.9083	0.0893	1.9193	0.0190	0.0175
50	4.2	19.4631	0.8950	0.1198	3.0238	0.0306	0.0318
60	5.0	21.4932	0.9043	0.0984	0.3572	0.0153	0.0113
70	5.8	24.9859	0.9116	0.0969	1.1704	0.0197	0.0149
85	7.1	10.7037	0.7808	0.3989	0.8687	0.0299	0.0510
100	8.4	8.6408	0.6293	0.6151	0.6658	0.0275	0.0314
20	1.7	4.9508	0.2789	0.5437	0.6329	0.0367	0.0290
35	2.9	20.9114	0.6559	0.1973	1.0992	0.0576	0.0238
50	4.2	21.4247	0.7004	0.1753	1.3753	0.0579	0.0236
60	5.0	21.4484	0.6844	0.1893	1.1042	0.0499	0.0209
70	5.8	20.6709	0.6703	0.1780	1.5356	0.0635	0.0268
85	7.1	5.0812	0.2562	0.5080	0.5992	0.0256	0.0256
100	8.4	5.3503	0.2574	0.5087	0.6625	0.0224	0.0222

6.3 Qualitative Evaluation

Figure 11 shows one rendering result out of 100 for focal lengths ranging from 20 mm to 100 mm. When the focal lengths are 20 mm, 85 mm, and 100 mm, the rendering is significantly distorted to the point where the original shape is unrecognizable. From this, it can be inferred that a realistic shooting distance for this model would be within the range of 2.9 m to 5.8 m.

Table 5. Evaluation results of novel view images obtained from 16 multi-view images captured using the circular arrangement. It has the highest maximum accuracy value among the four types of arrangements. However, the overall variance is not small. This is likely due to the lack of vertical viewpoint information.

Focal length [mm]	Distance [m]	PSNR↑	SSIM↑	LPIPS↓	SD PSNR	SD SSIM	SD LPIPS
20	1.7	9.6917	0.7051	0.4991	1.8690	0.1131	0.1436
35	2.9	27.9909	0.9455	0.0492	0.9530	0.0051	0.0049
50	4.2	29.4486	0.9503	0.0474	0.3915	0.0049	0.0061
60	5.0	19.0877	0.9128	0.1145	2.1242	0.0157	0.0286
70	5.8	18.8952	0.8844	0.1447	2.0699	0.0214	0.0338
85	7.1	10.3469	0.7579	0.4209	0.7653	0.0296	0.0536
100	8.4	10.0022	0.7121	0.5069	0.8694	0.0371	0.0661
20	1.7	5.2330	0.2621	0.5527	0.8876	0.0397	0.0353
35	2.9	22.3819	0.7826	0.1437	1.4061	0.0343	0.0119
50	4.2	23.4983	0.7976	0.1422	0.5902	0.0268	0.0111
60	5.0	23.4416	0.7759	0.1545	0.5716	0.0248	0.0122
70	5.8	20.7527	0.6943	0.1794	1.4341	0.0307	0.0156
85	7.1	4.8601	0.2686	0.5207	0.6213	0.0309	0.0305
100	8.4	5.3295	0.2419	0.5028	0.6284	0.0291	0.0284

Table 6. Evaluation results of novel view images obtained from 16 multi-view images captured using the Fibonacci hemisphere arrangement. The cameras are evenly distributed around the subject, leading to high accuracy. Additionally, the overall low variance indicates a high-quality set of images.

Focal length [mm]	Distance [m]	PSNR↑	SSIM↑	LPIPS↓	SD PSNR	SD SSIM	SD LPIPS
20	1.7	10.2728	0.7588	0.4317	1.1084	0.0577	0.0827
35	2.9	27.8783	0.9345	0.0571	0.8423	0.0096	0.0077
50	4.2	27.9752	0.9360	0.0748	1.6802	0.0098	0.0149
60	5.0	21.7969	0.9206	0.1033	0.6567	0.0106	0.0234
70	5.8	23.7068	0.9011	0.1069	0.8012	0.0152	0.0162
85	7.1	10.4774	0.6019	0.5661	0.7039	0.0264	0.0232
100	8.4	10.0382	0.6787	0.5517	0.7984	0.0304	0.0450
20	1.7	5.1226	0.2723	0.5449	0.7781	0.0340	0.0277
35	2.9	22.1902	0.7385	0.1653	0.9798	0.0338	0.0142
50	4.2	23.2315	0.7578	0.1636	0.4580	0.0208	0.0140
60	5.0	23.3645	0.7622	0.1622	0.4073	0.0216	0.0151
70	5.8	20.2617	0.6496	0.1952	1.1539	0.0403	0.0193
85	7.1	9.4598	0.2128	0.4120	1.2311	0.0201	0.0312
100	8.4	5.5237	0.2407	0.4912	0.7552	0.0315	0.0309

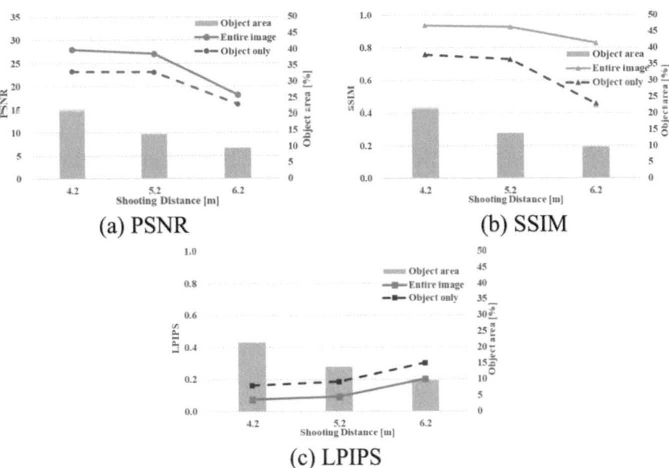

Fig. 9. Shooting Distance and Target Object Area. When using a standard lens, a closer shooting distance allows for capturing more feature points of the subject, resulting in highly accurate reconstruction outcomes.

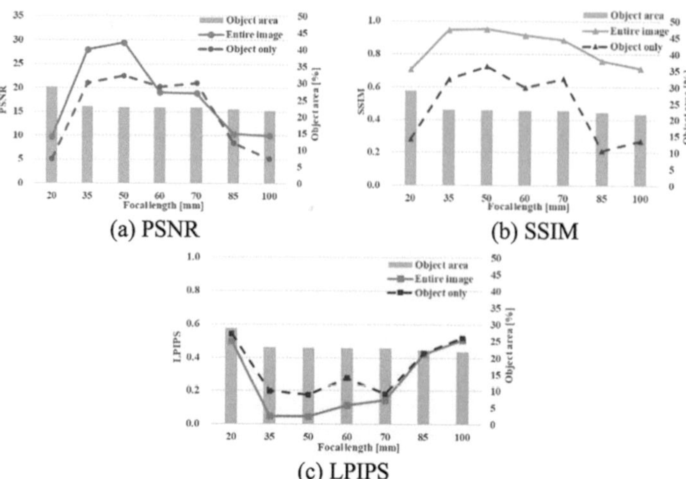

Fig. 10. Focal Length and Target Object Area. Using a lens with low impact from projection distortion and perspective compression results in highly accurate reconstruction outcomes.

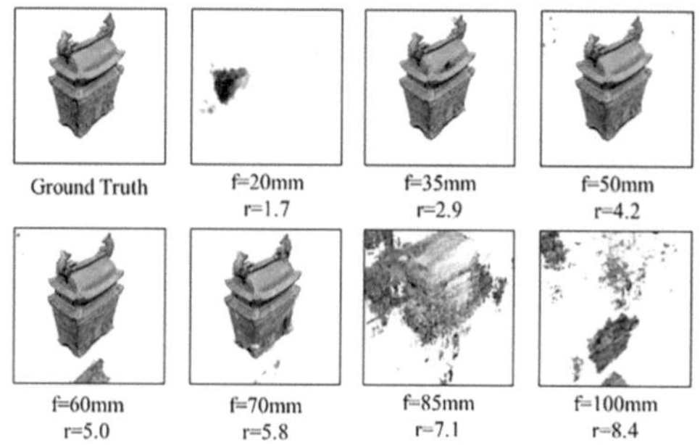

Fig. 11. Rendering results of Mip-NeRF for each focal length. f represents the focal length, and r indicates the shooting distance (radius).

7 Conclusion

This research explored a shooting configuration method for multi-view image acquisition aimed at the digitization of cultural heritage. By utilizing Blender to configure lighting control and camera layouts, the environment was quantitatively optimized for free-viewpoint generation.

The results revealed that arranging cameras densely to cover the target object improves accuracy. Additionally, the relationship between the field of view and focal length indicates that acquiring multi-view images at shooting distances appropriate for the focal length is one of the factors contributing to improved accuracy.

From the perspective of reproducibility, grid arrangements, circular arrangements, and Fibonacci hemisphere arrangements are available options. However, when considering implementation in real-world photography, the complex configuration of the

Fibonacci hemisphere arrangement is expected to be challenging. Therefore, circular arrangements, which are relatively easier to set up, are considered more suitable for real-world photography.

References

1. Agency for Cultural Affairs: Cultural Properties. In: Agency for Cultural Affairs Website. https://www.bunka.go.jp/seisaku/bunkazai/index.html. Accessed 20 Nov 2024
2. National Institutes for Cultural Heritage: Official Website. In: National Institutes for Cultural Heritage Website. https://www.nich.go.jp/. Accessed 20 Nov 2024
3. Snavely, N., Seitz, S. M., & Szeliski, R. (2006). Photo tourism: Exploring photo collections in 3D. In *ACM SIGGRAPH 2006 Papers* (pp. 835–846)
4. Schonberger, J.L., Frahm, J.-M.: Structure-from-motion revisited. CVPR (2016)
5. Segawa, O.: 3D Structure reconstruction using image processing: automatic generation of 3D point clouds using photo images. Technical Development News, No. 163. Energy Applications Research and Development Center (2020)
6. Ito, T., Kodama, S., Kokubo, A.: 3DCG model production of cultural properties and exhibition contents using photogrammetry: example of Hachinohe City Museum exhibition. Bull. Hachinohe Inst. Technol. **41**, 103–109 (2022)
7. 3Dflow. 3DF Zephyr - photogrammetry software: 3D models from photos. 3Dflow, Verona (2024). https://www.3dflow.net/
8. Capturing Reality. RealityCapture - 3D Models from Photos and/or Laser Scans. Capturing Reality, Bratislava (2024). https://www.capturingreality.com/
9. Mildenhall, B., Srinivasan, P.P., Tancik, M., Barron, J.T., Ramamoorthi, R., Ng, R.: NeRF: Representing scenes as neural radiance fields for view synthesis. In: ECCV (2020)
10. x, N.: Optical models for direct volume rendering. IEEE Transactions on Visualization and Computer Graphics (1995)
11. Barron, J.T., Mildenhall, B., Tancik, M., Hedman, P., Martin-Brualla, R., Srinivasan, P.P.: Mip-NeRF: a multiscale representation for anti-aliasing neural radiance fields. In: ICCV (2021)
12. OAK Corporation. Agisoft Metashape. OAK Corporation, Tokyo (2024). https://oakcorp.net/agisoft/
13. Zhang, X., et al.: Toward Global Sensing Quality Maximization: A Configuration Optimization Scheme for Camera Networks (2023)
14. Li, Q.: Light Field Generation Methods Using Multiple Omnidirectional Cameras. Doctoral dissertation, University of Tsukuba (2023)
15. Edmund Optics: Understanding Focal Length and Field of View. In: Edmund Optics Knowledge Center. https://www.edmundoptics.jp/knowledge-center/application-notes/imaging/understanding-focal-length-and-field-of-view/. Accessed 12 Feb 2024
16. Blender Online Community. Blender- a 3D modelling and rendering package. Blender Foundation, Stichting Blender Foundation, Amsterdam (2023)
17. Wang, Z., Bovik, A.C., Sheikh, H.R., PSimoncelli, E.: Image quality assessment: from error visibility to structural similarity. IEEE TIP (2004)
18. Zhang, R., Isola, P., Efros, A.A., Shechtman, E., Wang, O.: The unreasonable effectiveness of deep features as a perceptual metric. CVPR (2018)

Cherry Packing Skill Proficiency Classification Using Hand Motion Analysis

Ricardo Cerrud(✉), Hiromi Watanabe, and Shinji Kotani

Yamanashi University, 4-4-37 Takeda, Kofu, Yamanashi 400-8510, Japan
g23dtsa6@yamanashi.ac.jp

Abstract. The decline in the number of farmers and the consequent loss of agricultural expertise poses a major challenge in passing on important skills to the next generation. The art of cherry mirror-packing, which requires many years of training and dexterity, is a typical example of this challenge. In this study, we research and develop a skill acquisition system to support the transmission and acquisition of the mirror-packing technique. Two expert and one novice packers from Yamagata Prefecture, one of Japan's major cherry-producing regions, were filmed and the 3D hand landmark coordinates of their hands were tracked using Mediapipe. Angular changes between the finger joints were calculated as a time series while the cherries were being packed. To handle time series of various lengths, kNN classification models were trained using DTW similarity distance, and separate models were created for the left and right hands. Based on the test results, classification achieved an accuracy of 0.86 for the left hand and 0.78 for the right hand. These results highlight the feasibility of automatic expertise evaluation for skill transfer and acquisition systems.

Keywords: Video Analysis · Skill Evaluation · Cherry Mirror-packing

1 Background

Agriculture is facing significant challenges in the modern era, including the diminishing number of farmers and the gradual loss of critical agricultural skills. In Japan, the agricultural workforce is aging rapidly, having 70% of farmers aged over 65 years old [1]. Meanwhile, younger generations increasingly gravitate toward urban areas and non-agricultural careers. This demographic shift results in a shrinking pool of skilled farmers capable of sustaining agricultural productivity. As a consequence, there is a gradual loss of traditional agricultural knowledge and skills, often passed down through generations. As experienced farmers retire, specialized techniques, such as fruit harvesting, processing and packing, are at risk of disappearing. These skills, mastered by years of experience, are difficult to replicate or transfer without direct mentorship.

Cherry mirror-packing represents a highly specialized packing method, reserved for large, premium cherries exceeding 25 mm in diameter, classified as 2L or greater [2]. This technique involves the manual arrangement of cherries into decorative layers, carefully positioned with stems oriented inwards, to achieve the desired weight and

B. Kim (Ed.): IW-FCV 2025, CCIS 2769, pp. 100–107, 2026.
https://doi.org/10.1007/978-981-95-4578-0_8

structure. Skilled artisans, often with over a decade of experience, hand-pack each cherry to create a seamless, gap-free presentation, resulting in a pack where the cherries appear to elegantly overflow. This method underscores the precision and craftsmanship required for high-quality cherry presentation (Fig. 1).

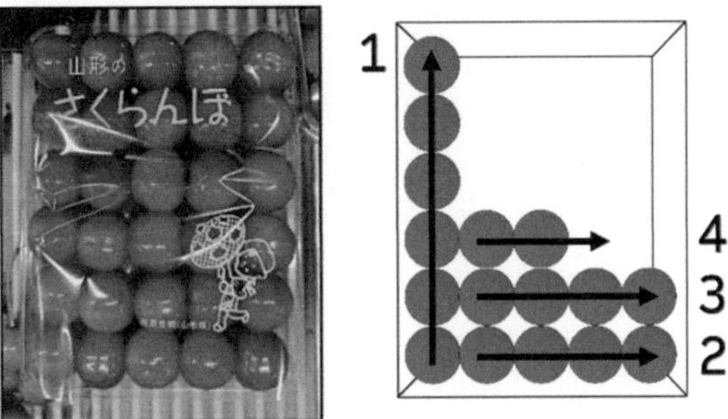

Fig. 1. Cherry Mirror-packed product example. The order in which cherries are packed is as follows: beginning from the bottom left corner of the container, pack cherries in a column while moving to the top. Next, beginning beside the first-placed cherry, pack cherries in a row moving to the right. Finally, fill in the container using the previous procedure.

Therefore, the development of a technique acquisition system based on automatic evaluation to hand down the art of mirror-packing to new generations is proposed. This system is an initiative to preserve traditional agricultural practices by embedding the knowledge of experts into the system and encourage younger generations to engage in agriculture as a viable and rewarding career path. Based on Fig. 2, the proposed system consists of two main cameras that are in charge of tracking the work and motion of the trainees. The pickup of correct cherries and the discarding of not suitable cherries are also taken into consideration for mirror-packing. Additionally, users will be able to learn, practice and get an evaluation of their performance and progress. In this study, hand movement analysis is used to classify the skill level of the master craftsmen in mirror-packing, which is the main evaluation criteria for the proposed system.

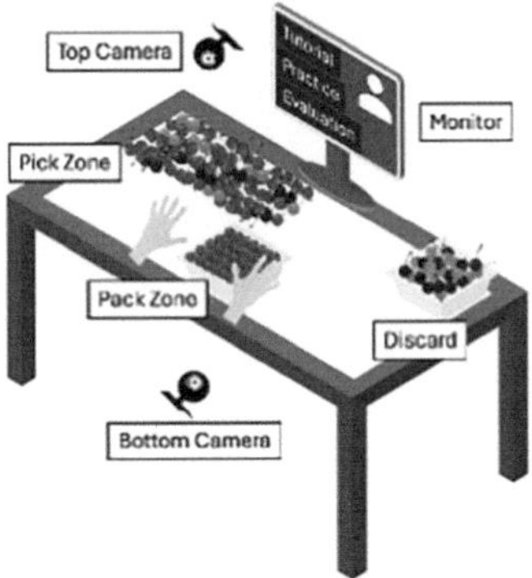

Fig. 2. Proposed skill transfer and acquisition system.

2 Mirror-Packing Work Analysis

2.1 Data Collection

Since Yamagata Prefecture is the primary cherry production region in Japan, craftsmen specializing in mirror-packing were recorded during the cherry harvest season. Using a wide-angle camera positioned for a bird's-eye view, the packing work of two experts (with 20 and 10 years of experience, respectively) and one beginner (with 2 years of experience) was captured in Yamagata Prefecture. To better understand their interaction with their surroundings, the entire workbench, including additional tools, was included in the filming area, as illustrated in Fig. 3. The expert with 20 years of experience presented the higher skill level by utilizing multiple fingers to create a claw-like posture with the hands, providing a more efficient method for placing cherries. Meanwhile, the 10 years of experience expert presented a less efficient methodology by only utilizing two fingers for picking and packing the fruits. On the other hand, the beginner was not able to properly pack cherries, carelessly scattering the cherries inside pack. In total, four videos of expert craftsmen (two for each expert) and four videos of the beginner were obtained. Due to the unavailability of additional participants, the sample size was limited to three craftsmen. As a result, the findings may not fully represent the broader population. Despite this limitation, efforts were made to ensure a representative sample within the available constraints.

Fig. 3. Workbench used for mirror-packing (Expert).

2.2 Hand Tracking

To analyze the hand dexterity of expert craftsmen during the mirror-packing of cherries, hand movements were tracked, and feature angles were extracted from the recordings.

Hand Landmarks. In this study, the Mediapipe library [3] was utilized to track the hands of the craftsmen that appeared on the recordings. Mediapipe has been shown to be efficient for evaluating manual tasks that require an excellently finished product in previous studies [4]. Furthermore, unlike traditional motion tracking systems, which require users to attach equipment to their bodies, our approach relies solely on video data. This allows users to perform activities more naturally, thereby improving the quality of the collected data. Using this library, the 3D coordinates of 21 different landmarks, each from both hands, were collected. The landmarks represent the 3D position of the joints of the hands, while each finger is represented by a total of five landmarks and three joints formed by a pair of vectors that join the landmarks. A total of 15 landmarks were used to represent each hand movement, as shown on Fig. 4. The nomenclature of the fingers follows the digits number for each finger: D1 for the thumb, D2 for the index finger, D3 for the middle finger, D4 for the ring finger, and D5 for the pinky finger. Meanwhile, joints were named according to their respective anatomical names: Basal Carpometacarpal (CMC), Metacarpophalangeal (MCP), Interphalangeal (IP), Proximal Interphalangeal (PIP), and Distal Interphalangeal (DIP).

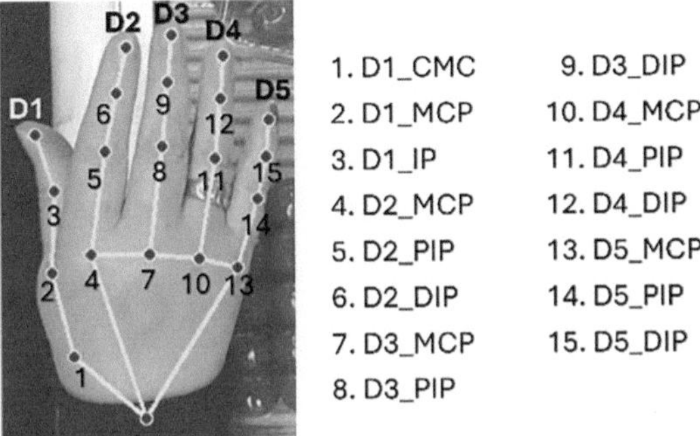

Fig. 4. Landmarks representing each hand in this study.

Angle Calculation. For each frame of the recording, the angle formed at each landmark by the pair of vectors was calculated. A Region of Interest (ROI) was defined to track the position of the hand over the workbench, allowing the extraction of only the angles corresponding to the hand's movement over the cherry pack. Additionally, the entry and exit of each hand into and out of the ROI were recorded as the beginning and end of a time series representing changes in finger angles during cherry packing. Consequently, the motion of each craftsman's hand, used to pack individual cherries, was compiled into separate datasets for the beginner and the experts. A total of 398 sequences for the beginner and 396 sequences for the experts were obtained.

Formula (1) was used to calculate the acute angle θ between two vectors $\overrightarrow{AB}$ and $\overrightarrow{BC}$, which are formed by three consecutive points A, B and C in a given space. After calculating the magnitude of the angle, formula (2) was applied to determine the direction of the angle θ between the same two vectors, $\overrightarrow{AB}$ and $\overrightarrow{BC}$. A visualization of the angle orientations is presented in Fig. 5. Furthermore, the limits of fingers motion were defined based on the anatomy of the human body [5], as shown in Table 1.

$$\theta = arccos(\frac{\overrightarrow{AB} \bullet \overrightarrow{BC}}{\|\overrightarrow{AB}\| \, \|\overrightarrow{BC}\|}) \tag{1}$$

$$\theta = \overrightarrow{AB} \times \overrightarrow{BC} \tag{2}$$

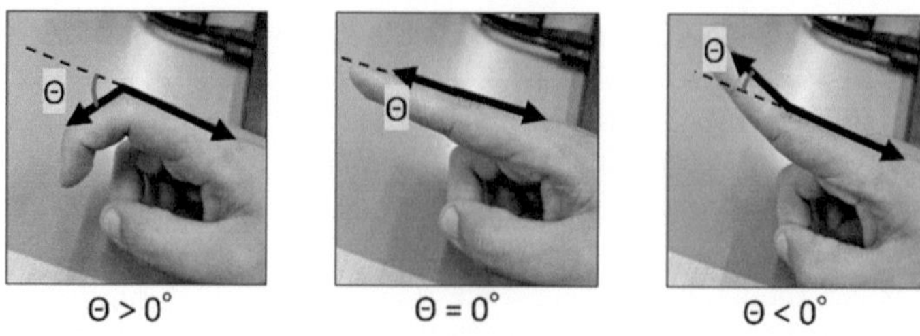

Fig. 5. Orientation of the angles on flexion (left), extension (center) and hyperextension (right).

Table 1. Maximum and minimum permissible angles per joint.

Finger	Joint	Range
D1	CMC, MCP	−10~55°
	IP	−15~80°
D2, D3, D4, D5	MCP	−45~90°
	PIP	0~100°
	DIP	0~80°

3 Classification of Packing Skill Level

3.1 Classification Method

To classify experts and beginners, the distance-based k-Nearest Neighbors (kNN) classification algorithm was implemented. Due to the varying lengths of the time series, Dynamic Time Warping (DTW) was used as the distance metric to measure the similarity between the time series. DTW evaluates the similarity between two sequences of data points recorded over time by overcoming differences in length through stretching or compressing segments to achieve optimal alignment (one-to-many or many-to-one), unlike traditional distance measures such as Euclidean distance, which relies on a one-to-one point comparison.

In kNN classification, once DTW distances are computed for every pair of time series and each distance is labeled, the k-nearest neighbors are identified. Compared to other machine learning methods, DTW is particularly effective in handling temporal distortions, making it well-suited for the given dataset. This adaptability allows the model to accommodate future data where time and speed may vary. Additionally, since two styles of packing were observed among the experts, this method demonstrates robustness to pose variations, as DTW captures the overall shape of the time series rather than focusing on individual points.

Training Settings. Since the left and right hands perform differently during mirror-packing, separate classification models were trained for each hand. A total of 495 time series were obtained for the left hand (249 for experts and 246 for novices) and 299 for the right hand (147 for experts and 152 for novices). The data were split in a ratio of 1:3 for testing and training, respectively. Tuning of parameters was performed using a grid search for the *k*-value, on a range of 3 to 10.

3.2 Classification Results

The accuracy for the left and right hands was calculated, ranging from 0.0 to 1.0, with values closer to 1.0 indicating better classification performance of the model. Accuracy results for *k*-values of 3, 5, 7, and 10 are shown in Table 2. According to the results, a *k*-value of 10 performed the best for the left-hand data, achieving an accuracy of 0.86. Meanwhile, *k*-values of 3 and 5 performed the best for the right-hand data, both with an accuracy of 0.78. Skill classification for mirror-packing is a challenging task, as it is closely related to the quality of the final product. A classification rate of 70% (0.70) is considered sufficient; however, it is important to complement this rate with additional evaluation metrics that directly assess the final product. This approach ensures a more comprehensive and accurate evaluation of the classification model's effectiveness.

Table 2. Accuracy results according to *k*-value and handedness.

k-value	Handedness	Accuracy	Error Rate
3	Left	0.85	0.15
	Right	**0.78**	**0.22**
5	Left	0.84	0.16
	Right	**0.78**	**0.22**
7	Left	0.85	0.15
	Right	0.76	0.24
10	Left	**0.86**	**0.14**
	Right	0.68	0.32

The classification model performs better for left-handed mirror-packing compared to right-handed mirror-packing, reflecting differences in performance during packing. Experts use their left hand to occasionally pack but mostly to arrange cherries while packing with their right hand. In contrast, beginners primarily use their left hand to hold the packing box, moving it less than experts. Furthermore, the choice of *k*-value has little impact on the accuracy of left-hand data, suggesting that the model is robust to varying *k*-values.

For right-hand data, accuracy decreases as *k*-values increase from 3 to 10, indicating that the model's performance may be sensitive to higher *k*-values. The higher error rate further suggests that the model struggles more with classifying right-handed mirror-packing. This may be due to similarities in hand motions between beginners and experts when packing cherries with the right hand.

Previous studies have attempted to classify the productivity of soldering workers using threshold-based classification [6]. This method utilized the distance between the head and the right hand, as well as the angle between the right hand and the soldering position. The classification process involved clustering the data into four sequential classes, revealing distinct characteristics between experts and beginners. Although the results demonstrated a significant classification rate, this method lacks adaptability, as new data would require recalculating thresholds. In contrast, our proposed methodology allows the system to adapt dynamically and perform new classifications using kNN as additional data is introduced.

4 Future Considerations

Plans for photographing new craftsmen are on track; however, due to the short cherry harvest season (only two months per year), their availability might be limited. Introducing new data from both experts and beginners into the system would enhance its robustness by accommodating different hand poses. Additionally, scaling this method to another skill would require the collection of new data, which could be time- and resource-intensive, depending on the niche of the skill.

One of the challenges in deploying the proposed methodology is the high computation time, primarily due to the time required by DTW to compute comparisons between time series, which increases with the dataset size. Another challenge is hand occlusion caused by objects during mirror-packing, which makes it difficult to track hand movements accurately. During data collection, there was a high contrast between the hands and the background; however, backgrounds with similar tones or the use of low-contrast gloves could reduce the accuracy of hand joint detection.

5 Conclusion

This study demonstrates the possibility of using hand motion analysis and classification models to classify special skills, such as cherry mirror-packing. By analyzing changes in finger angles during packing per hand, the proposed classification system accurately distinguished expert and beginner data, achieving a promising accuracy rate of 0.86 for the left hand and 0.78 for the right hand. These findings demonstrate the effectiveness of using left-hand data to classify experts and beginners in cherry mirror-packing. The results also provide a foundation for the research and development of a skill acquisition system that bridges gaps in the transfer of expertise and supports the next generation in acquiring agricultural techniques.

Based on this study, further evaluation criteria will be determined, including time to complete the task, accuracy rate of sorting fine cherries for packing, completion of final product, and accuracy rate of mirror-packing technique. Furthermore, plans are in place to collect more data to enhance the robustness of the training dataset. By integrating these evaluation criteria and new data with the proposed skill classification method, future research aims to facilitate the training and evaluation of novice mirror-packing operators and to systematically analyze their progress toward proficiency.

6 Disclosure of Interests.

The authors have no competing interests to declare that are relevant to the content of this article.

Acknowledgments. This work was supported by JST SPRING, Grant Number JPMJSP2133.

References

1. Ministry of Agriculture, Forestry and Fisheries Census (2020). https://www.maff.go.jp/j/tokei/census/afc/index.html. Accessed 9 Dec 2024
2. How to pack cherries: What are the differences|Aji no Koen. https://www.ajfarm.com/13611/. Accessed 9 Dec 2024
3. Lugaresi, C., et al.: MediaPipe: A Framework for Building Perception Pipelines. ArXiv, 1906.08172 (2019)
4. Jinkawa, K., Mori, K.: Skill evaluation of precision manual tasks using hand tracking and fuzzy inference. In: Proceedings of the Fuzzy System Symposium, vol.39, pp.349–351. Japan Society for Fuzzy Systems and Intelligent Informatics, Japan (2023)
5. Ngeo, J.G., Tamei, T., Shibata, T.: Continuous and simultaneous estimation of finger kinematics using inputs from an EMG-to-muscle activation model. Journal of NeuroEngineering and Rehabilitation, vol. 11, 122. BMC (2014)
6. Mori, K., et al.: A Relationship Between Product Quality and Body Information of Worker and its Application to Improvement of Productivity. In: IEEE International Conference on Systems, Man, and Cybernetics (SMC), pp. 1433–1438. Japan (2018)

Visual Feedback Control of an Underactuated Hand for Grasping Objects of Varying Stiffness

Ryogo Kai[1(✉)], Yuzuka Isobe[1], Sarthak Pathak[2], and Kazunori Umeda[2]

[1] Course of Precision Engineering, Graduate School of Science and Engineering, Chuo University, 1-13-27 Kasuga, Bunkyo-ku, Tokyo, Japan
{kai,isobe}@sensor.mech.chuo-u.ac.jp

[2] Department of Precision Mechanics, Faculty of Science and Engineering, Chuo University, 1-13-27 Kasuga, Bunkyo-ku, Tokyo, Japan
{pathak,umeda}@mech.chuo-u.ac.jp

Abstract. This paper presents a novel method for grasping objects with varying stiffness using an underactuated hand and a stereo camera. In factories, robots are required to handle a wide variety of objects. Tasks such as grasping soft objects without causing damage are particularly important in industries like food processing. While many existing approaches equip robotic hands with sensors, such as force or pressure sensors, these methods are unsuitable for food items due to hygiene concerns. To address the challenges of grasping various objects without causing damage or dropping them, underactuated hands that can conform to object shapes have gained attention.

In this study, we propose a method for controlling an underactuated hand using only a stereo camera as an external sensor. First, the target object is detected using a background subtraction method. Next, the contact between the hand and the object is detected. Then, the object is grasped with appropriate force, calculated based on four elements: the centroid shifts of the hand and the object, the deformation rate of the object, and the occlusion rate of the hand. Finally, drop detection is performed to ensure the object is not dropped during pick-and-place tasks. Experiments were conducted using six different objects to validate the proposed method.

Keywords: Robot vision · Underactuated hand · Manipulation

1 Introduction

With the advancement of mass production of many models in small quantities, the demand for robots to handle a wide variety of objects is increasing. Therefore, robots need to grasp not only hard objects, such as metal products, but also soft objects, such as food items. Moreover, there are objects with hard surfaces that may crush if the grasping force is too large. Similarly, if soft objects are

B. Kim (Ed.): IW-FCV 2025, CCIS 2769, pp. 108–119, 2026.
https://doi.org/10.1007/978-981-95-4578-0_9

not grasped with the proper force, it may cause the object to drop and lead to damage. Thus, it is necessary to grasp objects of varying stiffness with the proper force.

To grasp various objects, the underactuated hands are gaining attention [1]. These hands have a high degree of freedom, allowing them to deform according to the shape of the object. Thanks to this characteristic, the contact area between the hand and the object becomes larger, enabling stable grasping and allowing the handling of easily damaged objects. However, due to their adaptability, it is difficult to detect the grasping state, such as the contact area, grasping force, or potential damage and dropping of the object.

Many studies use tactile sensors and force sensors for grasping objects [2–4]. Some studies equip a small camera on the finger [5,6]. By obtaining force information from sensors, it may be possible to grasp objects without applying excessive force. However, the contact area between the sensor and the object becomes small, which means the deformation of the entire object might not be detected, potentially resulting in damage to the object. Furthermore, there are issues such as the inability to detect the appropriate force due to sensor contamination, as well as the increased complexity of the system caused by the integration of sensors.

Instead of embedding sensors in the hand, some research uses a camera as an external sensor to observe the hand from the outside [7,8]. These methods recognize the grasping state by using markers attached to the hand and the object. However, it is impossible to attach markers to food items or everyday products. In the previous research, we proposed visual feedback control method for underactuated hand [9]. However, this method requires the color of the object beforehand. In addition, because a monocular camera was used, only two-dimensional image information could be acquired, making it impossible to accurately detect crushed objects or falling objects.

In this paper, we propose a visual feedback control method for an underactuated hand using a stereo camera. Using the background subtraction method, the target object can be detected even when its color information is unknown. Additionally, utilizing depth information acquired by stereo camera, enabling the detection of the 3D deformation and movement of the object. To demonstrate the effectiveness of the proposed method, grasping experiments are conducted using objects with various colors and stiffness.

2 Visual Feedback Control Method

2.1 Overview of the Method

The feedback control of the underactuated hand is performed using images obtained from a stereo camera. A two-finger underactuated hand, without any embedded sensors, is used. To control the underactuated hand, both the object and the hand are captured by the stereo camera.

An overview of the proposed method is shown in Fig. 1. In this method, four types of detection are introduced for the visual feedback control of the underactuated hand: object detection, contact detection, grasping state detection, and drop detection. First, the target object is identified using a background subtraction method. After object detection, the hand begins to close. Then, contact between the hand and the object is detected based on their contour information. Next, during the grasping process, the grasping state is observed. The grasping state is represented using four indices: the centroid shifts of the hand and the object, the deformation rate of the object, and the occlusion rate of the hand. Using these indices, the object is grasped with sufficient force without causing damage. Once the grasping is completed, the object is lifted. During the lifting process, droppage and rotation of the object are detected. By conducting these detections, the proposed method enables the stable grasping and transportation of objects with various sizes and stiffness without causing damage or dropping them.

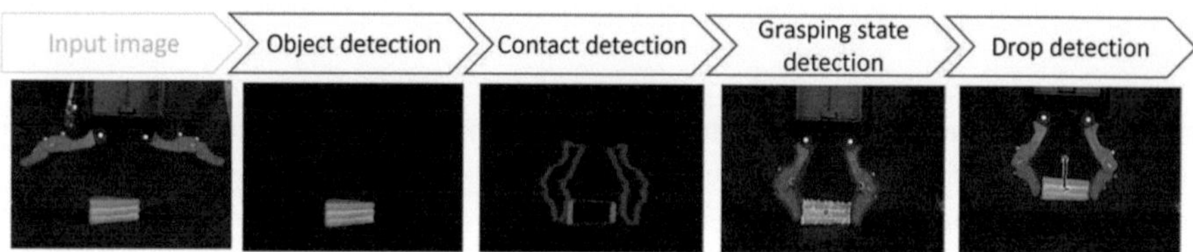

Fig. 1. Overview of the visual feedback control method.

2.2 Object Detection

Object detection is a method to identify the target object from an image. In this study, we use background subtraction to detect the object to be grasped. An overview of the object detection process is shown in Fig. 2. First, as shown in Fig. 2(a), an image is captured before the object is placed. Next, an image is captured after the object is placed (Fig. 2(b)). Then, the two images are converted into grayscale image, and the difference between them is calculated(Fig. 2(c)). From this difference image, contours are detected. Among these contours, the largest contour is considered as the target object for grasping. Based on the contour of the largest object in Fig. 2(b), an HSV color threshold is calculated to extract only the region of the object. Using this HSV threshold, the target object is detected from the color image in Fig. 2(b), as shown in Fig. 2(d).

2.3 Contact Detection

Contact detection identifies the contact between the hand and the object based on images. An overview of the contact detection process is shown in Fig. 3. Figure 3(a) shows an input image. First, the input image is converted into the HSV color space. Using the HSV information of the object calculated in Sect. 2.2 and the HSV information of the hand which is known beforehand, each region

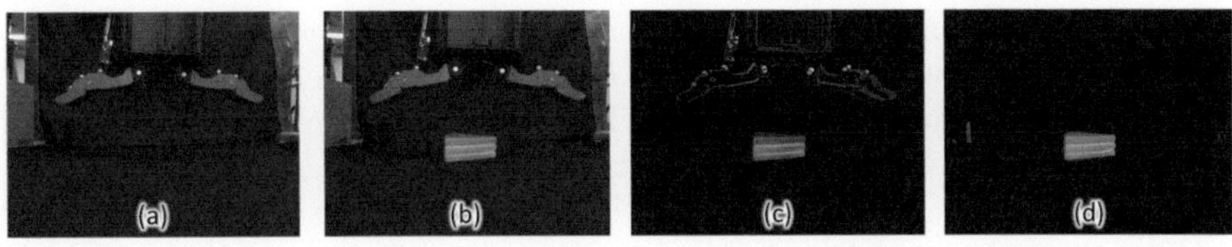

Fig. 2. Example of object detection: (a) Background image, (b) Foreground image, (c) Difference image between (a) and (b), and (d) Extracted object.

is extracted respectively. Next, the contours of both the hand and the object are obtained from the extracted regions. Afterwards, both contours are drawn in different colors, as shown in Fig. 3(b). In Fig. 3(b), the hand's contour is drawn in blue, the object's contour is drawn in red. When the hand and the object come into contact, their contours overlap. In Fig. 3(c), the overlapping contours are represented in magenta. For each finger of the hand, if the overlap of the contours exceeds a certain threshold, it is detected as contact between the hand and the object.

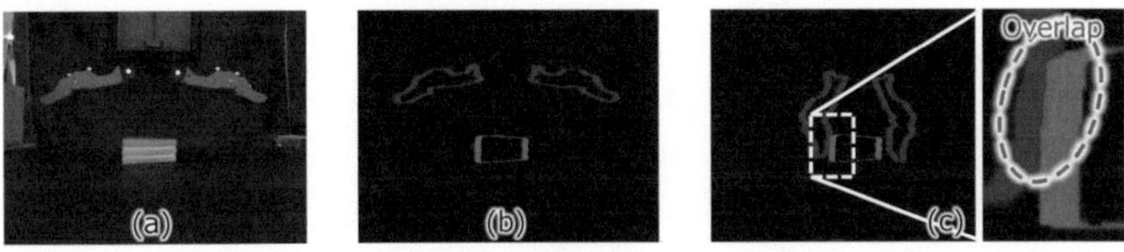

Fig. 3. Example of contact detection: (a) Input image, (b) Contours of the hand and the object, (c) Detection of contact through the overlap of both contours.

2.4 Grasp State Detection

To grasp objects without causing damage, the movement of the hand and deformation of the object are detected during grasping. Some objects, such as potato chips or box-shaped items, have hard surfaces but are fragile. On the other hand, such as tofu or balloons, have soft surfaces and are easy to be damaged. To adapt to objects of various stiffness, four indices are introduced as IfG (Index for Grasping). Indices described in Sects. 2.4.1 and 2.4.2 are designed for grasping objects with hard surfaces, while those in Sects. 2.4.3 and 2.4.4 are intended for grasping objects with soft surfaces. Grasping is considered complete if any of the IfG indices are satisfied.

IfG$_1$: Centroid Shift of The Hand IfG$_1$ involves calculating the movement of the hand. When grasping objects with hard surfaces, the hand is expected to stop moving after the contact with the object. If the object is brittle, continuing to apply force may cause it to break. Therefore, it is necessary to observe whether the hand is still moving.

Here, the movement of the hand is calculated based on the centroid information from each finger. In Fig. 4, the centroid of the left and right fingers are represented by blue circles. Assuming that the hand moves along the xy-plane as shown in the upper left of Fig. 4, the 2D movement of the centroid is calculated. Denoting the centroid of the left and right fingers as (x_l, y_l) and (x_r, y_r), respectively. Then, the movement of the left and right fingers, denoted as diff_l and diff_r, can be calculated by the following equations:

$$\mathrm{diff}_l = (x_l(t-1) - x_l(t))^2 + (y_l(t-1) - y_l(t))^2 \quad (1)$$

$$\mathrm{diff}_r = (x_r(t-1) - x_r(t))^2 + (y_r(t-1) - y_r(t))^2 \quad (2)$$

Here, t and $t-1$ represent the image frames. The index IfG_1 is then calculated as follows:

$$\mathrm{IfG}_1 = \mathrm{diff}_l + \mathrm{diff}_r \quad (3)$$

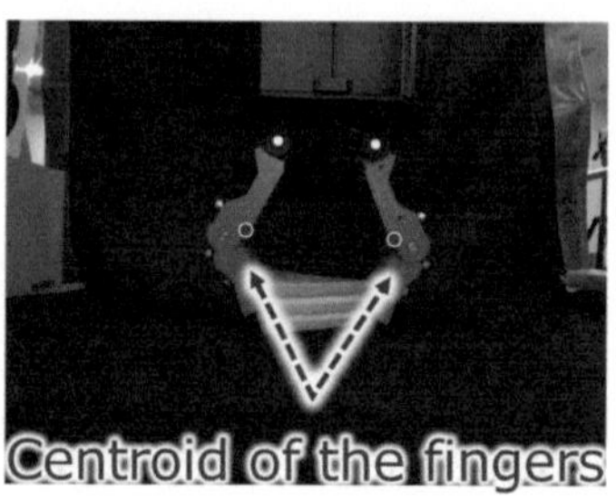

Fig. 4. IfG_1: Centroid Shift of The Hand.

IfG_2: Centroid Shift of The Object The second index IfG_2 is the calculation of the movement of the object's centroid.When the object has a soft surface, applying grasping force causes the force to spread and deform the object. However, in the case of objects with a hard surface, the force does not escape towards the object but rather towards the hand, creating a torque in the passive joints of the hand. This results in rotational motion in the passive joints, which leads to the movement of the object.Therefore, it is necessary to observe the movement of the object. The movement of the object is determined by the centroid of the object in the image. In Fig. 5, the centroid of the object is shown as a red circle. When the centroid of the object is denoted as (x_{obj}, y_{obj}), IfG_2 can be calculated using the following equation:

$$\mathrm{IfG}_2 = (x_{obj}(0) - x_{obj}(t)) + (y_{obj}(0) - y_{obj}(t)) \quad (4)$$

Here, t represents the image frame, and $t = 0$ denotes the first frame where the calculation of IfG_2 begins. This allows us to calculate the movement of the object during the grasping process.

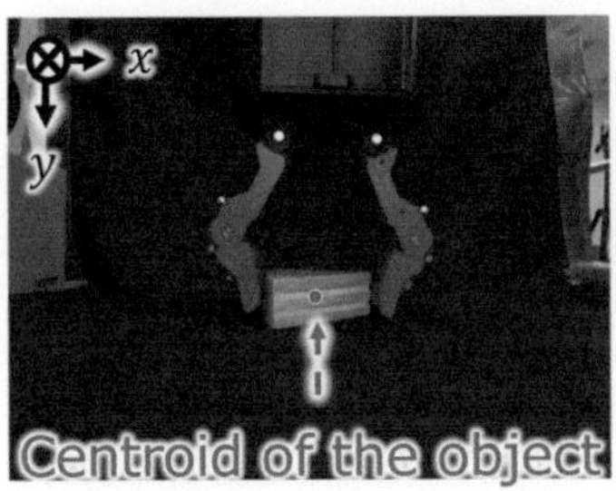

Fig. 5. IfG$_2$: Centroid Shift of The Object.

IfG$_3$: Deformation of The Object The third index, IfG$_3$, represents the deformation of the object. For soft objects, excessive deformation may cause damage. Therefore, it is important to calculate the overall deformation of the object.

Previous studies have calculated the two-dimensional deformation of objects [9]. However, when grasping soft objects, it is also possible that the object deforms along the depth direction in the image. Thus, we calculate the deformation based on the object's contour and the three-dimensional movement of the points inside the contour. In Fig. 5, the object's contour and internal points are shown in green circles. When calculating the deformation, handling three-dimensional point clouds requires time-consuming processes such as point correspondence and downsampling. To address this problem, optical flow is applied using the Lukas-Kanade method [10]. The object's contour is obtained from the object region, and internal points are randomly distributed with a constant density. Using optical flow, the points are tracked, and three-dimensional deformation is calculated by acquiring depth information through a stereo camera. Represent point for optical flow as $\mathbf{P_i} = (x_i, y_i, z_i)$, and the total number of points N, IfG$_3$ is calculated using the following equation:

$$\text{IfG}_3 = \frac{1}{N}\sum_{i=1}^{N} ||\mathbf{P_i(t)} - \mathbf{P_i(t-1)}|| \tag{5}$$

The displacement of each point on the object is normalized by dividing by the total number of point N. This allows to detect the deformation in objects of different sizes, even if they belong to the same category. With this approach, the deformation of the object can be successfully detected (Fig. 6).

IfG$_4$: Occlusion of the Object. The fourth index, IfG$_4$, represents the percentage of the hand's area that is occluded by the object. Since only one camera is used, certain areas where the object may deform cannot be captured by the image. Therefore, by detecting the change in the area of the hand, it is possible to prevent excessive force from being applied to the object, even if it is occluded. In Fig. 7, the contour of the hand is shown in blue. The index IfG$_4$, which indicates the occlusion rate of the hand with respect to the object region, can be

Fig. 6. IfG$_3$: Deformation of The Object.

calculated using the following equation.

$$\text{IfG}_4 = \frac{A_{hand}(0) - A_{hand}(t)}{A_{obj}(0)} \tag{6}$$

Here, A_{hand} is the area of the hand, A_{obj} is the area of the object, and t is the image frame. Since the force required for grasping differs depending on the size of the object. Therefore, evaluating only the change in the hand's occlusion area is not sufficient. Therefore, in IfG$_4$, the change in the hand's area is normalized by the object's area. This approach enables to adjust grasping force for objects of varying sizes within the same category.

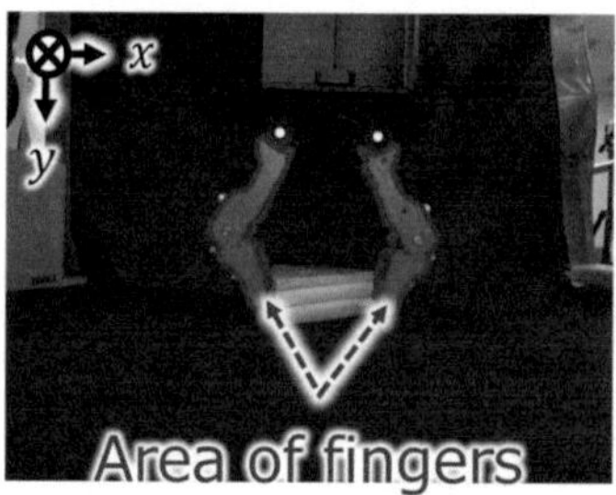

Fig. 7. IfG$_4$: Occlusion of The Object.

2.5 Drop Detection

After grasping completion, the object lifting action is performed. During this process, drop detection is conducted. The drop detection consists of two parts: object drop detection and object rotation detection.

Object Drop Detection. In object drop detection, not only the movement of the object outside the hand's workspace is considered, but also the state where the object is sliding while moving within the hand is detected. When an object is dropping, the relative position between the hand and the object changes. Therefore, the hand and object's centroid information is used for drop detection. The contour information is obtained from the input image, and the average centroid of the object and the two fingers of the hand is calculated. The distance between these two points is computed for each frame. In Fig. 8, the object's centroid is shown in red, the average centroid of the hand's two fingers is marked with a blue dot, and the line connecting the two points is drawn in black. The change in distance between the two points, d_{diff}, is calculated using the following equation.

$$d_{diff} = d(t) - d(0) \tag{7}$$

Here, $d(0)$ represents the distance before the arm movement, and $d(t)$ represents the distance during the movement. If d_{diff} exceeds a certain threshold, the object is considered as dropped. In this case, the value of $d(t)$ is updated by substituting it for $d(0)$, enabling continuous drop detection in subsequent frames.

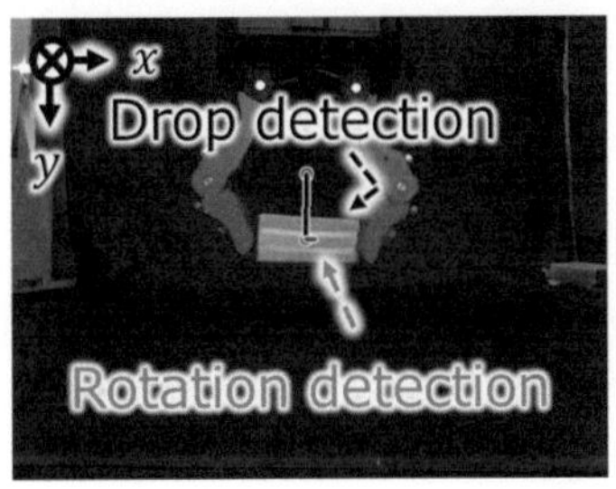

Fig. 8. Object drop and rotation detection.

Object Rotation Detection. In rotation detection, the sliding of the object is detected. In this method, principal component analysis (PCA) is applied to the object's contour, and the rotation of the object is determined by the change in the angle between the first principal component and the horizontal axis. In Fig. 8, the direction of the object's first principal component is shown with a green line. The change in angle θ_{diff} can be calculated using the following equation:

$$\theta_{diff} = \theta(t) - \theta(0) \tag{8}$$

Here, $\theta(0)$ represents the angle before the arm movement, and $\theta(t)$ represents the angle during the movement. If θ_{diff} exceeds a threshold, the object is detected to be sliding while rotating. At that time, $\theta(t)$ is updated by substituting it for $\theta(0)$, allowing for repeated rotation detection.

3 Experiments

3.1 Experimental Condition

To verify the effectiveness of the proposed method, grasping experiments were conducted. The experimental environment is shown in Fig. 9. In this experiment, the Yale OpenHand Project Model T-42 [10] was used for the underactuated hand, the DOBOT MG400 for robotic arm, and the Intel RealSense D405 for stereo camera.

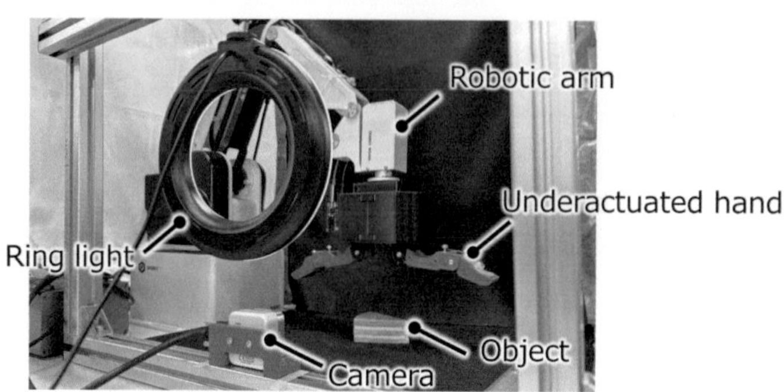

Fig. 9. Experimental environment.

The objects used in the experiment are shown in Fig. 11, and five trials were performed for each object (Fig. 10). The objects included two multi-colored toys and four actual food items, arranged to display the xy plane as shown in the top-left corner of Fig. 11.

Fig. 10. Objects for the experiment.

After successfully grasping the objects, the robotic arm followed a predefined path, simulating a situation where disturbances were applied while lifting the object. The effectiveness of the method was evaluated using the success rate, which represents the proportion of successful experiments in which the object was grasped without dropping it. Additionally, for the food items shown in Fig. 11, the number of visible damages was evaluated.

3.2 Experimental Results

The results are shown in Table 1. The successful grasping results are shown in Fig. 11. From the results, all objects were grasped successfully without being dropped, except for the potato chips and hamburger. This is due to the ability to adapt the grasping force according to the hardness of the object in the object state detection during grasping. Moreover, drop detection was well performed so as not to drop the object during the arm control. Furthermore, for the food items, no noticeable damage was observed visually during the grasping of any object. This suggests that the object deformation and hand occlusion detection in the object state detection were effective in preventing damage to the items.

Table 1. Experimental result

Object	success rate [%]	number of visible damages
Toy cake	100	-
Toy cupcake	100	-
Sausage	100	0
Potato chip	80	0
Cream puff	100	0
Hamburger steak	90	0

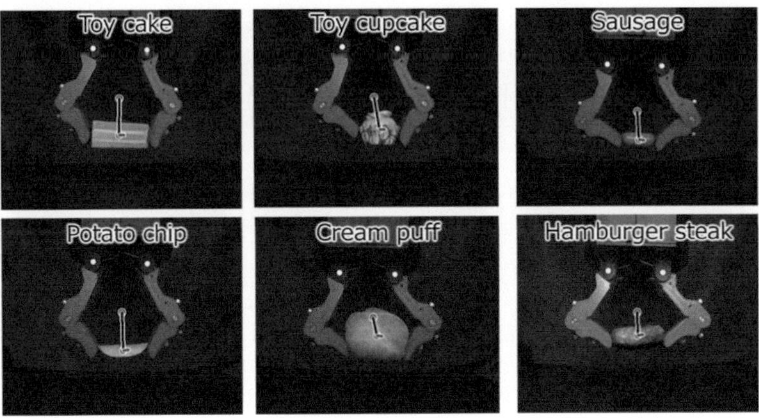

Fig. 11. Examples of successful grasps for objects.

Next, consider the failed attempts with the hamburger and potato chips. The examples of failure scenarios are shown in Fig. 12.

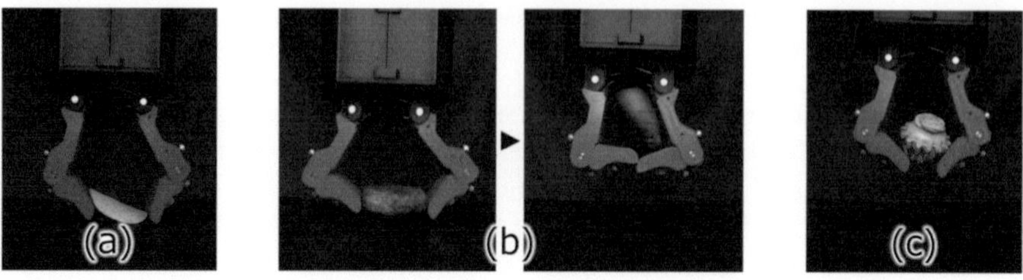

Fig. 12. Examples of failure in grasping.

In Fig. 12(a), with the potato chips, the object's posture changes during the grasping process. This is the factor that caused the failure of grasping the object due to insufficient force applied to the object. Therefore, it seems necessary to improve the method by observing the posture of the object during the grasp. Additionally, it is necessary to add control that performs a re-grasp if the force is not effectively added to the object.

In Fig. 12(b), with the hamburger, the object slips and drops during the lifting process. The hamburger was covered with a fatty layer, making it slippery, and it had some elasticity. The grasp was made near the fingertips, resulting in a small contact area. Due to the physical properties of the hamburger, the grasping force was not sufficiently applied, causing the object to slip and fall. Therefore, in the future, controlling the grasping point by considering the direction and magnitude of the force applied to the object will help for a more stable grasp.

Additionally, there was also failure with toy cupcake, as shown in Fig. 12(c). Although it did not fall, it seems to be in a state where it was not effectively grasped, almost leading to a drop. This indicates that, despite the underactuated hand having characteristics that allow it to conform to the object, it was unable to fully utilize those conforming capabilities. Therefore, it seems necessary to consider the deformation of the underactuated hand and calculate a grasping position that can conform to the shape of the object, enabling more stable grasping.

4 Conclusion

In this study, we proposed an visual feedback control method for grasping objects using an underactuated hand and a stereo camera. The proposed method enables the grasping of objects with various stiffness without using any internal sensors or attaching markers to the objects. To prevent excessive grasping force, we calculated the movements of the hand and the object, object deformation, and the occlusion of the hand. Additionally, during the lifting process by a robotic arm, object slippage was detected. In experiments, we successfully grasped objects without dropping them, except for potato chips and hamburgers. Furthermore, for food items, we confirmed that the objects could be grasped without causing visible damage.

In future work, we aim to improve the system by calculating the object's posture during grasping. This will allow regrasping when no force is applied to the object. Additionally, we plan to calculate the optimal grasping position by considering the forces applied to the object and the underactuated hand's adaptability to the object. This will enhance the stability of object grasping.

References

1. Birglen, L., Laliberté, T., Gosselin, C.: Underactuated Robotic Hands. Springer Tracts in Advanced Robotics **40** (2008)
2. Azulay, O., Ben-David, I., Sintov, A.: Learning Haptic-based Object Pose Estimation for In-hand Manipulation with Underactuated Robotic Hands. arXiv:2207.02843. (2020)
3. Prado da Fonseca, V., Jiang, X., Emil, M. P., Eustaquio Alves de Oliveira, T.: Tactile object recognition in early phases of grasping using underactuated robotic hands. Intell. Serv. Robot. **15**, 513–525 (2022)
4. Lu, Z., Guo, H., Zhang, W., Yu, H.: GTac-gripper: a reconfigurable under-actuated four-fingered robotic gripper with tactile sensing. IEEE Robot. Autom. Lett. **7**(3), 7232–7239 (2022)
5. She, Y., Liu, S. Q., Yu, P., Adelson, E. H.: Exoskeleton-covered soft finger with vision-based proprioception and tactile sensing. In: 2020 IEEE International Conference on Robotics and Automation (ICRA), pp. 10075–10081. IEEE, Paris, France (2020)
6. Liu, S.Q., Yañez, L.Z., Adelson, E.H.: GelSight EndoFlex: a soft endoskeleton hand with continuous high-resolution tactile sensing. In: 2023 IEEE International Conference on Soft Robotics (RoboSoft), pp. 1–6. IEEE, Singapore, Singapore (2023)
7. Andrew, S. M., Walter, G. M., Aaron, M. D.: Towards generalized manipulation learning through grasp mechanics-based features and self-supervision. IEEE Trans. Robot. **37** (2021)
8. Van, P. N., Quan Khanh, L., Yuzuru, T., Van Anh, H.: Wet adhesion of micro-patterned interfaces for stable grasping of deformable objects. In: 2020 IEEE/RSJ International Conference on Intelligent Robots and Systems (IROS), pp. 9213–9219. IEEE, Las Vegas, NV, USA (2020)
9. Ryogo, K., Yuzuka, I., Sarthak, P., Kazunori, U.: Visual feedback control of an underactuated hand for grasping brittle and soft foods. In: 2024 IEEE International Conference on Robotics and Automation (ICRA), pp. 7332–7338. IEEE, Yokohama, Japan (2024)
10. Bruce D. L., Takeo, K.: An iterative image registration technique with an application to stereo vision. In: Proceedings of the 7th International Joint Conference on Artificial Intelligence, pp. 674—679. Morgan Kaufmann Publishers Inc., Vancouver, BC, Canada (1981)
11. Raymond, R.M., Lael, U.O., Aaron, M.D.: A Modular, Open-Source 3D Printed U nderactuated Hand. In: 2013 IEEE International Conference on Robotics and Automation (ICRA), pp. 2737–2743. IEEE, Karlsruhe, Germany (2013)

CATS+: Cultural Heritage Data Augmentation and Transformation System with Correlation Analysis

Hyerin Hwnag, Seohyun Baek, Chan-Woo Park, Hee-Kwon Kim, and Jae-Ho Lee(✉)

Electronics and Telecommunications Research Institute (ETRI), Daejeon, Korea
{hyerin,b_seohy,gamer,hkkim79,jhlee3}@etri.re.kr

Abstract. Due to the continuous digitization of cultural heritage, many users can now experience their own museums. However, most digitization work is currently done manually, making it inefficient in terms of time and cost. This manual process underscores the necessity of automation to keep pace with the speed of digitization. Cultural heritage items are categorized into various groups, but the metadata information for each item varies, making it difficult to infer specific classification criteria. This study aims to automate classification by utilizing visual data. We addressed the issue of imbalanced datasets by generating a training dataset for cultural heritage using generative models. A dictionary was created to use appropriate prompts randomly, ensuring consistency in image generation. To validate the performance of the training model using the generated dataset, a multi-label classification model is used. The results demonstrate the potential for automating classification using visual features derived from text in the cultural heritage domain.

Keywords: Text-to-Image Generative Models · Multi-Label Classification · Cultural Heritage

1 Introduction

Cultural heritage is a valuable asset that reflects the history and culture of humanity, encompassing a wide range of materials accumulated over centuries. Through the digitization process, cultural heritage can be more widely shared and preserved, enabling its use in academic research, education, and more. However, to effectively manage and utilize the vast amount of cultural heritage data, a systematic and efficient data classification and management system is essential. Currently, most cultural heritage data has an inconsistent structure and insufficient information, making it crucial to establish a systematic classification. This problem persists in the process of digitizing and systematically managing the vast amount of cultural heritage data.

To address this issue, it is essential to introduce an automated classification system that leverages various characteristics of metadata. Cultural heritage data includes various forms and information, and a customized system that can systematically classify

C.-W. Park and H.-K. Kim—Contributing authors.

B. Kim (Ed.): IW-FCV 2025, CCIS 2769, pp. 120–135, 2026.
https://doi.org/10.1007/978-981-95-4578-0_10

and manage this data according to the characteristics of each cultural heritage item is necessary. Text-based classification methods have limitations for cultural heritage data that lack information or have incomplete records. To overcome these limitations, generative AI, which has recently gained attention, is a model that learns the characteristics of large-scale data and analyzes meaningful patterns and relationships within images. Using visual materials to extract features within images can fill the gaps in data. This approach can significantly improve efficiency in terms of time and cost compared to traditional manual digitization methods. By utilizing text-to-image generation models, unique images based on the provided text information can be created and used as a training dataset. This study proposes a method to analyze the relationships between data using training cultural heritage data generated from a text-to-image generation model by employing a multi-label classification model. The multi-label classification model can predict multiple attributes for a single data point simultaneously, thus overcoming the limitations that arise from text-only classification and enabling data analysis. Even when text information is insufficient, image-based classification can complement the data, helping to mitigate the shortcomings of inadequate text information. The ultimate goal of this study is to automatically infer and classify cultural heritage data based on its forms and incomplete information, and to present a data management system implementation based on this classification. For cases with insufficient image data, generated images are utilized to prepare various digitized cultural heritage content. The contributions of this paper are as follows:

1. We validated the performance of the multi-label classification model applied to cultural heritage data. We propose methods for using the augmented generated dataset either as a standalone training dataset or combined with actual datasets.
2. We introduce the use of visual materials to complement incomplete data. By employing image-based analysis techniques for cultural heritage data with insufficient text information, we propose an approach to enhance data classification accuracy.
3. We propose a design method for an automated cultural heritage data management and utilization system. Based on the multi-label classification model, we analyze the relationships between data, and through automated classification and recommendation systems, we suggest new possibilities for the digitization process.

2 Related Work

Computer Vision for Cultural Heritage

Recent research utilizing cultural heritage data has addressed various issues based on deep learning algorithms. DeFi [1] proposes a method for hole boundary detection training by generating synthetic datasets to form accurate 3D point clouds [11] through the acquisition of 3D data using 3D sensors or multi-view reconstruction for the preservation of digital cultural heritage. ConvSRGAN [2] suggests a method for restoring and enhancing traditional Chinese paintings by applying a high-frequency retention module that maintains high-frequency components and restores detailed features of images using residual blocks and high-frequency emphasis loss functions. MROPM [3] utilizes Photorealistic Style Transfer (PST) to style old photos through multiple references and enhances the results to create modern images. ArchGPT [4] focuses on tailored tasks for the repair and preservation of traditional buildings by leveraging large language models (LLMs). Another method [5] proposes the augmentation of images using a generative model and captioning of cultural heritage to apply a retrieval technique using the CLIP model [6]. Various techniques are emerging to address the issues arising from cultural heritage data. This study presents a method for extracting meaningful patterns and relationships from cultural heritage data using generative models [7].

Text-to-Image Synthesis

Text-to-Image models are a rapidly growing generative technology in the field of artificial intelligence. These models combine Natural Language Processing (NLP) [12] with diffusion-based image generation algorithms to create images based on text prompts provided by users. The diffusion process generates images by gradually removing noise, starting with random noise and progressively refining it into a clear image. The core of this technology is learning the relationship between text input and image output. For this, it trains on large datasets that contain both text descriptions and corresponding images. During the training process, the model learns to understand the meaning of the text and how to connect it to the visual elements of the image. As a result, the model can generate realistic and detailed images based on the given text descriptions. A representative model of Text-to-Image is the Latent Diffusion Model (LDM) [7]. The DDPM (Denoising Diffusion Probabilistic Models) [8] used in the Latent Diffusion Model is an algorithm that stabilizes and finely tunes the generation process. It models the data distribution by adding noise in stages and then removing it inversely to restore the data, generating images through this process. DDIM (Denoising Diffusion Implicit Models) [9] is utilized to accelerate the generation process, using a non-Markovian approach instead of DDPM is Markov chain method to produce high-quality images with fewer computational steps. In other papers, editing tools were complex and manipulation methods for specific regions were very limited. Thus, this paper proposes a method for semantically editing specific regions of an image solely through the manipulation of text prompts in a Text-to-Image Diffusion model. Openjourney [23] was developed with the goal of providing precise control over generated content and is based on the open-source Stable Diffusion v1.5 model. Imagen [24] demonstrates that using T5 [25], a text-only pre-trained encoder, has a more significant impact on overall performance compared to scaling the decoder within the diffusion model. Additionally, they highlight that the final generated images achieve super-resolution through the application of a super-resolution upsampler model [26]. Prompt-to-Prompt [10] loads the pre-trained Stable Diffusion model and controls the cross-attention layer to adjust object changes, textures, and the number of objects.

This study proposes a methodology for utilizing image data generated from a Text-to-Image generation model as a training dataset through a multi-label classification model [13]. The goal is to solve the classification and management problems of cultural heritage data based on the generated data.

3 Methodology

This section introduces the specific methods of how data is generated using a text-to-image generation model, augmented, and then used as a training dataset.

3.1 Visualization of Cross-Attention Maps by Text

The text-specific visualization method proposed in this paper modifies the layers involved in editing images by injecting cross-attention maps during the diffusion process. This approach enables the identification of which pixels attend to specific tokens of the prompt text during each diffusion step. The general method for generating cross-attention maps is described in Eq. (1):

$$Attention(Q, K, V) = softmax\left(\frac{QK^T}{\sqrt{d_k}}\right) \cdot V, with$$
$$Q = W_Q^{(i)} \cdot \phi_z(x), K = W_K^{(i)} \cdot \tau_y(x), V = W_V^{(i)} \cdot \tau_y(x). \tag{1}$$

The query represents the noisy image, while the key and value correspond to the text prompt. To calculate the similarity between the query and the key, the dot product of their respective vectors is performed, where a higher value indicates greater similarity. This allows the analysis of the relationship between the query and the key. The computed similarity scores are then passed through a softmax function, which generates weights that indicate how well each key aligns with the query. These generated weights are subsequently applied to the value through a dot product operation, extracting the most relevant information. This method enables users to control cross-attention maps through a simple and intuitive interface. The proposed approach includes the process of generating images based on text descriptions, as described in Eq. (2):

$$I = f(D; \theta) \tag{2}$$

The generated image is denoted as I, the input prompt (text data) as D, and the model parameters as θ. The model is represented as a function f, where f generates an image based on the input data and the model parameters. Thus, this process represents how the model utilizes its parameters to generate an image that corresponds to the given input text data.

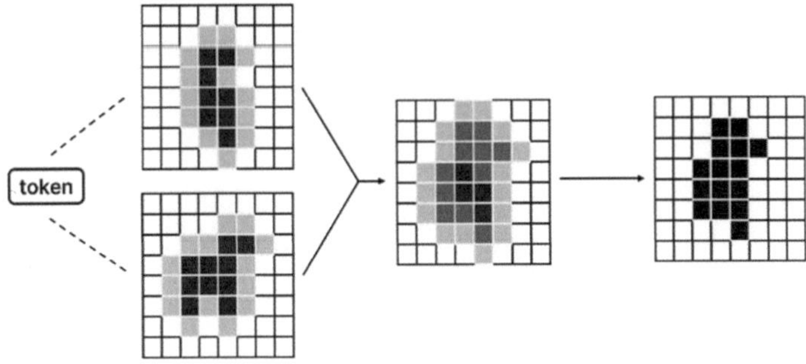

Fig. 1. Combination of Input Tokens [14].

As shown in Fig. 1, the input text prompt is tokenized, and attention scores are calculated for each token. These attention scores are expanded and aggregated to create a larger map, with heatmaps from each layer being combined to generate the final heatmap. Features are extracted from the input image at the pixel level, and these features are used to generate pixel queries. The token keys derived from the text prompt are matched with the pixel queries, calculating the attention scores that represent interactions between tokens and image patches. These computed attention scores are combined with the token values and are used by the model to construct the final output image. During the image generation phase, the Stable Diffusion model progressively refines a noisy image by predicting its alignment with the text prompt, forming cross-attention maps to ensure semantic relevance.

In this study, we use the Prompt-to-Prompt model [10] as the baseline for our research. This model introduces a novel approach to image editing within text-to-image generation models. The primary focus of the Prompt-to-Prompt model lies in analyzing the relationships between text prompts. Specifically, cross-attention maps are employed to examine how the model responds to each input text prompt, enabling visual verification of which words or phrases are associated with specific parts of the generated image. The model leverages methods to control the cross-attention layers, allowing fine-tuned adjustments to the generated images. By incorporating cross-attention maps, interactions between pixels and tokens are seamlessly integrated, providing insights into the semantic relationships that significantly influence the final output.

3.2 Improving Image Resolution in the Latent Space

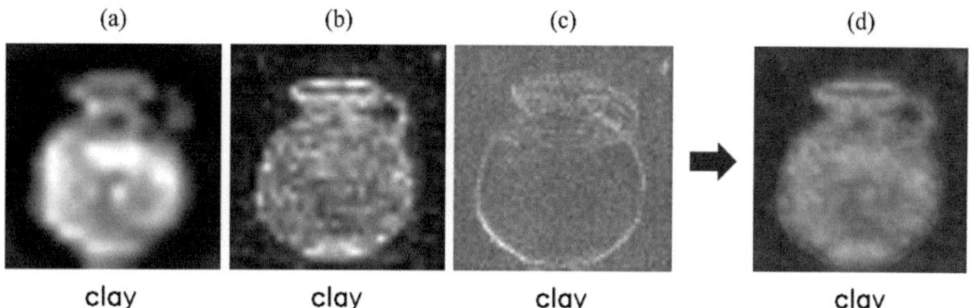

Fig. 2. Visualization of Methods for Adjusting the Resolution of Cross Attention Maps.

In this paper, we designed an additional method to improve the visualization of 16 × 16 resolution images (Fig. 2a) in the latent space, as it is difficult to capture detailed features. We extracted a single image from the latent space in three different sizes: 16 × 16 (Fig. 2a), 32 × 32 (Fig. 2b), and 64 × 64 (Fig. 2c), and visualized it by averaging them (32 × 32) (Fig. 2d). As shown in Fig. 4, while the 16 × 16 resolution allows the shape of the object ("clay") to be distinguished but not clearly, the 32 × 32 resolution shows relatively clearer results. The 64 × 64 resolution makes it easier to distinguish the contours of the object. Therefore, averaging the three cross-attention maps yields the average map as shown in Fig. 2(d). By cropping only the object from the image in Fig. 2(d), labeling tasks can be performed using this image. Utilizing the generated average map allows for clearer identification of the object's detailed visual features, enabling more accurate labeling tasks.

3.3 Multi-Label Classification

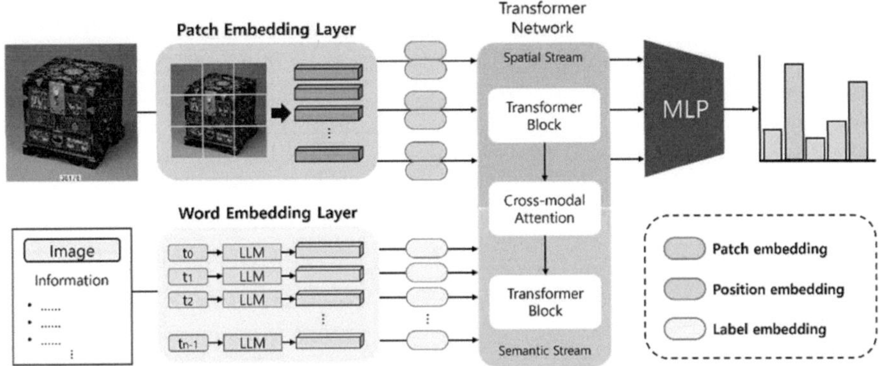

Fig. 3. Transformer-based [13] multi-label classification architecture [15].

Multi-label classification is a technique used to predict multiple labels simultaneously for a single data instance. For example, when an image contains multiple objects or attributes, the objective is to predict all labels corresponding to those objects or attributes. Unlike single-label classification, this approach has the advantage of capturing complex information structures. Multi-label classification is employed in image retrieval systems to enable efficient classification and search. The dataset used is structured in the COCO [16] format, with multiple labels assigned to each image, categorized under higher-level categories. When focusing solely on the textual information of cultural heritage, each image represents the subcategories of each category predicted by the model through multi-label classification. These results allow the model to learn shared features among cultural heritage sites where textual information has been visualized. Based on this, it becomes possible to identify and link similar cultural heritage items. Consequently, the system can analyze the relationships between images and provide recommended images, facilitating a visual understanding of the relevance of cultural heritage information.

Figure 3 illustrates the architecture of the multi-label classification model [13] based on a transformer framework, categorized by higher-level categories. This architecture consists of two primary streams: the Spatial Stream and the Semantic Stream. The Spatial Stream employs a Vision Transformer (ViT) [17] to process cultural heritage image data generated in the earlier stages. The images are divided into patches, and the visual features of each patch are extracted, transformed into vectors, and encoded into a learnable format. The process of dividing images into patches preserves detailed visual information while enabling the model to learn relationships between patches. The transformer then models the global relationships among these patches, effectively capturing the complex visual characteristics of cultural heritage images. These visual features are processed through the transformer model, playing a critical role in the classification process. The Semantic Stream leverages a large-scale language model, BERT [18], to process textual information. The input text data includes the actual multi-label classes of cultural heritage items, which are aligned with the generated images. BERT encodes the text into embedding vectors that reflect the contextual meaning of each word, allowing the model to capture semantic relationships within the text. These embeddings are crucial inputs for the multi-label prediction process. The Semantic Stream learns the alignment between the generated images and the actual categories of cultural heritage (e.g., age, material, life-style) by analyzing textual and visual data. It also identifies contextual and semantic relationships among the labels. The two streams operate independently, collecting visual and textual features, which are then integrated through an Integration Layer. In this layer, the outputs of both streams are combined, allowing the model to learn the latent relationships between visual and textual information. This integration enhances the semantic connections between images and text, improving the accuracy of multi-label predictions. As a result, the model can classify cultural heritage data more effectively and with greater precision.

3.4 Dataset

MUCH Dataset

(See Table 1).

Table 1. Classification Based on Korean Age, Materials, and Lifestyles Using the MUCH Dataset.

Super Categories	Class Name	Number
Age	Bronze Age, Early Iron Age, Proto-Three Kingdoms, Baek-je, Silla, Three Kingdoms, Unified Silla, Go-ryeo, Late Joseon, Joseon, Japanese colonial period	11
Material	Wood, stone, soil, paper, mineral, fossil, seed, chilgi, leaf, leather, bone, fiber, ceramic, rubber	14
Life style	Transportation/communication, culture/art, social life, industry/livelihoods, dietary life, clothing life, daily life	7

The MUCH (Multi-purpose Universal Cultural Heritage) dataset is composed of 9,600 filtered images from Korean cultural heritage metadata that fall under three categories. Using these as prompts, a total of 96,000 augmented images were generated, with 10 images created per prompt. Of these, 86,400 images were used for training and 9,600 images were used for validation. The dataset was created by processing text data provided by the National Museum of Korea. This dataset is categorized into three main categories: age, material, and lifestyle, and includes a total of 32 classes. We used the age, material, and lifestyle categories to perform experiments with minimal metadata information. Each main category includes various detailed sub-classes. Firstly, the 'Age' category includes classes that distinguish historical periods of Korea. Secondly, the 'Material' category represents the material characteristics of each cultural heritage item, classified based on surface texture or material. Lastly, the ‘Lifestyle’ category describes the social or industrial background reflected by the respective cultural heritage.

4 Results

4.1 Implementation Details

(Table 2).

Table 2. Multi-Label Classification Model Key Parameters.

Parameters	Value
Learning rate	1e-5
Batch size	128
Epoch	100
Resolution	448 × 448
(Train, Valid, Test)	(8: 1: 1)
Optimizer	AdamW
Weight Decay	1e-5
Loss Function	BCE

The proposed approach was evaluated through experiments conducted on the MUCH dataset. The evaluation metrics included average precision (AP) for each category and mean average precision (mAP) across all categories. To further assess model performance, the F1-score (OF1) was employed. The experiments utilized a transformer-based multi-label classification model, with all input images resized to a resolution of 448 × 448 to ensure a balance between computational efficiency and detail preservation. The AdamW optimizer [19] was applied with a learning rate of $1 \times 10^{-5} 1 \times 10^{-5}$ and a weight decay of $1 \times 10^{-5} 1 \times 10^{-5}$.. Binary cross-entropy (BCE) [20] was adopted as the loss function, given its effectiveness for multi-label classification tasks.

4.2 Quantitative Result

Table 3 shows the performance results of the model trained solely on the generated dataset. The MUCH dataset, composed of 9,600 images generated by converting metadata into prompts, showed performance differences across categories. When analyzing the performance of each super-category, the mAP value for the ‘Age’ category was 45.7%. This may be because the characteristics of different historical periods in Korea are difficult to represent visually, resulting in a lower classification accuracy due to the lack of visual cues for distinguishing epochs. The mAP value for the ‘Life Style’ category was 44.4%. This is likely due to the concept of lifestyle being inherently challenging to define as a clear visual object. Additionally, the number of classes in this category

Table 3. Experimental results on datasets showing a performance (mAP in %).

Dataset	Resolution	Super Category	Class	mAP	OF1
MUCH(Ours)	448 × 448	All	32	56.3	50.1
MUCH(Ours)	448 × 448	Age	11	45.7	41.1
MUCH(Ours)	448 × 448	Material	14	78.8	69.5
MUCH(Ours)	448 × 448	Life style	7	44.4	39.7

is seven, which is fewer than in other categories, and the dataset size for each class is limited, possibly leading to insufficient training. On the other hand, the 'Material' category had the highest performance with an mAP value of 78.8%. This is because the types of materials are relatively easier to distinguish visually, making inter-class classification more straightforward. The visual cues provided by the characteristics of materials, such as color and texture, likely contributed to achieving higher accuracy in image-based classification compared to other categories. However, as shown in Fig. 6, there are still challenges in classifying fragments of pottery into 'ceramic' and 'soil' within the Material category. The differences in mAP values across super-categories indicate that performance varies based on the visual information of the classification targets, the number of datasets, and the number of classes. Setting distinguishable age for abstract concepts such as age and lifestyle could lead to even higher performance.

Table 4. Experimental results of testing the model trained with augmented generative data with original data (mAP in %).

Dataset	Super Category	Class	Baseline mAP	Augm mAP
e-Museum	All	15	56.7	**58.1**
e-Museum	Age	5	46.6	**46.7**
e-Museum	Material	5	62.3	**64.1**
e-Museum	Life style	5	61.2	**63.5**

Table 4 shows the results of evaluating a pre-trained model with the augmented MUCH dataset on an actual cultural heritage dataset. The actual cultural heritage dataset was crawled from the National Museum of Korea's e-Museum site [21], targeting public type 1 and 2 images that are available for commercial use and research. The dataset used in the experiment consists of a total of 96,500 images, and the sub-classes are included in the MUCH dataset. The sub-classes for 'Age' are Bronze Age, Three Kingdoms, Unified Silla, Goryeo, and Joseon. The sub-classes for 'Material' are wood, stone, ceramic, paper, and soil. The sub-classes for 'Life style' are social life, industry/livelihoods, dietary life, clothing life, and culture/art. These classes were set up because there is not a lot of data that includes all three multi-label categories, and filtering them this way prevents overfitting.

Baseline mAP represents the mAP performance of the model trained on the original cultural heritage dataset, while Augm mAP (Augmented Dataset mAP) is the result of the model trained by loading the pre-trained model with the augmented dataset. When applying the model trained with the augmented dataset to the actual cultural heritage dataset, an overall improvement in performance was observed. The use of augmented data helped improve performance in the classification of material and lifestyle categories. However, for the age classification, the model struggled to understand features related to the age in the images, resulting in relatively lower performance improvement. This is because the augmented dataset included characteristics similar to the actual data, contributing to the model's generalization ability. The comparison of performance by sub-class showed that the model using the augmented dataset performed consistently well across all sub-classes, demonstrating that it can address the issue of class imbalance due to data scarcity.

Table 5. Experimental results of the model trained by combining augmented and original data (mAP in %).

Dataset	Super Category	Class	mAP
Augm + e-Museum	All	15	**60.5**
Augm + e-Museum	Age	5	**52.7**
Augm + e-Museum	Material	5	**66.4**
Augm + e-Museum	Life style	5	**62.4**

Table 5 shows the results of tests conducted on a model trained by combining the augmented dataset with the original dataset. Compared to previous experimental methods, this approach demonstrated the highest performance. The augmented data compensated for the insufficient number of datasets and improved image classification performance across various situations. Including the augmented dataset enabled the model to learn a wider range of visual patterns, enhancing its generalization ability. This indicates that the use of the augmented dataset is effective in allowing the model to predict new data with high accuracy. Therefore, the method proposed in this paper suggests its applicability across various domains.

4.3 Qualitative Result

Figure 4(a) illustrates a coin, with the output from the SDXL 1.0 [22] model demonstrating the highest similarity to the real image, particularly in its accurate texture representation. While other models also produced comparable results, SDXL 1.0 exhibited superior fidelity in reproducing textures akin to the original. Figure 4(b) depicts celadon, with the generated output closely aligning with the overall appearance of the original

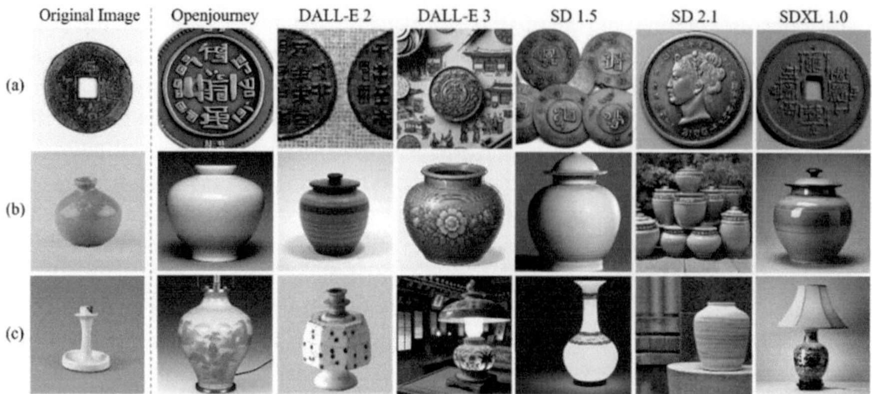

Fig. 4. Compare the visualization results [15] of text-to-image generative models when using translated English sentences as input; (a) coins, (b) celadon bottles, (c) white porcelain lanterns.

artifact. Figure 4(c) presents a porcelain lamp, effectively capturing the distinctive characteristics of both porcelain and the lamp itself. In summary, considering the quality of the generated outputs alongside computational efficiency and runtime, SDXL 1.0 emerges as a suitable model for data generation and augmentation tasks. This model not only delivers high performance but also possesses practical usability, enabling system administrators to efficiently apply it across diverse domains.

Fig. 5. Compare images generated using SDXL 1.0 **(top)** with actual cultural heritage images **(bottom)**; (a) a duck sculpture, (b) fragments of a jar, (c) bead bracelets.

Figure 5 is a comparison between the image generated through the proposed method and the actual image. The amount of metadata information for each cultural heritage varies significantly. However, it can be observed that the images generated after switching to English descriptions are highly similar to the actual images. Specifically, (a) plate (굽다리접시), (b) porcelain jar (청화백자용문호), and (c) dining table (목제나전소반). The generated images are so similar to the original ones that it is challenging to distinguish the generated versions of (a), (b), and (c) in Fig. 5 from the actual images. Utilizing these images for model training is expected to further enhance the automatic classification of newly added cultural heritage items.

Fig. 6. Comparison of Ceramic and Soil in Cultural Heritage; (a) ceramic, (b) soil.

Figure 6 shows real-world cultural heritage images of 'ceramic' and 'soil'. These images are often difficult to distinguish with the naked eye, which can contribute to poor learning performance when the model performs a classification task. If the textures or colors are similar, it is likely that the model will not be able to clearly distinguish the boundaries between the two classes. Establishing clear standards to solve this problem remains a future research task.

Figure 7 compares the automated and manual processing methods of the cultural heritage search and recommendation system. Figure 7(a) shows how a model trained on user input data in a GUI environment analyzes images and automatically categorizes and recommends them based on the evaluation results. Figure 7(b) shows the cultural heritage information page of the e-Museum site [21] operated by the National Museum of Korea, displaying the same items as in Fig. 7(a). This page requires all images to be manually uploaded and organized. Implementing an automated method like that in Fig. 7(a) could reduce the costs associated with manual tasks. This system automatically analyzes the various textual information of each cultural heritage item and classifies them into appropriate categories, demonstrating the commercial potential of deep learning-based models.

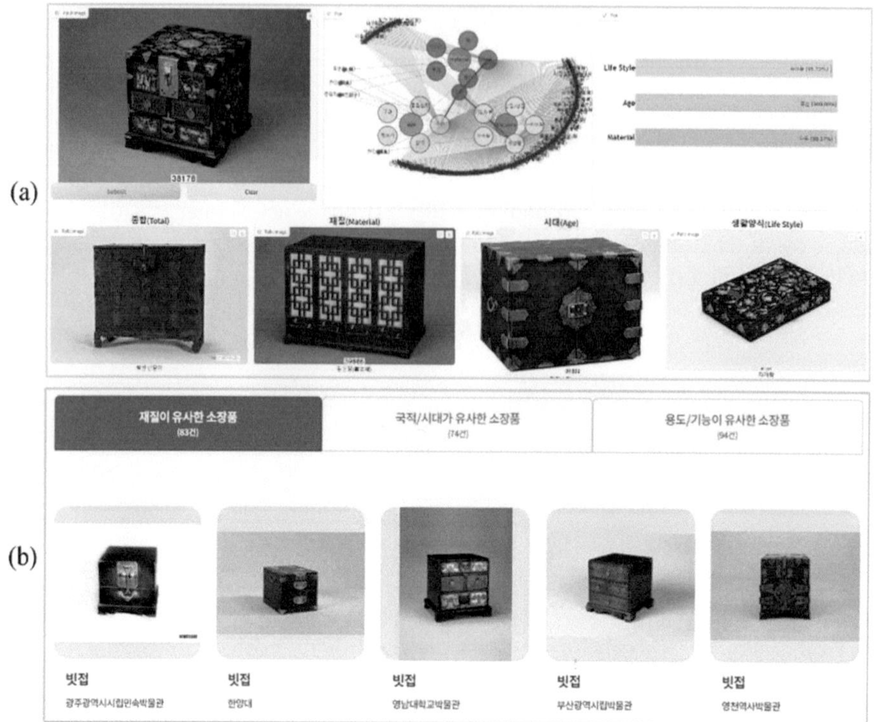

Fig. 7. Visualization [15] of Association Analysis and Recommendation System Application Results in a GUI Environment; (a) Site constructed in the GUI environment, (b) National Museum of Korea e-Museum site [21].

5 Conclusions

This study proposed a method based on the Stable Diffusion model to visualize cross-attention maps and automatically assign labels to generated images. The proposed approach demonstrated its effectiveness in analyzing the relationship between text and images, contributing to the efficient management and classification of data with varying amounts of information. Through the application of multi-label classification techniques and augmented datasets, the potential for automated classification and management systems was validated. The results indicate that the proposed method can effectively classify cultural heritage data and analyze the relationships between text and images, facilitating the processing of newly added data. This highlights its applicability not only in large-scale search and recommendation systems but also in specialized fields such as cultural heritage management. In particular, by leveraging text-based image generation, the proposed approach provides practical tools for system administrators to automatically classify new information and quickly identify its relevance.

Future research will focus on constructing an expanded dataset to enable application to a wider range of cultural heritage systems. This dataset will include a more diverse set of cultural heritage data, encompassing temporal, material, and lifestyle characteristics, to improve the model's generalization performance. Beyond its role as a training dataset, this resource will serve as a standardized dataset for cultural heritage research and management systems. Additionally, we aim to incorporate previously unaddressed classes and improve the classification of abstract and higher-level concepts through algorithmic enhancements. Furthermore, experiments on more complex domains and large-scale datasets will be conducted to establish the feasibility of the proposed method as a foundation for commercialized automated data management and recommendation systems.

Acknowledgements. This research is supported by Ministry of Culture, Sports and Tourism and Korea Creative Content Agency (Project Number: RS-2023-00219579).

Authors' Contributions. H was responsible for writing the main manuscript, designing the experiments, creating the figures, and conducting the main model experiments. P assisted with experimental design and performed data pre-processing. K, B assisted with experimental design and setting up the experiments. L reviewed the manuscript and contributed to the experimental design. All authors read and approved the final manuscript.

Funding. This research is supported by Ministry of Culture, Sports and Tourism and Korea Creative Content Agency (Project Number: RS-2023-00219579).

Availability of Data and Materials. The dataset used in this study was generated using a generative model. The code used for data generation and analysis will be made available in a future release.

Competing Interests

The authors declare that they have no competing interests.

Authors' Information

Hyerin Hwang: First Author, Electronics and Telecommunications Research Institute (ETRI), Daejeon, Korea. E-mail: hyerin@etri.re.kr.

Seohyun Baek: First Author, Electronics and Telecommunications Research Institute (ETRI), Daejeon, Korea. E-mail: b_seohy@etri.re.kr.

Chan-Woo Park: Contributing Author, Electronics and Telecommunications Research Institute (ETRI), Daejeon, Korea. E-mail: gamer@etri.re.kr.

Hee-Kwon Kim: Contributing Author, Electronics and Telecommunications Research Institute (ETRI), Daejeon, Korea. E-mail: hkkim79@etri.re.kr.

Jae-Ho Lee: Corresponding author, Electronics and Telecommunications Research Institute (ETRI), Daejeon, Korea. E-mail: jhlee3@etri.re.kr.

References

1. Tabib, R.A., et al.: DeFi: detection and filling of holes in point clouds towards restoration of digitized cultural heritage models. In: Proceedings of the IEEE/CVF International Conference on Computer Vision, 2023

2. Hu, Q., et al.: ConvSRGAN: super-resolution inpainting of traditional Chinese paintings. Herit. Sci. **12**(1), 176 (2024)
3. Gunawan, A., et al.: Modernizing old photos using multiple references via photorealistic style transfer. In: Proceedings of the IEEE/CVF Conference on Computer Vision and Pattern Recognition (2023)
4. Zhang, J., et al.: ArchGPT: harnessing large language models for supporting renovation and conservation of traditional architectural heritage. Herit. Sci. **12**(1), 220 (2024)
5. Cioni, D., Berlincioni, L., Becattini, F., Del Bimbo, A.: Diffusion Based Augmentation for Captioning and Retrieval in Cultural Heritage, pp. 1699–1708 (2023)
6. Radford, A., et al.: Learning transferable visual models from natural language supervision. In: International Conference on Machine Learning. PMLR, 2021
7. Rombach, R., et al.: High-resolution image synthesis with latent diffusion models. In: Proceedings of the IEEE/CVF Conference on Computer Vision and Pattern Recognition (2022)
8. Ho, J., Jain, A., Abbeel, P.: Denoising diffusion probabilistic models. Adv. Neural. Inf. Process. Syst. **33**, 6840–6851 (2020)
9. Song, J., Meng, C., Ermon, S.: Denoising diffusion implicit models. arXiv preprint arXiv: 2010.02502 (2020)
10. Hertz, A., et al.: Prompt-to-prompt image editing with cross attention control. arXiv preprint arXiv:2208.01626 (2022)
11. Guo, Y., et al.: Deep learning for 3D point clouds: a survey. IEEE Trans. Pattern Anal. Mach. Intell. **43**(12), 4338–4364 (2020)
12. Collobert, R., et al.: Natural language processing (almost) from scratch. J. Mach. Learn. Res. **12**, 2493–2537 (2011)
13. Zhu, X., Cao, J., Ge, J., Liu, W., Liu, B.: Two-stream transformer for multi-label image classification. In: Proceedings of the 30th ACM International Conference on Multimedia, pp. 3598–3607, 2022
14. Hwnag, H., et al.: Data labeling and test-bed for analyzing correlations between input text prompt and output image. J. Inst. Electron. Inf. Eng. **61**(6), 93–102 (2024)
15. Hwang, H.: CATS: cultural-heritage classification using LLMs and distribute model. Heritage Science. (in press)
16. Lin, T.Y., et al.: Microsoft COCO: common objects in context. In: Fleet, D., Pajdla, T., Schiele, B., Tuytelaars, T. (eds.) Computer Vision – ECCV 2014. ECCV 2014. LNCS, vol. 8693, pp. 740–755. Springer, Cham (2014). https://doi.org/10.1007/978-3-319-10602-1_48
17. Dosovitskiy, A.: An image is worth 16 × 16 words: transformers for image recognition at scale. arXiv preprint arXiv:2010.11929 (2020)
18. Devlin, J., et al.: Bert: pre-training of deep bidirectional transformers for language understanding. arXiv preprint arXiv:1810.04805 (2018)
19. Loshchilov, I., Hutter, F.: Decoupled weight decay regularization. arXiv preprint arXiv:1711.05101, 2017
20. Zhang, Z., Sabuncu, M.: Generalized cross entropy loss for training deep neural networks with noisy labels. Adv. Neural Inf. Process. Syst. **31** (2018)
21. National museum of korea e-museum. https://www.emuseum.go.kr/main
22. Podell, D., et al.: SDXL: improving latent diffusion models for high-resolution image synthesis. arXiv preprint arXiv:2307.01952 (2023)
23. Prompthero. Openjourney. Hugging Face, n.d. Web, 12 July 2024. https://huggingface.co/prompthero/openjourney

24. Saharia, C., et al.: Photorealistic text-to-image diffusion models with deep language understanding. Adv. Neural Inf. Process. Syst. **35**, 36479–36494 (2022)
25. Raffel, C., et al.: Exploring the limits of transfer learning with a unified text-to-text transformer. J. Mach. Learn. Res. **21**(140), 1–67 (2020)
26. Saharia, C., et al.: Image super-resolution via iterative refinement. IEEE Trans. Pattern Anal. Mach. Intell. **45**(4), 4713–4726 (2022)

Mask-Guided Region-Specific Editing in Diffusion Models

Muhammad Shaheryar(✉), Jinhyeong Park, and Soon Ki Jung

School of Computer Science and Engineering, Kyungpook National University, Daegu, Republic of Korea
{shaheryar,hini2245,skjung}@knu.ac.kr

Abstract. Diffusion models have emerged as state-of-the-art generative frameworks, capable of producing high-quality realistic images. However, achieving precise and localized editing within specific regions of an image while preserving global consistency remains a significant challenge. In this paper, we propose a mask-based region-specific editing framework that leverages the latent space of diffusion models. Our approach enables fine-grained semantic modifications within a designated region of interest (ROI) while ensuring the unmasked regions remain unaffected. To achieve this, we compute the Jacobian matrix $\mathbf{J}_{\mathcal{M},t}$ restricted to the masked region and employ Singular Value Decomposition (SVD) to identify the most influential directions in the latent space. These directions are further refined via nullspace projection to eliminate undesired changes outside the ROI. By efficiently manipulating the latent space along the identified directions, our method achieves localized edits without requiring external labels, retraining, or additional supervision. Extensive experiments demonstrate that our framework produces visually consistent and semantically meaningful edits across diverse attributes, masks, and scale levels. The proposed method provides a mathematically principled, and highly controllable solution for localized image editing, advancing the capabilities of diffusion models in practical applications.

Keywords: Face Editing · Diffusion Models · Latent Space · Image Editing · Face Mask

1 Introduction

The growing demand for facial image editing in the era of selfies and personalized media has driven significant advancements in both research and industry [1–3]. Widely adopted in applications such as Snapchat and Facetune, these tools enable precise and creative facial enhancements, transforming how users interact with and modify digital portraits. Facial image editing using generative models has achieved remarkable progress in modifying facial attributes with high realism. Recent advancements focus on leveraging diverse auxiliary conditions, such as text, masks, and images, to guide editing tasks [4–7]. However, methods that generate entirely new images prior to editing often require additional processes, such as masking and blending, to retain attributes from the original images [8, 9]. To address this, partial editing techniques have emerged, offering

B. Kim (Ed.): IW-FCV 2025, CCIS 2769, pp. 136–147, 2026.
https://doi.org/10.1007/978-981-95-4578-0_11

solutions that selectively edit specific attributes while preserving the majority of details in the original image. These approaches eliminate the need for re-training the model and enable flexible conditional editing.

In particular, generative adversarial net-based (GAN-based) models demonstrated the ability to edit images [2, 7, 10–12]. For example, InterFaceGAN [11] explores the latent space of GANs to manipulate facial attributes such as ethnicity, age, and expression. StarGAN [2] modifies multiple attributes at once with a single model, known as multi-domain image-to-image translation. Nevertheless, in the sense of image editing, GAN-based methods struggle with disentanglement, which is one of the abilities to separate independent attributes of an image effectively. On the other hand, diffusion models revealed themselves as a rivaling alternative to GANs, showing better quality and detail in image synthesis [13–16]. This edge-cutting quality is implemented by the iterative process of adding noise and denoising, offering fine controllability pixel-wise. Extensive research on diffuson-based image editing has been conducted based on theoretical and novel findings. For instance, Asyrp [17] introduced the h-space as a representative latent space of diffusion models, taking place of the deepest layer in the backbone U-Net [18]. The backbone constructs a rich latent space after encoding raw data through multiple layers, enabling interpretable and disentagled editing. Meanwhile, boundary diffusion [19] proposed a single-attribute editing framework by finding semantic boundaries and eventually edit the image in the latent states, where this latent refers to the intermediate (i.e., noisy) states of an image.

While modern diffusion models excel at generating high quality images research on multi-attribute editing with diffusion models remains limited, and achieving disentangled, localized control over content generation is still challenging. Unlike generative adversarial networks (GANs), the semantic spaces of diffusion models are not yet well understood, and current editing approaches often rely on additional training or heuristic-based techniques, limiting their practicality [20–23]. Generative models, such as GANs, have revealed the rich structure of latent spaces, where manipulating latent codes along specific directions can result in meaningful attribute changes in generated images [24]. This enables control over the generation process by discovering semantically relevant subspaces. Traditional methods for latent semantic discovery often involve generating a dataset of synthesized images, labeling them for a target attribute, and then training a classifier to identify a separation boundary in the latent space [25]. However, this supervised approach is limited by its dependence on predefined labels, which may fail to capture subtle or highly localized attributes [26]. Techniques such as PCA, while unsupervised, compute directions based on global sample statistics and often identify broad changes, such as pose or gender, but lack the ability to address finer, region-specific edits, such as adjusting eye shape or closing eyes [26]. To address these limitations, we leverage the Jacobian matrix as a powerful tool for identifying precise, region-specific editing directions in the latent space. By calculating the Jacobian with respect to a region of interest (ROI) specified by a segmentation mask, we can isolate the influence of the latent variables on the targeted region. This enables the discovery of orthogonal directions in the latent space (h-space) that induce the most significant changes in the prediction of clean image for ROI. We operate within the linear subspace of the Jacobian, providing disentangled and localized control over edits without requiring additional labels or text-based supervision. This approach effectively combines the advantages of unsupervised learning with the precision of Jacobian-based analysis, offering a scalable and robust solution for fine-grained ROI editing. The key contributions are as follows:

- We propose a mask-based ROI editing framework that effectively modifies regions within the latent space of diffusion models while preserving the semantic integrity of unmasked regions.
- Our method demonstrates strong generalizability by applying editing directions derived from one image to diverse inputs and exhibits robustness across various mask configurations and scales.
- Rigorous evaluations using FID, MSE, and ID metrics validate the method's effectiveness, showing strong performance in producing semantically consistent and visually realistic edits.

2 Related Work

2.1 Diffusion Models

While GANs served as one of the generative models providing high-quality samples, diffusion models emerged as a new generative model that outperforms GANs in terms of sample quality. Starting from pure Gaussian noise, diffusion models learn to gradually recover a clear image, which introduces sophisticated control over multiple timesteps. This detail controlled by iterative denoising enabled various diffusion-based applications such as image generation [14, 15], semantic segmentation [27, 28], and editing [6, 29].

2.2 Mask-Based Editing

Among the advances in editing images using generative models, mask-based image editing gained significant attention due to the strong localization of ROI to edit. Masked-based editing can concentrate more on the regions given a segmentation mask, preserving the rest of the region more stable. MaskFaceGAN [30] directly operates within the StyleGAN2 [31] latent space and utilizes additional face masks from a face parser, addressing the previous limitations of image editing methods: entangled attribute editing, low-resolution manipulation, and artifacts introduced in result images. Mask-Guided Portrait Editing with Conditional GANs [32] proposed a face mask-guided portrait editing scheme based on conditional GANs [33]. The GAN is conditioned on masked regions that enable fine control over the modification while preserving backgrounds better than in previous works. These methods demonstrated mask-guided GAN-based image editing, providing a more refined condition by mask condition. Meanwhile, DiffEdit [6], a diffusion model-based editing scheme, introduces an automated mask generation module. This mask generator automatically finds the region to edit based on the given text condition, eliminating the need for explicit mask conditions. DiffEdit showcased the superiority of diffusion-based methods over GAN-based with more controllability and detail. Different from the above approaches, in this paper, we perform image editing tasks within the latent space of diffusion models.

3 Methodology

3.1 Diffusion Model Basics

Diffusion models are generative frameworks that transform data through a sequence of noisy latent states. In the forward process, a clean image $\mathbf{x}_0$ is gradually corrupted by adding Gaussian noise over T steps, following a predefined noise schedule. The forward diffusion step at time t is expressed as:

$$\mathbf{x}_t = \sqrt{\alpha_t}\mathbf{x}_0 + \sqrt{1-\alpha_t}\boldsymbol{\epsilon},\ \boldsymbol{\epsilon} \sim \mathcal{N}(0, \mathbf{I}),$$

where α_t controls the proportion of noise added at each step. The reverse process aims to recover $\mathbf{x}_0$ from $\mathbf{x}_T$ by iteratively denoising the latent states. The reverse diffusion step is parameterized as:

$$\mathbf{x}_{t-1} = \frac{1}{\sqrt{\alpha_t}}\left(\mathbf{x}_t - \frac{1-\alpha_t}{\sqrt{1-\overline{\alpha}_t}}\boldsymbol{\epsilon}_\theta(\mathbf{x}_t, t)\right) + \sigma_t\mathbf{z},$$

where $\boldsymbol{\epsilon}_\theta(\cdot)$ is a neural network trained to predict the added noise, $\overline{\alpha}_t = \prod_{s=1}^{t}\alpha_s$, and $\mathbf{z} \sim \mathcal{N}(0, \mathbf{I})$ introduces stochasticity. Diffusion models approximate data distributions by learning this reverse stochastic process.

3.2 Editing in Diffusion Models

Editing in the latent space $\mathbf{h}_t$ of a diffusion model can be formulated as identifying a meaningful direction $\mathbf{n}$ in the latent space and perturbing $\mathbf{h}_t$ along this direction to achieve a desired modification in the output image. This process is expressed as:

$$\mathbf{h}_t^{\text{edit}} = \mathbf{h}_t + \alpha\mathbf{n},$$

where $\mathbf{h}_t$ is the latent code at timestep t, $\alpha \in \mathbb{R}$ is a scalar controlling the magnitude of the edit, $\mathbf{n} \in \mathcal{H}$ is the editing direction, typically derived from sensitivity analysis or learned attributes in the model.

$$\mathbf{x}_0^{\text{edit}} = \epsilon^\theta(\mathbf{h}_t^{\text{edit}}, t),$$

This approach enables precise editing in specific regions of the image by carefully selecting the direction $\mathbf{n}$, which is often derived from region-specific gradients or precomputed latent directions.

3.3 Mask-Based Region-Specific Editing in Diffusion Models

In Mask-Based Region-Specific Editing, our goal is to edit a specific region of interest (ROI) in the image while keeping the rest of the image unchanged. The goal is to identify an editable direction $\mathbf{n}$ in the latent space of diffusion models to selectively modify (ROI), denoted as masked region $\mathcal{M}$, in an image while ensuring no changes occur in the complement of the masked region, denoted as $\overline{\mathcal{M}}$. To achieve this, we divide the image into two parts: $\mathbf{x}_{\mathcal{M}}$: The masked region corresponding to $\mathcal{M}$, where changes are desired, $\mathbf{x}_{\overline{\mathcal{M}}}$: The unmasked region, complement of $\mathcal{M}$, which should remain unchanged. These regions form a partition of the image:

$$\mathbf{x} = \mathbf{x}_{\mathcal{M}} \cup \mathbf{x}_{\overline{\mathcal{M}}}, \mathbf{x}_{\mathcal{M}} \cap \mathbf{x}_{\overline{\mathcal{M}}} = \varnothing.$$

Finding Editable Directions Using the Jacobian: Let us extend the role of the Jacobian $\mathbf{J}_t$ in the context of mask-based editing, explicitly incorporating the masked ($\mathcal{M}$) and unmasked ($\overline{\mathcal{M}}$) regions. The goal is to enable localized changes in the masked region $\mathcal{M}$ $||\mathbf{x}^{\text{edit}}_{\mathcal{M}} - \mathbf{x}_{\mathcal{M}}||_2^2 > 0$. while ensuring that the unmasked region $\overline{\mathcal{M}}$ remains unaffected $||\mathbf{x}^{\text{edit}}_{\overline{\mathcal{M}}} - \mathbf{x}_{\overline{\mathcal{M}}}||_2^2 = 0$.

3.4 Jacobian-Based Approximation

The Jacobian matrix $\mathbf{J}_t$, which captures the relationship between the latent space $\mathbf{h}_t$ and the predicted image $\boldsymbol{\epsilon}_\theta(\mathbf{x}_t, \mathbf{h}_t)$, can be partitioned to reflect the influence on the masked region $\mathcal{M}$ and the unmasked region $\overline{\mathcal{M}}$. This is expressed as:

$$\mathbf{J}_{\mathcal{M},t} = \nabla_{\mathbf{h}_t} \boldsymbol{\epsilon}_\theta(\mathbf{x}_{\mathcal{M},t}, \mathbf{h}_t), \mathbf{J}_{\overline{\mathcal{M}},t} = \nabla_{\mathbf{h}_t} \boldsymbol{\epsilon}_\theta(\mathbf{x}_{\overline{\mathcal{M}},t}, \mathbf{h}_t).$$

where $\mathbf{J}_{\mathcal{M},t}, \mathbf{J}_{\overline{\mathcal{M}},t}$ are the Jacobian capturing the effect of latent space perturbations on the masked region $\mathcal{M}$ and the unmasked region $\overline{\mathcal{M}}$ respectively (Fig. 1).

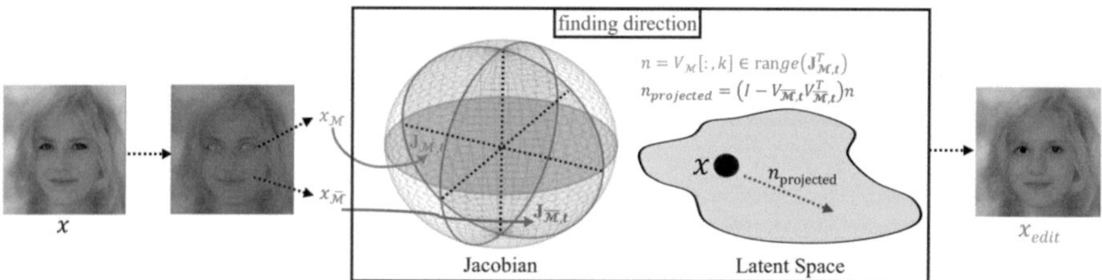

Fig. 1. The figure illustrates the workflow of our mask-guided editing approach in the latent space of diffusion models. Given an input image $\boldsymbol{x}$, we first segment it into the masked region $\boldsymbol{x}_{\mathcal{M}}$ (region of interest, ROI) and the unmasked region $\boldsymbol{x}_{\overline{\mathcal{M}}}$. We then compute the Jacobian $\boldsymbol{J}_{\mathcal{M},t}$ of the masked region, as expressed in the SVD decomposition $\boldsymbol{J}_{\mathcal{M},t} = \boldsymbol{U}_{\mathcal{M}} \boldsymbol{\Sigma}_{\mathcal{M}} \boldsymbol{V}^\top_{\mathcal{M},t}$. Using the singular vectors $\boldsymbol{V}_{\mathcal{M},t}$, we determine the optimal editing direction $\boldsymbol{n}$, which induces the largest semantic changes in the masked region. The direction $\boldsymbol{n}$ is then projected onto the nullspace of the unmasked region $\boldsymbol{J}_{\overline{\mathcal{M}},t}$ to preserve its content. Finally, the image is edited in the latent space of the diffusion model by perturbing it along the identified direction $\boldsymbol{n}_{\text{projected}}$, resulting in the edited output $\boldsymbol{x}_{\text{edit}}$.

The editing task involves finding a latent direction $\mathbf{n}$ that maximizes the change in the masked region $\mathcal{M}$ while minimizing changes in the unmasked region $\overline{\mathcal{M}}$. Mathematically, this can be formulated as:

$$\text{maximize}_{\mathbf{n}} \ \mathbf{n}^\top \mathbf{J}^\top_{\mathcal{M},t} \mathbf{J}_{\mathcal{M},t} \mathbf{n}.$$
$$\text{minimize}_{\mathbf{n}} \ \mathbf{n}^\top \mathbf{J}^\top_{\overline{\mathcal{M}},t} \mathbf{J}_{\overline{\mathcal{M}},t} \mathbf{n}.$$

To achieve both objectives simultaneously, we combine them into a single Rayleigh quotient [34]:

$$\text{maximize}_{\mathbf{n}} \frac{\mathbf{n}^\top \mathbf{J}_{\mathcal{M},t}^\top \mathbf{J}_{\mathcal{M},t} \mathbf{n}}{\mathbf{n}^\top \mathbf{J}_{\overline{\mathcal{M}},t}^\top \mathbf{J}_{\overline{\mathcal{M}},t} \mathbf{n}}.$$

This optimization identifies the direction $\mathbf{n}$ in latent space that strongly affects the masked region $\mathcal{M}$ while minimally altering the unmasked region $\overline{\mathcal{M}}$. To identify the direction $\mathbf{n}$, we reformulate to solve the following optimization problem:

$$\mathbf{n}^* = \underset{\mathbf{n}}{\text{argmax}} \frac{\mathbf{n}^\top \mathbf{J}_{\mathcal{M},t}^\top \mathbf{J}_{\mathcal{M},t} \mathbf{n}}{\mathbf{n}^\top \mathbf{J}_{\overline{\mathcal{M}},t}^\top \mathbf{J}_{\overline{\mathcal{M}},t} \mathbf{n}}.$$

To identify the editing direction $\mathbf{n}$ in our method, we calculate the Jacobian $\mathbf{J}$ restricted to the masked region $\mathcal{M}$.. Specifically, we project the model's prediction onto the region of interest (ROI) $\mathcal{M}$. Mathematically, this is expressed as:

$\mathbf{J}_{\mathcal{M},t} = \nabla_{\mathbf{h}_t} \epsilon_0(\mathbf{x}_{\mathcal{M},t}, \mathbf{h}_t) = \mathbf{U}_{\mathcal{M}} \mathbf{\Sigma}_{\mathcal{M}} \mathbf{V}_{\mathcal{M}}^\top$. where, $\mathbf{U}_{\mathcal{M}}$, $\mathbf{\Sigma}_{\mathcal{M}}$, and $\mathbf{V}_{\mathcal{M}}$ are obtained from the Singular Value Decomposition (SVD) of the Jacobian. To find the editing direction $\mathbf{n}$, we select one of the top singular vectors from $\mathbf{V}_{\mathcal{M}}$, corresponding to the largest singular values. This direction is defined as:

$$\mathbf{n} = \mathbf{V}_{\mathcal{M}}[:, k] \in \text{range}(\mathbf{J}_{\mathcal{M},t}^\top),$$

where k is the index of the singular vector within the top-r singular vectors. This process ensures that the identified direction $\mathbf{n}$ induces the largest semantic changes in the masked region $\mathcal{M}$ while maintaining mathematical efficiency and precision. To ensure that $\mathbf{n}$ does not introduce changes in $\overline{\mathcal{M}}$, we project $\mathbf{n}$ onto the nullspace of $\mathbf{J}_{\overline{\mathcal{M}},t}$ [35, 36], which is basically the subspace associated with zero singular values.$\mathbf{n}_{\text{projected}} = \left(\mathbf{I} - \mathbf{V}_{\overline{\mathcal{M}},t} \mathbf{V}_{\overline{\mathcal{M}},t}^\top\right) \mathbf{n}$.

4 Experimental Results

In this section, we detail the experimental setup designed to validate the robustness and effectiveness of our proposed method for mask-based region-specific editing in diffusion models. The experiments are performed using DDPM [37] trained on the CelebA dataset [38], framework renowned for their capabilities in high-quality image generation and manipulation. To quantitatively evaluate the method's performance, we employ three metrics: Fréchet Inception Distance (FID) [39], which assesses the quality of generated images by comparing their distribution to the original dataset; Masked Mean Squared Error (MSE), which evaluates the accuracy of edits within the masked region while ensuring minimal changes in unmasked areas; and Identity Similarity (ID), which measures how well the edited images preserve the original identity and we use arcFace [40] to calculate the identity similarity.

For segmentation and mask generation, we utilize BiSeNet [41], a segmentation model pre-trained on CelebA, to identify and generate masks for specific facial regions such as eyes, nose, mouth, and hair. These masks guide the editing process, ensuring changes remain confined to the designated areas, leaving unmasked regions unaffected.

To validate the effectiveness of our method, we conduct two key experiments. First, direction generalization is tested by deriving editing directions from one image and applying them across various inputs, verifying the method's ability to produce consistent edits across different images. Second, the scalability of edits is demonstrated by varying scale levels, showcasing the method's capability for fine-grained control over the intensity of changes within the masked regions.

5 Results

Figure 2. Illustrates the effectiveness of our ROI-based editing method, where the edits are confined to a specific region of interest (ROI) highlighted by the blue mask. The edits were performed using a single direction derived from one image, and the results were then applied across a variety of other input images. The rows represent different input images, demonstrating the robustness and generalizability of the editing direction. The edits are consistent and localized within the masked region, ensuring that the unmasked areas remain unaffected. These results emphasize the method's ability to provide precise and transferable modifications while maintaining high semantic integrity in unedited regions.

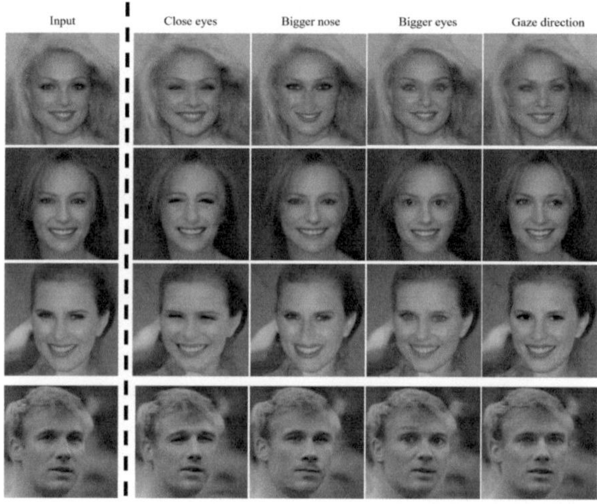

Fig. 2. Controlled ROI-based editing results demonstrating the application of a single editing direction derived from one image to various other input images. The blue mask highlights the region of interest (ROI) where the edits are confined. Each row corresponds to a specific input image, showcasing consistent and localized edits within the masked region while preserving the semantic integrity of the unmasked areas. These results validate the transferability and robustness of the editing direction across diverse images.

Figure 3 illustrates the impact of scaling singular vectors on the nose region, revealing distinct editing effects across different rows. In the first row, positive scaling towards

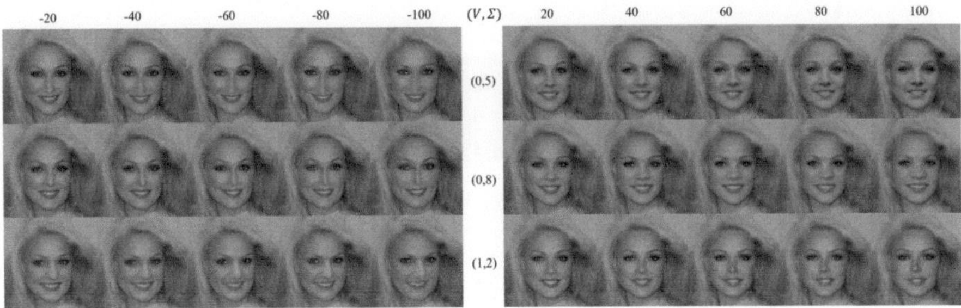

Fig. 3. This grid showcases the editing results obtained by modifying the image using directions derived from singular vectors ($\boldsymbol{V}$) and singular values ($\boldsymbol{\Sigma}$) in the Jacobian subspace. The columns correspond to different singular vector dimensions, with the associated scaling values ranging from -100 to 100, and the rows represent varying magnitudes of the scaling factors applied to these directions.

the right enhances the nose, making it **broader and more defined**, with a noticeable lift in the tip and a more pronounced bridge. Conversely, negative scaling towards the left **compresses the nose region**, reducing its prominence, resulting in a smaller and narrower shape. The second row primarily affects the **width of the nose**. Positive scaling broadens the nose structure, while negative scaling **shrinks it**, emphasizing a narrower profile. In the third row, the edits focus on the **tilt of the nose tip**. Positive scaling tilts the tip upward, creating a lifted appearance, whereas negative scaling tilts the nose downward, giving it a retracted or downward-sloping look. Together, these edits demonstrate how specific singular vectors and scaling values can target unique aspects of the nose's geometry, such as size, width, and orientation, within the latent space. In Fig. 3 we demonstrate mask-based region-specific editing using a semantic latent space framework. Each row corresponds to a distinct region of interest (ROI) indicated by the blue mask: the mouth, hair, and eyes, respectively. The edits applied to these regions showcase the versatility of the proposed editing method. In the first row, edits focus on transforming the mouth's shape, including subtle adjustments to the lips' curvature and smile intensity. The second row illustrates modifications to the hair, where edits involve varying textures, volume, and overall style. Finally, the third row highlights changes to the eyes, such as widening, narrowing, or altering the gaze intensity. The blue overlay represents the masked regions targeted for editing, ensuring precise control while preserving the unmasked areas. These results emphasize the robustness of the method in producing diverse yet realistic alterations (Fig. 4).

Table 1 presents the quantitative evaluation of our method across different attributes, including "Close Eyes," "Big Nose," "Bigger Eyes," and "Gaze Direction." Our approach consistently achieves the highest identity similarity (ID) scores after editing for all these attributes, demonstrating its ability to preserve identity while performing attribute-specific modifications. Our algorithm operates without any additional supervision or annotations, making it more versatile and efficient in practical applications. This robustness highlights the capability of our framework to effectively isolate and edit region-specific attributes in a principled and unsupervised manner.

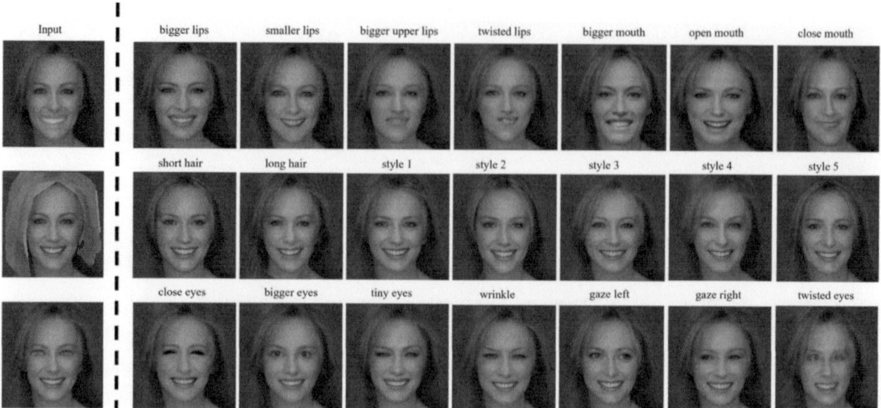

Fig. 4. Visualization of mask-based region-specific edits using semantic latent space. Each row corresponds to a distinct ROI (mouth, hair, and eyes), with the blue mask indicating the region under transformation. The edits demonstrate precise control over the targeted area while maintaining realistic and versatile results.

Table 1. Performance Comparison on Different Tasks

Metric	Close Eyes	Big Nose	Bigger Eyes	Gaze Direction
FID ↓	**22.80**	25.12	24.37	26.65
MSE ↓	2.90	2.64	**2.08**	3.21
ID ↑	**0.87**	0.79	0.81	0.84

6 Limitations and Discussion

While our framework enables precise mask-based region-specific editing in diffusion models, a few limitations remain intact. The method relies heavily on the quality of segmentation masks; inaccuracies can introduce unintended changes outside the target area. The linear approximation of Jacobian directions, while effective for small perturbations, may lead to artifacts for larger edits due to its inability to model non-linear relationships. Additionally, computing the Jacobian and performing SVD across multiple timesteps adds computational overhead, which can hinder real-time applications. Extending this approach to simultaneously handle multiple overlapping attributes or regions remains challenging, as disentangling their respective directions without interference is non-trivial. Future work could address these limitations by incorporating robust mask refinement, improving computational efficiency, and exploring non-linear direction modeling for broader and more efficient applicability.

7 Conclusion

In this work, we presented a mask-based region-specific editing framework for diffusion models, enabling precise and localized control over image edits. By leveraging the Jacobian matrix restricted to masked and unmasked regions, our method identifies orthogonal editing directions in the latent space through Singular Value Decomposition (SVD). This allows targeted semantic modifications within a region of interest while preserving the integrity of unmasked regions. Our approach ensures mathematically grounded, disentangled edits, and demonstrates strong generalizability across multiple images for same ROI editing. Despite minor limitations, such as computational overhead and sensitivity to mask quality, this work establishes a robust foundation for advancing region-specific editing in diffusion models. Future directions include improving computational efficiency, handling non-linear edits, and extending the method to multiple overlapping regions and diverse generative frameworks.

Acknowledgment. This work was partly supported by Innovative Human Resource Development for Local Intellectualization program through the Institute of Information & Communications Technology Planning & Evaluation(IITP) grant funded by the Korea government(MSIT) (IITP-2024-RS-2022–00156389, 50%) and the ICT R&D program of MSIT/IITP. [RS-2024–00336663, Development of AI technology for tracking and investigating drug criminals through multimedia sources].

References

1. Chen, Y.-C., et al.: Semantic component decomposition for face attribute manipulation. In: Proceedings of the IEEE/CVF Conference on Computer Vision and Pattern Recognition, pp. 9859–9867 (2019)
2. Choi, Y., Choi, M., Kim, M., Ha, J.-W., Kim, S., Choo, J.: Stargan: unified generative adversarial networks for multi-domain image-to-image translation. In: Proceedings of the IEEE Conference on Computer Vision and Pattern Recognition, pp. 8789–8797 (2018)
3. He, Z., Zuo, W., Kan, M., Shan, S., Chen, X.: Attgan: facial attribute editing by only changing what you want. IEEE Trans. Image Process. **28**, 5464–5478 (2019)
4. Huang, Z., Chan, K.C., Jiang, Y., Liu, Z.: Collaborative diffusion for multi-modal face generation and editing. In: Proceedings of the IEEE/CVF Conference on Computer Vision and Pattern Recognition, pp. 6080–6090 (2023)
5. Andonian, A., Osmany, S., Cui, A., Park, Y., Jahanian, A., Torralba, A., Bau, D.: Paint by word. arXiv preprint arXiv:2103.10951. (2021)
6. Couairon, G., Verbeek, J., Schwenk, H., Cord, M.: Diffedit: Diffusion-based semantic image editing with mask guidance. arXiv preprint arXiv:2210.11427. (2022)
7. Xia, W., Yang, Y., Xue, J.-H., Wu, B.: Tedigan: text-guided diverse face image generation and manipulation. In: Proceedings of the IEEE/CVF Conference on Computer Vision and Pattern Recognition, pp. 2256–2265 (2021)
8. Lee, C.-H., Liu, Z., Wu, L., Luo, P.: Maskgan: towards diverse and interactive facial image manipulation. In: Proceedings of the IEEE/CVF Conference on Computer Vision and Pattern Recognition, pp. 5549–5558 (2020)
9. Kim, K., et al.: Diffface: Diffusion-based face swapping with facial guidance. arXiv preprint arXiv:2212.13344. (2022)

10. Patashnik, O., Wu, Z., Shechtman, E., Cohen-Or, D., Lischinski, D.: Styleclip: text-driven manipulation of stylegan imagery. In: Proceedings of the IEEE/CVF International Conference on Computer Vision, pp. 2085–2094 (2021)
11. Shen, Y., Yang, C., Tang, X., Zhou, B.: Interfacegan: Interpreting the disentangled face representation learned by gans. IEEE Trans. Pattern Anal. Mach. Intell. **44**, 2004–2018 (2020)
12. Shaheryar, M., Laishram, L., Lee, J.T., Jung, S.K.: Latent space navigation for face privacy: A case study on the MNIST dataset. Presented at the (2023)
13. Ho, J., Jain, A., Abbeel, P.: Denoising diffusion probabilistic models. Adv. Neural. Inf. Process. Syst. **33**, 6840–6851 (2020)
14. Dhariwal, P., Nichol, A.: Diffusion models beat gans on image synthesis. Adv. Neural. Inf. Process. Syst. **34**, 8780–8794 (2021)
15. Stypułkowski, M., Vougioukas, K., He, S., Zięba, M., Petridis, S., Pantic, M.: Diffused heads: Diffusion models beat gans on talking-face generation. In: Proceedings of the IEEE/CVF Winter Conference on Applications of Computer Vision, pp. 5091–5100 (2024)
16. Shaheryar, M., Lee, J.T., Jung, S.K.: IDDiffuse: dual-conditional diffusion model for enhanced facial image anonymization. In: Proceedings of the Asian Conference on Computer Vision, pp. 4017–4033 (2024)
17. Kwon, M., Jeong, J., Uh, Y.: Diffusion models already have a semantic latent space. arXiv preprint arXiv:2210.10960. (2022)
18. Ronneberger, O., Fischer, P., Brox, T.: U-net: convolutional networks for biomedical image segmentation. In: Medical Image Computing and Computer-assisted Intervention–MICCAI 2015: 18th International Conference, Munich, Germany, october 5–9, 2015, Proceedings, Part III 18. pp. 234–241. Springer (2015)
19. Zhu, Y., Wu, Y., Deng, Z., Russakovsky, O., Yan, Y.: Boundary guided learning-free semantic control with diffusion models. Adv. Neural Inform. Process. Syst. **36** (2024)
20. Zhang, L., Rao, A., Agrawala, M.: Adding conditional control to text-to-image diffusion models. In: Proceedings of the IEEE/CVF International Conference on Computer Vision, pp. 3836–3847 (2023)
21. Kouzelis, T., Plitsis, M., Nicolaou, M.A., Panagakis, Y.: Enabling local editing in diffusion models by joint and individual component analysis. arXiv preprint arXiv:2408.16845. (2024)
22. Haas, R., Huberman-Spiegelglas, I., Mulayoff, R., Graßhof, S., Brandt, S.S., Michaeli, T.: Discovering interpretable directions in the semantic latent space of diffusion models. In: 2024 IEEE 18th International Conference on Automatic Face and Gesture Recognition (FG), pp. 1–9. IEEE (2024)
23. Shaheryar, M., Laishram, L., Lee, J.T., Jung, S.K.: Multi-attributed face synthesis for one-shot deep face recognition. In: Frontiers of Computer Vision, pp. 1–13 (2023)
24. Shen, Y., Gu, J., Tang, X., Zhou, B.: Interpreting the latent space of gans for semantic face editing. In: Proceedings of the IEEE/CVF Conference on Computer Vision and Pattern Recognition, pp. 9243–9252 (2020)
25. Shen, Y., Zhou, B.: Closed-form factorization of latent semantics in gans. In: Proceedings of the IEEE/CVF Conference on Computer Vision and pAttern Recognition, pp. 1532–1540 (2021)
26. Härkönen, E., Hertzmann, A., Lehtinen, J., Paris, S.: Ganspace: Discovering interpretable gan controls. Adv. Neural. Inf. Process. Syst. **33**, 9841–9850 (2020)
27. Amit, T., Shaharbany, T., Nachmani, E., Wolf, L.: Segdiff: Image segmentation with diffusion probabilistic models. arXiv preprint arXiv:2112.00390. (2021)
28. Baranchuk, D., Rubachev, I., Voynov, A., Khrulkov, V., Babenko, A.: Label-efficient semantic segmentation with diffusion models. arXiv preprint arXiv:2112.03126. (2021)
29. Kim, G., Kwon, T., Ye, J.C.: Diffusionclip: text-guided diffusion models for robust image manipulation. In: Proceedings of the IEEE/CVF Conference on Computer Vision and Pattern Recognition, pp. 2426–2435 (2022)

30. Pernuš, M., Štruc, V., Dobrišek, S.: Maskfacegan: high resolution face editing with masked gan latent code optimization. IEEE Trans. Image Process. (2023)
31. Karras, T., Laine, S., Aittala, M., Hellsten, J., Lehtinen, J., Aila, T.: Analyzing and improving the image quality of stylegan. In: Proceedings of the IEEE/CVF Conference on Computer Vision and Pattern Recognition, pp. 8110–8119 (2020)
32. Gu, S., Bao, J., Yang, H., Chen, D., Wen, F., Yuan, L.: Mask-guided portrait editing with conditional gans. In: Proceedings of the IEEE/CVF Conference on Computer Vision and Pattern Recognition, pp. 3436–3445 (2019)
33. Mirza, M.: Conditional generative adversarial nets. arXiv preprint arXiv:1411.1784. (2014)
34. Ramesh, A., Choi, Y., LeCun, Y.: A spectral regularizer for unsupervised disentanglement. arXiv preprint arXiv:1812.01161. (2018)
35. Banerjee, S., Roy, A.: Linear algebra and matrix analysis for statistics. Crc Press Boca Raton (2014)
36. Zhu, J., et al.: Low-rank subspaces in gans. Adv. Neural. Inf. Process. Syst. **34**, 16648–16658 (2021)
37. von Platen, P., et al.: Diffusers: State-of-the-art diffusion models (2022)
38. Liu, Z., Luo, P., Wang, X., Tang, X.: Large-scale celebfaces attributes (celeba) dataset 11 (2018), Retrieved August 15
39. Heusel, M., Ramsauer, H., Unterthiner, T., Nessler, B., Hochreiter, S.: Gans trained by a two time-scale update rule converge to a local nash equilibrium. Adv. Neural Inform. Process. Syst. **30** (2017)
40. Deng, J., Guo, J., Xue, N., Zafeiriou, S.: Arcface: additive angular margin loss for deep face recognition. In: Proceedings of the IEEE/CVF Conference on Computer Vision and Pattern Recognition, pp. 4690–4699 (2019)
41. Yu, C., Wang, J., Peng, C., Gao, C., Yu, G., Sang, N.: Bisenet: bilateral segmentation network for real-time semantic segmentation. In: Proceedings of the European Conference on Computer Vision (ECCV), pp. 325–341 (2018)

Lighting Condition Discrimination Based on Hyperspectral Images

Shumpei Chochi(✉), Youta Noboru(✉), and Yuko Ozasa

Tokyo Denki University, 5 Senju Asahi-Cho, Adachi-Ku, Tokyo, Japan
{24amj27,24amj29}@ms.dendai.ac.jp, ozasa@mail.dendai.ac.jp

Abstract. In image-based authentication systems designed to protect physical assets, the lighting conditions under which images are captured typically remain consistent. Therefore, if an image captured under different lighting conditions is input into the system, it can be considered an indication of unauthorized access. This paper presents a system to discriminate whether the image used for authentication and the image registered in the authentication database is captured under differing lighting conditions using hyperspectral imaging. Specifically, we construct a dataset for this task and train a feature extractor for the identification based on metric learning, enabling robust and accurate discrimination of lighting conditions.

Keyword: hyperspectral imaging · lighting condition discrimination · metric learning

1 Introduction

In image-based authentication systems that secure physical assets like safes, the lighting conditions during image capture typically remain unchanged. Even if the room layout is changed, the type of lighting rarely differs. Therefore, if an image captured under lighting conditions different from those during biometric registration is input into the authentication system, it can be considered an indication of unauthorized access. We aim to leverage this fact to enhance the security of authentication systems.

We set up a task to determine whether two images were captured under different lighting conditions. Specifically, we focus on biometric authentication using hand images, where the task involves analyzing the dorsal side of the hand. Identifying whether the lighting conditions of the registered hand image and the input hand image are consistent can significantly enhance the security of biometric authentication systems.

While it is challenging to capture differences in lighting conditions using RGB images, hyperspectral (HS) images can effectively distinguish such differences [6].

HS imaging involves capturing images across a continuous range of wavelengths of light incident on the camera, effectively combining spatial information with spectral data. This rich spectral information makes HS images well-suited for identifying variations in lighting conditions with high precision.

B. Kim (Ed.): IW-FCV 2025, CCIS 2769, pp. 148–155, 2026.
https://doi.org/10.1007/978-981-95-4578-0_12

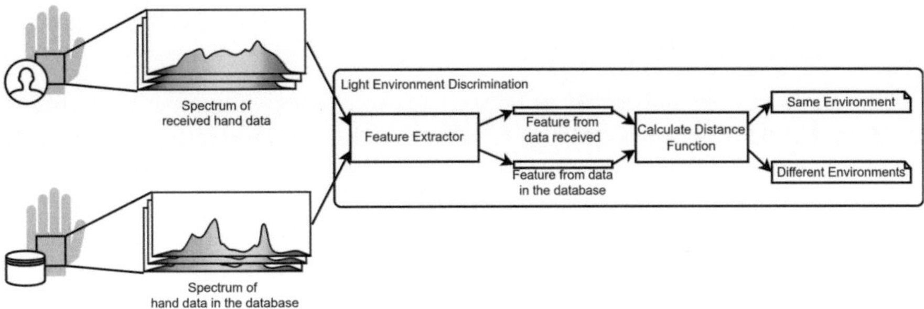

Fig. 1. Overview of the proposed method.

In this paper, we address the task of discriminating whether the lighting conditions of two input images are identical using HS imaging. To achieve this, we construct an HS image dataset and present the discrimination system for lighting conditions.

The proposed system for lighting condition discrimination consists of a feature extraction module and a classifier. The feature extraction module extracts features from the input HS images, while the classifier determines whether the images share the same lighting conditions. Training the feature extraction module requires many images captured under different lighting conditions. However, capturing a large dataset with diverse lighting conditions is labor-intensive. To address this, we generate a dataset of HS images with varying lighting conditions from a limited number of lighting environments and use it for training.

In the experiments, we conducted experiments to detect differences in lighting between two HS images, yielding the following results. The accuracy improved by approximately 1.5 times when using HS images compared to RGB images. By applying the proposed method, the accuracy increased by 10 times compared to when it was not applied.

2 Proposed Method

2.1 Lighting Environment Discrimination

Overview. A lighting environment discrimination system is proposed to detect differences in ambient light between two HS images $\mathbf{I}_1$ and $\mathbf{I}_2$, where $\mathbf{I} \in \mathbb{R}^{C \times H \times W}$. As shown in Fig. 1, the system consists of a feature extraction module and a classifier. Features are extracted from the spectrum of the pixels in the HS images using the feature extraction module, and the lighting environment similarity is assessed through a classifier. The distance between the features of the two HS images is calculated by the classifier. If the distance is below a certain threshold, the images are considered to have the same lighting environment.

Feature Extraction The feature extraction module uses a convolutional neural network (SpectralConv) to extract spectral features from the HS images. SpectralConv is a one-dimensional convolutional neural network (CNN) effective for HS images due to its ability to capture spectral information [4]. Convolution operations are applied along the spectral dimension of the HS images by this network to capture the spectral characteristics of the lighting environment.

HS images can be considered as three-dimensional data with dimensions (bands, height, width). However, since this work aims to extract spectral information without considering spatial information, we use a one-dimensional convolutional neural network (1D-CNN). Three convolutional layers are used to extract spectral features from the spectra. Each convolutional layer is followed by the ReLU activation function, batch normalization, dropout, and fully connected layers. The output size of the fully connected layer was adjusted to match the output size of the preceding layer.

Training Data Generation. For training the feature extraction module, we generate a dataset of HS images from many different lighting environments. Generating this dataset requires HS images of just a few lighting environment types.

We first capture HS images of the same object under a few different lighting environments. For each captured HS image, we generate a transformation vector $\mathbf{T}_n$ that follows a normal distribution with a mean of 1 and a variance of σ^2. $\mathbf{T}_n$ is used to modify the original HS images to simulate various lighting conditions. The transformation vector is generated as follows:

$$\mathbf{T}_n \in \mathcal{N}(1, \sigma^2)(n = 1, 2, ..., N) \tag{1}$$

where $\mathbf{T}_n$ is the transformation vector. By increasing N, we can generate a greater variety of lighting environments. We then multiply the original spectrum $\mathcal{D} = \left\{\mathbf{i}^1_{1,1}, \ldots, \mathrm{i}^1_{H,w}, \mathrm{i}^2_{1,1}, \ldots, \mathrm{i}^2_{H,W}, \ldots, \mathrm{i}^M_{H,w}\right\}$ of HS images by the transformation vector to create the training dataset. Here, H and W denote the height and width of each HS image, respectively, and M represents the number of HS images to be transformed. Since real HS images have correlations between adjacent wavelength bands, we apply a Gaussian filter to smooth them. We use a Gaussian filter with the standard deviation of σ to smooth the HS images. The Gaussian filter is applied to each pixel in the spectral dimension.

$$\mathbf{i}^n = \mathbf{i} \cdot \mathbf{T}_n \tag{2}$$

$$\mathbf{i}^{n'} = \mathbf{i}^n * \mathbf{G} \tag{3}$$

where $\mathbf{i}^n$ is the HS image with the transformation vector $\mathbf{T}_n$, $\mathbf{G}$ is the Gaussian filter, and $*$ denotes the convolution operation. These processes encourage the feature extractor to learn to distinguish between different lighting environments effectively.

To efficiently train the feature extraction module, we randomly sample a subset of the generated data. We randomly sample $\alpha \times 1/N$ of the data from the transformed dataset $D = \left\{\mathrm{i}^{1,1}_{1,1}, \ldots, \mathrm{i}^{M,1}_{H,W}, \ldots, \mathrm{i}^{M,1}_{H,W}\right\}$ This sampling ratio ensures that the training process remains computationally feasible while providing sufficient data diversity for effective learning. The sampled dataset S is defined as follows:

$$S = \mathrm{RandomSample}\left(D, \alpha \times \frac{1}{N}\right) \tag{4}$$

The random sampling process was implemented using the numpy library's 'numpy.random.choice' function[9].

2.2 Baseline Methods

To evaluate the performance of the proposed method, we compared it with several baseline methods. The baseline methods include:

- Spectra: The spectral information of the HS images is used as the feature. The spectral information is standardized using the mean and covariance of the training data.
- PCA-3D[8]: Principal Component Analysis (PCA) is applied to the HS images to reduce the dimensionality to three. The three principal components are used as features. PCA is expected to enhance the discrimination of lighting environments by extracting the main features of the data and reducing the dimensionality of the high-dimensional spectral data. Specifically, we fit the PCA model using the training data D to ensure that the principal components capture the most significant variance in the data. The cumulative contribution rate of PCA on the training data reaches 96.5% in three dimensions.
- Autoencoder [10]: An autoencoder is used to extract features from the spectra of the HS images. The autoencoder is expected to extract features that capture nonlinear relationships that PCA cannot, making it easier to distinguish between lighting environments. The autoencoder consists of three 1D convolutional layers for the encoder and three transposed convolutional layers for the decoder. Each layer is trained using the training data, and the encoder is used as the feature extractor. The output of the encoder is used as the feature. The encoder consists of three one-dimensional convolutional layers and ReLU activation functions, while the decoder consists of three one-dimensional transposed convolutional layers and ReLU activation functions. These are trained on the training data D. During evaluation, the features obtained from the encoder are input into the distance function.

3 Experiments

3.1 Dataset

To validate our method, we created a dataset of hand images captured under 4 different lighting environments. The dataset consists of 360 HS images of hands captured with an HS camera (NH-9, EBA JAPAN Co., Ltd.) [2] covering the spectral range of 350 to 1100 nm with a resolution of 5 nm. The subjects consisted of 15 individuals, and three images of both hands were captured under the same lighting environment for each individual. To ensure a fixed lighting environment, we used a light booth (byko-spectra standard, BYK) [1] equipped with Daylight D65, Incandescent light A, Department store light CWF, and TL84, installed in a darkroom for capturing the images. The data captured under the D65 environment was used as the training data, while the data captured under the remaining three lighting environments was used as the test data.

3.2 Experimental Setup

For training the feature extraction module, we used data captured under the D65 environment as the training data. Based on this data, we generated datasets for N different lighting environments. The transformation vector $\mathbf{T}_n$ was applied to the original HS images to simulate various lighting conditions, as described in the previous section. The value of N was set to 5000, and the total number of training data M was 90.

To evaluate the performance of our proposed method, we used the Equal Error Rate (EER) and Half Total Error Rate (HTER) as metrics. The EER is a point where the false acceptance rate (FAR) and false rejection rate (FRR) are equal. The HTER is the average of the FAR and FRR at a specific threshold θ. The threshold for calculating a HTER is determined based on the EER from the training data. The FAR and FRR are calculated based on the number of false positives (FP), false negatives (FN), true positives (TP), and true negatives (TN) at the determined threshold.

$$\mathrm{FAR}_{\theta_i} = \frac{\mathrm{FP}_{\theta_i}}{\mathrm{FP}_{\theta_i} + \mathrm{TN}_{\theta_i}} \tag{5}$$

$$\mathrm{FRR}_{\theta_i} = \frac{\mathrm{FN}_{\theta_i}}{\mathrm{FN}_{\theta_i} + \mathrm{TP}_{\theta_i}} \tag{6}$$

$$\mathrm{EER} = \frac{\mathrm{FAR} + \mathrm{FRR}}{2}, \quad \text{where } |\mathrm{FAR} - \mathrm{FRR}| = 0 \tag{7}$$

$$\mathrm{HTER} = \frac{\mathrm{FAR} + \mathrm{FRR}}{2} \tag{8}$$

The extracted features were compared using three different distance metrics: Z-score, Euclidean distance, and Mahalanobis distance. To calculate the distance between the received image ($\mathbf{I}_1$) and the image in the database ($\mathbf{I}_2$), we consider the HS images of both $\mathbf{I}_1$ and $\mathbf{I}_2$ to have a size of 151 channels, with a height and width of 200 each. These images are treated as data of size (40000, 151). The distance between the two data sets is calculated by considering the spectral groups of $\mathbf{I}_2$ as a known distribution and calculating the distance between all spectra of $\mathbf{I}_1$ and this known distribution, then averaging these distances.

The preprocessing of HS images was performed to stabilize the discrimination accuracy. The preprocessing involved smoothing each channel using a Gaussian filter and standardizing the data using the mean and covariance of the training data. The smoothing process helps to reduce noise introduced during image capture. The standardization process ensures that the data has a mean of zero and a standard deviation of one, making it more suitable for distance-based calculations by eliminating the effects of differing scales.

The feature extractor was trained using the following settings. The one- dimensional convolutional layers used a kernel size of 3, and the pooling size was set to 1 to ensure the shape remains unchanged. Each one-dimensional convolutional layer's output size was set to 256, 128, and 64, respectively. The dropout rate was set to 0.3. The number of generated lighting environments N was set to 5000. The training was conducted for 100 epochs, with early stopping applied when the validation loss reached 1.1 times the minimum loss. The optimizer used for training the feature extraction module was Adam [5], and the loss function was Triplet loss [3]. The Adam optimizer was configured with a learning rate of $0.001, \beta_1 = 0.9$, and $\beta_2 = 0.999$. The Triplet loss function encourages the feature extractor to minimize the distance between an anchor and a positive sample while maximizing the distance between the anchor and a negative sample. The margin parameter for the Triplet loss was set to 0.5. The sampling ratio α was set to 0.4.

3.3 Results

Lighting Environment Discrimination. To evaluate the performance of the proposed method, we compared its EER and HTER with those of the baseline methods. Table 1 shows the EER and HTER of the proposed method and the baseline methods. The proposed method achieves the lowest EER on the test data and the lowest HTER at the threshold obtained from the training data. However, for certain distance metrics (e.g., Z-score and Euclidean), the HTER, which indicates generalization performance, increases compared to HS. This increase is likely due to a significant difference between the spectral distribution of the lighting environment used for training and the actual test data.

Visualization. To verify the effectiveness of the feature extraction module, we visualized the feature space using T-distributed Stochastic Neighbor Embedding (t-SNE).[7]. Figure 2 shows the t-SNE visualization of the feature space before and after feature extraction for the same individual. The RGB data shows significant overlap among features from multiple lighting environments. In contrast, the HS images and the features extracted from HS images exhibit sufficient separation for discrimination. Although the dataset created in this work shows that HS images alone provide adequate feature separation, the proposed method, which is trainable, is expected to discriminate even similar lighting conditions effectively.

Table 1. Comparison of EER and HTER for the proposed method and baseline methods.

Method	Distance Method	EER ↓	HTER ↓
Spectra	Z-score	0.160	0.133
	Euclidean	0.140	0.336
	Mahalanobis	0.101	0.131
PCA-3D	Z-score	0.177	0.149
	Euclidean	0.261	0.277
	Mahalanobis	0.198	0.298
Autoencoder	Z-score	0.401	0.347
	Euclidean	0.303	0.339
	Mahalanobis	0.135	0.157
Ours	Z-score	0.165	0.500
	Euclidean	**0.007**	0.440
	Mahalanobis	0.057	**0.114**

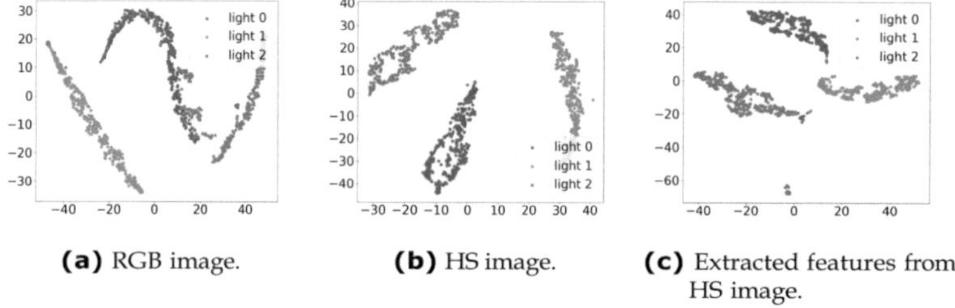

(a) RGB image. **(b)** HS image. **(c)** Extracted features from HS image.

Fig. 2. T-SNE visualization of the feature space.

4 Conclusion

This work contributes to the field by proposing a task setting aimed at detecting unauthorized access while taking into account variations in illumination environments. Additionally, it investigates and validates a training method for classifiers that utilizes data generated from a limited number of illumination conditions, ensuring robust performance under diverse lighting scenarios.

In this paper, we proposed a method for discriminating lighting conditions using features extracted from HS images. The feature extractor was trained using a dataset generated from a few lighting environments. The proposed method achieved a lower EER than the baseline methods, indicating effective discrimination of lighting conditions. The HTER was also lower, demonstrating the generalization performance of the proposed method. In future work, we plan to investigate the generalization performance of the proposed method by increasing the number of lighting environments used for training.

Acknowledgement. This research was supported by a research grant from the KDDI Foundation. We would like to express our sincere gratitude to the faculty and students of the Pattern and Media Informatics Laboratory and the Visual Perception & Recognition Laboratory in Tokyo Denki University for their invaluable support in data collection. Special thanks are also extended to all those who contributed to the data set photography.

References

1. BYKInstruments: byko-spectra standard. https://www.byk-instruments.com/en/Color-Control/byko-spectra-LightBooth/Cost-effective-light-booths-with-5-Illuminants/c/p-442?variant=6046
2. Eba Japan Co.Ltd.:Hyper spectral camera NH9. https://ebajapan.jp/products/hyper-spectral-camera/
3. Hoffer, E., Ailon, N.: Deep metric learning using triplet network. In: Feragen, A., Pelillo, M., Loog, M. (eds.) Similarity-Based Pattern Recognition, pp. 84–92. Springer International Publishing, Cham (2015). https://doi.org/10.1007/978-3-319-24261-3_7
4. Hu, W., Huang, Y., Wei, L., Zhang, F., Li, H.: Deep convolutional neural networks for hyperspectral image classification. J. Sensors **2015**(1), 258619 (2015)
5. Kingma, D.P.: Adam: A method for stochastic optimization. arXiv preprint arXiv:1412.6980 (2014)
6. Kobi, S.H., David, M., August, I., Bykhovsky, D.: Hyperspectral image prediction using a linear model in different illumination conditions. In: 2023 13th Workshop on Hyperspectral Imaging and Signal Processing: Evolution in Remote Sensing (WHISPERS), pp. 1–4 (2023). https://doi.org/10.1109/WHISPERS61460.2023.10430661
7. van der Maaten, L., Hinton, G.: Visualizing data using t-sne. J. Mach. Learn. Res. **9**(86), 2579–2605 (2008), http://jmlr.org/papers/v9/vandermaaten08a.html
8. Maćkiewicz, A., Ratajczak, W.: Principal components analysis (pca). Comput. Geosci. **19**(3), 303–342 (1993). https://doi.org/10.1016/0098-3004(93)90090-R, https://www.sciencedirect.com/science/article/pii/009830049390090R
9. NumPy Developers: numpy.random.choice. https://numpy.org/doc/2.1/reference/random/generated/numpy.random.choice.html
10. Tornyeviadzi, H.M., Seidu, R.: Leakage detection in water distribution networks via 1d cnn deep autoencoder for multivariate scada data. Eng. Appli. Artifi. Intell. **122**, 106062 (2023). https://doi.org/10.1016/j.engappai.2023.106062, https://www.sciencedirect.com/science/article/pii/S0952197623002464

Reflectance and Illumination Estimation from a Known Reflectance for Classification

Yuma Mabuchi(✉), Takuma Kaneko, and Yuko Ozasa

Tokyo Denki University, 5, Senju Asahi-Cho, Adachi-Ku, Tokyo 120-8551, Japan
{24amj34,24amj09}@ms.dendai.ac.jp, ozasa@mail.dendai.ac.jp

Abstract. Robust inference against fluctuations in illumination conditions remains a significant challenge in image sensing. Existing works aim to achieve illumination-invariant features by estimating optical properties such as reflectance. However, accurate estimation using RGB images, where the spectral distribution is encoded into three dimensions, is inherently difficult.

To address this limitation, approaches leveraging hyperspectral (HS) images, which provide richer wavelength information than RGB images, have been developed for reflectance estimation. Nonetheless, these methods often require the presence of a gray card with known diffuse reflectance within the image. Furthermore, the absence of publicly avail- able datasets combining reflectance values with real RGB or HS images constrains advancements in this field.

To overcome these challenges, we propose an intensity-based illumination and reflectance estimation grounded in the Retinex theory. This approach eliminates dependency on gray cards by being guided by objects with known reflectance within the image, enabling illumination- invariant inference across diverse datasets. Additionally, we construct an HS-reflectance dataset and validate its utility.

Through experiments, we evaluate our method and analyze its impact on classification using estimated reflectances. The results demonstrate the efficacy of the HS-reflectance dataset, our method, and its potential to enhance illumination robustness in visual systems.

Keyword: reflectance Estimation · lighting estimation · hyperspectral imaging

1 Introduction

Variations in the spectral distribution of illumination under different imaging conditions are a major challenge of image sensing. It is well-known that changes in spectral distribution—caused by lighting conditions such as temporal factors like daylight or nighttime, and differences in artificial lighting—can lead to do- main shifts, which degrade the performance of computer vision tasks. Sensor outputs are primarily determined by the reflectance of objects and the spectral distribution of illumination, thereby fluctuations in the latter introduce significant perturbations to the observed values.

Existing works [2, 5, 11–13] aim to achieve illumination-invariant features by estimating optical properties such as specular reflection, diffuse reflection, and scattering.

B. Kim (Ed.): IW-FCV 2025, CCIS 2769, pp. 156–168, 2026.
https://doi.org/10.1007/978-981-95-4578-0_13

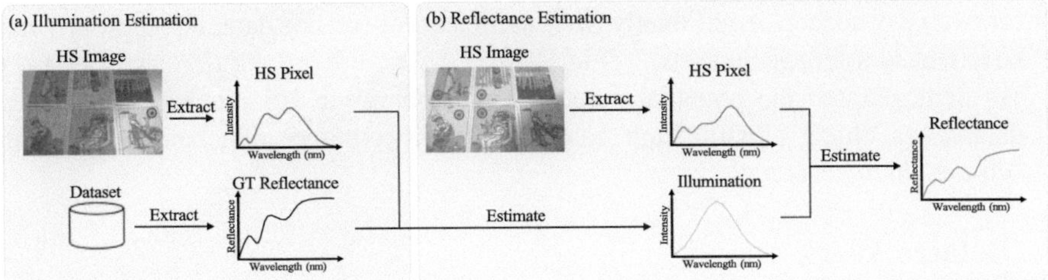

Fig. 1. Overview of the Our Method. Our intensity-based method estimates the spectral distribution of illumination and reflectance. (a) Illumination estimation is performed from an object with known reflectance using an HS pixel and GT reflectance to predict the spectral intensity of the illumination. (b) Reflectance estimation for an unknown object is performed using the predicted illumination and an HS image pixel to estimate the object's reflectance.

A prominent theoretical foundation for this approach is the Retinex theory [8], which models human vision and expresses intensity as the product of an object's reflectance and the spectral distribution of illumination.

There are two primary challenges associated with these optics-based approaches. The first challenge is estimating reflectance and spectral distribution from RGB images, where intensity is encoded into only three bands. To address this, Falcioni et al. [5] proposed an illumination-robust classification method that leverages intensity from hyperspectral (HS) images, which capture tens to hundreds of spectral bands, along with a gray card with known diffuse reflectance properties. However, the necessity of including a gray card in the image imposes strict constraints, limiting its applicability in general settings.

The second challenge is the scarcity of reflectance datasets. Publicly available datasets that include both real-world images and their corresponding ground- truth (GT) reflectance values are scarce. Similarly, no datasets currently exist that link the intensity of HS images to GT reflectance values. The development of this field critically depends on the availability of reflectance datasets.

In this paper, we construct a small-scale dataset comprising object reflectances and HS images of scene intensity, and propose a simple intensity-based reflectance estimation approach grounded in Retinex theory (Fig. 1). Although the optical decomposition method differs, our approach can be seen as a substitute for the role of a gray card in Falcioni et al.'s method [5] with objects of known reflectance to estimate the reflectance of unknown objects. This substitution facilitates illumination-invariant inference, making our method applicable to diverse image datasets.

In the experiments, we perform illumination and reflectance estimation and analyze the results. Using the estimated reflectance, we validate its effectiveness for classification tasks through a simple matching approach. Furthermore, these results demonstrate the validity and utility of the hyperspectral intensity- reflectance dataset.

Our contributions are as follows:

- We propose a reflectance and illumination estimation method that references objects within the image instead of relying on a gray card. For applications, by placing known objects within a scene, this method enables illumination and reflectance estimation

for everyday scenes. Additionally, with sufficient reflectance data, the approach can be extended to image datasets.
- We demonstrated the potential value of constructing an HS intensity reflectance dataset, as object classification based on intensity-based reflectance estimation achieved high accuracy.

2 Related Work

2.1 Illumination Robustness in Machine Learning

In machine learning, a significant challenge is the performance degradation observed when applying models trained on source datasets to target datasets captured under different illumination conditions. One solution to this issue involves leveraging large-scale datasets to achieve generalizable inference.

Recently developed large-scale vision-language models (VLMs) demonstrate remarkable generalization capabilities due to their large pre-trained data. How- ever, they have yet to achieve illumination-robust inference. Moreover, collecting data that encompasses all possible illumination conditions is infeasible, making data collection alone insufficient to address this problem.

Conventional approaches often involve input modifications such as preprocessing [1, 6, 9, 14] and image enhancement [10] or training strategies like domain adaptation [17] and customized loss functions [16]. Nonetheless, handcrafted feature designs inherently lack generalizability, and domain adaptation or image enhancement methods struggle to replicate and learn from all possible illumination environments.

2.2 Reflectance Estimation

Another promising approach for achieving illumination-robust inference is estimating the optical properties of objects. Existing studies have explored techniques to estimate reflectance maps [2, 5, 12] or decompose optical properties into detailed components such as reflection and scattering [11, 13].

While some of these studies construct synthetic or small-scale reflectance datasets, the unavailability of such datasets to the broader community has hundered progress in this research area.

2.3 Reflectance Estimation from Hyperspectral Intensity

Most existing works aiming to achieve illumination robustness in machine learning have focused on constructing datasets using RGB images as inputs. However, accurately estimating reflectance from RGB images, which encode spectral distributions into just three dimensions, remains a challenging task. To address this limitation, Falcioni, et al. [5] have employed hyperspectral (HS) cameras capable of capturing significantly more wavelength information than RGB cameras. Their approach involves estimating reflectance using HS images by leveraging gray card with known diffuse reflectance properties.

By linking HS intensity values to reflectance, this method highlights the relationship between intensity and reflectance more effectively than RGB-based approaches. However, a significant barrier to progress in this field is the lack of publicly available intensity-reflectance datasets, as well as the limited volume of research focusing on this area.

3 Proposed Method

Reflectance and Illumination Estimation from an Known Reflectance We estimate the spectral distribution of illumination and the reflectance of un-known objects based on Retinex theory, using objects with known reflectance in the image as references. Retinex theory, which models human perception, represents the intensity I: $[0, 1] \in R^{C\times H\times W}$ of the image, where C, H and$W$ represent the band, height and width of the image, as a product of reflectance R: $[0, 1] \in R^{C\times H\times W}$ and the spectral distribution of illumination L: $[0, 1] \in R^{C\times H\times W}$, expressed by the following equation:

$$I = R \times L \tag{1}$$

3.1 Illumination Estimation from an Known Reflectance

We estimate the spectral distribution of illumination L: $[0, 1] \in R^{C\times 1}$ from intensity I_k: $[0, 1] \in R^{C\times Pk}$ of known objects in the image, where P_k represent the pixel of known objects, and reflectance R_k: $[0, 1] \in R^{C\times Pk}$. This calculation is expressed by the following equation:

$$L = \frac{1_k}{R_k} \tag{2}$$

3.2 Reflectance Estimation for Object with Unknown Reflectance

Assuming a uniform spectral distribution of illumination across the image to simplify the problem, we estimate the reflectance of unknown objects R_{uk}: $[0, 1] \in R^{C\times Puk}$, where P_{uk} represent the pixel of unknown objects, using their intensity I_{uk}: $[0, 1] \in R^{C\times Puk}$ and the spectral distribution of illumination L with the following equation:

$$R_{\mathrm{uk}} = \frac{I_{\mathrm{uk}}}{L} = \frac{I_{\mathrm{uk}}}{I_{\mathrm{k}}} R_{\mathrm{k}} \tag{3}$$

4 Experiment

We constructed a small-scale intensity-reflectance dataset and proposed a simple intensity-based reflectance estimation method using known object reflectance. Using the proposed method, we validated the effectiveness of the dataset by an- alyzing errors in illumination and reflectance estimation. Furthermore, we validated the impact of estimation errors on classification performance by analyzing the matching between the estimated and GT reflectance.

Table 1. Imaging setting

	Spectrophotometer [7]	Hyperspectral Camera [4]
Targets	The spectral radiance S	The spectral intensity I
Targets Object	Six tarot cards, Standard reflectance board	Six tarot cards
Illumination Types	UV + Incandescent A	Fluorescent CWF, UV + Incandescent A, Daylight D65
Spectral Range	350 – 1000 nm	350 – 1100 nm
Optical Bandwidth	4.5 nm	5 nm
Resolution	1×1	2048×1080

4.1 Reflectance Dataset

We measured the spectral radiance S: $[0, 1] \in \mathrm{R}^{131\times1\times1}$ of the target scene using a spectroradiometer [7]. We used the accompanying software to interpolate the data at 1nm intervals and further processed the measurements into 5nm intervals.

Additionally, we measured the spectral intensity of the target scenes I: $[0, 1] \in \mathrm{R}^{151\times1080\times2048}$ using a hyperspectral camera [4]. We show imaging conditions are summarized in Table 1.

The target objects in our dataset are tarot cards. We selected these for two reasons that facilitate dataset validation: First, their flat shape simplifies the modeling of optical properties; Second, the consistent material across the cards results in similar reflectance distributions, making it more strictly to assess the impact of errors in the estimated reflectance.

We show six tarot cards in Fig. 2 labeled as "Gray", "Black", "Blue IX", "Blue KC", "Blue QC", and "Yellow". For each card, We measured relative reflectance data using a spectrophotometer, with reference to a gray card [3] featuring a diffuse reflectance of 18%.

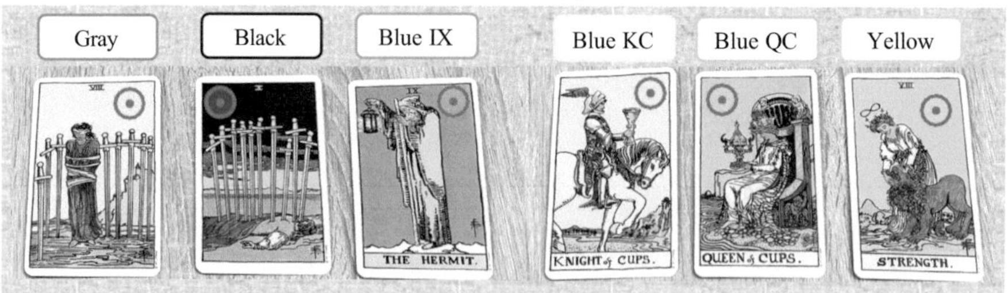

Fig. 2. The six types of tarot cards used in the dataset. Our measurement target is the background of the tarot, the center point of the red circle.

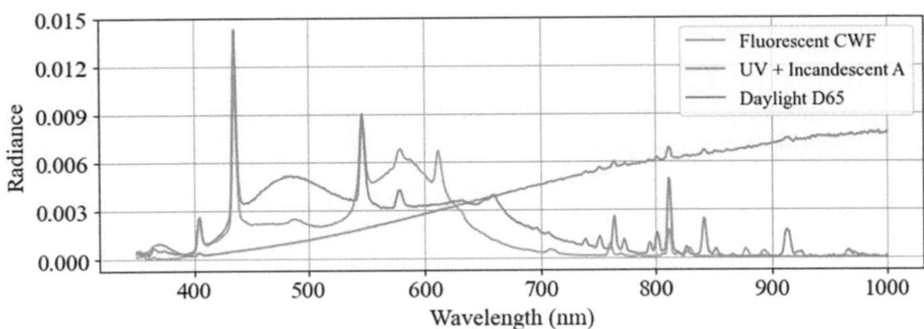

Fig. 3. The spectral radiance of illuminations. Using a spectrophotometer, we measured the relative reflectance with respect to a gray card with a known diffuse reflectance.

We utilized three types of illumination: "Fluorescent CWF" (CWF), "UV + Incandescent A" (UV + A), and "Daylight D65" (D65) provided by a light booth (byko-spectra lite) [15]. The spectral distributions of each illumination type, measured using the gray card, are shown in Fig. 3.

Measurement Environment. To minimize specular reflections, we set the illumination directly above the target objects, and the sensor at a 45-degree angle. The imaging setup is illustrated in Fig. 4.

Measurement of Reflectance (GT). We measure the spectral radiance S_{tarot}: [0, 1] $\in R^{131\times1\times1}$ of the tarot card and, S_{white}: [0, 1] $\in R^{131\times1\times1}$ of the gray card, using a spectrophotometer. The spectral reflectance R_{k}: [0, 1] $\in R^{131\times1\times1}$ of each tarot card is derived from the S_{tarot} and S_{white} as expressed in Eq. 4:

$$R_k = \frac{S_{tarot}}{S_{white}} \tag{4}$$

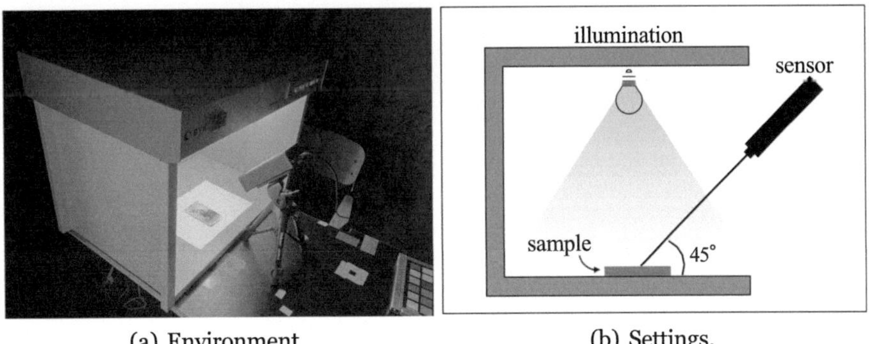

(a) Environment. (b) Settings.

Fig. 4. Details of imaging.

The radiance measured by the spectrophotometer and the computed reflectance values are shown in Fig. 5.

4.2 Estimation of Illumination and Reflectance

Using the proposed reflectance estimation method, we estimated the illumination and reflectance of unknown objects based on objects with known reflectance. The estimation follows these steps:

1. Select one tarot card as an object with known reflectance and retrieve its reflectance R_{k} from the dataset.
2. Estimate the spectral distribution of illumination L using the known object's reflectance R_{k} and intensity I_{k} (Eq. 2).
3. Estimate the reflectance R_{uk} of unknown objects using their intensity I_{uk} and the illumination L (Eq. 3).

The estimated reflectance values are shown in Fig. 5.

4.3 Classification

To evaluate the error in the estimated reflectance, we classified five tarot cards using one tarot card as the object with known reflectance.

The classification was performed by assigning each tarot card to the class with the minimum Mean Absolute Error (MAE), Spectral Angle Mapper (SAM) and Pearson Distance (PD) between the estimated and GT reflectance.

The MAE was calculated using the following equation:

$$\mathrm{MAE} = \frac{1}{n}\sum\nolimits_{i=1}^{n}\left|\widehat{R_{\mathrm{i}}} - R_{\mathrm{i}}\right|, \tag{5}$$

where n is the number of spectral bands, $\hat{R}\mathrm{i}$ is the estimated reflectance, and R_{i} is the GT reflectance.

The SAM was calculated using the following equation:

$$\mathrm{SAM} = \arccos\left(\frac{\sum\nolimits_{i=1}^{n}\widehat{R_{\mathrm{i}}}R_{\mathrm{i}}}{\sqrt{\sum\nolimits_{i=1}^{n}\widehat{R_{\mathrm{i}}^{2}}}\sqrt{\sum\nolimits_{i=1}^{n}R_{\mathrm{i}}^{2}}}\right). \tag{6}$$

The PD was calculated using the following equation:

$$\mathrm{PD} = 1 - \frac{\sum\nolimits_{i=1}^{n}\left(\widehat{R_{\mathrm{i}}} - \overline{\widehat{R}}\right)\left(R_{\mathrm{i}} - \overline{R}\right)}{\sqrt{\sum\nolimits_{i=1}^{n}\left(\widehat{R_{\mathrm{i}}} - \overline{\widehat{R}}\right)^{2}}\sqrt{\sum\nolimits_{i=1}^{n}\left(R_{\mathrm{i}} - \overline{R}\right)^{2}}}, \tag{7}$$

where $\overline{\widehat{R}}$ and $\overline{R}$ are the mean values of the estimated and GT reflectance.

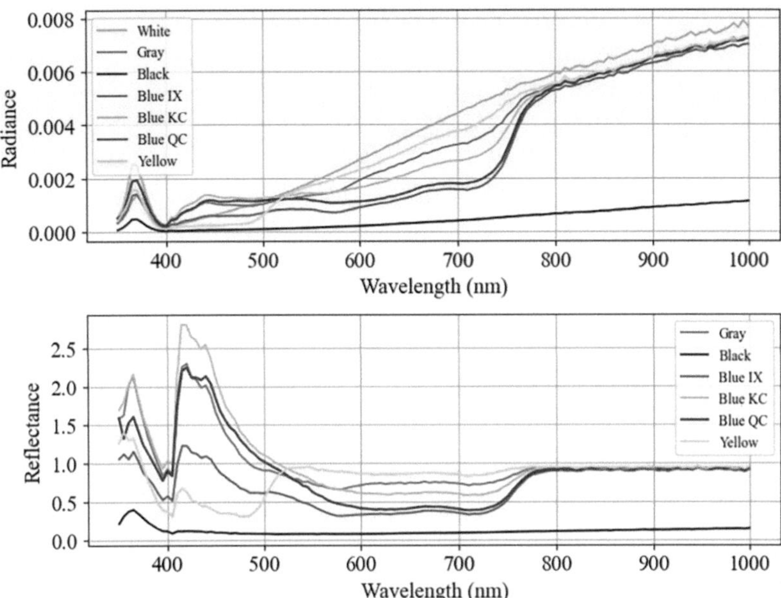

Fig. 5. Radiance (upper) and reflectance (lower) of standard reflectance board and tarot cards.

5 Result

5.1 Reflectance and Illumination Estimation

We evaluate the effectiveness of our method by the errors of illumination and reflectance estimations. We summarize the reflectance estimation errors in Table3, and the illumination estimation errors in Table 2. The rows correspond to the objects designated as reflectance-known, and the results are shown for inference across six tarot cards. Furthermore, we show the reflectance estimation results in Fig. 6 under conditions using UV + A illumination and the known reflectance object Blue_QC.

Illumination Estimation. The illumination estimation accuracy for UV + A, which covers the broadest wavelength range, is the lowest. However, as shown in Fig. 6, a qualitative evaluation reveals that, while CWF and D65 exhibit wave- length peaks that deviate significantly from the GT, UV + A shows relatively lower errors. This discrepancy is attributed to the reduced sensitivity of the HS camera beyond 800 nm. In the long wavelength range, the intensity of CWF and D65 approaches nearly zero, whereas UV + A exhibits increasing. Consequently, measurement errors have a greater impact on UV + A due to the amplified sensitivity to noise in these regions.

Reflectance Estimation. The accuracy of reflectance estimation surpasses that of illumination estimation. Additionally, since reflectance is calculated by dividing the intensity values, the influence of the camera's sensitivity can be effectively mitigated. Thereby, the UV + A illumination outperforms both qualitatively and quantitatively. Also, as shown in the GT spectral distributions of CWF and D65 (Fig. 3), the radiance significantly decreases beyond 400 nm and after 800 nm.

Table 2. Error of Illumination Estimation.

Known object	CWF	MAE ↓ UV + A	D65	CWF	PD ↓ UV + A	D65	CWF	SAM ↓ UV + A	D65
Black	0.001	0.001	0.003	0.327	0.444	0.016	0.642	0.636	0.103
Blue_IX	0.001	0.001	0.001	0.167	0.327	0.003	0.464	0.556	0.050
Blue_KC	0.001	0.001	0.000	0.219	0.510	0.002	0.530	0.680	0.041
Blue_QC	0.001	0.001	0.001	0.212	0.487	0.004	0.522	0.664	0.056
Gray	0.001	0.001	0.001	0.200	0.442	0.002	0.508	0.638	0.049
Yellow	0.001	0.001	0.000	0.168	0.283	0.003	0.467	0.522	0.042
Mean	**0.001**	**0.001**	**0.001**	0.216	0.415	**0.005**	0.522	0.616	**0.057**

Table 3. Error of Reflectance Estimation.

Known object	CWF	MAE ↓ UV + A	D65	CWF	PD ↓ UV + A	D65	CWF	SAM ↓ UV + A	D65
Black	0.328	0.336	0.360	0.672	0.267	0.516	0.512	0.263	0.384
Blue IX	0.256	0.098	0.189	0.458	0.098	0.291	0.489	0.178	0.331
Blue KC	0.246	0.119	0.172	0.389	0.093	0.260	0.492	0.176	0.338
Blue QC	0.217	0.092	0.153	0.402	0.103	0.261	0.475	0.169	0.318
Gray	0.238	0.094	0.155	0.387	0.106	0.245	0.507	0.192	0.329
Yellow	0.434	0.153	0.386	0.530	0.122	0.461	0.571	0.208	0.473
Mean	0.287	**0.149**	0.236	0.473	**0.131**	0.339	0.508	**0.198**	0.362

Table 4. Classification result (Accuracy ↑).

Known object	CWF	MAE UV+A	D65	CWF	PD UV+A	D65	CWF	SAM UV+A	D65	Mean
Black	0.167	0.167	0.167	0.667	0.500	0.500	0.667	0.500	0.500	0.426
Blue_IX	0.833	1.000	0.833	0.500	1.000	0.500	0.500	1.000	0.500	0.741
Blue_KC	0.833	1.000	0.833	0.667	1.000	0.833	0.833	1.000	0.833	**0.870**
Blue_QC	0.833	1.000	0.833	0.667	0.833	0.667	0.833	1.000	0.833	0.833
Gray	1.000	1.000	1.000	0.667	0.667	0.833	0.833	1.000	0.833	**0.870**
Yellow	0.833	0.833	0.833	0.500	0.833	0.500	0.500	0.667	0.500	0.667
Mean	0.750	**0.833**	0.750	0.611	**0.806**	0.639	0.694	**0.861**	0.667	0.735

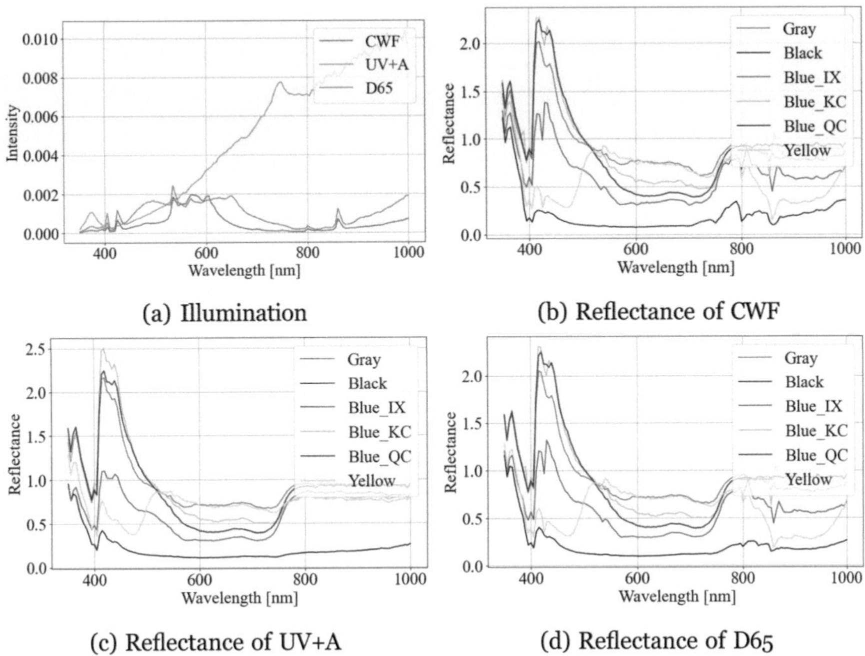

(a) Illumination

(b) Reflectance of CWF

(c) Reflectance of UV+A

(d) Reflectance of D65

Fig. 6. Estimation result of target is Blue_KC Moreover, CWF and D65 fail to cover critical regions around 350 nm and 420 nm, where GT reflectance (Fig. 5) exhibits notable differences.

5.2 Classification

We evaluate the impact of the errors in reflectance and illumination estimation, as presented in Sec.5.2, through a classification task. We present the classification results in Table 4. Using Blue or Gray as an object of known reflectance achieved consistently high accuracy, particularly under UV + A illumination, where the accuracy approached 1.0 in most cases.

Although the classification task involved a limited number of targets under a single ambient lighting condition, the method achieved satisfactory performance despite its simplified illumination estimation. This result shows the effectiveness of our estimation method based on known reflectance objects using the HS intensity-reflectance dataset for classification.

Objects with Known Reflectance. Selecting black as the object with known reflectance resulted in suboptimal performance. This is due to its overall low reflectance, which led to weak intensity signals and greater susceptibility to noise. Objects that reflect a broader range of wavelengths are more suitable as reference objects.

Evaluation Metrics. The evaluation primarily relies on MAE, which performs well in this context. Since the tarot cards are the same material, their spectral shapes exhibit similarities, and only the colors introduce variations in the reflectance distributions. For CWF and D65, which include minimal non-visible wavelengths, the localized changes in reflectance are more pronounced, making MAE particularly effective. However, for

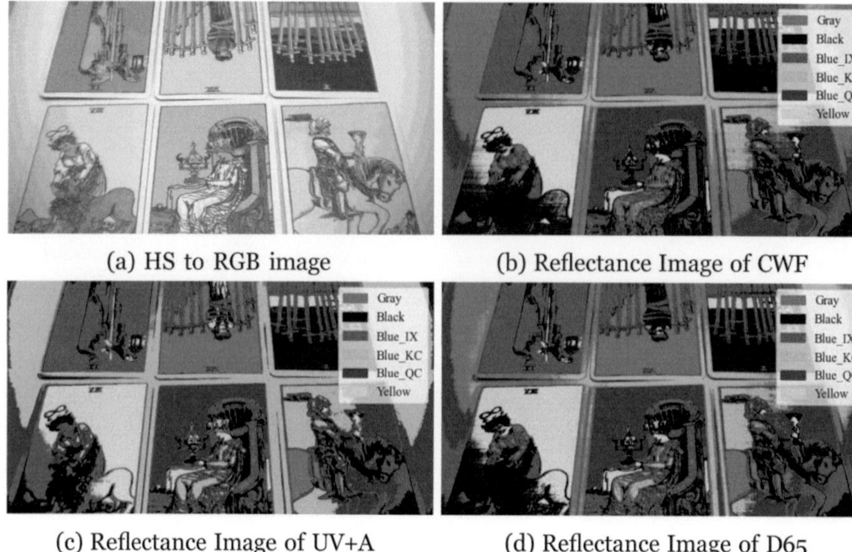

(a) HS to RGB image (b) Reflectance Image of CWF

(c) Reflectance Image of UV+A (d) Reflectance Image of D65

Fig. 7. Estimation result of target is Blue_QC

UV + A, which covers non-visible wave- lengths and results in fewer overall reflectance errors, SAM becomes the most accurate metric as it focuses on the spectral shape.

5.3 Classification for Overall Pixel

We show the classification results for the entire HS image, including nonbackground pixels, in Fig. 7. In this experiment, similar to the above classification, we classified the six background regions of the tarot cards. Consequently, areas out- side the cards were not accurately evaluated for classification. The background regions of the tarot cards were classified with high accuracy, demonstrating that the reflectance could be effectively estimated even for pixels beyond those used for GT measurements.

We observe significant misclassifications outside the camera's field of view. Notably, the outer edge of the "Yellow" region in the lower-left corner was classified as "Blue_IX". This discrepancy arises from differences between the GT measurements, where the sensor captured the target directly at a 45-degree angle from the center, and the HS imaging conditions, including variations in the angles of the camera, target, and illumination, as well as a reduction in peripheral light intensity. These differences caused spectral changes, resulting in classification errors.

6 Conclusion

We have constructed a hyperspectral intensity-reflectance dataset and proposed a method for estimating spectral illumination and reflectance to address the challenge of illumination perturbations in image classification tasks. Our method replaces the role of a gray card in illumination estimation with objects of known reflectance within the scene, aiming to extend its applicability to everyday scenes and datasets without gray card images.

Through experiments involving classification using the estimated illumination and reflectance, we demonstrated the effectiveness of the proposed method and the hyperspectral intensity-reflectance dataset. Future work will focus on expanding the dataset scale and developing advanced estimation methods that account for conditions such as spatial variations in spectral distribution and reflectance.

Acknowledgments. This work was supported by JSPS KAKENHI Grant Number 22K12081.

References

1. Akazawa, T., Kinoshita, Y., Kiya, H.: Template matching with white balance adjustment under multiple illuminants. In: 2022 IEEE 11th Global Conference on Consumer Electronics (GCCE), pp. 372–376
2. Amziane, A., Losson, O., Mathon, B., Dumenil, A., Macaire, L.: Reflectance estimation from multispectral linescan acquisitions under varying illumination— application to outdoor weed identification. Sensors **21**(11), 3601
3. CHUO PRECISION INDUSTRIAL Co.: Nd-filter gk-2. https://www.chuo.co.jp/contents/hp0103/list.php?CNo=103&ProCon=7613 (2024), Accessed 12-December-2024
4. EBA Japan Co.: Hyperspectral camera nh-9 (2023). https://ebajapan.jp/products/hyper-spectral-camera/ Accessed 12-December-2024
5. Falcioni, R., Antunes, W.C., Demattê, J.A.M., Nanni, M.R.: Reflectance spectroscopy for the classification and prediction of pigments in agronomic crops. Plants **12**(12), 2347
6. Jenicek, T., Chum, O.: No fear of the dark: image retrieval under varying illumination conditions. In: 2019 IEEE/CVF International Conference on Computer Vision (ICCV), pp. 9695–9703
7. JETI Technische Instrumente GmbH: specbos 1211–2 broadband spectroradiometer. https://www.jeti.com/Products/Spectroradiometer/specbos1211-2 (2024), Accessed 12-December-2024
8. Land, E.H., McCann, J.J.: Lightness and retinex theory. Josa **61**(1), 1–11 (1971)
9. Lu, Y., Tanaka, M., Kawakami, R., Okutomi, M.: Local brightness normalization for image classification and object detection robust to illumination changes. In: Yan, W.Q., Nguyen, M., Nand, P., Li, X. (eds.) Image and Video Technology, pp. 56–68. Springer Nature Singapore, Singapore (2024). https://doi.org/10.1007/978-981-97-0376-0_5
10. Ma, L., Jin, D., An, N., Liu, J., Fan, X., Luo, Z., Liu, R.: Bilevel fast scene adaptation for low-light image enhancement. Inter. J. Comput. Vis. (Oct 2023)
11. Maeda, R., Hiura, S.: Polarimetric light transport analysis for specular inter-reflection. IEEE Trans. Comput. Imaging **10**, 876–887
12. Rematas, K., Ritschel, T., Fritz, M., Gavves, E., Tuytelaars, T.: Deep reflectance maps. In: 2016 IEEE/CVF Conference on Computer Vision and Pattern Recognition (CVPR), pp. 4508–4516
13. Takatani, T., Mukaigawa, Y., Matsushita, Y., Yagi, Y.: Decomposition of reflection and scattering by multiple-weighted measurements. IPSJ Trans. Comput. Vis. Appli. **10**(1), 13
14. Tan, X., Triggs, B.: Enhanced local texture feature sets for face recognition under difficult lighting conditions. IEEE Trans. Image Process. **19**(6), 1635–1650
15. TETSUTANI Co.: Byko-spectra. https://www.tetsutani.co.jp/sokutei/pte/bykospectra.html (2024), Accessed 12-December-2024

16. Windrim, L., Melkumyan, A., Murphy, R., Chlingaryan, A., Nieto, J.: Unsupervised feature learning for illumination robustness. In: 2016 IEEE International Conference on Image Processing (ICIP), pp. 4453–4457 (2016)
17. Ye, J., Fu, C., Zheng, G., Paudel, D.P., Chen, G.: Unsupervised domain adaptation for nighttime aerial tracking. In: 2022 IEEE/CVF Conference on Computer Vision and Pattern Recognition (CVPR), pp. 8896–8905 (2022)

Detection of Red Tide Plankton in Automatic Microscope System Imaging Using Deep Learning

Tomoka Kawano(✉), Masahiro Migita, Tadashi Nakano, Akira Yamaguchi, Koki Yuasa, and Masashi Toda

Kumamoto University, 2-40-1. Kurokami Chuo-Ku, Kumamoto 860-8555, Japan
kawano@st.cs.kumamoto-u.ac.jp

Abstract. The occurrence of red tides causes mass mortality of farmed fish and leads to significant damage to the fishing industry, making early detection crucial. Currently, the detection and counting of phytoplankton, which are responsible for red tides, are mainly conducted through visual inspection using microscopes. However, this process requires time, effort, and knowledge of species identification. Therefore, in this study, we attempted to detect and count red tide plankton from microscope images of phytoplankton using the object detection method DINO.

Keywords: Object Detection · Red Tide · Deep Learning · DINO

1 Introduction

Red tides are phenomena in which the excessive growth of phytoplankton, triggered by an increase in nutrients or rising water temperatures due to global warming, changes the color of seawater. In Japanese coastal waters, harmful plankton frequently cause damage to fisheries, leading to significant losses for the aquaculture industry due to incidents such as fish asphyxiation. For example, harmful red tide plankton, such as those of the genera Chattonella and Karenia, have been responsible for massive fish kills in areas like the Yatsushiro Sea and the western waters of Kyushu. In the past, such incidents have resulted in economic losses exceeding several billion yen. The Yatsushiro Sea, where the data for this study was collected, is a highly enclosed bay characterized by high nutrient levels due to the influence of surrounding rivers. Consequently, red tides are more likely to occur during periods of high water temperatures, such as in summer, and mitigating their impact on fisheries has become a pressing issue.

To reduce the impact of red tides on fisheries, several measures can be implemented. These include the early identification of causative plankton, suspending the feeding of farmed fish in affected areas, and relocating fish pens to avoid the red tides. However, the occurrence of red tides has shown a trend toward increased frequency and chronicity in recent years, raising concerns about even greater future losses to fisheries. Thus, early detection of red tides and timely alerts to aquaculture operators are critical.

B. Kim (Ed.): IW-FCV 2025, CCIS 2769, pp. 169–180, 2026.
https://doi.org/10.1007/978-981-95-4578-0_14

Currently, the detection of red tides is conducted manually by experts. First, seawater samples are collected from various depths. These samples are then transported to a laboratory, where experts manually analyze the plankton using microscopes. During this analysis, the types and abundance of plankton, including harmful red tide plankton, are identified. If the concentration exceeds threshold values, such as 1,000 cells/mL for Karenia and 10–100 cells/mL for Chattonella, a red tide warning is issued, and aquaculture operators are alerted. During summer, when red tides are most frequent, water sampling is conducted every two days in the morning, and the microscopic analysis of samples from multiple survey sites can take an entire day.

Microscopic analysis is time-consuming and poses several challenges. Differences in judgment may arise among experts, and repetitive tasks often lead to fatigue. When red tides occur and the plankton count is exceptionally high, the area of observation under the microscope is sometimes reduced, and the results are extrapolated to estimate cell density. These factors can affect counting accuracy. The manual nature of the process requires specialized knowledge for species identification, and the significant time and labor involved present ongoing challenges. Consequently, there is an urgent need to automate the current microscopy-based analysis.

Automation of processes such as water sampling and image acquisition has been the focus of various studies. For example, the Video Plankton Recorder (VPR) is a device that records underwater images along with environmental data such as water temperature and depth while simultaneously collecting seawater samples [1]. Images captured by the VPR can be processed using software to extract object regions, enabling plankton classification by isolating individual organisms in each frame. Additionally, devices like FlowCam (Flow Cytometer and Microscope), which analyze manually collected water samples, can automatically classify plankton. FlowCam captures particles within a sample and utilizes image analysis software to extract morphological information (e.g., major and minor axis lengths) and numerical data (e.g., color metrics) from a large volume of images, facilitating plankton classification. While such devices have significantly reduced manual labor through automation, they often require different flow cells based on the size of the target species and are costly, limiting their versatility.

In contrast, optical microscope images taken with digital cameras offer a more accessible and affordable alternative. These images are captured with manually adjusted magnification and focus depending on the size of the plankton. In recent years, advances in deep learning have led to improvements in image classification accuracy, spurring research on automating plankton classification. Efforts include the use of convolutional neural networks (CNNs) for plankton classification and the creation of large-scale datasets [2–4]. However, most of these studies focus on recognizing individual phytoplankton from single-specimen images extracted using automated image acquisition devices. This approach primarily identifies the species of a given plankton. In contrast, studies addressing the detection and recognition of plankton from multi-specimen images remain limited.

For multi-specimen phytoplankton detection and recognition, some proposed methods separate detection and recognition as distinct processes. Examples include approaches that use fluorescence imaging [5], complex image acquisition pipelines, or optical microscope images (similar to those used in this study) for automated detection

[6, 7]. Notably, Figueroa et al. applied deep learning techniques, such as Faster R-CNN [8] and RetinaNet [9], to achieve end-to-end detection and recognition. By employing deep learning for both detection and recognition, their work demonstrated improved performance. Deep learning has already been widely applied in various fields, such as medicine, agriculture, and security, and has shown high potential for application in phytoplankton detection. However, its adoption in this domain remains limited.

This study aims to achieve the automated detection of harmful red tide plankton from microscope videos acquired using the seaMS system with samples collected from the Yatsushiro Sea. For object detection, we compare the performance of three methods: Faster R-CNN [8], RetinaNet [9] and DINO (DETR with Improved Denoising Anchor Boxes) [11]. The study evaluates detection accuracy and recognition performance for harmful red tide plankton and examines the feasibility of practical applications by estimating cell density in collaboration with experts. These methods were selected to comprehensively evaluate both one-stage and two-stage detectors as well as image processing approaches utilizing Transformers [12]. Through this comparative analysis, we assess the suitability of these techniques for detecting and recognizing harmful red tide plankton. Ultimately, this study aims to improve the accuracy and efficiency of plankton analysis compared to traditional manual microscopic observation. This is expected to facilitate the prompt issuance of warnings to aquaculture operators, enhancing their ability to respond quickly to potential threats.

2 Methodology

2.1 seaMS Video and Dataset

seaMS is an on-site automated microscope system capable of performing a series of operations, from water sampling to imaging and cleaning, without manual intervention. In traditional microscopic observation, water samples needed to be collected from red tide-affected areas by boat, requiring several hours to a full day before analysis could be performed. In contrast, the seaMS system is installed on-site, allowing seawater to be pumped from predetermined depths and imaged with its built-in microscope. As a result, video footage can be reviewed within just five minutes of sampling, eliminating the need to travel to the sampling site.

The workflow of the seaMS system is shown in Fig. 1. First, a portion of seawater or sample is introduced into the cell chamber, and the water flow is temporarily stopped to capture 30 s of video. Afterward, the sample is flushed through the chamber, and the process is repeated approximately 10 times for each sample. Each video is recorded at 1280×720 pixels, 30 frames per second (fps), and is approximately 30 s long.

The videos are categorized into the following two types:

- **Cultured Strain Videos**: These videos feature harmful red tide plankton species cultivated under controlled laboratory conditions. Each video contains only one plankton species.
- **Field Sample Videos**: These videos capture seawater collected from the Yatsushiro Sea. In addition to the three red tide plankton species mentioned above, they may include other phytoplankton, such as the genus Ceratium, as well as mud and debris.

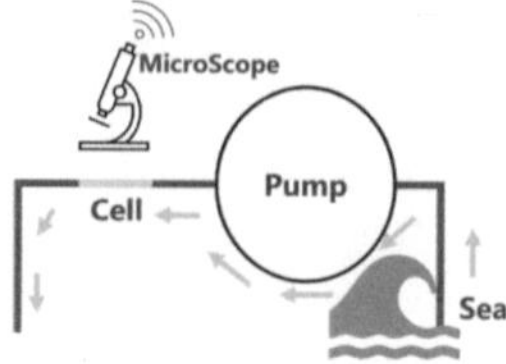

Fig. 1. Explanetion of SeaMS.1. Flow the sample. 2. Stop and capture images for 30 s. 3. Resume flow. Repeat the above steps 10 times.

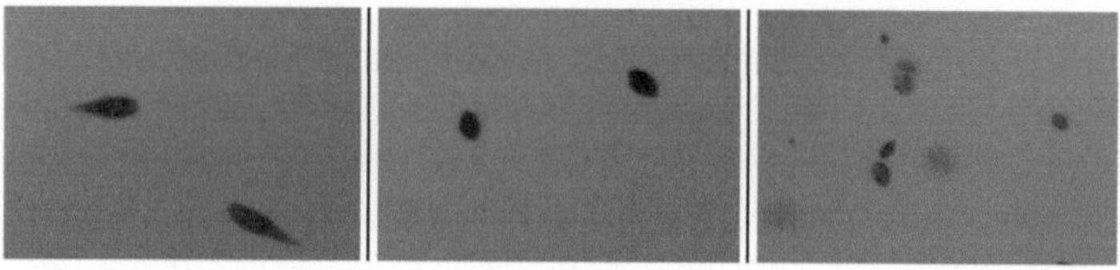

Fig. 2. Red tide plankton. From left to right: Chattonella Antiqua, Chattonella Marina, and Karenia.

From a 50 mL water sample, 49 mL was used for seaMS imaging, while the remaining 1 mL was reserved for microscopic examination.

In this study, we constructed a dataset based on seaMS videos. For the training dataset, cultured strain videos were used, and three species of red tide plankton, shown in Fig. 2, were designated as classes. For each class, one video was selected, and images were extracted every 2 s for annotation using LabelImg.

- **Chattonella antiqua**: A highly toxic species that is extremely harmful to fish. The minimum lethal cell density ranges from 30 to 50 cells/mL. The cell size is approximately 0.05 mm, and the shape is spindle-like with a pointed tail end. It swims slowly while rotating. Although morphologically similar to Chattonella marina, C. antiqua is larger and its shape can easily change due to environmental or external stimuli, making it indistinguishable when miniaturized.
- **Chattonella marina**: A harmful species with strong fish toxicity. The cell size is approximately 0.03 mm, and its shape is slightly flattened, with a tail end that may be either slightly pointed or rounded. It swims slowly while rotating. While morphologically similar to Chattonella antiqua, C. marina is smaller and can be differentiated by its overall roundness.
- **Karenia spp.**: A species harmful to fish and shellfish, known for forming dark brown-red tides that can cause mass mortalities at cell densities of several thousand cells/mL. The cell size is approximately 0.02 mm, with a circular shape when viewed from the front and an elongated oval shape when viewed from the side. It is flattened and moves forward while rotating.

One characteristic of the seaMS videos is that the microscope focus is fixed. As a result, plankton swimming within the chamber often appear out of focus. This poses a challenge, particularly for field sample videos, where misfocused footage makes it difficult for even experts to identify plankton species. Conversely, cultured strain videos contain only one species per video, allowing for all plankton, including out-of-focus specimens, to be annotated.

After annotation, data augmentation was performed by applying horizontal, vertical, and combined flips, resulting in 145 training images and 35 validation images. For testing, three images per class, for a total of nine images, were prepared to compare the performance of three object detection methods.

For cell density estimation, the object detection method with the best performance was employed. Regression analysis was conducted using 269 cultured strain videos, and the results were used to estimate cell density from 220 field sample videos.

2.2 Plankton Detection Using Deep Learning

In this study, we aim to detect harmful red tide plankton by applying various object detection algorithms, including the two-stage detector Faster R-CNN [8], the one-stage detector RetinaNet [9], and Transformer-based relational extraction models such as DINO (DETR with Improved denoising anchor boxes) [11]. Two-stage detectors separate the process into region proposal and object recognition, whereas one-stage detectors skip the region proposal step and perform detection and recognition simultaneously. Other well-known one-stage detectors include YOLO [13], which divides the image into a grid and predicts objects for each grid cell, and SSD (Single-Shot Detector) [14], which reduces the resolution of feature maps for efficient detection. In this study, we focus on Faster R-CNN, RetinaNet DINO due to their ability to share similar backbone architectures, allowing for a comprehensive comparison.

Faster R-CNN

Faster R-CNN is a two-stage detector that builds upon its predecessors, R-CNN [15] and Fast R-CNN [16]. It features a two-step detection process: (1) proposing regions of interest (ROIs) that likely contain objects and (2) refining these regions to predict accurate bounding boxes and object classes.

The network consists of three main components: the backend, the Region Proposal Network (RPN), and the head. The backend, typically a ResNet-based architecture, extracts features from the input image. The RPN generates candidate regions by evaluating anchor boxes at multiple positions in the feature map, calculating the probability of each anchor containing an object. The head processes these candidate regions to predict the class and precise location of the objects.

RetinaNet

RetinaNet is a one-stage detector that integrates region proposal and object recognition into a single process. While one-stage detectors are known for their simplicity and speed, they historically lagged behind two-stage detectors in accuracy due to class imbalance. To address this issue, RetinaNet introduces a novel loss function called Focal Loss, which prioritizes learning from objects rather than backgrounds, thereby improving detection accuracy.

The architecture of RetinaNet consists of a backbone for feature extraction and sub-networks for classification and bounding box regression. It employs a Feature Pyramid Network (FPN) [17] as its backbone. The FPN adds multi-scale skip connections to a

CNN encoder, enabling predictions at different scales. Anchors with an Intersection over Union (IoU) score above 0.5 are designated as positive samples, and their corresponding classes are treated as ground truth. The relative positions of anchors to object regions are used as targets for bounding box regression.

DINO

DINO is an improved method based on DETR [10] and Deformable-DETR [18]. These approaches utilize Transformers, a model architecture that has achieved significant success in natural language processing, and adapt it to object detection. This innovative strategy has garnered considerable attention in recent years. Unlike methods such as Faster R-CNN and RetinaNet, where detection results are inferred independently, DINO employs the attention mechanism of Transformers to capture relationships between objects within an image.

The foundation of DINO, DETR, predicts all objects in an image simultaneously by framing object detection as a bipartite matching problem between predictions and ground truths. This enables end-to-end processing, achieving both high accuracy and fast inference. DETR uses a Convolutional Neural Network (CNN), such as ResNet, to generate feature maps from input images, which are then passed through a Transformer. Positional encodings are supplied to the Transformer's encoder to provide location information, while object queries are used as input for the decoder. The output of the decoder is passed through a Feed Forward Network (FFN) to decode the object coordinates and class labels. By leveraging the Hungarian algorithm, DETR optimally matches predicted class labels and bounding boxes with ground truths, enabling it to learn relationships between features extracted by the encoder and object queries. This makes DETR an anchor-free method for object detection.

Building on DETR, DINO introduces a novel mechanism called Contrastive DeNoising Training. This method uses both positive samples, generated by adding slight noise to the labels, and negative samples, created by adding significant noise. This approach enables the model to learn more discriminative features. Additionally, DINO incorporates a mechanism known as Mixed Query Selection, which separates queries into positional and object-specific components. This mechanism addresses the issue of duplicate detections for a single object by learning positional information more effectively. As a result, DINO directly predicts object locations, differing from traditional CNN-based object detection methods. This architecture, based on Transformers, is particularly effective in scenes with complex backgrounds and objects of varying sizes, making it a promising approach for the automated detection of plankton.

2.3 Estimation of Cell Density

When red tides are detected, it is essential to promptly issue alerts to aquaculture operators. These alerts are based on the cell density of harmful red tide plankton, measured as the number of cells per milliliter of seawater. In Yatsushiro Sea, where data for this study were collected, the alert and warning thresholds for Chattonella red tides are set at 5 cells/mL and 10 cells/mL, respectively. For Karenia red tides, the thresholds are 100 cells/mL for alerts and 1,000 cells/mL for warnings. These cell densities are calculated by experts who count the number of red tide cells in a 1 mL water sample using optical microscopy.

In this study, we evaluated the practicality of automating red tide detection by selecting the best-performing object detection method and comparing its estimates of cell density with those obtained through microscopy.

The method for estimating cell density is as follows. First, the most accurate object detection method is applied to seaMS videos to infer the number of detections for each class in every frame. Next, a simple linear regression analysis is conducted using cultured strain videos. A regression line is derived by correlating the microscopic cell density measurements with the detection results from the object detection model. Separate regression lines are obtained for the genus Chattonella (combining Chattonella antiqua and Chattonella marina) and the genus Karenia. This approach is adopted because the microscopic results for field samples do not distinguish between C. antiqua and C. marina. Using these regression lines, cell density estimation is performed on field videos, and the estimates are compared with the actual microscopy results.

In this study, we attempted to detect red tide plankton using three object detection methods: Faster R-CNN, RetinaNet, and DINO. Both Faster R-CNN and RetinaNet, as well as DINO, were pre-trained on the COCO dataset [19]. For all methods, ResNet50 [20] was selected as the CNN backbone, which was pre-trained on the ImageNet dataset [21]. Training was conducted with an epoch setting of 300.

The evaluation of plankton detection performance was based on Average Precision (AP). The calculation of AP is described as follows: Intersection over Union (IoU), which measures the overlap between two bounding boxes, was used to determine whether a detection matches the ground truth. When the IoU between a detection and ground truth exceeded 0.5, it was classified as a True Positive (TP). Detections that did not meet this threshold were categorized as False Positives (FP), and instances where no detection was associated with the ground truth were considered False Negatives (FN). Using these metrics, Precision and Recall were calculated according to Eqs. (1) and (2). Next, detection results were ranked by their confidence scores, and based on these rankings, a Precision-Recall curve was generated. The area under this curve was calculated to determine AP.

$$Precision = \frac{TP}{TP + FP} \tag{1}$$

$$Recall = \frac{TP}{TP + FN} \tag{2}$$

For evaluating plankton classification performance, a confusion matrix was employed. The confusion matrix was computed for each class, providing a visualization of misclassifications and false detections. This allowed us to assess trends in misclassification. Additionally, for the method with the highest detection accuracy, we performed cell density estimation and compared the results with the actual microscopic observations conducted by experts.

3 Results and Discussion

3.1 Object Detection Results

Table 1 shows the AP results when the IoU threshold is set to 0.5. Testing on cultured plankton captured in controlled indoor experiments resulted in high accuracy exceeding 95% across all methods. Among these, DINO achieved the highest mAP of 98.5%.

Confusion matrices for each method are shown in Fig. 3. Misclassifications between species within the genus Chattonella and the genus Karenia were minimal (approximately 1–3%) for Faster R-CNN and DINO. However, RetinaNet exhibited a slightly higher misclassification rate of 8%, particularly when identifying Chattonella species as Karenia. Additionally, misclassification between C. Antiqua and C. Marina was observed. False negatives (i.e., missed detections of plankton against the background) were minimal for all methods, at around 2–3%. However, false positives, where the background was misclassified as plankton, were observed across all methods. This was attributed to the annotation process, which did not label plankton appearing partially at the edges of the images.

In previous research by Figueroa et al., Faster R-CNN and RetinaNet were used to detect and classify freshwater plankton, with Faster R-CNN yielding higher accuracy. Similarly, in this study, Faster R-CNN slightly outperformed RetinaNet, particularly in distinguishing the two morphologically similar species of Chattonella. The superior performance of DINO can be attributed to its ability to account for the relationships between plankton morphology and surrounding features, resulting in slightly higher accuracy. Given DINO's high AP score among deep learning methods, it was used to conduct cell density estimation experiments in collaboration with experts.

Table 1. AP for each class, and mAP for each method

	Average Predicion(%)		
	Faster R-CNN	RetinaNet	DINO
C. Antiqua	96.0	93.1	98.7
C. Marina	98.0	98.7	99.9
Karenia	96.7	96.1	97.0
Global	96.9	95.9	98.5

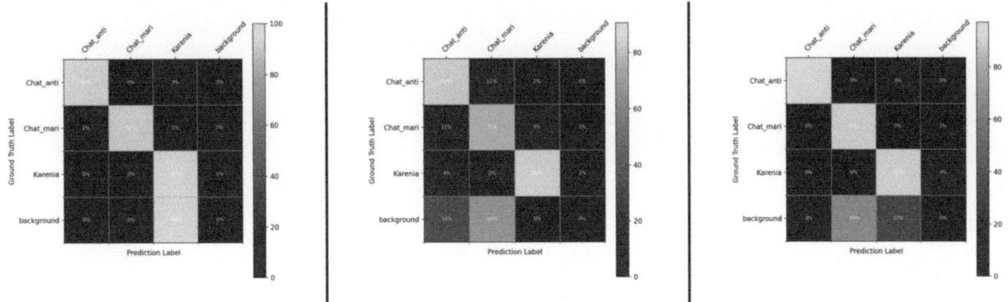

Fig. 3. Confusion matrix results: From left to right, Faster R-CNN, RetinaNet, DINO

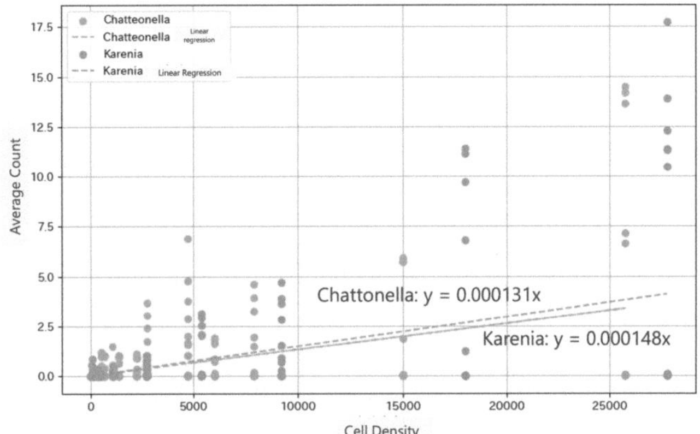

Fig. 4. Cell density vs. average count (average count = total detections per video / 900).

3.2 Cell Dencity Estimation Results

We used DINO for cell density estimation, with the results presented as regression lines in Fig. 4 and estimation outcomes in Fig. 5. Visualizing the average counts per frame for each cell density revealed significant variations in both Chattonella and Karenia, even at the same density. This variability was likely due to differences in plankton occurrence probability within the same sample. Regression lines were derived from the average counts and the expert-determined cell densities, yielding the following equations:

$$\text{Chattonella spp.} : y = 0.000131x$$

$$\text{Karenia spp.} : y = 0.000148x$$

The coefficient of determination (R^2) for Karenia was 0.495, while for Chattonella, it was -39.978. When analyzing only low-density samples, Karenia at ≤ 200 cells/ml showed an R^2 of -176.788, and Chattonella at ≤ 110 cells/ml resulted in an R^2 of -620. These results indicate that overall estimation accuracy was low, with particularly large discrepancies between predicted and actual values at low densities.

Several factors may have contributed to these discrepancies. First, misclassifications and false detections were observed. The seaMS video recordings included various.

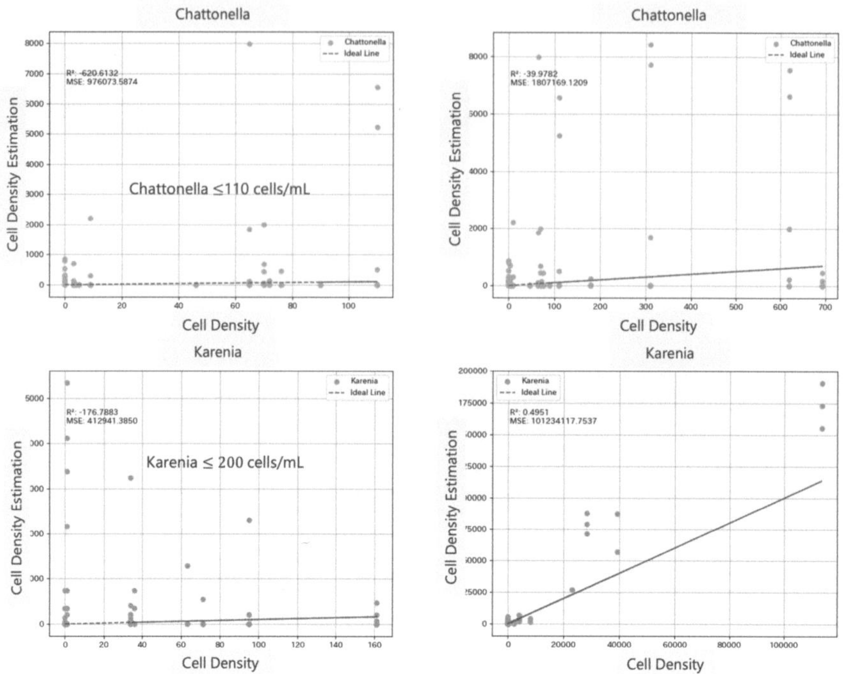

Fig. 5. Cell density estimation results: left shows results for low-density samples, and right shows results for overall cell density estimation.

plankton types and debris, which DINO occasionally misclassified. Second, the temporal representation of plankton in the seaMS videos may have affected accuracy. Each sample was divided into multiple videos, and images were captured using a 10x objective lens, which only covered a portion of the field. At lower densities, the time and likelihood of plankton appearing in the videos decreased, leading to greater divergence from expert microscopy results.

Although regression analysis based on average counts was used for estimation, future improvements will focus on aggregating videos for each sample and employing object tracking techniques to enhance the coefficient of determination.

4 Conclusion

This study evaluated the performance of deep learning-based object detection methods for the automatic detection and classification of red tide plankton, with a particular focus on Chattonella and Karenia genera. Among the tested methods, DINO achieved the highest mAP (98.5%) and demonstrated superior classification accuracy, particularly in distinguishing morphologically similar species. Faster R-CNN also performed well, but RetinaNet exhibited higher misclassification rates between certain species.

Despite DINO's high detection accuracy, challenges arose in cell density estimation, particularly for low-density samples. Regression analysis revealed significant discrepancies between predicted and expert-determined cell densities, attributed to factors such as misclassifications, partial annotations, and variations in plankton appearance probability within video frames. These issues were especially pronounced at lower densities, where the probability of plankton appearing in the field of view decreased, resulting in low coefficients of determination.

The results suggest that while DINO is effective for plankton detection in complex environments, additional improvements are needed for accurate cell density estimation. Potential future directions include the aggregation of videos for consistent sample representation and the integration of object tracking techniques to improve estimation accuracy. These findings provide a foundation for advancing automated plankton monitoring systems, contributing to ecological research and red tide management.

References

1. Davis, C.S., et al.: Rapid visualization of plankton abundance and taxonomic composition using the Video Plankton Recorder. Deep-Sea **43**(7–8) (1996)
2. Lumini, et al.: Deep learning and transfer learning features for plankton classification. Ecological informatics, vol. 51, pp.33–43 (2019)
3. Zheng, et al: Automatic plankton image classification combining multiple view features via multiple kernel learning. BMC Bioinformat. **18**, 1–18 (2017)
4. Zhao, et al.: Binary SIPPER plankton image classification using random subspace. Neurocomputing **73**(10), 1853–1860 (2010)
5. Schulze, K.: PlanktoVision - an automated analysis system for the identification of phytoplankton. BMC Bioinformatics **14**, 115 (2013)
6. Figueroa, J., et al.: Phytoplankton detection and recognition in freshwater digital microscopy images using deep learning object detectors. Heliyon, Vol. 10, Issue 3, 2024
7. Rivas-Villar, D., et al.: Fully automatic detection and classification of phytoplankton specimens in digital microscopy images. Comput. Methods Programs Biomed. **200** (2021)
8. Ren, S., et al.: Faster R-CNN: towards real-time object detection with region proposal networks. IEEE Trans. Pattern Anal. Mach. Intell. **39**(6), 1137–1149 (2017)
9. Lin, T.-Y., et al.: Focal loss for dense object detection. IEEE Trans. Pattern Anal. Mach. Intell. **42**(2), 318–327 (2020)
10. Carion, N., et al.: End-to-end object detection with transformers. European conference on computer vision. Cham: Springer International Publishing (2020)
11. Zhang, H., et al.: Dino: Detr with improved denoising anchor boxes for end-to-end object detection. arXiv preprint arXiv:2203.03605 (2022)
12. Vaswani, et al.: Attention is all you need. NeurIPS (2017)
13. Redmon, J., et al.: You only look once: unified, real-time object detection. In: IEEE Conference on Computer Vision and Pattern Recognition, pp. 779–788 (2016)
14. Liu, W., et al.: Ssd: single shot multibox detector. In: EECV, pp. 21–37 (2016)
15. Girshick, R., et al.: Rich feature hierarchies for accurate object detection and semantic segmentation. In: IEEE Conference on Computer Vision and Pattern Recognition, pp. 580–587 (2014)
16. Girshick, R.: Fast R-CNN. In: IEEE International Conference on Computer Vision, pp. 1440–1448 (2015)
17. Lin, T.-Y., et al.: Feature pyramid networks for object detection. In: European conference on computer vision. Cham: Springer International Publishing (2020)
18. Zhu, X., et al.: Deformable detr: Deformable transformers for end-to-end object detection. arXiv preprint arXiv:2010.04159 (2020)

19. Lin, T.-Y., et al.: Microsoft coco: common objects in context. In: Computer Vision – ECCV, pp. 740–755 (2014)
20. He, K., et al.: Deep residual learning for image recognition. In: IEEE Conference on Computer Vision and Pattern Recognition, pp.770–778 (2016)
21. Deng, J., et al.: Imagenet: a large-scale hierarchical image database. In: IEEE Conference on Computer Vision and Pattern Recognition, pp. 248–255 (2009)

Occlusion Robust 2D Pose-Based Gait Recognition

Takeshi Konno(✉), Shuji Awai, and Takahiro Yoshioka

Fujitsu Limited, 1-1, Kamikodanaka 4-Chome, Nakahara-Ku, Kawasaki, Japan
{konno.takeshi,awai.shuji,y.takahiro}@fujitsu.com

Abstract. In Japan, the number of elderly people who go missing has been increasing year by year. A delay in finding a missing person can lead to death. However, there are limits to the early detection that can be achieved through search efforts conducted by volunteers using visual observation. Therefore, there is hope that a method that utilizes information from security cameras and person matching technology can be used to track the whereabouts of missing persons and help with the early detection. In recent years, there has also been interest in person matching technology that utilizes 2D pose estimation. However, there is a problem that the person matching accuracy decreases due to the decrease in the pose estimation accuracy caused by the blocking of body parts due to the shooting angle of the security camera or the person's clothes. This paper proposes a method to improve the person matching accuracy by focusing on the parts that are susceptible to a decrease in pose estimation accuracy and by masking the pose estimation information. As a result of the evaluation, the average accuracy rate improved by 3.7% with the proposed method compared to the case without masking. In the future, this technology will facilitate the early discovery of missing persons and contribute to the creation of a society where the elderly can live safely and securely.

Keywords: Gait Recognition · 2D Pose Estimation · Occlusion

1 Introduction

1.1 Social Background

According to a report by the Cabinet Office, as of October 1, 2023, the total population of Japan was 124.35 million. The population aged 65 and over was 36.23 million, and the proportion of this group to the total population (i.e., the aging rate) was 29.1%, the highest in the world [1]. According to a report by the National Police Agency, the number of people with dementia who went missing in 2023 was 19,039 (21.1% of the total), an increase of 330 people over the previous year, the highest number on record (Fig. 1). In addition, the number of people with dementia who went missing in 2012 was 9,607, but in just over 10 years, this number has doubled [2].

The definition and causes of elderly people wandering off are as follows. At first glance, wandering off seems to be aimless wandering around, but this is not necessarily

B. Kim (Ed.): IW-FCV 2025, CCIS 2769, pp. 181–193, 2026.
https://doi.org/10.1007/978-981-95-4578-0_15

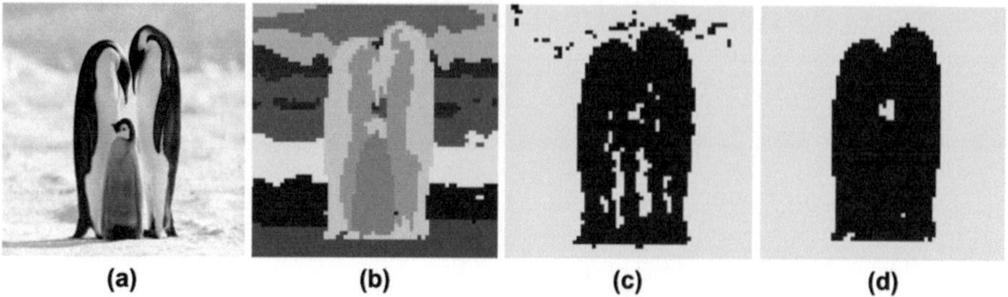

Fig. 1. The number of people with dementia who went missing.

the case for dementia patients. Wandering behavior often has a clear sense of purpose, such as "going home" or "going to work," but due to a decline in cognitive function, the person may forget the purpose at the point of departure or may be unable to follow the route to the destination. As a result, they become lost and wander around without being able to achieve their original goal, and this is observed as the behavior of "wandering." In other words, *wandering* is a secondary behavior that occurs as a result of cognitive impairment preventing the achievement of goals, and it does not occur independently of the patient's own intentions or will. Memory impairment and disorientation are said to be important factors that cause wandering. Memory impairment, particularly episodic memory (i.e., memory of past experiences) and semantic memory (i.e., memory of general knowledge), is a major factor in causing wandering behavior. Episodic memory impairment can cause people to forget their original destination or route. For example, if a person goes out with the intention of "going shopping," they may forget their original destination and become unable to find their way home. Semantic memory impairment can prevent people from correctly recognizing their surroundings, creating situations where they are likely to become lost. Furthermore, short-term memory impairment can cause a person to lose the ability to retain recent actions and information, which can lead to panic and induce wandering behavior. Behaviors like searching around the house for the toilet are often observed as precursors to wandering and suggest a decline in spatial cognitive ability. Disorientation, particularly spatial disorientation, is strongly associated with wandering. As a person is unable to recognize the location of their home, directions, and surrounding landmarks, they more likely to become lost and wander for longer periods of time. Disorientation in time is a factor that keeps them wandering because they lose track of the time they have been out and the time that has passed, and they do not know when to go home. These disorders are closely related to a dysfunction of the parietal and frontal lobes. One type of disorientation is the "dusk syndrome," which is a type of wandering that is time-of-day specific. When dusk falls, patients experiencing this syndrome suddenly become restless and may behave or wander in a way that is different from usual.

When dealing with elderly people who wander off, it is said that the rate of discovery decreases significantly after 9 h, and the mortality rate increases by about 37% after a day has passed and further increases after 2 to 3 days [3]. In addition, the causes of death are often senility and hypothermia. It has been reported that more than 40% of people who drown die on the day of the incident, and that people who suffer hypothermia die on the third or fourth day (Table 1).

Table 1. Missing persons reported and confirmed.

Category	Same day	2–3 days	4–7 days	8–14 days
Total	13,698	4,700	203	74
Location confirmed	13,517	4,471	131	33
Confirmed deaths	118	192	68	37
Mortality rate	0.9%	4%	33%	50%

Measures to prevent elderly people from wandering off are being taken both outdoors and indoors, but there are limits to their effectiveness. Outdoors, there are methods for obtaining location information using GPS devices that can be placed in smartphones or shoes. However, there are cases where the GPS battery runs out or the device is not carried around. Indoors, sensor mats and door/motion sensors are often used. However, although it is possible to tell when a person has passed through, it is not possible to tell when they have gone outside. In Japan, the police and local governments are working together to find missing people as quickly as possible through the SOS Network, a network for monitoring the whereabouts of elderly people. Those who wish to do so can register the characteristics of the elderly person in advance (e.g., height, weight, build, and hairstyle). However, because the search is carried out by volunteers visually, it takes an average of 15.8 h to find the person, and there are limits to finding them within 9 h.

The objective of this study is to develop an early detection system for missing persons by automatically mapping their whereabouts on a map using information from security cameras and person identification technology and notifying the police and volunteers (Fig. 2). In this early detection system, first, images of the elderly taken with a smartphone are registered. Next, when the police contact you because an elderly person has gone missing, images from security cameras are collected and compared with the registered images to identify the person. The results of the person identification are displayed on a map and provided to the police and volunteers. This helps to detect elderly people who have gone missing early.

1.2 Gait Recognition

In some cases, biometric technology is used to identify individuals by measuring their unique physical characteristics and comparing them with information registered in a database. There are two types of biometrics: 1) static biometrics (e.g., fingerprints, irises, blood vessels, and faces) that do not change over time and 2) dynamic biometrics (e.g., gait, voice, and handwriting) that do change over time. However, because the physical characteristics can vary depending on the surrounding environment and conditions when they are read by sensors, even with static biometrics, it is not always possible to achieve 100% accuracy. In addition, because dynamic biometrics involves

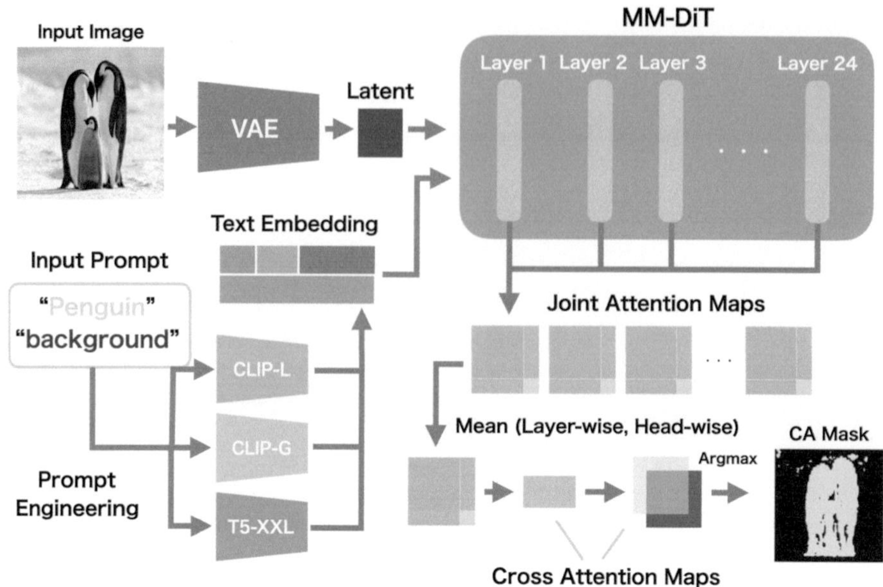

Fig. 2. System overview

changes in characteristics, the accuracy of identification is generally lower than with static biometrics.

The authors of this paper focused on a method of identifying people by extracting the characteristics of their gait, even when the person is far away and visible only on a security camera. Gait analysis has a long history, and in 1984, the first biometric gait recognition using camera images was introduced. Gait has been used as forensic evidence in court. In particular, in the case of a robbery that occurred in London in 2000, Hadyn Kelly was the first person to give expert testimony in court on the analysis of walking patterns [4]. In 2002, the Defense Advanced Research Projects Agency released HumanID, a large-scale dataset consisting of approximately 300 GB of data related to 452 sequences from 74 subjects, and this promoted research into gait recognition [5]. In October 2008, gait recognition was used as criminal evidence for the first time in the United Kingdom by Professor Mark Nixon of Southampton University [6]. In February 2009, gait recognition technology developed by Osaka University was used for the first time in Japan in a criminal investigation. Research into deep-learning-based gait recognition began in 2015.

There are two approaches to gait recognition: one that utilizes silhouette-type gait features and another that utilizes pose-estimation-type gait features.

The basic process of silhouette-based gait recognition consists of generating a sequence of person silhouette images from the walking video, converting them into normalized silhouette images, detecting the walking cycle, and extracting the gait features. Gait Energy Image (GEI) is a feature extracted as an average image over one gait cycle, obtained from a sequence of silhouette images extracted from a person's walking video, after size normalization and alignment. This image clearly reflects the magnitude of relative movement with respect to the torso. Frequency domain features (FDF) is a feature composed of three-channel images. The left channel is the GEI, the center channel represents the asymmetric component appearing once per gait cycle, and the right channel represents the symmetric component appearing twice per gait cycle. Gait Entropy Image (GEnI) is calculated by calculating the Shannon entropy for all pixels in the gait cycle. Even in situations where obtaining background differences for silhouette generation is difficult, the Intersection over Union (IoU), an indicator of the overlap between two areas, is 77.2%. However, the matching accuracy is less than 75% for the top 20 silhouettes. There are also reports that the speed of silhouette extraction takes an average of 15,567 ms per image, which is equivalent to 15 s [7]. In other words, it would take almost 40 min to extract the silhouettes of a 5-s video at 30 fps; therefore, it is not suitable for processing large amounts of video footage in real time.

For pose-based gait recognition, a pose estimation method that can extract person silhouettes at high speed and high accuracy has been proposed. Also known as a model-based approach, this method extracts detailed biomechanical parameters, such as joint angles and trunk movements, and uses these as feature values to identify people. Previously, Wang et al. [8] proposed a gait recognition method that used a motion model composed of 14 rigid body parts (e.g., head, neck, chest, abdomen, left and right upper arms, left and right lower arms, left and right thighs, left and right lower legs, left and right feet). There have also been other proposals, such as KinectGaitNet [9], which is a method based on 3D coordinate data using Kinect. In recent years, with the progress of 2D pose estimation technology, model-based approaches using pose estimation information have attracted attention. Since 2020, many gait recognition methods have been proposed using high-precision pose estimation models developed using deep learning. Typical methods include PoseGait [10], which combines 2D pose estimation and convolutional neural networks (CNN); GaitMixer [11] and GaitGraph [12], which combine 2D pose estimation information and graph convolutional networks; GaitFormer [13], a hybrid method that combines CNN and vision transformer (ViT); and Gait-D [14], which combines 2D pose estimation information and silhouette information. These methods each employ different architectures and feature extraction methods. HRNet [15], a 2D pose estimation model with higher accuracy than OpenPose, which was released in 2019, is used in many gait recognition studies. The biggest advantage of using 2D pose estimation is that it does not require complex preprocessing, such as silhouette extraction using background difference, as in conventional methods. This simplicity and high accuracy make it suitable for application to real-world data, such as security camera footage, and this study adopts a model-based approach, particularly a method based on 2D pose estimation.

In this paper, there is a problem where the person matching accuracy decreases due to a decline in pose estimation accuracy because the body parts are blocked by the shooting angle of the security camera or clothing. The proposed method aims to improve the person matching accuracy by focusing on body parts that are susceptible to a decrease in pose estimation accuracy and by masking the pose estimation information.

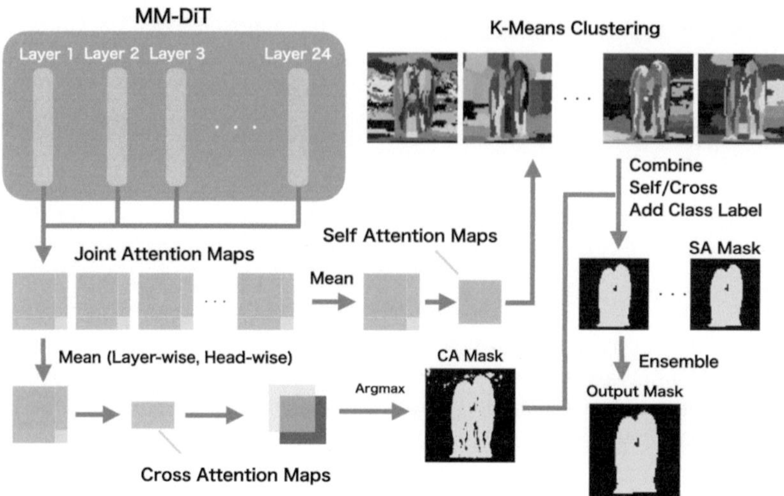

Fig. 3. Pose estimation information on HRNet

2 Occlusion Robust Gait Recognition Method

2.1 Conventional Method

In previous evaluation using CASIA-B [16], the conventional method GaitMixer had higher accuracy than GaitGraph in the pose estimation matching of gait features, and it was the most accurate algorithm at the time of evaluation. Therefore, this study will adopt GaitMixer, since it has almost the same accuracy as GaitPart [17], which is an appearance-based gait matching algorithm.

GaitMixer is a novel skeleton-based gait recognition model employing a heterogeneous multi-axial mixer architecture. This architecture comprises a spatial self-attention mixer, learning inter-joint interactions within each frame by capturing relationships between joints (spatial tokens) using self-attention mechanisms, thus effectively learning both high and low-frequency spatial features. Furthermore, a temporal large-kernel convolution mixer models interactions between temporal tokens (joint positions at different time indices) of each joint, utilizing large-kernel depthwise separable convolutions to capture short-term and long-term repetitive patterns (mid-frequency features) in the walking sequence. This dual approach enables robust gait representation learning, overcoming limitations of previous methods that struggled with variations in clothing or carrying objects. Given HRNet's demonstrated ability to generate the high-resolution representations critical for accurate joint localization, as shown in the GaitMixer paper's implementation and evaluation, and its significant impact on performance, this study also adopts HRNet for pose estimation.

The input is the pose estimation information of the human time series estimated by HRNet, and the output is a 128-dimensional feature quantity. The pose estimation information uses the 17-point 2D coordinates of the joints of the human body, as shown in Fig. 3.

2.2 Proposed Method

Taking into account the problem of the pose estimation accuracy decreasing due to the occlusion of body parts because of the shooting angle of the security camera or the person's clothing, the proposed method focused on the parts of the body that are likely to be occluded when walking. Specifically, the information of the arms, which are prone to occlusion when extracting gait features, was masked to extract gait features that are less susceptible to the effects of differences in clothing.

This study masks only right_elbow and right_wrist, which are prone to occlusion, as right-side arm information. While details are provided in Sect. 3.1, the dataset used for training and evaluation in this study consists of videos of subjects walking from right to left. The right hand, positioned further away from the camera, is frequently occluded by the body during walking, leading to an anticipated decrease in the reliability of skeletal position estimation. Conversely, the left hand, being closest to the camera and clearly visible, is considered crucial for representing temporal repetitions in GaitMixer and is therefore retained. Right_ear, right_shoulder, and right_hip, while potentially obscured like the right arm, were not excluded due to their empirically observed lack of significant cyclical changes during walking and their importance in representing the torso.

The processing flow is shown in Fig. 4. First, pose estimation was performed on the input video of the person, and the pose estimation information was obtained in chronological order. The HRNet method was used to obtain the 17 two-dimensional coordinates of the joints of the person. Next, the gait features were extracted from the model that has been trained on the gait features, except for the right_elbow and right_wrist arm joints, using the time-series pose estimation information as input. The degree of agreement was calculated using the cosine similarity from the obtained gait features. The model for learning the gait features is a model that can accept input excluding the arm joints, which is defined based on the conventional method.

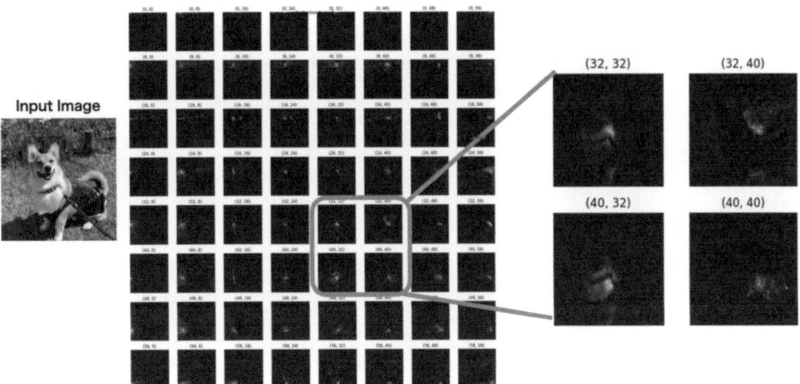

Fig. 4. Processing flow

3 Experiment

3.1 Dataset

The CASIA-B dataset was used for learning the gait features, and it is one of the widely used datasets in gait-related research. It contains images of 124 subjects walking, captured from 11 different angles, and includes patterns of subjects carrying bags and wearing coats. For training, 74 subjects were used. CASIA-B has a resolution of 320 × 240 pixels and a frame rate of 25 fps.

The Southampton Human ID (HID) database (hereafter, Southampton) was used as the evaluation dataset. This dataset is available in large [18] and small [19] versions. The small version contains 15 patterns of different clothing and walking speeds, with 11 subjects walking in front of a camera from four different angles, and it includes 15 patterns, such as differences in clothing and walking speed. The large dataset includes video footage of 116 subjects walking with a four-angle camera and of them walking on a treadmill with a two-angle camera. For the evaluation of the same attire condition, images of 115 people (excluding 1 person) in Normal attire in the Large dataset walked 2 times at the same angle. Using the walking video of the normal dress as a query, the similarity with all the walking video of the normal dress was calculated. If the ID of the video with the highest similarity matches the ID of the query, the correct answer is assumed. In the evaluation of the dress difference condition, the video of the Raincoat dress (walking 8 times at the same angle) was used. Using the walking video of the Normal outfit as a query, we calculated the similarity with all the walking videos of the Raincoat outfit in the Small dataset. If the ID of the video with the highest similarity matches the ID of the query, the correct answer is assumed. The video sample used for the evaluation is shown in Fig. 5. The walking direction was from right to left on the screen. The resolution of Southampton is 720 × 576 pixels, and the frame rate is 25 FPS.

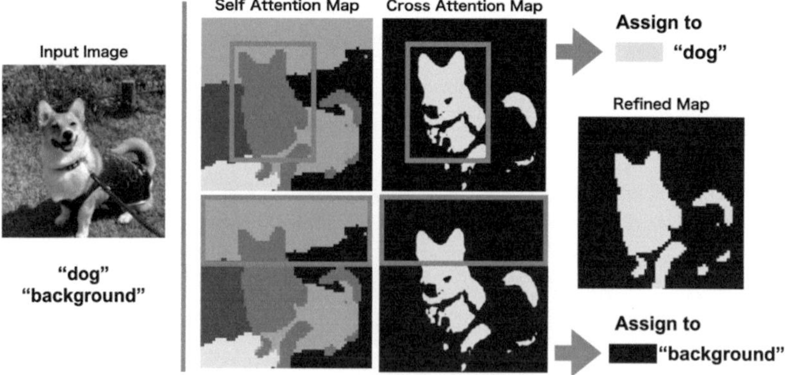

Fig. 5. Clothing patterns

4 Results

The evaluation results for the conventional method and the proposed method under the two clothing conditions are shown in Table 2. In both conditions, the average accuracy rate was improved by the proposed method. As a result of the evaluation, the average accuracy rate was improved by 3.7% with the proposed method compared to the case without a mask.

Table 2. Results of Collation Accuracy (%)

Method	Condition	Accuracy
GaitMixer	Normal × Normal	82.6
Proposed		**87.8**
GaitMixer	Normal × Raincoat	89.8
Proposed		**92.0**

5 Discussion

5.1 Normal × Normal

The mean, max (average of the top 5), and min (average of the bottom 5) of the confidence score for each part obtained from HRNet are shown in Fig. 6. The variance (var) is shown in Fig. 7. In standard clothing, the variance of the confidence scores for right_elbow and right_wrist is high. This means that occlusion is likely to occur because the right arm is hidden by the body when walking. As a result, masking this feature resulted in improved accuracy compared to the conventional method.

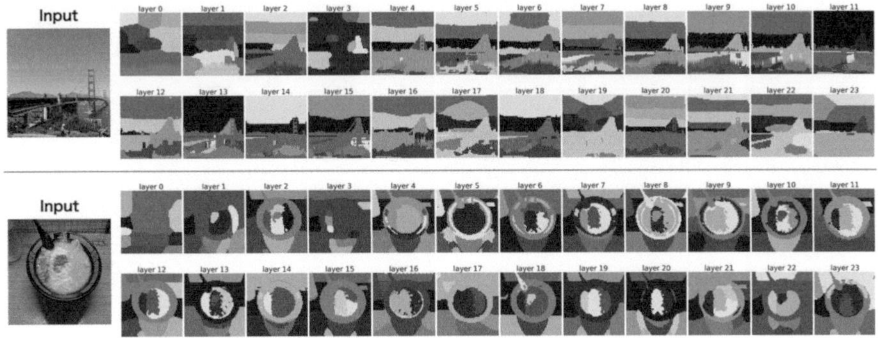

Fig. 6. The confidence scores (mean, max, min)

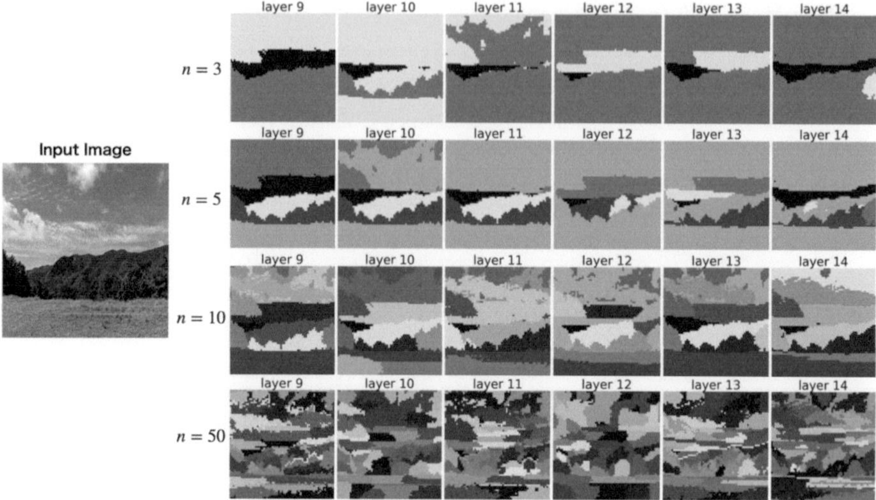

Fig. 7. The confidence scores (var)

5.2 Normal × Raincoat

Mean, max (average of the top 5), and min (average of the bottom 5) of the confidence score for each part obtained from HRNet are shown in Fig. 8. The variance (var) is shown in Fig. 9. As with the standard clothing, the variance of the confidence scores for right_elbow and right_wrist is high for the raincoat. By masking this feature, the authors were able to improve the accuracy over the previous method.

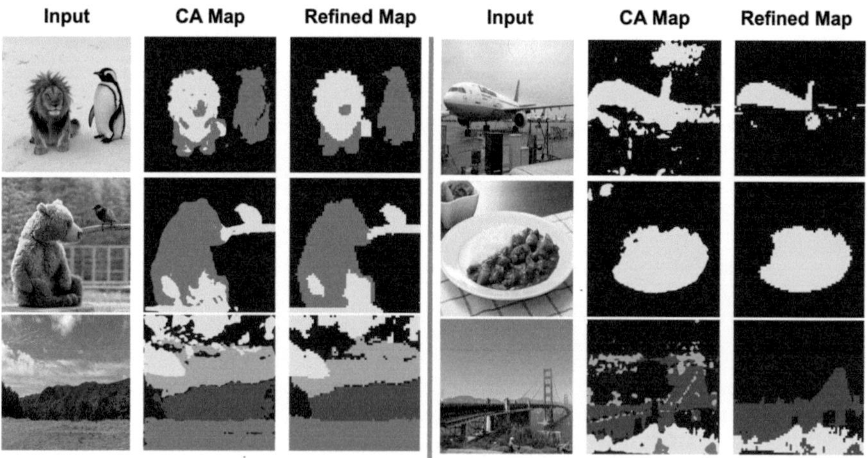

Fig. 8. The confidence scores (mean, max, min)

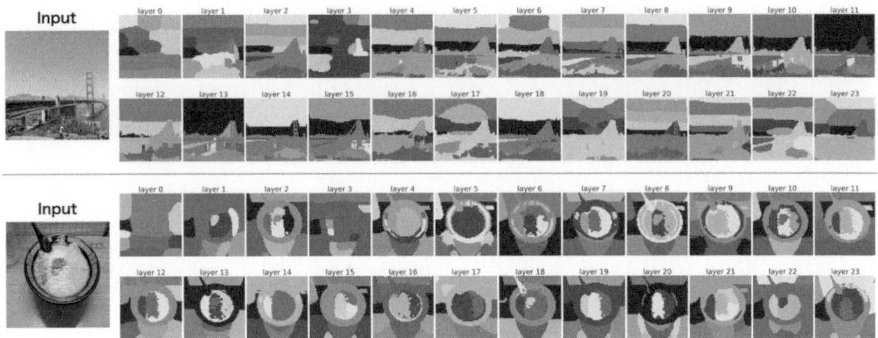

Fig. 9. The confidence scores (var)

5.3 Other Right-Side Parts

Further investigation into other right-side body parts, as discussed in Sect. 2.2, is warranted. For Normal × Normal, while the confidence scores for right_shoulder and right_hip are lower than those on the left side, they are comparable to left_hip score. Right_ear consistently exhibits low confidence scores due to near-constant occlusion. However, the variance of right_ear, right_shoulder, and right_hip is considerably smaller than that of right_elbow and right_wrist. Since the proposed method using 15 keypoints outperforms GaitMixer using all 17 keypoints in gait recognition accuracy, we hypothesize that high variance in confidence scores contributes more to accuracy degradation than low confidence scores themselves.

For Normal × Raincoat, the relationship between confidence scores and their variance for other right-side body parts is largely consistent with the findings in Sect. 5.1. Even with raincoat occlusion, the high variance in confidence scores likely contributed more to accuracy degradation than low confidence scores themselves.

Under both conditions, the variance in confidence scores for the crossing legs during walk was relatively high compared to other body parts. However, the confidence scores themselves remained relatively high, exceeding 0.6 even with raincoats. The confidence scores showed little difference between the left and right legs. While these keypoints, considered most influential for gait recognition, are clearly important even with somewhat lower detection confidence, the utilization of knee joints, which tend to be hidden especially with raincoats, remains a topic for future investigation.

6 Conclusion

The proposed method has improved the person matching accuracy by focusing on parts of the body that are susceptible to a decline in pose estimation accuracy and masking the pose estimation information. As a result of the evaluation, the average correct response rate improved by 3.7% with the proposed method compared to the case without masking.

However, the number of clothing variations was small in this verification. For example, in Southampton, there are also clothes that cover up to the ankles, such as trench coats. In the future, the authors will increase the number of clothing variations to be evaluated, with the belief that this will enable the creation of a general-purpose gait matching model that can handle different types of clothing.

In the future, this technology will make it easier to find missing people quickly and contribute to creating a society where the elderly can live safely and securely.

References

1. Cabinet Office: White Paper on the Aging Society (2019). https://www8.cao.go.jp/kourei/whitepaper/w-2024/html/gaiyou/s1_1.html. Accessed 18 Dec 2024
2. National Police Agency: Status of Missing Persons in 2023. https://www.npa.go.jp/safetylife/seianki/fumei/R05yukuefumeisha.pdf. Accessed 18 Dec 2024
3. Kikuchi, K., Ijuin, M., Awata, S., Suzuki, T.: A study on the mortality patterns of missing and deceased persons with dementia who died due to wandering. Nihon Ronen Igakkai Zasshi. Jpn. J. Geriatr. **53**(4), 363–373 (2016)
4. Guinness World Records: First use of forensic gait analysis evidence in court (2016). https://www.guinnessworldrecords.com/world-records/first-use-of-forensic-gait-analysis-evidence-in-court/. Accessed 18 Dec 2024
5. Phillips, P.J., Sarkar, S., Robledo, I., Grother, P., Bowyer, K.: The gait identification challenge problem: data sets and baseline algorithm. In: 2002 International Conference on Pattern Recognition, vol. 1, pp. 385–388. IEEE (2002)
6. BBC. http://news.bbc.co.uk/2/hi/programmes/click_online/7702065.stm. Accessed 18 Dec 2024
7. Iwamura, M., et al.: Individuality-preserving silhouette extraction for gait recognition and its speedup. IEICE Trans. Inf. Syst. **104**(7), 992–1001 (2021)
8. Wang, L., Ning, H., Tan, T., Hu, W.: Fusion of static and dynamic body biometrics for gait recognition. IEEE Trans. Circuits Syst. Video Technol. **14**(2), 149–158 (2004)
9. Bari, A.H., Gavrilova, M.L.: KinectGaitNet: kinect-based gait recognition using deep convolutional neural network. Sensors **22**(7), 2631 (2022)
10. Liao, R., Yu, S., An, W., Huang, Y.: A model-based gait recognition method with body pose and human prior knowledge. Pattern Recogn. **98**, 107069 (2020)
11. Pinyoanuntapong, E., Ali, A., Wang, P., Lee, M., Chen, C.: Gaitmixer: skeleton-based gait representation learning via wide-spectrum multi-axial mixer. In: ICASSP 2023–2023 IEEE International Conference on Acoustics, Speech and Signal Processing (ICASSP), pp. 1–5. IEEE (2023)
12. Teepe, T., Khan, A., Gilg, J., Herzog, F., Hörmann, S., Rigoll, G.: Gaitgraph: Graph convolutional network for skeleton-based gait recognition. In: 2021 IEEE International Conference on Image Processing (ICIP), pp. 2314–2318. IEEE (2021)
13. Li, J., Wang, Z., Wang, C., Su, W.: GaitFormer: leveraging dual-stream spatial–temporal Vision Transformer via a single low-cost RGB camera for clinical gait analysis. Knowl.-Based Syst. **295**, 111810 (2024)
14. Gao, S., Yun, J., Zhao, Y., Liu, L.: Gait-D: skeleton-based gait feature decomposition for gait recognition. IET Comput. Vision **16**(2), 111–125 (2022)
15. Sun, K., Xiao, B., Liu, D., Wang, J.: Deep high-resolution representation learning for human pose estimation. In Proceedings of the IEEE/CVF Conference on Computer Vision and Pattern Recognition, pp. 5693–5703 (2019)
16. Wu, Z., Huang, Y., Wang, L., Wang, X., Tan, T.: A comprehensive study on cross-view gait based human identification with deep CNNs. IEEE Trans. Pattern Anal. Mach. Intell. **39**(2), 209–226 (2016)

17. Fan, C., et al.: Gaitpart: temporal part-based model for gait recognition. In: Proceedings of the IEEE/CVF Conference on Computer Vision and Pattern Recognition, pp. 14225–14233 (2020)
18. Hayfron-Acquah, J.B., Nixon, M.S., Carter, J.N.: Automatic gait recognition by symmetry analysis. Pattern Recogn. Lett. **24**(13), 2175–2183 (2003)
19. Shutler, J.D., Grant, M.G., Nixon, M.S., Carter, J.N.: On a large sequence-based human gait database. In: Applications and Science in Soft Computing, pp. 339–346. Springer, Heidelberg (2004)

Character Restoration System for "Shihai-Monjo" in Ancient Document Images Based on Image Inpainting Technique

Haruto Izumi(✉), Masahiro Migita, Masashi Toda, and Masahiko Itoh

Kumamoto University, 2-39-1 Kurokami, Chuo-Ku, Kumamoto-Shi, Kumamoto 860-8555, Japan

izumi@st.cs.kumamoto-u.ac.jp, {migita,toda}@cc.kumamoto-u.ac.jp, mitoh@kumamoto-u.ac.jp

Abstract. There are some ancient documents that reuse paper due to the rarity of paper in the past, and that have different documents written on both sides. Among these documents, the ones that were first no longer needed and were left on the back side of the paper are called "Shihai-monjo," and it is known that historically important content has been left in them as well. However, it is difficult to read the Shihai-monjo by peering into the interior of a document with a bag-bound structure, from the perspective of preserving the document. In this study, we developed an image restoration system based on a deep learning-based image inpainting method to solve the problem of missing back side characters caused by overlapping characters, which is an issue when analyzing ancient document images taken from the top.

Keywords: Image Restoration · Image Inpainting · Ancient Document

1 Introduction

Many ancient documents are of high historical value because they contain information about the communication of people in past eras, family registry information, and records of government offices. When analyzing the contents of these ancient documents, great care must be taken to avoid physical damage to the documents, such as folds, tears, and stains. In the past, paper production was small and was considered a precious commodity, so it was often used again after it had been used. In this case, when a document is written using the blank space on the reverse side of a document, the document on the side that has become a waste of paper is called a "Shihai-monjo" or "Ura-monjo" [1].

According to Tarashima, a representative example of the Shihai-monjo in Japan is the "Shosoin-monjo" of the Nara period (710–794), in which discarded official documents such as family registers and account books were delivered to the Todaiji temple, and practical documents of the temple were written on the reverse side [2]. Furthermore, Iikura says that in the diaries of court nobles of the Kamakura and Muromachi periods, letters on the reverse side are often related to the body of the diary on the front side, and

B. Kim (Ed.): IW-FCV 2025, CCIS 2769, pp. 194–207, 2026.
https://doi.org/10.1007/978-981-95-4578-0_16

have great historical value as Ura-monjo [3]. For this reason, in analyzing the contents of ancient documents, it is necessary to treat not only the front side but also the back side of the documents as important objects for analysis.

Figure 1 is a 360° camera image of the inside of a bag of ancient documents with a bag-bound structure, in which a single sheet of paper is folded and bound at both ends.

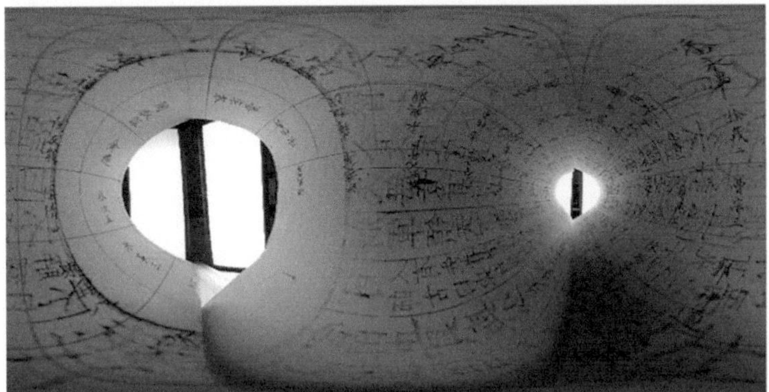

Fig. 1. Image of the inside of the bag-bound structure of an ancient document.

From the image, this ancient document contains characters not only on the surface of the document, but also inside the bag-bound. However, such a photographing method is extremely difficult for high-value documents because the document itself needs to be widely opened. Therefore, it is desirable to analyze both the front and back of a document using an image taken from the top of the document.

We have applied Semantic Segmentation, a type of image segmentation method, to the top-photographed image of such an ancient document with writing on both sides of the document to extract the region of the Shihai-monjo, i.e., the characters of the writing on the back side of the paper that appears in the image [4]. However, one of the major problems was that in regions where characters overlap on the front and back sides, the ink shading of the characters on the front side prevents extraction of the characters on the back side.

Based on this background, this study examined a system to improve the readability of ancient documents by restoring the loss of the back side characters region caused by overlapping characters, with the aim of analyzing them in a non-damaged. The process can be divided into two main parts: automatic mask generation for the region to be restored, and character restoration through inpainting. For the former, we applied Semantic Segmentation, which has been used to extract back side characters, to this task, and for the latter, we applied an image impainting method using deep learning. Furthermore, the effectiveness of the applied image inpainting model was quantitatively evaluated using image quality evaluation indices.

2 Related Work

In this chapter, an overview of previous study that focused on the restoration of characters in documents whose forms are different from those of the ancient documents subject to this study is presented. Shiono et al. [5] conducted a study on the restoration of characters in an ancient document called "Mokkan," which is a long, thin piece of wood on which characters and symbols are written in ink. They particularly focused on "Kezurikuzu mokkan," which are wood pieces produced by shaving used Mokkan at the time of reuse them. These items contain characters that were lost during the shaving process. Therefore, they applied a deep learning-based image inpainting method [6] to the images of them, for the purpose to restore information of missing characters. The results suggest that the applied method is useful for the analysis of the Mokkan, objects in the study, although the accuracy of character restoration depends on the size of the defects in the image.

We attempt to restore back side documents that are missing due to overlapping characters by training our own ancient document dataset in paper format against the inpainting model applied in this previous study [5].

3 Target Ancient Document

The ancient documents we focus on in this study are called "Kan-sho" documents, which are stored in the Seikado Bunko collection in Tokyo, Japan. Figure 2 shows an image of the document.

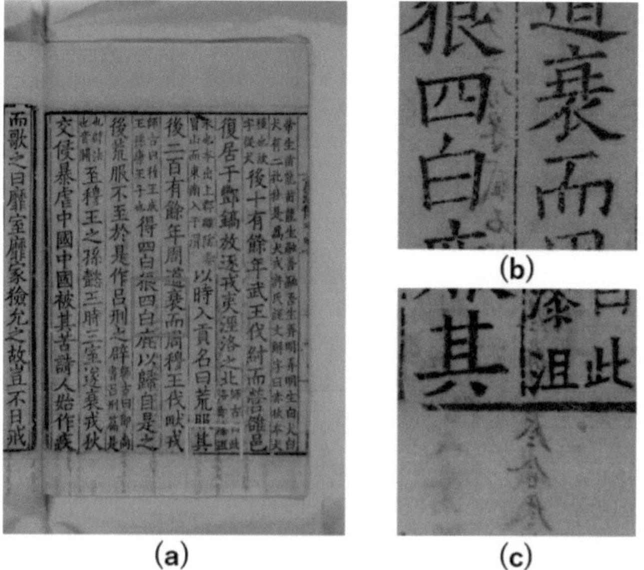

Fig. 2. Examples of ancient document images focus on this study. (a) is entire image. (b) and (c) are images focusing on the area where the back side characters appear in the image.

The original image shown in Fig. 2(a) was acquired by infrared imaging from the top of document with a bag-bound structure, with a size of 4912 × 7360 [pixels] and a resolution of 300 [dpi]. Figure 2(b) (is area of red rectangle of (a)) and (c) (is area of blue rectangle of (a)) shows the locations of back side document's characters in the original image, and it can be seen from each image that these characters exists widely around the body of the front side document and outside its frame.

4 Proposed Method

4.1 Overview of Processing

This section describes the flow of the method proposed in this study for recovering missing reverse side characters in old document images. Figure 3 shows the overall flow of the process.

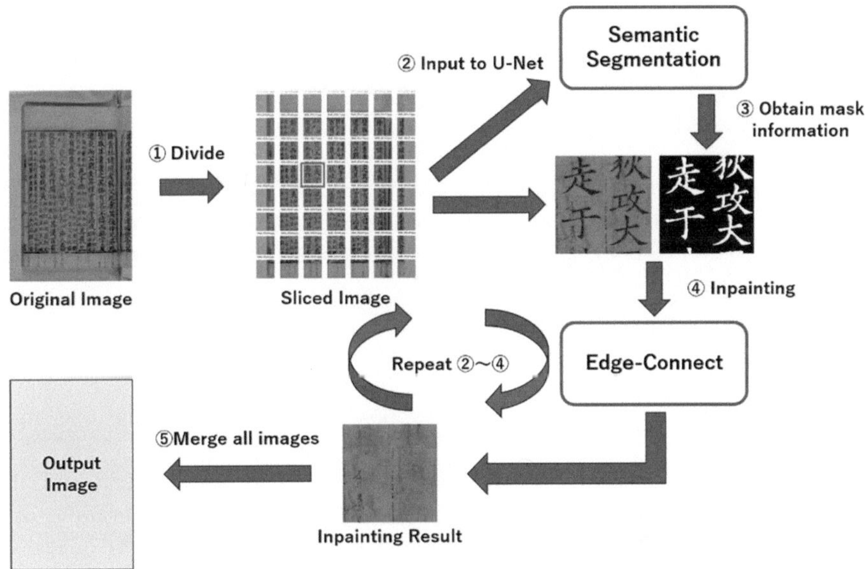

Fig. 3. Schematic diagram of the proposed system.

As described in Chapter 3, the images used in this study are so large that they cannot be processed all at once due to GPU memory capacity. Therefore, the method of dividing an image into pieces and processing each piece separately was adopted. In this study, the original image was divided into square areas of 768 x 768 [pixels] each. Padding is applied to the right and bottom edges of the image so that the image can be divided by the size of the square. Each slice image obtained in this way is processed one by one to restore the missing regions. Inpainting requires a mask image that represents the area to be complemented, in this case, only the surface characters. Initially, we attempted to generate this mask image using Otsu's binarization [7], but we found that this method omits the light surface characters and, conversely, excessively masks the dark back side characters. For this reason, Semantic Segmentation is applied using a model that has learned the features of surface characters in advance, so that an appropriate mask can be obtained. The mask image and the corresponding slice image are input to Edge-Connect for inpainting. This is applied to all slice images, and the results are combined to their original shape to obtain the final output image.

In the following, an explanation of the Semantic Segmentation applied for the purpose of mask image generation and the image inpainting model Edge-Connect employed in this study will be presented.

4.2 Semantic Segmentation

Semantic Segmentation is an image segmentation task in which each pixel of an input image is labeled and divided into regions. In this study, we constructed a model using U-Net [8], which is a type of FCN (Fully Convolutional Network). U-Net is an Encoder-Decoder architecture consisting of an Encoder that performs convolution of the input image and extracts its features, and a Decoder that generates a probability map of the output result. One of the major features of U-Net is a structure called "skip connection" in which the feature map of the Encoder is concatenated with that of the Decoder. This enables the preservation of object location information during upsampling, which results in improved segmentation accuracy.

In this case, Semantic Segmentation is used to generate a mask image to be input to the inpainting model. For this purpose, a U-Net model trained on the dataset described below was used to classify the input image into two classes: "surface text areas" or "other areas."

4.3 Edge-Connect

Edge-Connect is Generative Adversarial Networks (GANs) [9] based image inpainting model.

GANs is a model consisting of two types of neural networks: the Generator and the Discriminator. The Generator is a network that generates images from random noise data given as initial input, and is iteratively trained to determine that the generated image is a real image by the Discriminator. The Discriminator, on the other hand, is a network that determines whether a given image is real or not, and is iteratively trained to correctly determine that an image generated by the Generator is a fake. Learning proceeds in parallel in both the Generator and the Discriminator, thereby improving the accuracy of each network as they work against each other. Finally, the goal is for the Generators to produce more realistic data.

The Edge-Connect applied in this study is a model that consists of the above-mentioned GANs coupled in two stages. Figure 4 shows a schematic diagram of Edge-Connect.

In Fig. 4, the network consisting of generator G_1 and discriminator D_1 on the left side of the model (first stage) is called the "Edge generator", and the network consisting of generator G_2 and discriminator D_2 on the right side of the model (second stage)

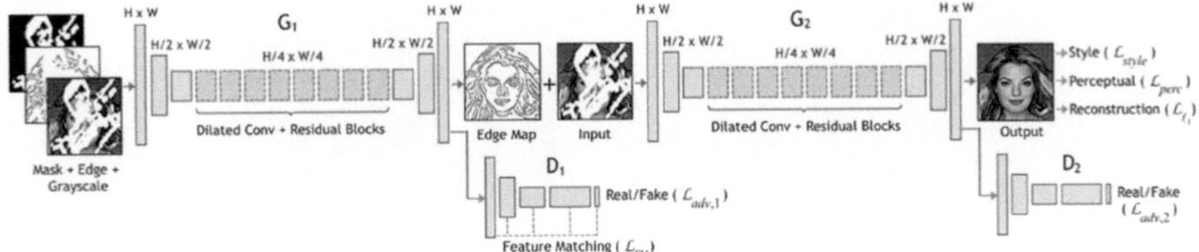

Fig. 4. Schematic diagram of Edge-Connect (cited from [6]).

is called the "Image completion network." As can be understood from the connections between these networks, Edge-Connect first estimates the edge information contained in the missing regions of the input image, and by using this information, it aims to provide a more appropriate inpainting for the missing regions. The overall training flow of the model is as follows.

1. Train an Edge generator using an input image (grayscale) containing defects, its edge image, and a mask image showing the missing regions of the input image.
2. Train an Image completion network in advance using an input image (color) that contains defects and the edge information of the ground truth image.
3. Train an Image completion network again using the edge-estimated image output by G_1 and deficient input image (color).

Thus, after first training each model separately, the Edge generator and the Image completion network are finally connected and trained again in End-to-End to apply inpainting that considers the edge information of the missing regions in the image. This is a major feature of this method.

5 Experiments

5.1 Generation of Mask Images

Datasets. As mentioned above, when inpainting ancient document images, it is necessary to generate a mask image that indicates the area to be inpainted, and in this study, semantic segmentation using was used to conduct this process. The details of the dataset used for training the model are described below.

To train the mask generation model, we use the image shown in Fig. 5(a), which is a cropped image of a region of an ancient document image in which the characters on the surface appear. The size of this image is 768 x 768 [pixels]. The surface character regions are annotated on these images using LabelMe [10], one of the annotation tools, to create the mask data shown in Fig. 5(b). In this study, 6 images were created and rotated 90°, 180°, and 270° as data expansion to increase the total amount of data to 24 images. The data set was then divided into 18 images for training and 6 images for validation.

Model Construction and Training. U-Net training is performed by fine-tuning a model that uses ResNet34, which has been pretrained on the large-scale image dataset Imagenet [11], as the backbone of the encoder, using the above-mentioned dataset. We

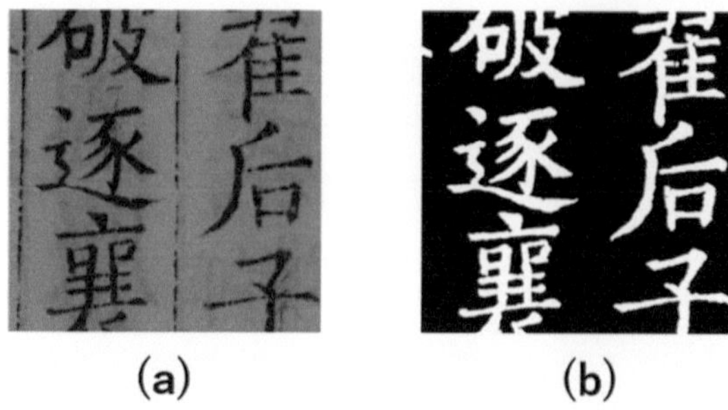

Fig. 5. Training dataset for mask generation. (a) is the cropped image of a character region on the surface. (b) is the mask data created by annotation.

set Dice loss as the loss function during learning and IoU (Intersection over Union) as the evaluation index, and trained for 50 epochs.

5.2 Inpainting

Datasets. Here a description of the dataset used for training Edge-Connect. The target areas for restoration are those where the characters on the back side of the document overlap with those on the front side, making them difficult to read. Taking this into account, a dataset for learning is created.

First, an image is created from the entire ancient document image by cropping a region such that the characters on the back side are without any defects, as shown in Fig. 6(a). This is the ground truth image. Next, thresholding and morphological processing are applied to the front side character areas of original image to generate a mask image in the shape of the them. An example is shown in Fig. 6(b). And overlay of these images is shown in Fig. 6(c). In this image, white areas are defects, and the model is trained to restore these areas correctly. The actual input images to the model are the ground truth image and the mask image.

In this study, 100 ground truth and mask images of the same format were created, and then rotated 90°, 180°, and 270° and flipped horizontally were applied as data expansion, resulting in a total of 800 images in the dataset. The entire dataset was divided into 560 images for training, 160 images for validation, and 80 images for testing. The size of these images is 256 x 256 [pixels].

Setting Up the Training Environment. Edge-Connect model training is performed by fine-tuning a pre-trained model with Places2 [12], a large landscape image dataset. The batch size was set to 10 and the number of epochs to 50 for all three training steps described in chapter 4. Other hyperparameters, such as the learning rate of the network and the weights of the loss function, were set to their default values.

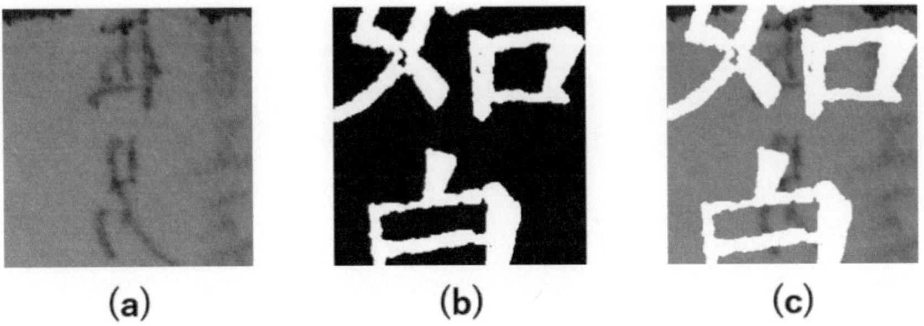

Fig. 6. Dataset for Edge-Connect model training. (a) is the ground truth image. (b) is a mask image showing missing regions to be added. (c) is a composite of (a) and (b).

6 Results

6.1 Processing Result of Sliced Images

First, the results for each slice image are discussed. Figure 7 shows a sample of the images processed in this study. The original image, the mask image created by segmentation, and the result of the inpainting process are shown side by side.

Each of the four samples shown in Fig. 7 is explained in the followings.

First, the images in the top row is an example of relatively successful restoration of missing characters, as both masking and inpainting processes were executed without any problems. The backside characters on the right side of the original image overlap with the front side characters, but the output image can be seen to be able to remove the influence of them.

The image in second row shows the example of processing when characters of the same size overlap on the front and back sides. The front side characters in the center of the original image are relatively smaller in size than the other front side characters, and in the case of overlapping such small characters, the missing area is also small. Therefore, the restoration can be done enough.

The images in third row shows the example in which, although the characters were restored, an overly masked portion of the back side characters located in the upper left corner of the image was erased in the output image. Since this was observed in some images, it is necessary to further improve the accuracy of front side character extraction during mask generation.

Finally, the bottom images show the example of unsuccessful character restoration in the output image due to a large overlap of characters on both sides on the left side of the image. As can be seen from this result, the accuracy of the restoration is affected by the area of the defect, and if local features of the characters are lost, restoration is difficult.

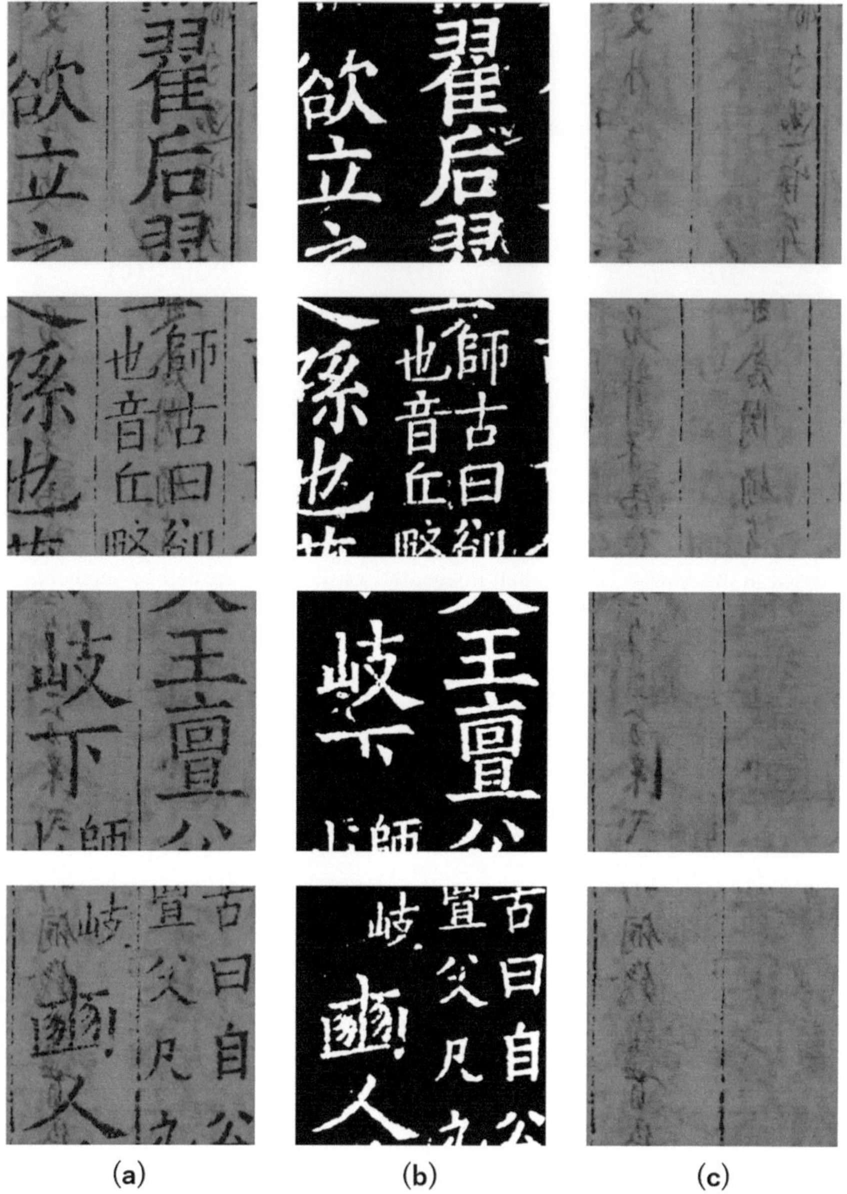

Fig. 7. Example of processing results in a sliced image. In each row, (a) is the original image, (b) is the mask image, and (c) is the inpainting result.

6.2 Processing Results of the Entire Image

Next, each slice image was processed according to the flow shown in Fig. 3, and then merged to obtain the inpainting result for the entire image. Figure 8 shows the result.

Comparing these images, the proposed method restores the information on the back side of the characters in the image, and removes the influence of the front side characters, although some of their textures remain. However, due to the characteristic of considering the surrounding pixel values when inpainting, the results are generally darker, especially in areas near the horizontal lines separating the document at the bottom of the image. Therefore, it is necessary to consider including the lines that separate documents in the processing target as well.

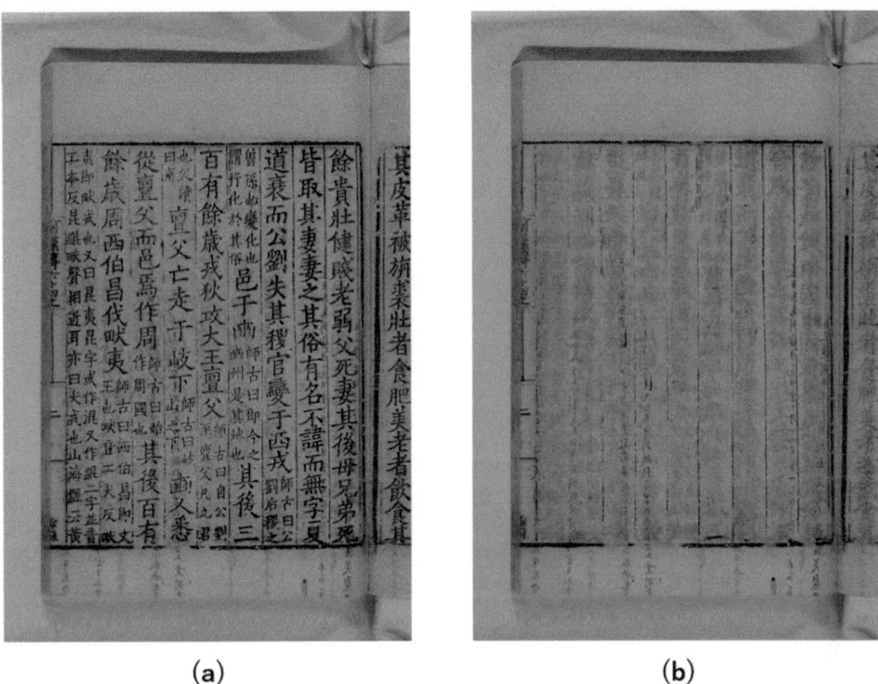

Fig. 8. Processing results for the entire image. (a) is the original image. (b) is the final output image.

6.3 Effectiveness of the Applied Inpainting Model

In this section, we conduct a quantitative evaluation of the effectiveness of the inpainting model applied in this study for restoring back side characters using image quality evaluation indices.

The evaluation uses 80 test images included in the Edge-Connect training dataset that were not used when training the model. Then, the inpainting process was performed on those images by with (Full model) and without (Inpainting only model) the Edge Generator in the first stage of the Edge-Connect, and the PSNR (Peak signal-to-noise ratio) and SSIM (Structural Similarity) between those results and the ground truth image were calculated and their averages were compared. The reason for using test images that simulate missing regions information instead of real images for evaluation, is that the ground truth of the back side characters does not exist in the real images due to the overlapping of characters.

Through this evaluation, we investigate whether the characteristic of Edge-Connect, inpainting through edge restoration of missing regions, is effective for the ancient documents targeted in this study, and demonstrate the validity of the applied method. Table 1 shows the average values of PSNR and SSIM calculated under each of the conditions described above.

Table 1. Quantitative evaluation results with 80 test images

Model	Full model	Inpainting only model
PSNR	**35.04**	34.35
SSIM	**0.949**	0.943

Table 1 shows that the Full model (with edge restoration) is superior in both indices calculated in this experiment, indicating that the inpainting model applied in this study is effective for restoring back side characters.

6.4 Extraction of Back Side Character Area

Finally, we conducted back side character region detection on the original image and the inpainted image using the model we constructed in our previous work on back side character segmentation [4], and compared the detected regions. Figure 9 shows the results.

In these images, the original images have adjacent characters on the front and back sides, and this has affected the segmentation result of the back side characters, which are partially missing. However, the inpainting process removes the influence of overlapping front side characters and restores the back side character information. This makes it possible to obtain previously undetectable character information in the segmentation result. These results indicate that the applied method improves the readability of the back side document area.

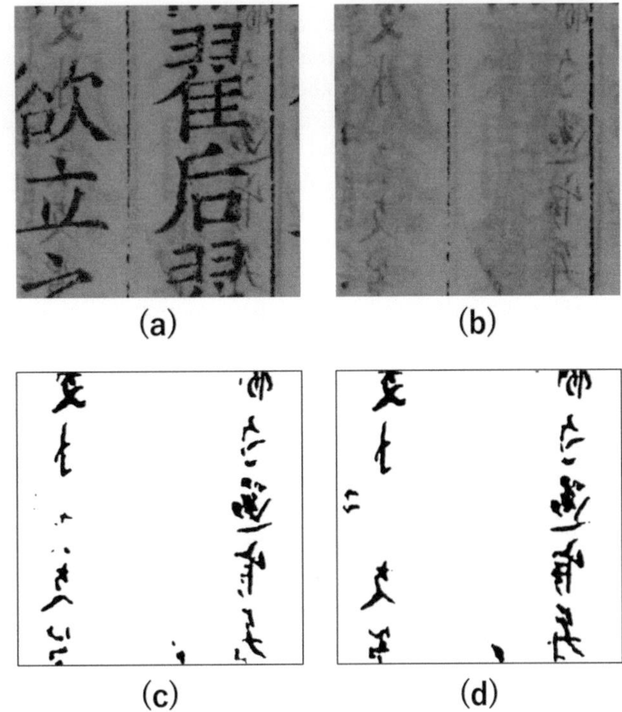

Fig. 9. Changes in back side character extraction results before and after applying inpainting process. (a) is the original image. (b) is the image after inpainting. (c) is the segmentation result of the original image. (d) is the segmentation result of the inpainted image.

Also Fig. 10 shows an image visualizing the difference in the detected area of the back side characters before and after the inpainting was applied.

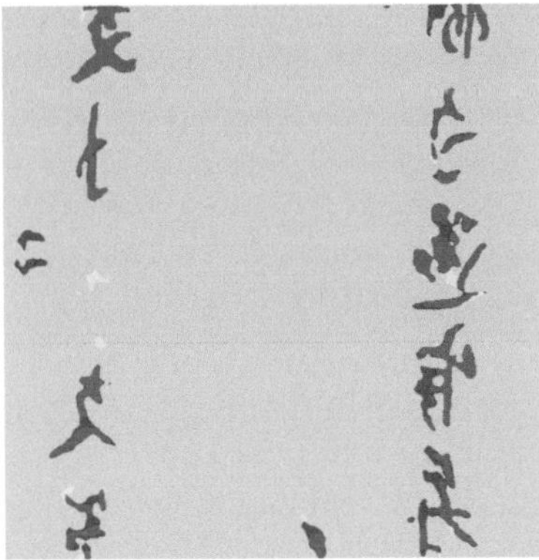

Fig. 10. Visualization of changes in back side character extraction results before and after inpainting process.

In the image shown in Fig. 10, the red regions indicate the areas that were determined to be back side characters both before and after the inpainting was applied, The blue regions indicate the areas that were determined to be the back side character areas only in the inpainted image, The yellow regions indicate the areas that were determined to be back side character areas only in the original image, And the green regions indicate the areas that were determined not to be back side character areas in both cases.

This figure visually represents that the application of the proposed method enables the detection of more back side character regions. However, in some cases, information of character regions that could be detected before inpainting was applied were lost (yellow areas in Fig. 10). This is thought to be due to the restored area is blurred when the character shading is large in the targeted missing regions, also the excessive masking of the back side character regions erases information that is necessary. Therefore, it is considered necessary to address this problem by eventually combining the character information present in the segmented images before and after processing without excess or deficiency.

7 Conclusion

In this study, we investigated an automatic image restoration system using Edge-Connect, a deep learning-based image inpainting model, to improve the readability of back side documents (called Shihai-monjo), which are missing in images captured from the top due to writing on both sides of the paper. As a result, the method was able to successfully restore the characters on the back side of the image when the overlapping area was small. However, there are still issues to be addressed, such as the accuracy of mask generation during processing and handling of cases in which the shaded area is large. Also, the segmentation of the restoration results increased the region of valid characters, suggesting the effectiveness of the method applied in this study.

Future work will include further expanding the dataset for both mask generation and inpainting processes to improve the accuracy of restoration, and evaluating the recognition rate of back side characters before and after processing using OCR (Optical Character Reader) to evaluate the effectiveness of the method.

References

1. Sato, S.: Shin-pan] komonjo-gaku nyumon [[New Edition] Introduction to Palaeography, pp. 26–27. Hosei University Press, Tokyo (1997)
2. Tarashima, S.: Quarry and rebirth of cultural assets information. J. Japan Soc. Inf. Knowl. **17**(4), 243–250 (2007)
3. Iikura, H.: Komonjo nyumon handbook [An Introductory Handbook to Ancient Documents], pp. 100–103. Yoshikawa Koubunkan, Tokyo (1993)
4. Izumi, H., Migita, M., Toda, M., Itoh, M.: Semantic Segmentation no tekiyou ni yoru komonjo gazou kara no shihai-monjo no chusyutu oyobi senmeika [Extraction and Sharpening of the "Shihai-monjo" from Ancient Document Images Using Semantic Segmentation]. In: Dynamic Image processing for real Application workshop 2024, pp. 218–222 (2024)
5. Shiono, K., Ohyama, W.: Image Completion for Missing Region of Mokkan Fragments by Deep Learning. In: Symposium on Humanities and Computers 2023, pp. 38–44 (2023)

6. Nazeri, K., Ng, E., Joseph, T., Qureshi, F, Z., Ebrahimi, M.: EdgeConnect: Generative Image Inpainting with Adversarial Edge Learning. https://arxiv.org/abs/1901.00212 (2019)
7. Otsu, N.: A Threshold Selection Method from Gray-Level Histograms. IEEE Trans. Syst. Man Cybern. **9**(1), 62–66 (1979)
8. Ronneberger, O., Fischer, P., Brox, T.: U-Net: Convolutional Networks for Biomedical Image Segmentation. https://arxiv.org/abs/1505.04597 (2015)
9. Goodfellow, I, J., Pouget-Abadie, J., Mirza, M., Xu, B., Warde-Farley, D., Ozair, S., Courville, A., Bengio, Y.: Generative Adversarial Nets. In: Advances in Neural Information Processing Systems 27, pp.2672–2680 (2014)
10. LabelMe. The Open annotation tool. http://labelme.csail.mit.edu/Release3.0/. Accessed 23 Dec 2024
11. Deng, J., Dong, W., Socher, R., Li, L., Li, K., Fei-Fei, L.: ImageNet: A large-scale hierarchical image database. In: 2009 Conference on Computer Vision and Pattern Recognition, pp.248–255 (2009)
12. Zhou, B., Lapedriza, A., Khosla, A., Oliva, A., Torralba, A.: Places: A 10 million Image Database for Scene Recognition. IEEE Transaction on Pattern Analysis and Machine Intelligence **40**(6), 1452–1464 (2018)

From Single to Unified Training: Evaluating Multi-organ Segmentation Techniques

Asad Imam(✉), Iftikhar Ahmad, Shahzad Ali, and Soon Ki Jung

School of Computer Science and Engineering, Kyungpook National University, Daegu, South Korea

{asadimam,iftikhar,shahzadali,skjung}@knu.ac.kr

Abstract. Expanding deep learning models to incorporate additional organ classes in medical image segmentation often requires costly retraining and significantly increases the risk of catastrophic forgetting of previously learned knowledge. Continual learning enables models to acquire new knowledge while retaining previously learned information progressively and has emerged as a promising solution to this challenge. In addition, to continual learning, another promising approach is multidata set training, which allows combining multiple organ classes from different datasets and training a deep learning model. This approach exposes the model to diverse datasets during training, significantly improving its ability to generalize to unseen data. The proposed study provides a detailed comparison of the three aforementioned approaches. We performed extensive experiments on two multi-organ segmentation datasets, FLARE22 and BTCV, to analyze the performance of each method. The multi-dataset training approach achieved an average Dice Similarity Score of 90.58% on FLARE22 and BTCV, outperforming the other two methods.

Keywords: Medical image segmentation · multi-dataset · multi-organ segmentation · Deep learning

1 Introduction

Medical image segmentation has become a crucial step in computer-aided diagnosis with the advancement in medical technology [1]. Segmentation on computed tomography (CT) images is an essential task in medical image analysis applications such as lesion detection, organ and tissue morphological analysis, disease prediction, and treatment planning. Manual interpretation and segmentation of medical images is time-consuming and expensive, requires a high level of expertise, and is prone to errors. Over the past few years, medical image segmentation has achieved significant progress due to convolutional neural networks (CNNs). U-Net [2] a convolution-based encoder-decoder architecture, is still considered one of the best networks for most medical image segmentation tasks. However, the success of medical image segmentation is highly dependent on the availability of large and diverse annotated medical image datasets [3].

The conventional training approach involves training a deep-learning network on a single dataset as shown in Fig. 1(a). The model trained on a single dataset often fails

B. Kim (Ed.): IW-FCV 2025, CCIS 2769, pp. 208–218, 2026.
https://doi.org/10.1007/978-981-95-4578-0_17

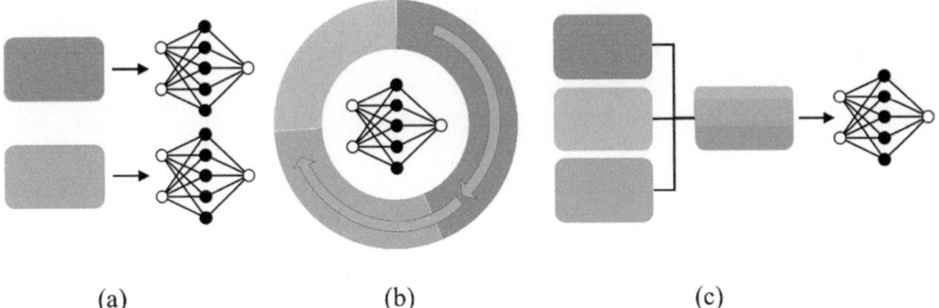

Fig. 1. Conventional, continual, and multi-dataset protocols for training and evaluating machine learning models. Each color represents a different dataset. a) The conventional training approach involves training separate models sequentially for different datasets. (b) Shows a continual learning approach where data from different datasets are added continuously. (c) Multi-dataset training approach leverages data from multiple datasets and combines it to train a single model.

to generalize well on unseen data due to differences in data distribution like imaging devices, protocols, and patient demographics. This approach works well on a single dataset, but it suffers from catastrophic forgetting [4]: the performance on a previously learned task or class in terms of multi-organ segmentation degrades as new tasks or classes are added. To mitigate the problem of catastrophic forgetting, the researcher introduced a new concept called continual learning [5]. Continual learning is also referred to as sequential learning [6], incremental learning [7], and, lifelong learning [8] This concept enables medical image segmentation models to learn from new data without forgetting the previously learned knowledge from previous data, as illustrated in 1(b). In a recent work, [5] the authors proposed continual learning for multi-organ and tumor segmentation. The proposed work introduced high-quality pseudo-labels to mitigate the catastrophic problem in multi-organ segmentation problems. To accommodate new classes, they replaced the conventional output layers with lightweight, class-specific heads to segment each class separately.

In another recent work [9], the authors introduced Lifelong nnU-Net, a continual learning approach for medical image segmentation based on the nnU-Net model. This medical image segmenter is well-equipped with all the necessary modules for sequential training and testing of data. With time, researchers continue to introduce and develop new techniques to address the limitations of existing methods, resulting in their eventual replacement as advancements are made. Continual learning emphasizes catastrophic forgetting but often at the expense of model adaptability and learning efficiency. Implementing knowledge preservation strategies in continual learning adds significant complexity to medical image segmentation tasks that are already resource intensive [10]. A new approach, multi-dataset training, has been introduced, enabling the training of a model on a dataset created by combining data from multiple datasets. This approach is illustrated in the 1(c).

To address the problems in continual learning, a new method is introduced called MultiTalent (MULTI daTAset LEarNing and pre-Training) [3]. In this approach, a single model is trained on multiple datasets and this model learns representations that generalize across datasets. This leads to improved performance across multiple datasets and minimizes redundancy by avoiding the need for various models. Among the previously mentioned techniques for medical image segmentation, multi-training strategies have proven to be resource-efficient while delivering better performance on medical image segmentation tasks. In this paper, we explore the above-mentioned training strategies for multi-organ segmentation tasks and perform extensive experiments to provide performance comparisons for each technique. The main contributions of this study are as follows:

- Performed extensive experiments on two publicly available datasets by training a model for the multi-organ segmentation task.
- Presented a detailed comparison of the multi-organ segmentation performance across conventional, continual, and multi-dataset training approaches.

The structure of this paper is as follows: Sect. 2 presents the related work to multi-organ segmentation, and Sect. 3 offers a comprehensive overview of the methodology proposed for this multi-dataset training approach. Section 4 provides a detailed explanation of the datasets, evaluation metrics, and experimental setup. Section 5 is dedicated to the results obtained and a concise discussion. Finally, the paper concludes with Sect. 6, where the conclusions are drawn.

2 Related Works

Multi-organ segmentation, particularly abdominal organ segmentation, has been extensively studied in the research community. Abdominal organ segmentation has attracted significant attention over the last decades [11]. Multi-organ segmentation has achieved excellent performance over the past few years due to the advancement in deep learning and medical imaging protocols. Abdominal multiorgan segmentation on CT (computed tomography) has been extensively explored using conventional, continuous, and multi-dataset training approaches. In this section, we will explore the work related to the mentioned approaches.

Conventional Method. Medical image segmentation has strong capabilities to learn image features in downstream tasks. Their outstanding performance is mainly contributed by extensive labeled data. Recently, they have achieved extraordinary performances and even outperformed human vision in medical imaging. U-Net [2] is one of the early works that introduced a Convolutional Neural Network (CNN) based encoder-decoder architecture for medical image segmentation. U-Net consists of an encoder that gradually down-samples and decoder which restores the original resolution and outputs the final segmentation mask. The input image. DoubleU-Net [12] is a combination of two U-Net architectures stacked on top of each other. A trained VGG-19 is used as the encoder, which has already learned features from ImageNet, and it can be transferred to another task easily. They trained and evaluated their model on four medical image datasets, covering various imaging modalities such as colonoscopy, dermoscopy, and microscopy. Their methods showed improved performance over the existing U-Net model. The conventional method has achieved state-of-the-art performance on most of the medical image tasks. However, there are certain limitations to single-dataset training strategies, such as being computationally expensive and high training inference time. To resolve these issues, the researchers proposed continual learning methods.

Continual Learning. Deep learning methods tend to forget the previously learned data when trained on new data. Continual learning enables the model to retain previously learned knowledge while training in new data classes. This approach has been applied to the abdominal multi-organ segmentation by [5] to segment the organs in the abdominal region. The proposed method is based on an encoder-decoder backbone, image-aware organ-specific heads, and text-driven head parameter generation. They trained and evaluated their proposed continual approach on three datasets: BTCV (Beyond the Cranial Vault) [13], LiTS (Liver Tumor Segmentation Benchmark) [14], and JHH (Johns Hopkins Hospital) [15]. In another method, the authors proposed a weakly-supervised paradigm for continual learning to extract useful features from noisy samples [16]. Similarly, [3] designed an algorithmic solution known as Batch-Level Distillation (BLD), a regularization-based continual learning approach to balance stability while learning from data streams.

Multi-dataset Approach. Deep neural networks heavily depend on large and diverse annotated datasets. Data annotation for medical image segmentation tasks is highly time-consuming, costly, and requires specialized expertise. Therefore, only a small number of samples are annotated by the experts. This results in partially labeled datasets: only a subset of the data samples is annotated or labeled, while the rest remain unlabeled. However, the small sizes and partially labeled nature of these datasets often limit the model to specific organs, ignoring the semantics of anatomical structures. To address these challenges, the CLIP-Driven Universal Model [17] leverages text embeddings from Contrastive Language-Image Pre-training (CLIP) to segment 6 types of tumors across 25 organs. Similarly, the authors of paper [18] proposed a "Multi-Decoder Network (MDNet)". This network employs a pre-trained MiT-B2 encoder connected to multiple decoders via multiscale feature enhancement dilated blocks. Each decoder progressively enhances the network's depth, refining segmentation masks by incorporating features from earlier decoders. In a recent work, the authors introduced MultiTalent (MULTI dataset learning and pre-Training) [3], a new and adaptable multi-dataset training framework. In this approach, a single model is trained on multiple datasets and this model learns representations that generalize across datasets.

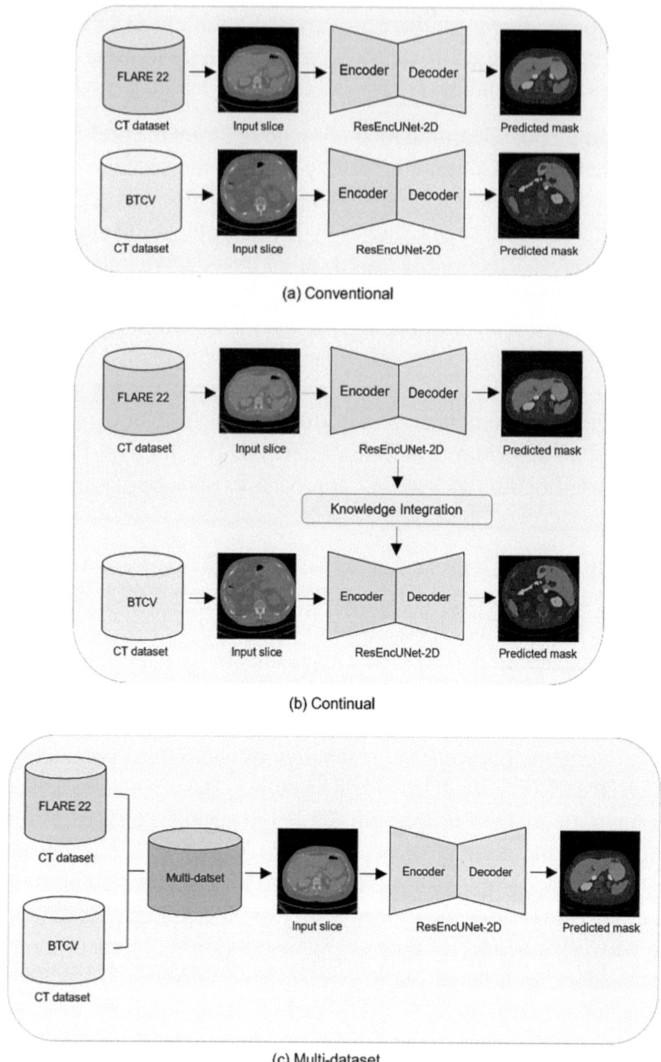

Fig. 2. An Overview of Training Scheme Comparison for multi-organ segmentation using ResUNet2D model: (a) Conventional training approach involves training the same model on different datasets individually. (b) Shows a continual learning approach where data from different datasets are added continuously to the model (c) multi-dataset training approach leverages data from multiple datasets and combines it to train the model.

3 Proposed Method

3.1 Model Architecture

The section briefly describes the methodology and model architecture for conventional training, continual learning, and a multi-dataset approach. The proposed training scheme for each approach is illustrated in 2. We adopted ResEncUNet3D [3] a Residual Encoder-Decoder architecture and modified it for use as ResEncUNet2D to perform slice-based segmentation, resulting in a network with 14.1 million parameters. This architecture leverages the ResNet [19] encoder and nn-UNet [20] decoder. We used ResEncUNet2D for all the there training schemes with modifications in the output layer.

Conventional Training Scheme. The conventional training approach involves standard supervising training, in which the model is trained on an individual dataset with multiple classes separately without any transfer of knowledge between the classes. This approach is also referred to as a one-by-one training scheme. In our method, we first trained the ResEncUNet2D model on the BTCV dataset's training data, evaluated it on the test dataset, and obtained the results. For the FLARE22 dataset, we adopted a similar methodology but trained a new ResEncUNet2D model from scratch. Figure 2 (a) shows the conventional training scheme.

While this training scheme is effective for handling individual datasets, it has certain limitations. The main challenge is the lack of shared knowledge, which prevents the model from leveraging shared features across the datasets.

Continual Training Scheme Continual training helps an already trained deep learning network to learn new classes without forgetting the knowledge it has previously learned. It adds progressively new classes to the model while retaining the old ones. We performed continual learning in two steps: first, we trained the model on all classes from the FLARE22 dataset. In the second step, we used the same trained model to add the classes from the BTCV dataset without forgetting the previous classes. The model uses the previously learned knowledge during the first training stage and segments the classes of the second dataset.

Multi-dataset Training Scheme Figure 2 (b) shows the multi-dataset training approach for multi-organ segmentation. We created a multi-dataset by combining 13 and 14 organ classes from the FLARE22 and BTCV datasets respectively. The FLARE22 and BTCV consist of 3D volumes and corresponding labels for abdominal organ segmentation. So, in total 27 organ classes will be segmented in this approach. We trained the ResUNet2D model, an encoder-decoder-based network, using the CT slices from the multi-dataset. We evaluated our framework on the test data from both datasets and obtained better segmentation results than conventional and continual training approaches.

4 Experiments

4.1 Datasets

We conducted our experiments on two publicly available datasets. The FLARE22 dataset [21], presented in the MICCAI grand challenge. We used 50 diverse abdominal CT scans with annotations for 13 organ classes for our experiment. Additionally, we used the BTCV (Beyond the Cranial Vault) dataset [22], which consists of 30 annotated abdominal CT scans covering 14 organ classes. We extracted the 2D slices from the CT volumes and downsampled the slices to 256 × 256 using bilinear interpolation. For the multi-dataset training, we merged the 2D slices with FLARE22 and BTCV to form a unified dataset. This was accomplished by sampling each case with a probability that is inversely proportional to $\sqrt{n}$, where n represents the number of training slices in the source dataset [3]. This approach helps balance the representation of data from different sources, ensuring fair and effective model training.

4.2 Loss Function

In our work, we used the combination of binary cross entropy loss $\mathcal{L}_{bce}$ and Dice similarity loss $\mathcal{L}_{dsc}$. The total segmentation loss $\mathcal{L}_{seg}$ was calculated as:

$$\mathcal{L}_{seg} = \lambda_1 \mathcal{L}_{BCE} + \lambda_2 \mathcal{L}_{dsc},$$
$$\mathcal{L}_{dsc} = 1 - 2\frac{\sum_i t_i p_i}{\sum_i t_i \sum_i p_i},$$
$$\mathcal{L}_{bce} = -\sum_i (t_i \ln(p_i) + (1 - t_i)\ln(1 - p_i)),$$

where t_i represents the ground truth label, p_i is the predicted probability, and λ_1 and λ_2 are the weights balancing parameters.

4.3 Evaluation Metrics

In this work, we compared the performance comparison of three training schemes on the abdominal organ segmentation task. We used two diverse and challenging datasets, FLARE22 and BTCV for this task. For the comparison of the target mask against the segmentation mask we used the Dice Similarity Coefficient (DSC) metric which is given as

$$\text{DSC} = \frac{2\,TP}{2\,TP + FP + FN},$$

The Dice Similarity Coefficient (DSC) is the common metric used for the model evaluation of segmentation tasks. DSC gives an insight into how well the model performs for each anatomical structure, especially on smaller or complex organs that pose segmentation challenges.

4.4 Implementation Details

We performed all of our experiments on NVIDIA TITAN XP GPU, with 12 GB of memory with i7 -9th gen CPU and 32 Gb of RAM. We used an input size of 256 × 256 pixels during the training of each model. During training, the network was trained for 100 epochs with a constant batch size of 4. Adam optimizer [23] was used to update the network parameters. Py-Torch [24] framework was employed for all experiments.

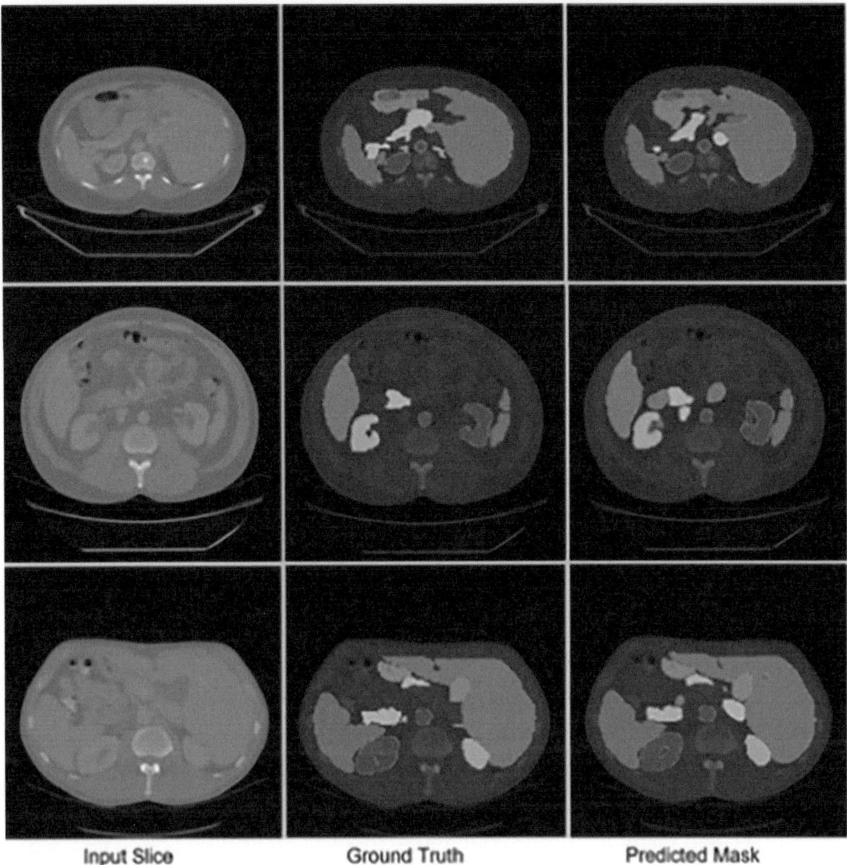

Fig. 3: Qualitative results for the abdominal organ segmentation: Input slices from FLARE22 and BTCV datasets (left column) with corresponding target masks (middle column) and predicted masks for multi-dataset training approach (end column).

Table 1. Performance evaluation, measured in % terms, of the three training schemes: Multi-Dataset, Continual, and Conventional approaches on FLARE22 and BTCV datasets across different organs. The multi-dataset training approach obtained better results across the three training schemes.

Organs	Conventional	Conventional	Continual	Multi-Dataset
	FLARE22	BTCV	FLARE22/BTCV	FLARE22/BTCV
Liver	94.94	89.91	87.44	93.54
Right Kidney	93.49	88.23	84.77	96.58
Spleen	92.97	89.23	92.97	95.06
Pancreas	79.74	81.09	76.22	88.09

(continued)

Table 1. (*continued*)

Organs	Conventional	Conventional	Continual	Multi-Dataset
Aorta	95.45	95.30	92.23	95.12
IVC	92.61	91.00	87.44	90.32
RAG	78.34	64.25	84.06	83.46
LAG	77.21	63.75	89.71	79.70
Gallbladder	86.02	68.68	86.02	94.43
Esophagus	88.08	79.56	73.19	93.62
Stomach	91.13	80.60	95.33	91.58
Duodenum	80.54	63.72	84.06	87.58
Left Kidney	93.26	89.82	89.71	95.04
Portal Vein	-	69.20	88.46	84.03
Average	87.98	79.59	86.54	**90.58**

5 Results

The Table 1 shows a performance comparison of the three training methods. The multi-dataset training approach outperformed the conventional and continual training schemes on FLARE22 and BTCV datasets for the multi-organ segmentation task. The multi-dataset training approach achieves an average score of 90.58 as shown in 1 on both FLARE22 and BTCV datasets. Hence, it proves that the multi-dataset training is better than the other two methods for the abdominal organ segmentation task. The continual learning performed better than the conventional training scheme. However, it still suffers from catastrophic forgetting when the model is re-trained for the new class. This limitation impacts its ability to retain previously learned information effectively, making it less optimal than the multi-dataset training method. In contrast, the multi-dataset approach addresses these challenges by integrating data from multiple sources, allowing the model to learn more generalizable features. The enhanced performance underscores its suitability for complex medical imaging tasks, where accurate and consistent segmentation across various organs is critical.

The qualitative results for the multi-dataset training are shown in Fig. 3. The figure shows the input slice which is fed to the model to get the prediction. We reported slices with the maximum number of abdominal organs. The model trained using the multi-dataset approach demonstrates better generalizability compared to both conventional and continual learning approaches.

6 Conclusion

In this research, we explored three different training schemes for multi-organ segmentation in medical imaging. We conducted a comprehensive study to evaluate their impact on the performance of a segmentation model on the abdominal organ segmentation task.

Through multiple experiments, we concluded that multi-dataset training performs the best for specific datasets. The multi-dataset approach enables the model to perform well across a variety of classes by combining multiple distinct datasets with diverse class distributions into a single dataset. Continual learning performs better in scenarios where new classes need to be sequentially added to an already trained model, and it performs better than conventional training methods. For future work, the comparison can be extended to include more organs for segmentation.

Acknowledgements. This work was supported by the National Research Foundation of Korea (NRF) grant funded by the Korean government (MSIT) (RS-2024–00360226) and also supported by the MSIT (Ministry of Science and ICT), Korea, under the ITRC (Information Technology Research Center) support program (IITP-2024-RS-2024–00437718) supervised by the IITP (Institute for Information & Communications Technology Planning & Evaluation).

References

1. Aljundi, R., Rohrbach, M., Tuytelaars, T.: Selfless sequential learning. arXiv preprint arXiv:1806.05421 (2018)
2. Antonelli, M., et al.: The medical segmentation decathlon. Nat. Commun. **13**, 4128 (2022)
3. Bilic, P., et al.: The liver tumor segmentation benchmark (lits). Med. Image Anal. **84**, 102680 (2023)
4. Chaudhry, A., Dokania, P.K., Ajanthan, T., Torr, P.H.: Riemannian Walk for incremental learning: Understanding forgetting and intransigence. In: Proceedings of the European Conference on Computer Vision (ECCV), pp. 532–547 (2018)
5. Chen, Z., Liu, B.: Lifelong machine learning. Morgan & Claypool Publishers (2018)
6. French, R.M.: Catastrophic forgetting in connectionist networks. Trends Cogn. Sci. **3**, 128–135 (1999)
7. Gibson, E., et al.: Automatic multi-organ segmentation on abdominal CT with dense v-networks. IEEE Trans. Med. Imaging **37**, 1822–1834 (2018)
8. Gonzalez, C., Lemke, N., Sakas, G., Mukhopadhyay, A.: What is wrong with continual learning in medical image segmentation? arXiv preprint arXiv:2010.11008. (2020)
9. González, C., Ranem, A., Pinto dos Santos, D., Othman, A., Mukhopadhyay, A.: Lifelong nnU-net: a framework for standardized medical continual learning. Sci. Rep. **13**, 9381 (2023)
10. He, K., Zhang, X., Ren, S., Sun, J.: Deep residual learning for image recognition. In: Proceedings of the IEEE Conference on Computer Vision and Pattern Recognition, pp. 770–778 (2016)
11. Isensee, F., et al.: Nnu-net: self-adapting framework for u-net-based medical image segmentation. arXiv preprint arXiv:1809.10486 (2018)
12. Jha, D., Riegler, M.A., Johansen, D., Halvorsen, P., Johansen, H.D.: Doubleu-net: a deep convolutional neural network for medical image segmentation. In: 2020 IEEE 33rd International Symposium on Computer-Based Medical Systems (CBMS), pp. 558–564. IEEE (2020)
13. Jha, D., et al.: MDNet: multi-decoder network for abdominal CT organs segmentation. arXiv preprint arXiv:2405.06166. (2024)
14. Kingma, D.P.: Adam: a method for stochastic optimization. arXiv preprint arXiv:1412.6980. (2014)
15. Landman, B., Xu, Z., Igelsias, J., Styner, M., Langerak, T., Klein, A.: Miccai multi-atlas labeling beyond the cranial vault–workshop and challenge. In: Proceedings of MICCAI Multi-atlas Labeling Beyond Cranial Vault—Workshop Challenge, p. 12 (2015)

16. Liao, M., Tang, H., Li, X., Vijayakumar, P., Arya, V., Gupta, B.B.: A lightweight network for abdominal multi-organ segmentation based on multi-scale context fusion and dual self-attention. Inf. Fusion **108**, 102401 (2024)
17. Liu, J., et al.: Clip-driven universal model for organ segmentation and tumor detection. In: Proceedings of the IEEE/CVF International Conference on Computer Vision, pp. 21152–21164 (2023)
18. Ma, J., et al.: Abdomenct-1k: is abdominal organ segmentation a solved problem? IEEE Trans. Pattern Anal. Mach. Intell. **44**, 6695–6714 (2021)
19. Maracani, A., Michieli, U., Toldo, M., Zanuttigh, P.: Recall: replay-based continual learning in semantic segmentation. In: Proceedings of the IEEE/CVF International Conference on Computer Vision, pp. 7026–7035 (2021)
20. Paszke, A., et al.: Pytorch: an imperative style, high-performance deep learning library. Adv. Neural Inf. Process. Syst. **32** (2019)
21. Ranneberger, O., Fischer, P., Brox, T.: U-net: convolutional networks for biomedical image segmentation. In: Medical image computing and computer-assisted intervention–MICCAI 2015: 18th International Conference, Munich, Germany, 5–9 October 2015, Proceedings, part III 18, pp. 234–241. Springer, Heidelberg (2015)
22. Ulrich, C., Isensee, F., Wald, T., Zenk, M., Baumgartner, M., Maier-Hein, K.H.: Multitalent: a multi-dataset approach to medical image segmentation. In: International Conference on Medical Image Computing and Computer-Assisted Intervention, pp. 648–658. Springer, Heidelberg (2023)
23. Xia, Y., et al.: The felix project: Deep networks to detect pancreatic neoplasms. medRxiv. 2022–09 (2022)
24. Zhang, Y., Li, X., Chen, H., Yuille, A.L., Liu, Y., Zhou, Z.: Continual learning for abdominal multi-organ and tumor segmentation. In: International Conference on Medical Image Computing and Computer-Assisted Intervention, pp. 35–45. Springer, Heidelberg (2023)

Occlusion Robust 2D Pose-Based Gait Recognition

Takeshi Konno(✉), Shuji Awai, and Takahiro Yoshioka

Fujitsu Limited, 1-1, Kamikodanaka 4-chome, Nakahara-ku, Kawasaki, Japan
{konno.takeshi,awai.shuji,y.takahiro}@fujitsu.com

Abstract. In Japan, the number of elderly people who go missing has been increasing year by year. A delay in finding a missing person can lead to death. However, there are limits to the early detection that can be achieved through search efforts conducted by volunteers using visual observation. Therefore, there is hope that a method that utilizes information from security cameras and person matching technology can be used to track the whereabouts of missing persons and help with the early detection. In recent years, there has also been interest in person matching technology that utilizes 2D pose estimation. However, there is a problem that the person matching accuracy decreases due to the decrease in the pose estimation accuracy caused by the blocking of body parts due to the shooting angle of the security camera or the person's clothes. This paper proposes a method to improve the person matching accuracy by focusing on the parts that are susceptible to a decrease in pose estimation accuracy and by masking the pose estimation information. As a result of the evaluation, the average accuracy rate improved by 3.7% with the proposed method compared to the case without masking. In the future, this technology will facilitate the early discovery of missing persons and contribute to the creation of a society where the elderly can live safely and securely.

Keywords: Gait Recognition · 2D Pose Estimation · Occlusion

1 Introduction

1.1 Social Background

According to a report by the Cabinet Office, as of October 1, 2023, the total population of Japan was 124.35 million. The population aged 65 and over was 36.23 million, and the proportion of this group to the total population (i.e., the aging rate) was 29.1%, the highest in the world [1]. According to a report by the National Police Agency, the number of people with dementia who went missing in 2023 was 19,039 (21.1% of the total), an increase of 330 people over the previous year, the highest number on record (Fig. 1). In addition, the number of people with dementia who went missing in 2012 was 9,607, but in just over 10 years, this number has doubled [2].

The definition and causes of elderly people wandering off are as follows. At first glance, wandering off seems to be aimless wandering around, but this is not necessarily

B. Kim (Ed.): IW-FCV 2025, CCIS 2769, pp. 219–231, 2026.
https://doi.org/10.1007/978-981-95-4578-0_18

the case for dementia patients. Wandering behavior often has a clear sense of purpose, such as "going home" or "going to work", but due to a decline in cognitive function, the person may forget the purpose at the point of departure or may be unable to follow the route to the destination. As a result, they become lost and wander around without being able to achieve their original goal, and this is observed as the behavior of "wandering". In other words, *wandering* is a secondary behavior that occurs as a result of cognitive impairment preventing the achievement of goals, and it does not occur independently of the patient's own intentions or will. Memory impairment and disorientation are said to be important factors that cause wandering. Memory impairment, particularly episodic memory (i.e., memory of past experiences) and semantic memory (i.e., memory of general knowledge), is a major factor in causing wandering behavior. Episodic memory impairment can cause people to forget their original destination or route. For example, if a person goes out with the intention of "going shopping", they may forget their original destination and become unable to find their way home. Semantic memory impairment can prevent people from correctly recognizing their surroundings, creating situations where they are likely to become lost. Furthermore, short-term memory impairment can cause a person to lose the ability to retain recent actions and information, which can lead to panic and induce wandering behavior. Behaviors like searching around the house for the toilet are often observed as precursors to wandering and suggest a decline in spatial cognitive ability. Disorientation, particularly spatial disorientation, is strongly associated with wandering. As a person is unable to recognize the location of their home, directions, and surrounding landmarks, they more likely to become lost and wander for longer periods of time. Disorientation in time is a factor that keeps them wandering because they lose track of the time they have been out and the time that has passed, and they do not know when to go home. These disorders are closely related to a dysfunction of the parietal and frontal lobes. One type of disorientation is the "dusk syndrome", which is a type of wandering that is time-of-day specific. When dusk falls, patients experiencing this syndrome suddenly become restless and may behave or wander in a way that is different from usual.

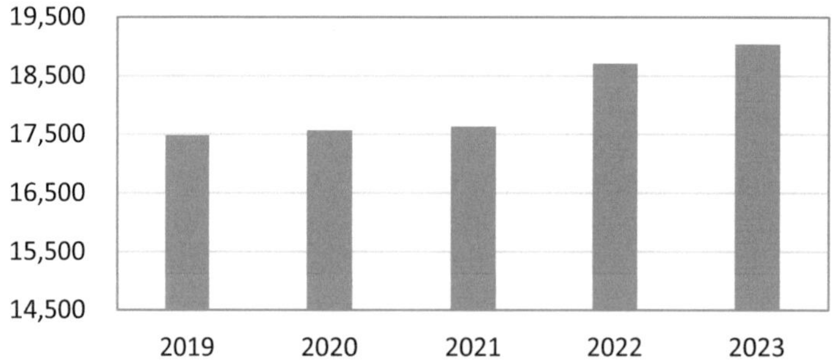

Fig. 1. The number of people with dementia who went missing.

When dealing with elderly people who wander off, it is said that the rate of discovery decreases significantly after 9 h, and the mortality rate increases by about 37% after a day has passed and further increases after 2 to 3 days [3]. In addition, the causes of death are often senility and hypothermia. It has been reported that more than 40% of people who drown die on the day of the incident, and that people who suffer hypothermia die on the third or fourth day (Table 1).

Table 1. Missing persons reported and confirmed.

Category	Same day	2–3 days	4–7 days	8–14 days
Total	13,698	4,700	203	74
Location confirmed	13,517	4,471	131	33
Confirmed deaths	118	192	68	37
Mortality rate	0.9%	4%	33%	50%

Measures to prevent elderly people from wandering off are being taken both outdoors and indoors, but there are limits to their effectiveness. Outdoors, there are methods for obtaining location information using GPS devices that can be placed in smartphones or shoes. However, there are cases where the GPS battery runs out or the device is not carried around. Indoors, sensor mats and door/motion sensors are often used. However, although it is possible to tell when a person has passed through, it is not possible to tell when they have gone outside. In Japan, the police and local governments are working together to find missing people as quickly as possible through the SOS Network, a network for monitoring the whereabouts of elderly people. Those who wish to do so can register the characteristics of the elderly person in advance (e.g., height, weight, build, and hairstyle). However, because the search is carried out by volunteers visually, it takes an average of 15.8 h to find the person, and there are limits to finding them within 9 h.

The objective of this study is to develop an early detection system for missing persons by automatically mapping their whereabouts on a map using information from security cameras and person identification technology and notifying the police and volunteers (Fig. 2). In this early detection system, first, images of the elderly taken with a smartphone are registered. Next, when the police contact you because an elderly person has gone missing, images from security cameras are collected and compared with the registered images to identify the person. The results of the person identification are displayed on a map and provided to the police and volunteers. This helps to detect elderly people who have gone missing early.

Fig. 2. System overview

1.2 Gait Recognition

In some cases, biometric technology is used to identify individuals by measuring their unique physical characteristics and comparing them with information registered in a database. There are two types of biometrics: 1) static biometrics (e.g., fingerprints, irises, blood vessels, and faces) that do not change over time and 2) dynamic biometrics (e.g., gait, voice, and handwriting) that do change over time. However, because the physical characteristics can vary depending on the surrounding environment and conditions when they are read by sensors, even with static biometrics, it is not always possible to achieve 100% accuracy. In addition, because dynamic biometrics involves changes in characteristics, the accuracy of identification is generally lower than with static biometrics.

The authors of this paper focused on a method of identifying people by extracting the characteristics of their gait, even when the person is far away and visible only on a security camera. Gait analysis has a long history, and in 1984, the first biometric gait recognition using camera images was introduced. Gait has been used as forensic evidence in court. In particular, in the case of a robbery that occurred in London in 2000, Hadyn Kelly was the first person to give expert testimony in court on the analysis of walking patterns [4]. In 2002, the Defense Advanced Research Projects Agency released HumanID, a large-scale dataset consisting of approximately 300 GB of data related to 452 sequences from 74 subjects, and this promoted research into gait recognition [5]. In October 2008, gait recognition was used as criminal evidence for the first time in the United Kingdom by Professor Mark Nixon of Southampton University [6]. In February 2009, gait recognition technology developed by Osaka University was used for the first time in Japan in a criminal investigation. Research into deep-learning-based gait recognition began in 2015.

There are two approaches to gait recognition: one that utilizes silhouette-type gait features and another that utilizes pose-estimation-type gait features.

The basic process of silhouette-based gait recognition consists of generating a sequence of person silhouette images from the walking video, converting them into normalized silhouette images, detecting the walking cycle, and extracting the gait features. Gait Energy Image (GEI) is a feature extracted as an average image over one gait cycle, obtained from a sequence of silhouette images extracted from a person's walking video, after size normalization and alignment. This image clearly reflects the magnitude of relative movement with respect to the torso. Frequency domain features (FDF) is a feature composed of three-channel images. The left channel is the GEI, the center channel represents the asymmetric component appearing once per gait cycle, and the right channel represents the symmetric component appearing twice per gait cycle. Gait Entropy Image (GEnI) is calculated by calculating the Shannon entropy for all pixels in the gait cycle. Even in situations where obtaining background differences for silhouette generation is difficult, the Intersection over Union (IoU), an indicator of the overlap between two areas, is 77.2%. However, the matching accuracy is less than 75% for the top 20 silhouettes. There are also reports that the speed of silhouette extraction takes an average of 15,567 ms per image, which is equivalent to 15 s [7]. In other words, it would take almost 40 min to extract the silhouettes of a 5-s video at 30 fps; therefore, it is not suitable for processing large amounts of video footage in real time.

For pose-based gait recognition, a pose estimation method that can extract person silhouettes at high speed and high accuracy has been proposed. Also known as a model-based approach, this method extracts detailed biomechanical parameters, such as joint angles and trunk movements, and uses these as feature values to identify people. Previously, Wang et al. [8] proposed a gait recognition method that used a motion model composed of 14 rigid body parts (e.g., head, neck, chest, abdomen, left and right upper arms, left and right lower arms, left and right thighs, left and right lower legs, left and right feet). There have also been other proposals, such as KinectGaitNet [9], which is a method based on 3D coordinate data using Kinect. In recent years, with the progress of 2D pose estimation technology, model-based approaches using pose estimation information have attracted attention. Since 2020, many gait recognition methods have been proposed using high-precision pose estimation models developed using deep learning. Typical methods include PoseGait [10], which combines 2D pose estimation and convolutional neural networks (CNN); GaitMixer [11] and GaitGraph [12], which combine 2D pose estimation information and graph convolutional networks; GaitFormer [13], a hybrid method that combines CNN and vision transformer (ViT); and Gait-D [14], which combines 2D pose estimation information and silhouette information. These methods each employ different architectures and feature extraction methods. HRNet [15], a 2D pose estimation model with higher accuracy than OpenPose, which was released in 2019, is used in many gait recognition studies. The biggest advantage of using 2D pose estimation is that it does not require complex preprocessing, such as silhouette extraction using background difference, as in conventional methods. This simplicity and high accuracy make it suitable for application to real-world data, such as security camera footage, and this study adopts a model-based approach, particularly a method based on 2D pose estimation.

In this paper, there is a problem where the person matching accuracy decreases due to a decline in pose estimation accuracy because the body parts are blocked by the shooting angle of the security camera or clothing. The proposed method aims to improve the person matching accuracy by focusing on body parts that are susceptible to a decrease in pose estimation accuracy and by masking the pose estimation information.

2 Occlusion Robust Gait Recognition Method

2.1 Conventional Method

In previous evaluation using CASIA-B [16], the conventional method GaitMixer had higher accuracy than GaitGraph in the pose estimation matching of gait features, and it was the most accurate algorithm at the time of evaluation. Therefore, this study will adopt GaitMixer, since it has almost the same accuracy as GaitPart [17], which is an appearance-based gait matching algorithm.

GaitMixer is a novel skeleton-based gait recognition model employing a heterogeneous multi-axial mixer architecture. This architecture comprises a spatial self-attention mixer, learning inter-joint interactions within each frame by capturing relationships between joints (spatial tokens) using self-attention mechanisms, thus effectively learning both high and low-frequency spatial features. Furthermore, a temporal large-kernel convolution mixer models interactions between temporal tokens (joint positions at different time indices) of each joint, utilizing large-kernel depthwise separable convolutions to capture short-term and long-term repetitive patterns (mid-frequency features) in the walking sequence. This dual approach enables robust gait representation learning, overcoming limitations of previous methods that struggled with variations in clothing or carrying objects. Given HRNet's demonstrated ability to generate the high-resolution representations critical for accurate joint localization, as shown in the GaitMixer paper's implementation and evaluation, and its significant impact on performance, this study also adopts HRNet for pose estimation.

The input is the pose estimation information of the human time series estimated by HRNet, and the output is a 128-dimensional feature quantity. The pose estimation information uses the 17-point 2D coordinates of the joints of the human body, as shown in Fig. 3.

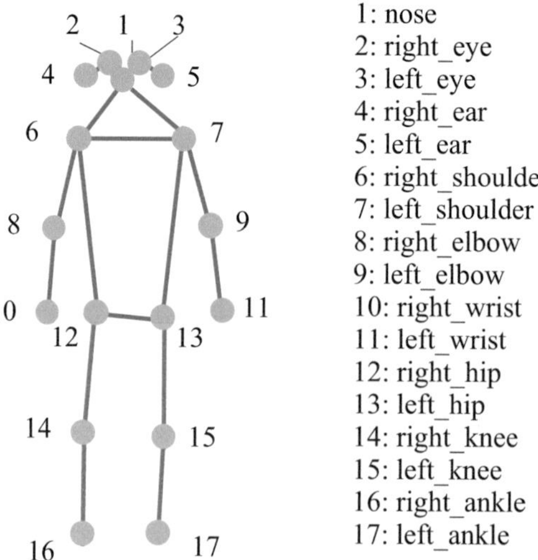

Fig. 3. Pose estimation information on HRNet

2.2 Proposed Method

Taking into account the problem of the pose estimation accuracy decreasing due to the occlusion of body parts because of the shooting angle of the security camera or the person's clothing, the proposed method focused on the parts of the body that are likely to be occluded when walking. Specifically, the information of the arms, which are prone to occlusion when extracting gait features, was masked to extract gait features that are less susceptible to the effects of differences in clothing.

This study masks only right_elbow and right_wrist, which are prone to occlusion, as right-side arm information. While details are provided in Sect. 3.1, the dataset used for training and evaluation in this study consists of videos of subjects walking from right to left. The right hand, positioned further away from the camera, is frequently occluded by the body during walking, leading to an anticipated decrease in the reliability of skeletal position estimation. Conversely, the left hand, being closest to the camera and clearly visible, is considered crucial for representing temporal repetitions in GaitMixer and is therefore retained. Right_ear, right_shoulder, and right_hip, while potentially obscured like the right arm, were not excluded due to their empirically observed lack of significant cyclical changes during walking and their importance in representing the torso.

The processing flow is shown in Fig. 4. First, pose estimation was performed on the input video of the person, and the pose estimation information was obtained in chronological order. The HRNet method was used to obtain the 17 two-dimensional coordinates of the joints of the person. Next, the gait features were extracted from the model that has been trained on the gait features, except for the right_elbow and right_wrist arm joints, using the time-series pose estimation information as input. The degree of agreement was calculated using the cosine similarity from the obtained gait features. The model for learning the gait features is a model that can accept input excluding the arm joints, which is defined based on the conventional method.

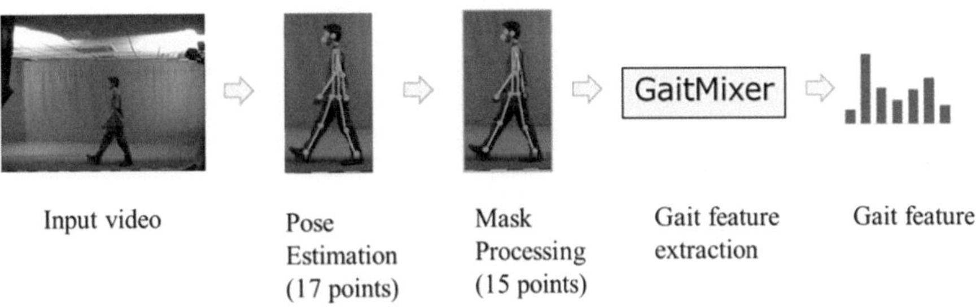

Fig. 4. Processing flow

3 Experiment

3.1 Dataset

The CASIA-B dataset was used for learning the gait features, and it is one of the widely used datasets in gait-related research. It contains images of 124 subjects walking, captured from 11 different angles, and includes patterns of subjects carrying bags and wearing coats. For training, 74 subjects were used. CASIA-B has a resolution of 320 × 240 pixels and a frame rate of 25 fps.

The Southampton Human ID (HID) database (hereafter, Southampton) was used as the evaluation dataset. This dataset is available in large [18] and small [19] versions. The small version contains 15 patterns of different clothing and walking speeds, with 11 subjects walking in front of a camera from four different angles, and it includes 15 patterns, such as differences in clothing and walking speed. The large dataset includes video footage of 116 subjects walking with a four-angle camera and of them walking on a treadmill with a two-angle camera. For the evaluation of the same attire condition, images of 115 people (excluding 1 person) in Normal attire in the Large dataset walked 2 times at the same angle. Using the walking video of the normal dress as a query, the similarity with all the walking video of the normal dress was calculated. If the ID of the video with the highest similarity matches the ID of the query, the correct answer is assumed. In the evaluation of the dress difference condition, the video of the Raincoat dress (walking 8 times at the same angle) was used. Using the walking video of the Normal outfit as a query, we calculated the similarity with all the walking videos of the Raincoat outfit in the Small dataset. If the ID of the video with the highest similarity matches the ID of the query, the correct answer is assumed. The video sample used for the evaluation is shown in Fig. 5. The walking direction was from right to left on the screen. The resolution of Southampton is 720 × 576 pixels, and the frame rate is 25 FPS.

Fig. 5. Clothing patterns

4 Results

The evaluation results for the conventional method and the proposed method under the two clothing conditions are shown in Table 2. In both conditions, the average accuracy rate was improved by the proposed method. As a result of the evaluation, the average accuracy rate was improved by 3.7% with the proposed method compared to the case without a mask.

Table 2. Results of Collation Accuracy (%)

Method	Condition	Accuracy
GaitMixer	Normal × Normal	82.6
Proposed		**87.8**
GaitMixer	Normal × Raincoat	89.8
Proposed		**92.0**

5 Discussion

5.1 Normal × Normal

The mean, max (average of the top 5), and min (average of the bottom 5) of the confidence score for each part obtained from HRNet are shown in Fig. 6. The variance (var) is shown in Fig. 7. In standard clothing, the variance of the confidence scores for right_elbow and right_wrist is high. This means that occlusion is likely to occur because the right arm is hidden by the body when walking. As a result, masking this feature resulted in improved accuracy compared to the conventional method.

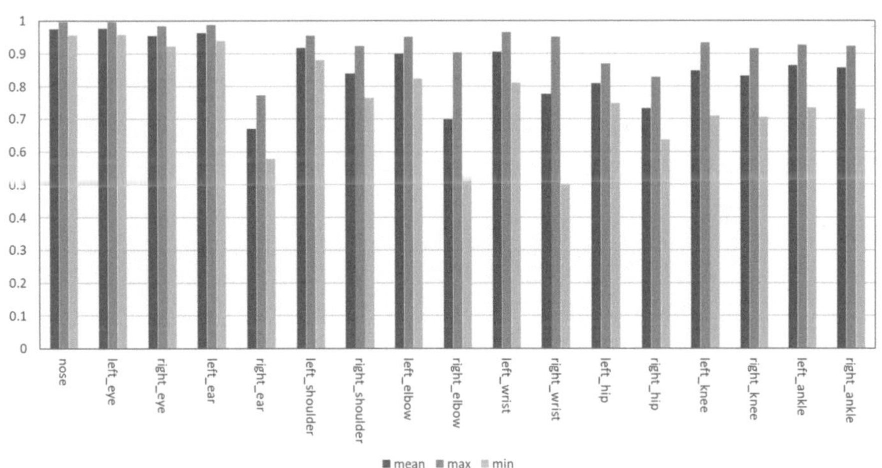

Fig. 6. Confidence scores (mean, max, min)

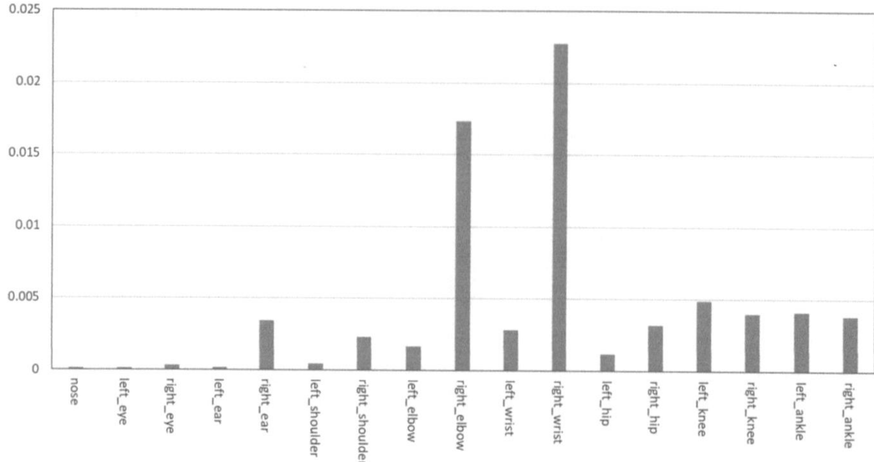

Fig. 7. Variance of confidence scores

5.2 Normal × Raincoat

The mean, max (average of the top 5), and min (average of the bottom 5) of the confidence score for each part obtained from HRNet are shown in Fig. 8. The variance (var) is shown in Fig. 9. As with the standard clothing, the variance of the confidence scores for right_elbow and right_wrist is high for the raincoat. By masking this feature, the authors were able to improve the accuracy over the previous method.

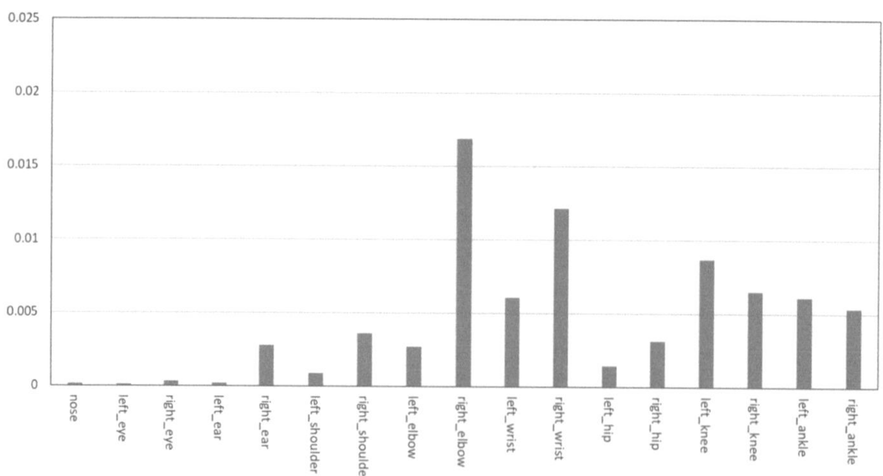

Fig. 8. Variance of confidence scores (raincoat condition)

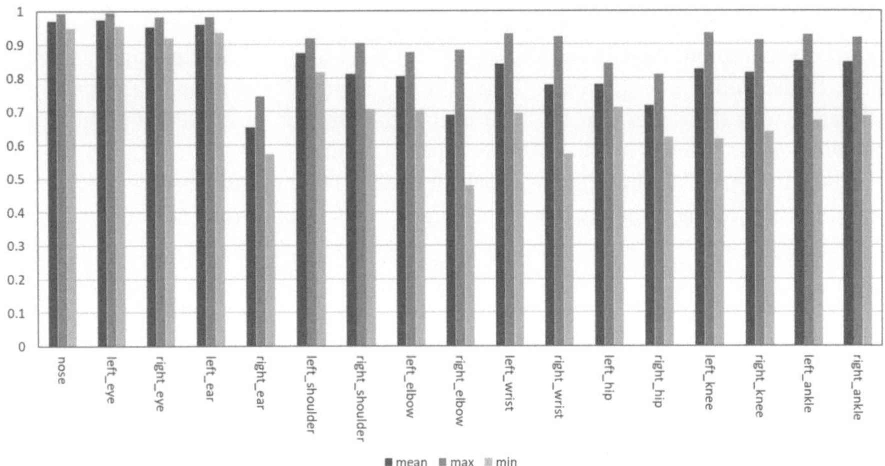

Fig. 9. Confidence scores (mean, max, min) (raincoat condition)

5.3 Other Right-Side Parts

Further investigation into other right-side body parts, as discussed in Sect. 2.2, is warranted. For Normal × Normal, while the confidence scores for right_shoulder and right_hip are lower than those on the left side, they are comparable to left_hip score. Right_ear consistently exhibits low confidence scores due to near-constant occlusion. However, the variance of right_ear, right_shoulder, and right_hip is considerably smaller than that of right_elbow and right_wrist. Since the proposed method using 15 keypoints outperforms GaitMixer using all 17 keypoints in gait recognition accuracy, we hypothesize that high variance in confidence scores contributes more to accuracy degradation than low confidence scores themselves.

For Normal × Raincoat, the relationship between confidence scores and their variance for other right-side body parts is largely consistent with the findings in Sect. 5.1. Even with raincoat occlusion, the high variance in confidence scores likely contributed more to accuracy degradation than low confidence scores themselves.

Under both conditions, the variance in confidence scores for the crossing legs during walk was relatively high compared to other body parts. However, the confidence scores themselves remained relatively high, exceeding 0.6 even with raincoats. The confidence scores showed little difference between the left and right legs. While these keypoints, considered most influential for gait recognition, are clearly important even with somewhat lower detection confidence, the utilization of knee joints, which tend to be hidden especially with raincoats, remains a topic for future investigation.

6 Conclusion

The proposed method has improved the person matching accuracy by focusing on parts of the body that are susceptible to a decline in pose estimation accuracy and masking the pose estimation information. As a result of the evaluation, the average correct response rate improved by 3.7% with the proposed method compared to the case without masking.

However, the number of clothing variations was small in this verification. For example, in Southampton, there are also clothes that cover up to the ankles, such as trench coats. In the future, the authors will increase the number of clothing variations to be evaluated, with the belief that this will enable the creation of a general-purpose gait matching model that can handle different types of clothing.

In the future, this technology will make it easier to find missing people quickly and contribute to creating a society where the elderly can live safely and securely.

References

1. Cabinet Office. White Paper on the Aging Society (2019). https://www8.cao.go.jp/kourei/whitepaper/w-2024/html/gaiyou/s1_1.html. Accessed 18 Dec 2024
2. National Police Agency. Status of Missing Persons in 2023. https://www.npa.go.jp/safetylife/seianki/fumei/R05yukuefumeisha.pdf. Accessed 18 Dec 2024
3. Kikuchi, K., Ijuin, M., Awata, S., Suzuki, T.: A study on the mortality patterns of missing and deceased persons with dementia who died due to wandering. Nihon Ronen Igakkai Zasshi. Jpn. J. Geriatr. **53**(4), 363–373 (2016)
4. Guinness World Records, First use of forensic gait analysis evidence in court. 2016. https://www.guinnessworldrecords.com/world-records/first-use-of-forensic-gait-analysis-evidence-in-court/. Accessed 18 Dec 2024
5. Phillips, P.J., Sarkar, S., Robledo, I., Grother, P., Bowyer, K.: The gait identification challenge problem: data sets and baseline algorithm. In: 2002 International Conference on Pattern Recognition, vol. 1, pp. 385–388. IEEE (2002)
6. BBC. http://news.bbc.co.uk/2/hi/programmes/click_online/7702065.stm. Accessed 18 Dec 2024
7. Iwamura, M., et al.: Individuality-preserving silhouette extraction for gait recognition and its speedup. IEICE Trans. Inf. Syst. **104**(7), 992–1001 (2021)
8. Wang, L., Ning, H., Tan, T., Hu, W.: Fusion of static and dynamic body biometrics for gait recognition. IEEE Trans. Circuits Syst. Video Technol. **14**(2), 149–158 (2004)
9. Bari, A.H., Gavrilova, M.L.: KinectGaitNet: kinect-based gait recognition using deep convolutional neural network. Sensors **22**(7), 2631 (2022)
10. Liao, R., Yu, S., An, W., Huang, Y.: A model-based gait recognition method with body pose and human prior knowledge. Pattern Recogn. **98**, 107069 (2020)
11. Pinyoanuntapong, E., Ali, A., Wang, P., Lee, M., Chen, C.: Gaitmixer: skeleton-based gait representation learning via wide-spectrum multi-axial mixer. In: ICASSP 2023–2023 IEEE International Conference on Acoustics, Speech and Signal Processing (ICASSP), pp. 1–5 IEEE (2023)
12. Teepe, T., Khan, A., Gilg, J., Herzog, F., Hörmann, S., Rigoll, G.: GaitGraph: graph convolutional network for skeleton-based gait recognition. In: 2021 IEEE international conference on image processing (ICIP), pp. 2314–2318. IEEE (2021)
13. Li, J., Wang, Z., Wang, C., Su, W.: GaitFormer: leveraging dual-stream spatial–temporal vision transformer via a single low-cost RGB camera for clinical gait analysis. Knowl.-Based Syst. **295**, 111810 (2024)
14. Gao, S., Yun, J., Zhao, Y., Liu, L.: Gait-D: skeleton-based gait feature decomposition for gait recognition. IET Comput. Vision **16**(2), 111–125 (2022)
15. Sun, K., Xiao, B., Liu, D., Wang, J.: Deep high-resolution representation learning for human pose estimation. In: Proceedings of the IEEE/CVF Conference on Computer Vision and Pattern Recognition, pp. 5693–5703 (2019)

16. Wu, Z., Huang, Y., Wang, L., Wang, X., Tan, T.: A comprehensive study on cross-view gait based human identification with deep CNNs. IEEE Trans. Pattern Anal. Mach. Intell. **39**(2), 209–226 (2016)
17. Fan, C., et al.: GaitPart: temporal part-based model for gait recognition. In: Proceedings of the IEEE/CVF Conference on Computer Vision and Pattern Recognition, pp. 14225–14233 (2020)
18. Hayfron-Acquah, J.B., Nixon, M.S., Carter, J.N.: Automatic gait recognition by symmetry analysis. Pattern Recognit. Lett. **24**(13), 2175–2183 (2003)
19. Shutler, J.D., Grant, M.G., Nixon, M.S., Carter, J.N.: On a large sequence-based human gait database. In: Applications and Science in Soft Computing, pp. 339–346. Springer, Heidelberg (2004)

Vision-Based Human Fall Detection with Pre-trained YOLO Models: Comparison and Application

Duy-Linh Nguyen, Xuan-Thuy Vo, Adri Priadana, Jehwan Choi, and Kang-Hyun Jo(✉)

Department of Electrical, Electronic and Computer Engineering, University of Ulsan, Ulsan 44610, South Korea
{ndlinh301,xthuy,priadana}@mail.ulsan.ac.kr, {cjh1897,acejo}@ulsan.ac.kr

Abstract. Human fall detection has been studied and applied in health care and human monitoring systems. Falls often occur in the elderly, and people with neurological and musculoskeletal diseases. It can also appear in heavy work environments, slippery surfaces, or human carelessness. Falls cause many serious health injuries, especially to the spine and brain. Developing tools to warn of falls early is essential and reduces many unnecessary risks. This paper proposes vision-based human fall detection and warning systems using person detection pre-trained models. Thereby, evaluating and comparing the performance between three nano versions of the YOLO (You Only Look Once) architecture, including YOLOv5n, YOLOv8n, and YOLOv11n. The YOLOv8n model achieved the best speed at 109.06 fps (FPS) on an NVIDIA GeForce GTX 1080Ti 11GB GPU as a real-time test result. The demo video can be accessed at this link: https://bit.ly/4flU7Xv.

Keywords: Convolutional neural network (CNN) · Human fall detection · Person detection · YOLO

1 Introduction

Human falls are the second leading cause of death due to unintentional injuries and are a common reason for hospitalization of the elderly and sick [1]. The World Health Organization (WHO) estimates that 684,000 people die from falls each year globally, with a high concentration in older adults over 60 years old [21]. The main causes of falls include weak musculoskeletal systems, bone and joint injuries, neurological and cardiovascular diseases, etc. Human falls cause a lot of physical, mental, and economic damage and can lead to death. Therefore, research, prevention, and early warning of falls are essential to reduce risks to humans.

B. Kim (Ed.): IW-FCV 2025, CCIS 2769, pp. 232–243, 2026.
https://doi.org/10.1007/978-981-95-4578-0_19

Many studies have been developed to support medical care and monitor patients at high risk of falling, based on ambient sensors and wearable devices [4]. These technologies collect and analyze electrocardiograms, electroencephalograms, blood pressure, heart rate, body temperature, and patient interaction with the environment to provide warnings and prevent falls. The accuracy of diagnostic results through these methods is often quite high and accurate. However, wearable devices and other types of sensors cause discomfort to users, hindering movement and mobility. On the other hand, it requires expensive equipment and complicated installation. In addition, the devices have to maintain operating energy by power supply devices or batteries.

Using the non-invasive approach [6], vision-based techniques show many advantages with the development of convolutional neural networks (CNN) and artificial intelligence (AI) [5,15]. Vision-based methods analyze images or videos obtained from cameras to make predictions based on human pose. Typically, these methods often apply human skeleton and human pose detection algorithms. These techniques require deeply designed models consisting of many complex modules. In addition, the datasets must also be labeled and processed carefully and meticulously to ensure the training process. That creates a burden on labor and deployment in real-time monitoring systems. Based on these observations, this paper provides a simpler approach to detecting human falls based on person detection with pre-trained models from Ultralytics. This study leverages the architecture of YOLO models [7–9] trained on the COCO dataset [12], integrating with mobile messaging applications (e.g., WhatApps) to provide early warning of human falls. The proposed systems can be deployed in hospital and house healthcare care, child monitoring in kindergartens, or worker monitoring in industrial production environments.

The core contributions of this paper are as follows:
1 - Building human fall monitoring and warning systems based on pre-trained YOLO models to leverage available resources and datasets.
2 - Evaluating and comparing the performance of three YOLO nano models to provide an overview and effective application directions.

The remainder of the paper is as follows: Sect. 2 introduces the related works to human fall detection and recognition. Section 3 provides the proposed system in detail. Section 4 analyzes and compares the experimental results. Section 5 is the conclusion and future work orientation.

2 Related Works

The related works section reviews the research on human fall detection and recognition. Methods are considered from two perspectives, including traditional machine learning-based methods and YOLO-based methods.

2.1 Traditional Machine Learning-Based Methods

Traditional machine learning-based methods widely use typical image processing algorithms to recognize human falls. The authors in [22] integrated the hidden

Markov model and curvelets for classifying the human fall and non-human fall. The work [13] used the K-Nearest Neighbor algorithm to build a human fall classification system. The research [2] designed the real-time human fall surveillance system by geometric features and temporal covariance motion. Another approach [14] applied a CNN-LSTM deep neural network model aggregate with three Ultra-WideBand (UWB) radars for human fall detection in reality. Then, a large vision-based system using the Spatial-Temporal Graph Convolutional Networks (ST-GCN) algorithm was proposed in [10]. The above techniques rely on feature analysis and evaluation from images or videos, which require careful and laborious manual data processing steps. However, the low accuracy of fall detection and recognition hinders the deployment in real-time applications.

2.2 YOLO-Based Methods

YOLO-based methods leveraged the advantage of YOLO architecture for human pose estimation by using human keypoint detection. A human fall detection system was proposed by the authors in [20] by the YOLO model and OpenPose algorithm. The work [18] applied YOLOv1 and YOLOv4 to build a human fall detector for edge devices. The experiment [3] used the spatial attention module to improve the YOLOv5s architecture for human fall detection. The authors in [23] aggregated the Coordinate Attention and Shuffle Attention to build novel attention that enhances the YOLOv7's human fall detection performance. The researcher in [17] offered a one-stage skeleton estimator based on the YOLOv8-pose architecture for detecting human falls. These methods have taken the YOLO network's advantage to detect human falls with high accuracy and negligible latency. However, the human keypoint datasets need to be carefully processed and annotated to ensure that the training and evaluation stages achieve the desired results.

3 Methodology

The proposed Human Fall Detection system structure is shown in Fig. 1. This system consists of three modules: Person Detection, Fall Estimation, and Alarm messages.

3.1 Person Detection Module

Person detection is the first module in the proposed system architecture. This module is a combination of a GPRO-QHD800 4K camera and a pre-trained YOLO nano network model. The main task of the camera is to capture images or videos at the installation site and transmit the image signal to the YOLO model. Here, the YOLO model has been trained on the COCO dataset to detect the main object as the person in the captured image. The input of the human detection module is the image or video from the camera and the output is the person bounding box including height (H) and width (W). This research uses

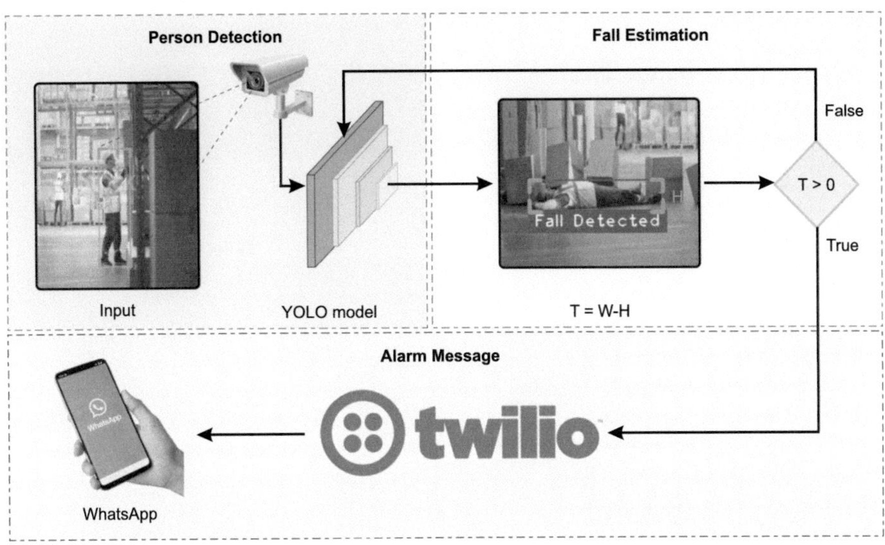

Fig. 1. The proposed Human Fall Detection system.

three different versions of the YOLO nano network architecture (v5, v8, and v11) for person detection. The general architecture of the YOLO network is shown in Fig. 2 comprises of Backbone, Neck, and Detection Head. The Backbone network plays an important role in the initial feature extraction process for the entire network. This module utilizes the advantage of Convolution block (Conv), Cross Stage Partial (CSP) networks (CSP in YOLOv5, C2f in YOLOv8, and C3K2 in YOLOv11), and Spatial Pyramid Pooling Fast (SPPF) module to generate multi-scale feature maps. The Neck module applies the Path Aggregation Network (PAN) operating principles and the Bi-directional Feature Pyramid (Bi-FPN). Combining these two architectures supports aggregating the current and previous feature maps. Therefore, the feature map is enriched with more information before being passed to the next stage. The detector module uses the output from three different feature maps of the Neck module for large, medium, and small objects. Each detector is designed based on two Conv blocks and a standard convolution to provide parameters for bounding box regression and classification processes. The YOLOv5 network implements the couple detection heads with anchor boxes and a Non-Maximum Suppression (NMS) algorithm for object detection. Later, these techniques were replaced by decouple detection heads and the free-anchor method in the YOLOv8 and YOLOv11 networks to improve the speed of object detection. The detail of each architecture is shown in Table 1.

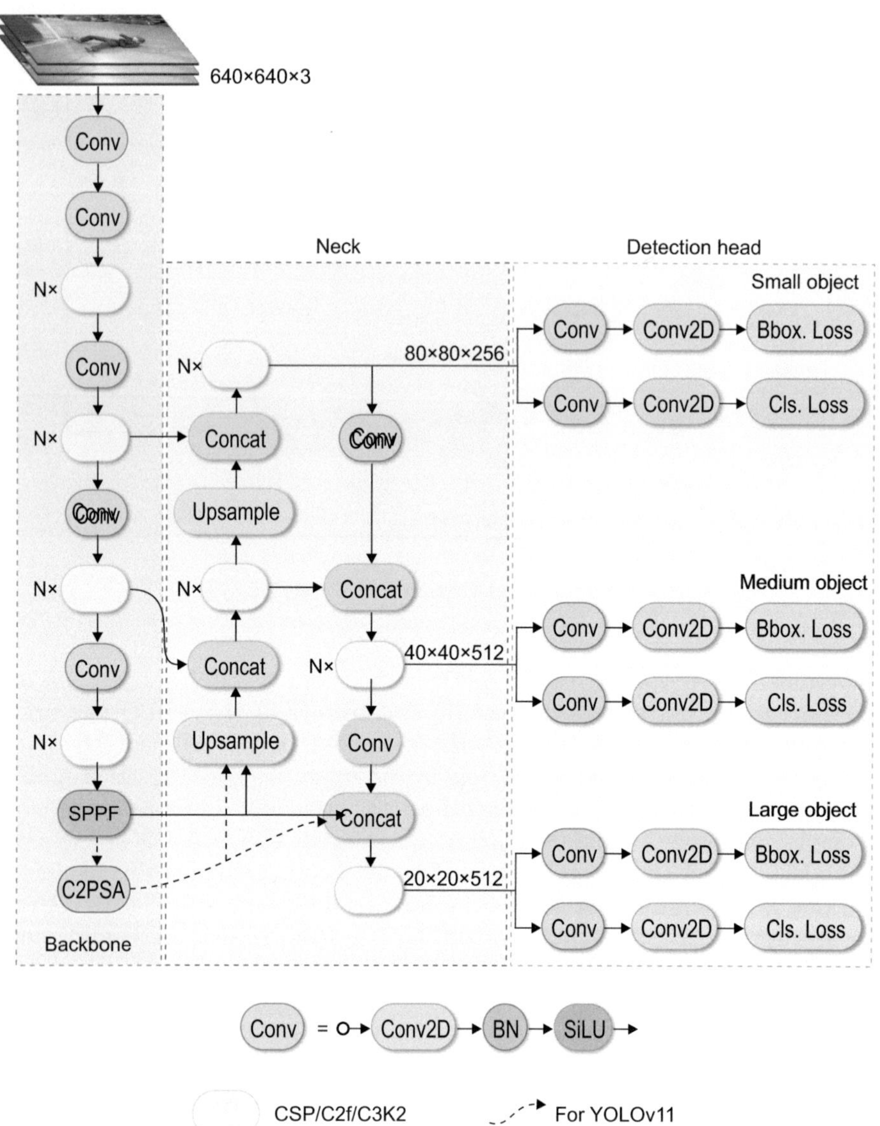

Fig. 2. The general architecture of YOLO series.

Table 1. The detail of three versions in the YOLO models.

Models	Blocks						
	Conv	CSP	C2f	C3K2	SPPF	Anchor	Free-anchor
YOLOv5n	✓	✓			✓	✓	
YOLOv8n	✓		✓		✓		✓
YOLOv11n	✓			✓	✓		✓

3.2 Fall Estimation Module

This step applies a simple mathematical model to estimate human falls. Given $W\,(Width) \times H\,(Height)$ is the output person bounding box dimension from the Person Detection module. A difference of W and H (called threshold $\mathcal{T} = W - H$) is considered. If the threshold $\mathcal{T}$ is larger than a certain limit number (in this case set $\mathcal{T} > 0$), the human fall will be detected and vice versa. This process repeats until the system detects one human fall situation. The pseudo-code of the fall estimation module is present in the Algorithm 1.

Algorithm 1. The pseudo-code of fall estimation process

Input: $W\,(Width), H\,(Height)$
Output: Fall Detected
  Compute $\mathcal{T}\,(Threshold) = W - H$;
  if $\mathcal{T} > 0$ **then**
    Fall Detected;
  else
    Return to compute $\mathcal{T}$.
  end if

3.3 Alarm Message Module

The final module in the fall detection system is the Alarm messages. This module receives the fall detection signal from the Fall Detection module and sends the warning message to the mobile phone via the WhatsApp messaging software. The experiment uses the Twilio platform as an intermediary to transmit the message for free while still ensuring the content of the warning.

4 Experiments

4.1 Dataset

COCO Dataset: The COCO (Common Objects in Context) dataset [12] is a large-scale dataset mainly used in the Computer Vision field. It contains over 330,000 images and 200,000 are labeled, including 80 object categories, making it diverse and comprehensive. The COCO dataset regards the detection of objects in complex real-world scenes with significant contextual information. The COCO dataset is implemented to evaluate models on challenging tasks, such as detecting small and occlusion objects.

HumanParts Dataset: The Human-Parts dataset [11] consists of 14,962 images and 106,879 annotated labels. It is split into three classes, including person, face, and hand. The big set of images from IA-Challenger are collected and annotated following the PASCAL VOC dataset format. To make the ablation study, this work utilizes 10,035 images including 8,038 images for the training and 1,997 images for the evaluation phases.

People Detection Computer Vision Project (PDCVP) Dataset: This dataset is downloaded from the RoboFlow website [19]. It contains 17,401 images with only one class (person). The images are divided into three subsets including 15,210 for training, 1,431 for evaluation, and 760 for testing. This work also uses the PDCVP dataset for system performance evaluation in the ablation study section.

Table 2. Comparison results on COCO dataset.

Models	Parameters (M)	GFLOPs	mAP@0.5:0.95	Latency*
YOLOv5n [7]	2.6	7.7	34.3	1.8
YOLOv5s [7]	9.1	24.0	43.0	1.9
YOLOv5m [7]	25.1	64.2	49.0	4.0
YOLOv5l [7]	53.2	135.0	52.2	6.6
YOLOv5x [7]	97.2	246.4	53.2	11.9
YOLOv8n [9]	3.2	8.7	37.3	1.6
YOLOv8s [9]	11.2	28.6	44.9	2.6
YOLOv8m [9]	25.9	78.9	50.2	5.8
YOLOv8l [9]	43.7	165.2	52.9	9.1
YOLOv8x [9]	68.2	257.8	53.9	14.4
YOLOv11n [8]	2.6	6.5	39.5	1.65
YOLOv11s [8]	9.4	21.5	47.0	2.55
YOLOv11m [8]	20.1	68.0	51.5	5.4
YOLOv11l [8]	25.3	86.9	53.4	6.8
YOLOv11x [8]	56.9	194.9	54.7	12.6

* Latency on T4 TensorRT10 (ms).

4.2 Experimental Setup

The overall human fall detection system is developed using Python, Pytorch, and Ultralytics libraries. In addition, to implement the Message Alarm module, this work also integrates the Twilio platform and WhatsApp message software. The proposed system is tested in real-time and a series of videos on an NVIDIA GeForce GTX 1080Ti 11GB GPU. All pre-trained models on the COCO dataset are collected from the Ultralytics website. Besides, this experiment borrows a pre-trained model on the HumaParts dataset from [16], and re-trained using the YOLOv8n model and PDCVP dataset for ablation study. The confidence and IoU thresholds of all person detectors are set at 0.5.

4.3 Experimental Result

The evaluation results of the YOLO family models on the COCO dataset with 80 classes are available on the Ultralytics website. This research selects three YOLO

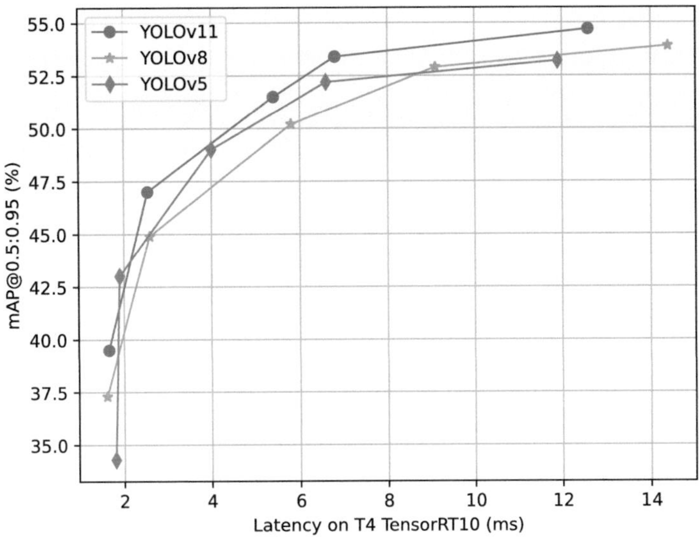

Fig. 3. The mAP and Latency comparison on the COCO dataset.

models including YOLOv5, YOLOv8, and YOLOv11 for performance comparison as shown in Table 2. As a result, the latest version of YOLO achieves outstanding detection performance of up to 54.7% of mAP in the extra large version (YOLOv11x). On the other hand, when comparing the remaining model sizes with previous versions, YOLOv11 still dominates. Especially, in the nano model size, YOLOv11 is also superior to YOLOv5 (larger 5.2% of mAP) and YOLOv8 (larger 2.2% of mAP). Furthermore, the latency of YOLOv11n evaluated on the T4 TensorRT10 library environment is comparable to YOLOv8n (0.05ms difference) and faster than YOLOv5n (0.15ms faster). The performance details of each model are presented in Fig. 3. This is the reason why this work chooses nano models in the YOLO family to build the fall detection application.

Table 3. The speed comparison with different video resolution.

Models	Speed (FPS)		
	VGA	HD	FHD
YOLOv5n	97.51	89.90	77.30
YOLOv8n	109.06	91.51	80.01
YOLOv11n	89.09	83.21	75.81

* **VGA:** 640 × 480 pixels.
* **HD:** 1280 × 7200 pixels.
* **FHD:** 1920 × 1080 pixels.

On the other hand, this work also conducts speed tests of each person detector on the real-time system as shown in Table 3. In which, the YOLOv8n network achieves the best speed compared to other networks on all three camera resolutions including VGA, HD, and FHD. Although YOLOv11n achieves the best detection performance when tested in the real-time system, the speed is slightly worse than the other two networks on all three resolutions. Several qualitative results are introduced in Fig. 4. The 1st row is the real-time testing results in the laboratory environment. The 2nd row to 4th row shows the testing results on various scene videos.

4.4 Ablation Study

To evaluate the effectiveness of different datasets on real-time systems, this experiment implements several ablation studies with the YOLOv8n network and

Fig. 4. The qualitative results on videos with YOLOv11n model.

Table 4. The ablation study on the YOLOv8n model with different video resolutions and datasets. The speed is measured by FPS.

Datasets	Resolution		
	VGA	HD	FHD
PDCVP dataset (1 class) [19]	84.87	76.67	66.28
HumanParts dataset (3 classes) [16]	104.57	89.94	79.34
COCO dataset (80 classes) [9]	109.06	95.10	80.01

the three datasets described in Subsect. 4.1. As a result in Table 4, the network trained on the large COCO dataset achieves superior speed compared to the models trained on other medium and small datasets. Especially with VGA resolution, the YOLOv8n network with the COCO dataset achieves the best speed at 109.06 FPS, larger than the PDCVP dataset (24.19 FPS better) and the HumanParts dataset (4.49 FPS better). In addition, the above results also show that the number of classes in the dataset does not affect the detection speed of the network. Therefore, leveraging YOLO models pre-trained on large and diverse datasets like COCO has the potential to develop real-time object detection applications.

5 Conclusion

This paper proposes a human fall detection and warning system based on pre-trained models on large available datasets. The proposed system comprises three main modules: Person Detection, Fall Estimation, and Warning Message. The system achieves high speed and accuracy when tested with GPU in real-time. However, for practical deployment, the system needs to be improved to respond to complex situations in the real world. In the future, the system will be further developed to solve several challenges such as multiple and overlapping individuals, and tested with low-computing, mobile, and edge devices. In addition, this work will also extend the comparison beyond the limits of the YOLO family to select the optimal model for the later human fall system.

Acknowledgement. This result was supported by "Regional Innovation Strategy (RIS)" through the National Research Foundation of Korea (NRF) funded by the Ministry of Education (MOE)(2021RIS-003)

References

1. Alam, E., Sufian, A., Dutta, P., Leo, M.: Vision-based human fall detection systems using deep learning: A review (2022). https://arxiv.org/abs/2207.10952
2. Ali, S.F., Khan, R., Mahmood, A., Hassan, M.T., Jeon, M.: Using temporal covariance of motion and geometric features via boosting for human fall detection. Sensors **18**(6), 1918 (2018)

3. Chen, T., Ding, Z., Li, B.: Elderly fall detection based on improved yolov5s network. IEEE Access **10**, 91273–91282 (2022). https://doi.org/10.1109/ACCESS.2022.3202293
4. Chen, Y., Tian, Y., He, M.: Monocular human pose estimation: A survey of deep learning-based methods. CoRR abs/2006.01423 (2020). https://arxiv.org/abs/2006.01423
5. Chen, Y., Tian, Y., He, M.: Monocular human pose estimation: A survey of deep learning-based methods. CoRR abs/2006.01423 (2020). https://arxiv.org/abs/2006.01423
6. Gutiérrez, J., Rodríguez, V., Martin, S.: Comprehensive review of vision-based fall detection systems. Sensors **21**(3) (2021). https://doi.org/10.3390/s21030947, https://www.mdpi.com/1424-8220/21/3/947
7. Jocher, G., et al.: ultralytics/YOLOv5: v3.1 - Bug Fixes and Performance Improvements (2020). https://doi.org/10.5281/zenodo.4154370
8. Jocher, G., et al.: Ultralytics YOLOv11 (2024). https://github.com/ultralytics/ultralytics
9. Jocher, G., Chaurasia, A., Qiu, J.: Ultralytics YOLOv8 (2023). https://github.com/ultralytics/ultralytics
10. Keskes, O., Noumeir, R.: Vision-based fall detection using ST-GCN. IEEE Access **9**, 28224–28236 (2021)
11. Li, X., Yang, L., Song, Q., Zhou, F.: Detector-in-detector: Multi-level analysis for human-parts. CoRR abs/1902.07017 (2019). http://arxiv.org/abs/1902.07017
12. Lin, T.Y., et al.: Microsoft COCO: Common objects in context (2015). https://arxiv.org/abs/1405.0312
13. Liu, C.L., Lee, C.H., Lin, P.M.: A fall detection system using k-nearest neighbor classifier. Expert Syst. Appl. **37**(10), 7174–7181 (2010)
14. Maitre, J., Bouchard, K., Gaboury, S.: Fall detection with UWB radars and CNN-LSTM architecture. IEEE J. Biomed. Health Inform. **25**(4), 1273–1283 (2020)
15. Munea, T.L., Jembre, Y.Z., Weldegebriel, H.T., Chen, L., Huang, C., Yang, C.: The progress of human pose estimation: a survey and taxonomy of models applied in 2D human pose estimation. IEEE Access **8**, 133330–133348 (2020). https://doi.org/10.1109/ACCESS.2020.3010248
16. Nguyen, D.L., Vo, X.T., Priadana, A., Nguyen, D.V., Nguyen, T.L.H., Jo, K.H.: Simple human fall surveillance system based on person detection. In: 2024 International Workshop on Intelligent Systems (IWIS), pp. 1–6 (2024). https://doi.org/10.1109/IWIS62722.2024.10706061
17. Noor, N., Park, I.K.: A lightweight skeleton-based 3D-CNN for real-time fall detection and action recognition. In: Proceedings of the IEEE/CVF International Conference on Computer Vision (ICCV) Workshops, pp. 2179–2188 (2023)
18. Raza, A., Yousaf, M.H., Velastin, S.A.: Human fall detection using YOLO: a real-time and AI-on-the-edge perspective. In: 2022 12th International Conference on Pattern Recognition Systems (ICPRS), pp. 1–6 (2022). https://doi.org/10.1109/ICPRS54038.2022.9854070
19. Ueno, L.: People detection computer vision project. https://universe.roboflow.com/leo-ueno/people-detection-o4rdr. Accessed 01 Dec 2024
20. Wang, B.H., Yu, J., Wang, K., Bao, X.Y., Mao, K.M.: Fall detection based on dual-channel feature integration. IEEE Access **8**, 103443–103453 (2020). https://doi.org/10.1109/ACCESS.2020.2999503
21. WHO: Falls. https://www.who.int/news-room/fact-sheets/detail/falls. Accessed 01 Dec 2024

22. Zerrouki, N., Houacine, A.: Combined curvelets and hidden markov models for human fall detection. Multimedia Tools Appl. **77**, 6405–6424 (2018)
23. Zhao, D., Song, T., Gao, J., Li, D., Niu, Y.: YOLO-fall: a novel convolutional neural network model for fall detection in open spaces. IEEE Access **12**, 26137–26149 (2024). https://doi.org/10.1109/ACCESS.2024.3362958

Improving Impurity Detection in Laver Images Through Data Augmentation

Byungjoon Kim[1,2](✉) and Yongduek Seo[2]

[1] Sogang University, Mapo-gu, Seoul 04091, Republic of Korea
atbem@sogang.ac.kr

[2] Korea AI Certification, Seongdong-gu, Seoul 04769, Republic of Korea
yndk@sogang.ac.kr

Abstract. This study focuses on enhancing impurity detection in laver images through advanced data augmentation and tailored dataset design. The irregular texture of laver and the microscopic size of impurities present significant challenges for traditional detection methods. To address these issues, a comprehensive dataset was constructed using StyleGAN to generate 10,000 synthetic laver images, coupled with traditional augmentation techniques for impurity data. The YOLOv8 model was employed for impurity detection, achieving a precision score of 0.96 under IoU 75, a substantial improvement from the 30% observed without augmented data. While occasional misclassifications of natural laver gaps as impurities were observed, the model demonstrated robust performance in detecting and excluding impurities. These results highlight the critical role of data design and augmentation in improving detection accuracy. This research provides a scalable foundation for automated impurity detection systems in the laver industry and suggests future opportunities for real-time applications and extended impurity types.

Keywords: Data Augmentation · Object Detection · Laver Impurity

1 Introduction

The laver industry is one of South Korea's key exports, accounting for approximately 70% of the global market share. As a highly valued product, laver production demands rigorous quality control. However, microscopic foreign objects, such as plastic fragments, shell debris, and fishing net pieces, frequently contaminate the production process, posing a significant challenge. These impurities are often small, diverse in shape, and irregularly distributed, blending into the complex texture of laver, making them difficult to detect using traditional methods [1]. Current inspection processes heavily rely on manual efforts, which are time-consuming, labor-intensive, and prone to human error. The need for an automated and efficient solution to ensure consistent quality has therefore become critical.

This study addresses this challenge by focusing on the design of high-quality training data through careful analysis of both laver images and impurity characteristics. Instead

B. Kim (Ed.): IW-FCV 2025, CCIS 2769, pp. 244–252, 2026.
https://doi.org/10.1007/978-981-95-4578-0_20

of developing a novel model or heavily modifying existing architectures, we propose a data-driven approach that leverages tailored augmentation and synthesis techniques. Specifically, the irregular patterns of laver and the rigid structures of impurities were incorporated into a framework that generates diverse and realistic training datasets. By applying these datasets to state-of-the-art object detection models, such as YOLOv8 and Faster R-CNN, we achieved a substantial improvement in detection accuracy, increasing it from an initial 55% to 94% [2, 3].

The contributions of this research lie in its emphasis on understanding the data's characteristics and employing augmentation to bridge the gap between limited real-world data and the demands of deep learning models. This approach not only facilitates the development of automated quality control systems for the laver industry but also demonstrates a scalable solution for similar data scarcity challenges in other fields.

2 Related Work

2.1 Object Detection

Object detection models have evolved significantly with the rise of deep learning, particularly in tasks requiring precision and efficiency. Region-based Convolutional Neural Networks (R-CNN) were among the first to demonstrate robust performance by extracting region proposals and classifying objects within them. Faster R-CNN further optimized this approach by introducing a Region Proposal Network (RPN), which integrates the detection and proposal stages into a single, unified framework [1, 2]. These advancements have proven effective in detecting small and intricate objects, making them suitable for tasks like impurity detection.

On the other hand, single-shot detectors such as YOLO (You Only Look Once) offer a trade-off between speed and accuracy. YOLO models divide an image into a grid and predict bounding boxes and class probabilities for each grid cell simultaneously, enabling real-time object detection [3, 4]. Recent iterations, such as YOLOv8, incorporate transformer-based backbones and enhanced feature extraction, improving accuracy while maintaining computational efficiency. These models are particularly advantageous for large-scale industrial applications requiring high-speed processing.

Despite their effectiveness, both Faster R-CNN and YOLO face limitations when dealing with highly irregular patterns or extremely small objects, such as impurities in laver images. Their performance heavily relies on the quality and diversity of training datasets, emphasizing the importance of proper data design and augmentation.

2.2 Data Augmentation

Data augmentation plays a crucial role in overcoming the limitations of small or imbalanced datasets by artificially expanding the training set. Traditional augmentation methods, such as flipping, rotation, scaling, and brightness adjustment, have been widely employed due to their simplicity and effectiveness. These techniques introduce variability into the training data, allowing models to generalize better across different scenarios. However, while they can address basic transformations, they often fail to capture the complex patterns and textures inherent in real-world data, such as the irregular structure of laver or the diverse shapes of impurities [5, 6].

To address these limitations, generative approaches, such as Generative Adversarial Networks (GANs), have emerged as powerful tools for data augmentation. GANs generate realistic synthetic data by learning the underlying distribution of the original dataset, making them particularly effective for applications where traditional augmentation methods fall short [3, 7]. For example, GANs can be trained to replicate the irregular patterns of laver, producing images that closely resemble real samples while maintaining variability. Similarly, impurities with distinct structural characteristics can be augmented using targeted transformations, creating diverse training examples (Fig. 1).

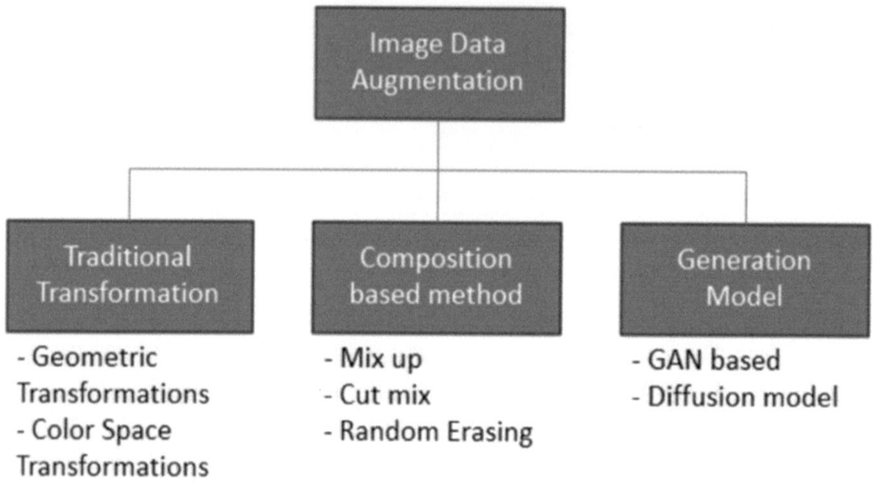

Fig. 1. Image Data Augmentation Techniques Categorized by Method.

More recently, diffusion models have gained attention for their ability to produce high-quality, diverse synthetic data. These models progressively add and remove noise during the generation process, resulting in detailed and realistic outputs [8, 9]. While diffusion models offer promising results, they often require significant computational resources, which may limit their applicability in large-scale industrial settings.

In this study, both traditional and generative augmentation techniques are employed. GANs are utilized to generate synthetic laver images, effectively mimicking the irregular patterns of real samples. For impurity augmentation, traditional methods such as rotation and scaling are applied to create diverse variations. The combination of these approaches ensures that the dataset is both realistic and sufficiently diverse, addressing the challenges posed by limited and imbalanced real-world data.

2.3 Limitations of Existing Research

Object detection and data augmentation techniques have significantly advanced over the years, with applications across diverse fields. State-of-the-art object detection models, such as YOLOv8 and Faster R-CNN, deliver impressive accuracy and speed, excelling on large-scale datasets [2, 4]. Similarly, data augmentation has become a cornerstone in addressing data scarcity, with traditional techniques such as flipping, scaling, and rotation effectively increasing dataset diversity and supporting robust model training [5, 6].

However, these technologies are not universally applicable to all domains. For instance, traditional augmentation methods often struggle to capture the unique characteristics of laver images, such as their irregular texture patterns, or to represent the diverse and rigid structures of microscopic impurities. In specific domains requiring detailed and realistic data, these limitations become more pronounced. Generative approaches, such as GANs and Diffusion Models, offer a promising solution by synthesizing domain-specific data that closely mimics real-world scenarios [7–9]. Despite their potential, these techniques often require extensive computational resources and advanced expertise, making their practical integration into industrial workflows challenging.

This study addresses these limitations by emphasizing data design and augmentation tailored to the unique characteristics of laver and impurities. Using GANs for laver image augmentation and traditional methods for impurity variations, we ensure a realistic and diverse dataset that supports effective model training. By shifting the focus from model-centric improvements to data-centric design, this approach bridges the gap between research innovations and industrial applications.

3 Data Design and Augmentation for Laver Impurity Detection

3.1 Object Detection

Laver images exhibit distinct characteristics that complicate impurity detection. The irregular texture patterns of laver, coupled with natural tissue gaps and overlapping structures, create a highly complex visual background. These features often cause impurities to blend seamlessly into the laver's patterns, making it difficult for conventional image processing methods or even advanced object detection models to distinguish between the two. The background complexity and variability of patterns across samples further exacerbate these challenges (Fig. 2).

Impurities in laver images add another layer of complexity due to their diverse sizes, shapes, and textures. Common contaminants include plastic fragments, shell debris, fish scales, and fishing net pieces. These impurities often exhibit rigid and distinct features, but their small size and variability in appearance make them particularly challenging to detect. For instance, plastic fragments are often translucent and irregularly shaped, making them appear as part of the natural laver pattern under certain lighting conditions. Shell debris, on the other hand, may have sharp edges but can reflect light, causing it to resemble bright laver tissues. Thin and thread-like fishing net pieces further complicate detection as they mimic the natural linear structures within laver (Fig. 3).

The inconsistent distribution of impurities across samples presents additional obstacles. Some laver images contain multiple impurities, while others are entirely free of contaminants, leading to class imbalance issues in datasets. Furthermore, the impurities' highly variable appearances necessitate the use of diverse training datasets that accurately capture both their distinct characteristics and the irregularities of laver patterns.

Fig. 2. Original Laver Image and Magnified Laver Pattern.

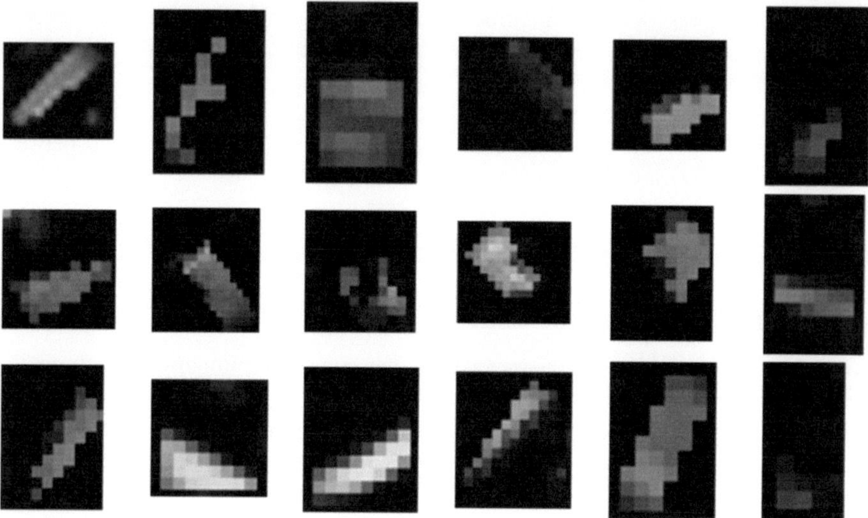

Fig. 3. Examples of Impurity Images.

To address these challenges, this study focuses on analyzing the unique features of both laver and impurities. By designing a dataset that incorporates these distinctive characteristics and employing advanced augmentation techniques, the goal is to create a robust and diverse training set that facilitates effective impurity detection.

3.2 Data Augmentation Framework

To address the challenges posed by irregular laver patterns and the limited variability of impurity data, this study employed a comprehensive data augmentation framework. The framework integrates synthetic laver image generation, impurity image augmentation, and Mixup techniques to create a robust dataset for impurity detection.

The process began with the generation of 10,000 synthetic laver images using StyleGAN. This model effectively captured the structural characteristics of laver while introducing randomized patterns, simulating real-world variations. Of these, 1,000 images were retained as clean samples without impurities to serve as negative examples. The remaining 9,000 images were used as the base for generating impurity-laden images (Fig. 4).

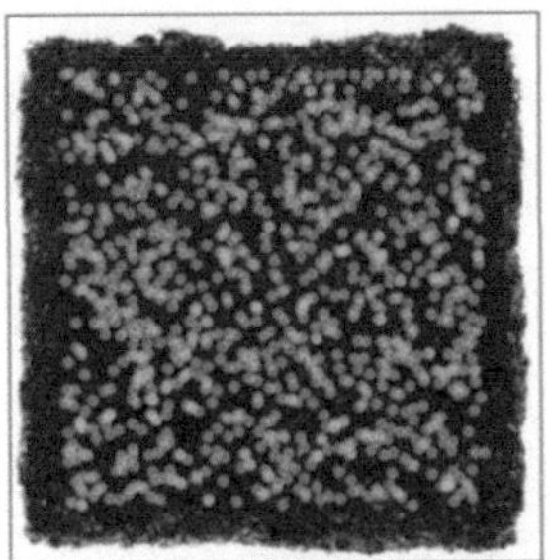

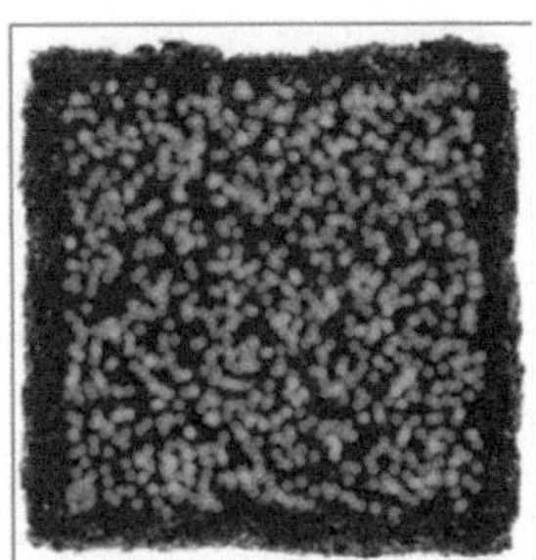

Fig. 4. Impurity Object Heatmap by Impurity Type

Impurity augmentation was performed on 100 original impurity images using a combination of traditional techniques, including rotation, flipping, scaling, color jittering, Gaussian noise, and distortion. These methods enhanced the diversity of impurity appearances, ensuring that the dataset accurately reflected real-world variability. By augmenting the impurities, the dataset was expanded to include a wide range of impurity conditions, enabling the creation of diverse and realistic training scenarios.

The augmented impurities were then integrated with the synthetic laver images using Mixup techniques. During this process, a blending parameter between 0.6 and 0.9 controlled the degree of integration between impurities and laver backgrounds. This approach initially produced 3,000 images with a single impurity object per image. Subsequently, 6,000 additional images were generated, containing 5 to 30 impurities distributed randomly across the laver patterns. This synthesis process was critical for replicating real-world contamination scenarios, where impurities are inconsistently distributed and blend into complex backgrounds.

The final dataset, consisting of 10,000 images, was split into training, validation, and testing subsets in an 8:1:1 ratio. All images were resized to 512x512 resolution to standardize input dimensions for the detection model. This dataset represents a realistic and diverse sample of impurity conditions in laver images, ensuring robustness in model training and evaluation.

4 Data Design and Augmentation for Laver Impurity Detection

This study employed YOLOv8 as the primary model for impurity detection in laver images. YOLOv8 was selected due to its balance between accuracy and speed, making it particularly suitable for detecting small and irregular objects like impurities in complex backgrounds. The ability of YOLOv8 to handle diverse object distributions and its efficiency in real-time processing align well with the requirements of this research.

The model was configured with input images resized to 256 × 256 and trained using a batch size of 16. The learning rate was set at 0.001, with the Adam optimizer minimizing the loss. A higher IoU threshold (IoU 75) was applied during evaluation to emphasize precise object localization, as impurities are often microscopic and require accurate detection. YOLOv8's anchor settings and feature map resolutions were adjusted to better accommodate small object detection, ensuring the network effectively captured the irregularities of laver patterns and impurities. The model was trained over 200 epochs, leveraging the large dataset to achieve robust performance across various impurity conditions (Fig. 5).

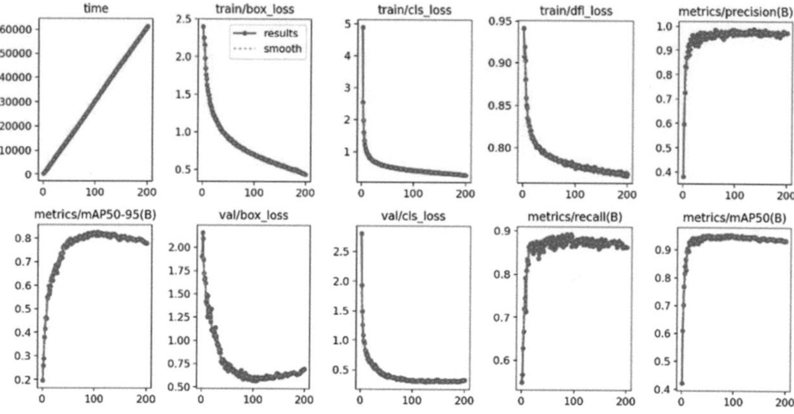

Fig. 5. Performance Metrics over Epochs

The dataset of 10,000 images was divided into training (8,000 images), validation (1,000 images), and testing (1,000 images) subsets. The training set included a mix of clean images (1,000) and impurity-laden images (7,000) to ensure balanced representation. Validation and test sets were similarly structured, with random distribution ensuring no data leakage between subsets.

Evaluation metrics included IoU 75-based precision, recall, and mean average precision (mAP). The model achieved a precision of 0.96, a significant improvement from the 30% precision recorded when using unaugmented data. This result highlights the effectiveness of the data augmentation framework in enhancing the model's ability to detect diverse impurities (Fig. 6).

While the model demonstrated high performance, certain limitations were observed. In some cases, the wide, empty spaces in the generated laver images were misclassified as impurities. These spaces, which frequently occur in real laver images, present challenges for distinguishing between natural gaps and contamination. Despite these occasional misclassifications, the primary objective of detecting and excluding impurities was successfully addressed, demonstrating the model's robustness and practical applicability.

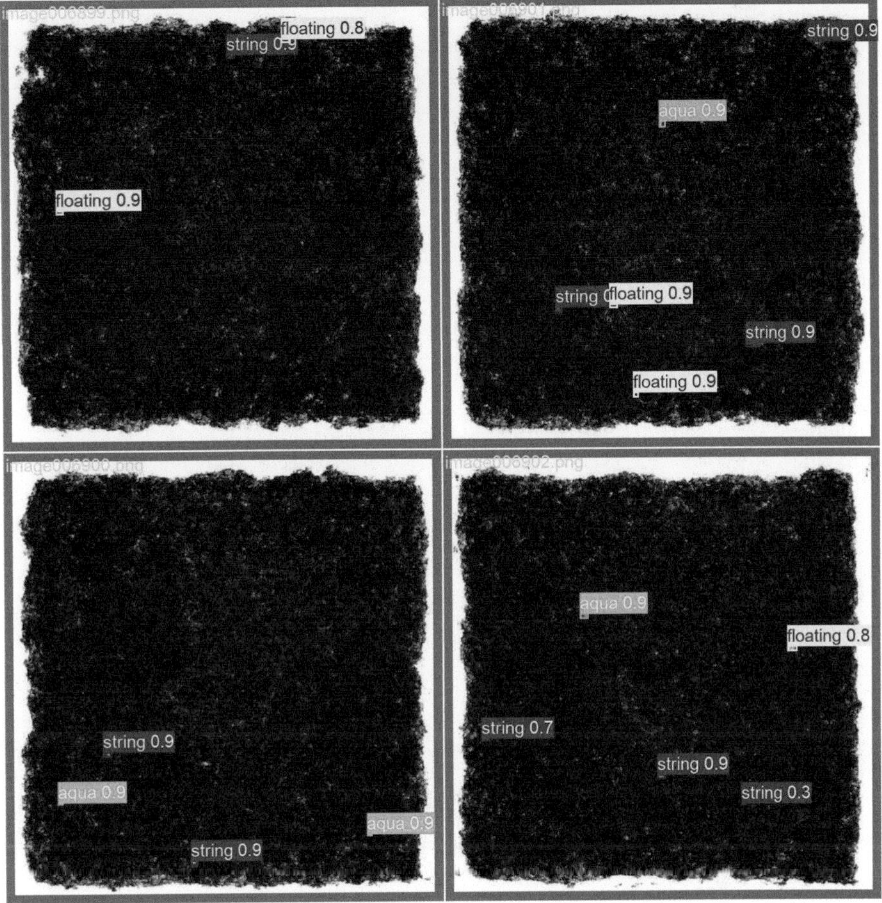

Fig. 6. Visualization of Actual Detection Results

5 Conclusion

This study demonstrates the effectiveness of data augmentation and tailored dataset design in improving impurity detection for laver images. By employing StyleGAN to generate realistic laver patterns and leveraging traditional augmentation techniques for impurities, the dataset achieved sufficient diversity to enhance the performance of YOLOv8, resulting in a precision score of 0.96 under IoU 75. This represents a significant improvement over the 30% precision observed without augmented data. The results highlight the critical role of robust data design in addressing challenges posed by the irregular texture of laver and the microscopic size of impurities. Despite these successes, certain limitations were identified, such as the misclassification of wide, empty spaces in the generated laver images as impurities. These issues underline the need for further refinement in distinguishing between natural laver gaps and contamination. This research contributes to advancing automated impurity detection systems for the laver industry, providing a scalable solution for quality control. Future work may explore the inclusion of additional impurity types, real-time system implementation, and further optimization for handling complex contamination scenarios.

Acknowledgments. This work was supported by the Technology development Program (S3440487) funded by the Ministry of SMEs and Startups (MMS, Korea).

Disclosure of Interests. The authors have no competing interests to declare that are relevant to the content of this article.

References

1. Smith, J.: Deep learning applications. J. AI Res. **25**(4), 123–145 (2022)
2. Redmon, J., Farhadi, A.: YOLOv3: an incremental improvement. arXiv preprint arXiv:1804.02767 (2018)
3. Goodfellow, I., Bengio, Y., Courville, A.: Deep Learning, 2nd edn. MIT Press, Cambridge (2016)
4. Bochkovskiy, A., Wang, C.Y., Liao, H.Y.M.: YOLOv4: optimal speed and accuracy of object detection. arXiv preprint arXiv:2004.10934 (2020)
5. Shorten, C., Khoshgoftaar, T.M.: A survey on image data augmentation for deep learning. J. Big Data **6**(1), 60 (2019)
6. Taylor, L., Nitschke, G.: Improving deep learning using generic data augmentation. arXiv preprint arXiv:1708.06020 (2017)
7. Goodfellow, I., Pouget-Abadie, J., Mirza, M., et al.: Generative adversarial nets. In: NeurIPS 2014, pp. 2672–2680 (2014)
8. Dhariwal, P., Nichol, A.: Diffusion models beat GANs on image synthesis. arXiv preprint arXiv:2105.05233 (2021)
9. Ho, J., Jain, A., Abbeel, P.: Denoising diffusion probabilistic models. arXiv preprint arXiv:2006.11239 (2020)

3D Annotation System for Work Assistance in Living Environments

Haruya Ishigami[1,2](✉), Tomomi Sato[1], Kenji Iwata[1], and Yutaka Satoh[1,2]

[1] National Institute of Advanced Industrial Science and Technology (AIST), Tsukuba, Japan
ishigami.h2002@aist.go.jp

[2] University of Tsukuba, Tsukuba, Japan

Abstract. Recently, 3D data generation techniques using neural networks are widely used in a variety of fields. In our study, we propose an efficient interactive annotation system by combining two 3D models: a high-quality 3D scene model generated by 3D Gaussian splatting and a model with surface information such as a mesh model. The system allows users to annotate the 3D space with intuitive operations. This system is expected to promote the effective use of 3D data and information sharing, and to be deployed in a wide range of scenes such as living environments.

Keywords: 3D Gaussian Splatting · Annotation system · Work Assistance

1 Introduction

Recently, the use of 3D data is rapidly developing in various areas such as architecture, entertainment, healthcare, and robotics. This is because of new methods using neural networks. One important method is Neural Radiance Fields (NeRF) [1], which creates photorealistic quality 3D scene models from multiple photos. However, NeRF and its related methods have a critical issue: they require too much computing power for real-time rendering.

On the other hand, 3D Gaussian Splatting [2] uses Gaussian distributions to represent scenes, making the rendering much faster. In contrast to NeRF, which needs complex calculations with multilayer perceptron, 3D Gaussian Splatting is much quicker and still generates images of the same high-quality as NeRF. This advancement facilitates the rapid and effective utilization of 3D data, making it highly promising for a wide range of applications.

In this study, we propose an interactive annotation system that allows users to place objects on a board with text labels or notes directly in 3D scenes created from the latest video data captured at home or in the office, using familiar tools such as smartphones and webcams. In the system, users point to any point of the 3DGS model as the target of annotation, and the system locates an annotation object at the point. However, a model generated by 3DGS does not have surface information like a mesh model, making it difficult to identify the point that the user specified. Therefore, we combine a surface

B. Kim (Ed.): IW-FCV 2025, CCIS 2769, pp. 253–257, 2026.
https://doi.org/10.1007/978-981-95-4578-0_21

model to obtain depth information with the Gaussian model. The system allows for efficient information sharing in everyday scenarios, such as when multiple individuals are rearranging a space. Specifically, during tasks like redecorating, information regarding task assignments and responsibilities can be shared seamlessly, providing each user with information from the most suitable viewpoint tailored to their role. Presenting task information and instructions in a visually intuitive manner enhances the clarity of communication among workers, thereby improving overall work efficiency.

Therefore, our research aims to develop a system that uses 3D Gaussian Splatting to create 3D data, enriches these models with depth information, and enables the addition of various annotations. This system facilitates easy browsing of annotated 3D data, making it a valuable tool for collaborative tasks in everyday environments (Figs. 1 and 4).

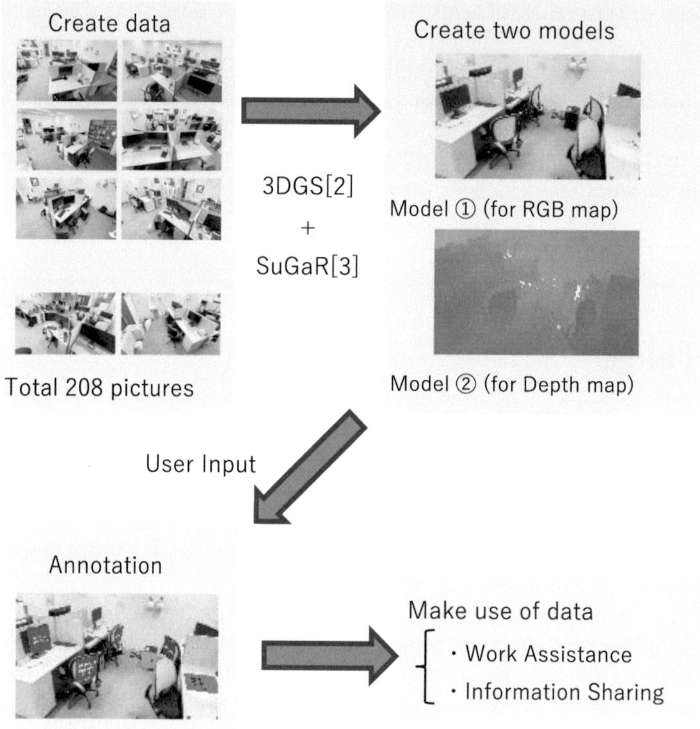

Fig. 1. System Overview

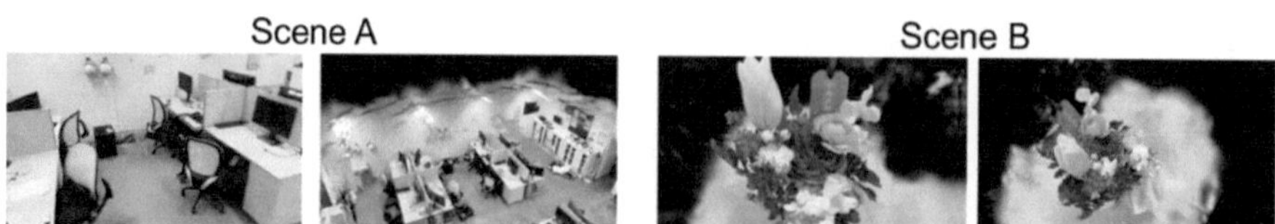

Fig. 2. Example of 3D Model for RGB data acquisition

Fig. 3. Example of 3D annotation

Fig. 4. Example of 3D Model for Depth data acquisition

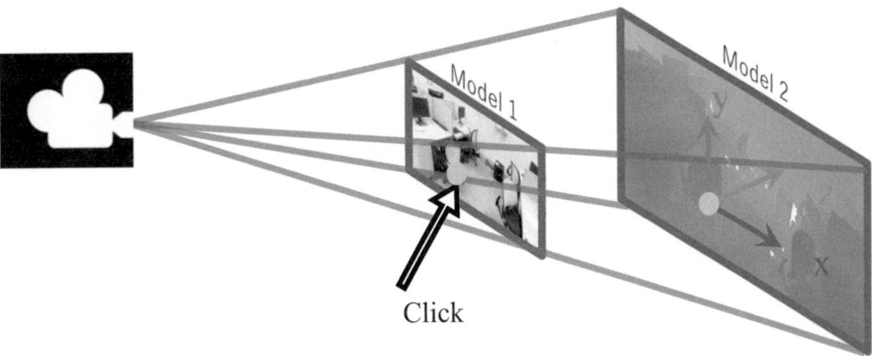

Fig. 5. Annotation Object Placement Method

2 Related Work

3DGS is a novel method to represent 3D objects, and efforts have been made to address various challenges. Some Techniques are advanced in 3DGS, such as initialization, attribute optimization, rendering, training methods, adaptive control, and post-processing. These improvements make 3DGS work better and handle various tasks. Additionally, 3DGS can be combined with other 3D representation methods, which makes it even better.

Point clouds use many points to represent 3D structures of a scene. 3DGS can fill in missing parts of point clouds. It is also possible to turn 3DGS into point clouds [4]. Meshes use triangles and polygons to represent 3D objects [3]. Triplanes use three perpendicular planes to efficiently represent 3D structure [5]. This makes 3DGS processing faster and more suitable for large scenes.

3 Methods

3.1 System Overview

In our system, users can browse 3D models generated with 3D Gaussian Splatting (3DGS) from free viewpoint. Users can also add annotation objects (3D plane with arbitrary text) by clicking any location on the screen.

As the first step in using this system, users generate two types of scene models (Model 1 and Model 2) from multiple images of the target scene. The first model (Model 1) is a Gaussian model generated by 3DGS for display purposes. The second model (Model 2) is a surface model generated by SuGaR [3] Model 2 is introduced to identify target positions of an annotations (see Sec. 3.2).

By inputting both Model 1 and Model 2 into the system, users can browse the scene from a free viewpoint. By clicking a point on the screen, users can place an annotation object at the point. The system retrieves the three-dimensional coordinates from the models and places an annotation object at that location. The annotation object is placed on the point where the user clicked and aligned with the posture along the surrounding surfaces of the point.

Figures 2 and 3 (Scene A: Room, Scene B: Flower) show examples of a use case. From a video recorded in 4K resolution (3840 × 2160 pixels), we extracted 208 images to generate the 3DGS model shown in Fig. 2 (Model 1). Figure 3 shows this scene model with annotations added. Users can freely place annotations that display attribute information of objects in the scene or work instructions intuitively.

3.2 Annotation Object Placement Method

We use two types of 3D models based on multiple photos taken with any camera. When users add annotations to a scene based on their input, the system needs to obtain 3D coordinates of target point from the models. Model 1, the 3DGS model, which is displayed on the screen, does not have surface information like a mesh model, making it difficult to get depth information. Thus, we introduce Model 2, the mesh model, which has surface information.

In our system, Model 1 and Model 2 are placed at the same coordinates. Only Model 1 is always visible to the user on the screen. When a user clicks on the screen to add an annotation, we determine the position and alignment of an annotation object by the following process. The user clicks on the location where they want to add an annotation on the screen showing Model 1, as shown in the center of Fig. 5. The system retrieves the screen coordinates of the clicked position and the area within a radius of n pixels around that click. Then, the system obtains the depth information corresponding to those coordinates from Model 2. The screen coordinates and depth information are combined and projected into 3D world coordinates to determine the target position. An annotation object is placed at this position.

Next, we align the object's normal direction with the surface's normal direction around the clicked position. To do this, we sample some number of points around the target position and perform principal component analysis on the 3D coordinates of sampled points. We determine the normal direction around the clicked position as the third principal component, and this allows the annotation to be placed along the surface's orientation.

4 Conclusion

In this paper, we propose an interactive system that allows the user to annotate the clicked location by combining the two models.

To solve the problem of difficulty in getting depth information from Model 1, we solved it by using Model 2 and constructed this system by enabling the acquisition of 3D coordinates.

We will improve the placement of annotation objects to make them more effective in the future. In addition, we are exploring methods to evaluate annotations that have been added and displayed. We also aim to improve the utility of our system by testing it in more complex environments.

References

1. Mildenhall, B., et al.: NeRF: representing scenes as neural radiance fields for view synthesis. Commun. ACM **65**(1), 99–106 (2021)
2. Kerbl, B., et al.: 3D gaussian splatting for real-time radiance field rendering. ACM Trans. Graph. **42**(4), 139–141 (2023)
3. Guédon, A., Lepetit, V.: Sugar: surface-aligned gaussian splatting for efficient 3D mesh reconstruction and high-quality mesh rendering. In: Proceedings of the IEEE/CVF Conference on Computer Vision and Pattern Recognition (2024)
4. Lei, X., Wang, M., Zhou, W., Li, H.: GaussNav: Gaussian splatting for visual navigation. arXiv preprint arXiv:2403.11625 (2024)
5. Xu, D., Yuan, Y., Mardani, M., Liu, S., Song, J., Wang, Z., Vahdat, A.: AGG: amortized generative 3D Gaussians for single image to 3D. arXiv preprint arXiv:2401.04099 (2024)

Personal Protective Equipment Detection Based on Improved YOLO11-Nano Using Multi-Perspective Attention

Adri Priadana, Duy-Linh Nguyen, Xuan-Thuy Vo, Jehwan Choi, Ge Cao, and Kang-Hyun Jo(✉)

Department of Electrical, Electronic and Computer Engineering, University of Ulsan, Ulsan, South Korea
{priadana3202,ndlinh301,backhammer5}@mail.ulsan.ac.kr, {cjh1897,acejo}@ulsan.ac.kr, caoge@islab.ulsan.ac.kr

Abstract. Personal Protective Equipment (PPE) detection is essential for strengthening intelligent surveillance systems and ensuring worker compliance with safety protocols in modern manufacturing facilities. A YOLO-based PPE detection model provides an efficient solution for resource-limited environments, supporting real-time operation at high speeds. This work proposes a Multi-Perspective Attention (MPA) module to enhance YOLO11n's performance in PPE detection, enabling its feature extractors to focus on critical elements. Hence, the improved YOLO11n achieves superior results compared to other methods on the PPE Detection (PPED) and Color Helmet and Vest (CHV) datasets, operating at 19.94 and 28.09 frames per second (FPS) on an Intel Core i7-9750H CPU and NVIDIA Jetson Orin Nano GPU devices, respectively, without significantly increasing parameters or computational cost.

Keywords: Multi-Perspective Attention · Personal Protective Equipmen · PPE Detection · Real-Time Detection · YOLO model

1 Introduction

Current technology in the manufacturing industry is evolving through enhanced human-machine integration, where automation, robotics, and AI work alongside human workers to improve efficiency, precision, and productivity. Collaboration between workers and intelligent systems allows for greater flexibility while maintaining the critical role of human oversight in complex production environments [18]. However, this scenario introduces new safety challenges [24]. As robots and automated systems work alongside human operators, risks, including human error, collisions, and physical injuries, can arise, especially in high-speed or heavy-duty operations [13]. Machines are programmed to follow specific instructions, which may not adapt to unpredictable human behavior in unknown cases, leading to potential accidents.

B. Kim (Ed.): IW-FCV 2025, CCIS 2769, pp. 258–272, 2026.
https://doi.org/10.1007/978-981-95-4578-0_22

Advanced technologies, such as computer vision, have been implemented to enhance worker safety in the manufacturing industry. Computer vision enables detection tasks through video surveillance to enforce compliance with safety protocols, including ensuring workers wear personal protective equipment (PPE) [25]. These systems use camera devices to capture real-time images or video feeds of the work environment, which AI algorithms then analyze to detect potential safety violations. By processing visual data from the cameras, the system can accurately identify if workers lack the necessary protection from required equipment [7]. This integration of safety technology ensures worker fulfillment with safety protocols in modern manufacturing facilities, helping to minimize the risk of accidents and injuries.

Computer vision based on deep learning has become a popular approach for personal protective equipment (PPE) detection, with models like YOLO (You Only Look Once) and its improvement frequently employed for rapid detection in real-time scenarios [3,12,17,21,22]. YOLO's architecture is designed for high-speed object detection, making it well-suited for monitoring dynamic environments where quick PPE detection is essential. Since its initial development, YOLO has evolved through multiple versions, with each iteration improving accuracy, speed, and robustness. In addition to these versions, YOLO offers various model sizes, particularly YOLO-Nano, to accommodate hardware and performance requirements for lightweight applications on inexpensive device setups in industrial environments. This versatility has made YOLO a preferred choice in PPE detection, ensuring reliable compliance monitoring across diverse implementation settings.

As the new version, YOLO11 [9] presents a considerable advancement over its predecessors in the YOLO series, providing enhanced speed, accuracy, and efficiency in real-time object detection. Unlike earlier versions, YOLO11 leverages a streamlined architecture with reduced computational burden and improved mean Average Precision (mAP) for object detection tasks. This architecture makes YOLO11 highly adaptable for low-cost devices, requiring efficient performance under limited resources. Nevertheless, there is room to improve YOLO11, especially in enhancing PPE detection performance, without significantly increasing the number of parameters or computational costs.

This work proposes a Multi-Perspective Attention (MPA) module to enhance YOLO11n for PPE detection performance. This work describes its contributions as follows:

1. A novel Multi-Perspective Attention (MPA) module is introduced to support feature extractors on YOLO11n architecture to concentrate on essential features, leading to improved detection performance.
2. The improved YOLO11n for PPE detection achieves better performance than other methods on PPE Detection (PPED) [14] and Color Helmet and Vest (CHV) [22] datasets.
3. The proposed network enables PPE detection to operate at 19.94 and 28.09 frames per second (FPS) on an Intel Core i7-9750H CPU and NVIDIA

Jetson Orin Nano GPU devices, respectively, delivering higher mean Average Precision (mAP) than the baseline YOLO11n model and other methods.

2 Related Work

Research on Personal Protective Equipment (PPE) detection has progressed significantly by leveraging various YOLO (You Only Look Once) architectures to balance speed and accuracy in real-world environments. Several studies utilize different YOLO versions to optimize performance for PPE detection in construction and industrial settings. A study [22] implemented YOLOv5 and demonstrated that the YOLOv5x model achieves high mAP, while the smaller variant, YOLOv5s, offers the fastest processing speed on construction site datasets. Samma et al. [17] improved YOLOv7 with a contrastive-based approach to better distinguish visually similar PPE items by incorporating a contrast loss branch, effectively improving classification accuracy for items like safety glasses.

Further advancements center on YOLOv8, which has gained traction for its precision and efficiency in detecting PPE [12], including helmets and vests, where the large variant (YOLOv8l) achieved a high mAP [3]. Another approach [21] emphasizes cross-level path aggregation on YOLOv8, improving feature fusion and enhancing small object detection while balancing accuracy with computational efficiency. Collectively, these studies highlight the versatility and continuous enhancements of the YOLO architecture, providing the proper solutions for the challenges of real-time PPE detection in safety-critical applications. As the latest version, YOLO11 [9] shows considerable potential for PPE detection applications, demonstrating superior performance in general object detection tasks.

3 The Proposed Method

Figure 1 shows the proposed improved YOLO11n [9] with a novel Multi-Perspective Attention (MPA) module applied on the Conv-MPA blocks. This architecture generates 2,583,517 parameters and 6.3 GFLOPs.

3.1 Multi-Perspective Attention (MPA)

An attention mechanism has proven highly effective in boosting model performance across various vision tasks [1,2]. It enables the feature extractor to dynamically concentrate on critical features in input images, enhancing its ability to capture and represent important information. This work proposed a Multi-Perspective Attention (MPA) module, as shown in Fig. 2. MPA utilizes Efficient Channel Attention (ECA) [20] and improves it by introducing Multi-Perspective Spatial Attention (MPSA). MPA uses ECA [20] to enhance important channels by applying global average pooling to compress spatial dimensions, generating a channel descriptor. This descriptor passes through a 1D convolution with a small

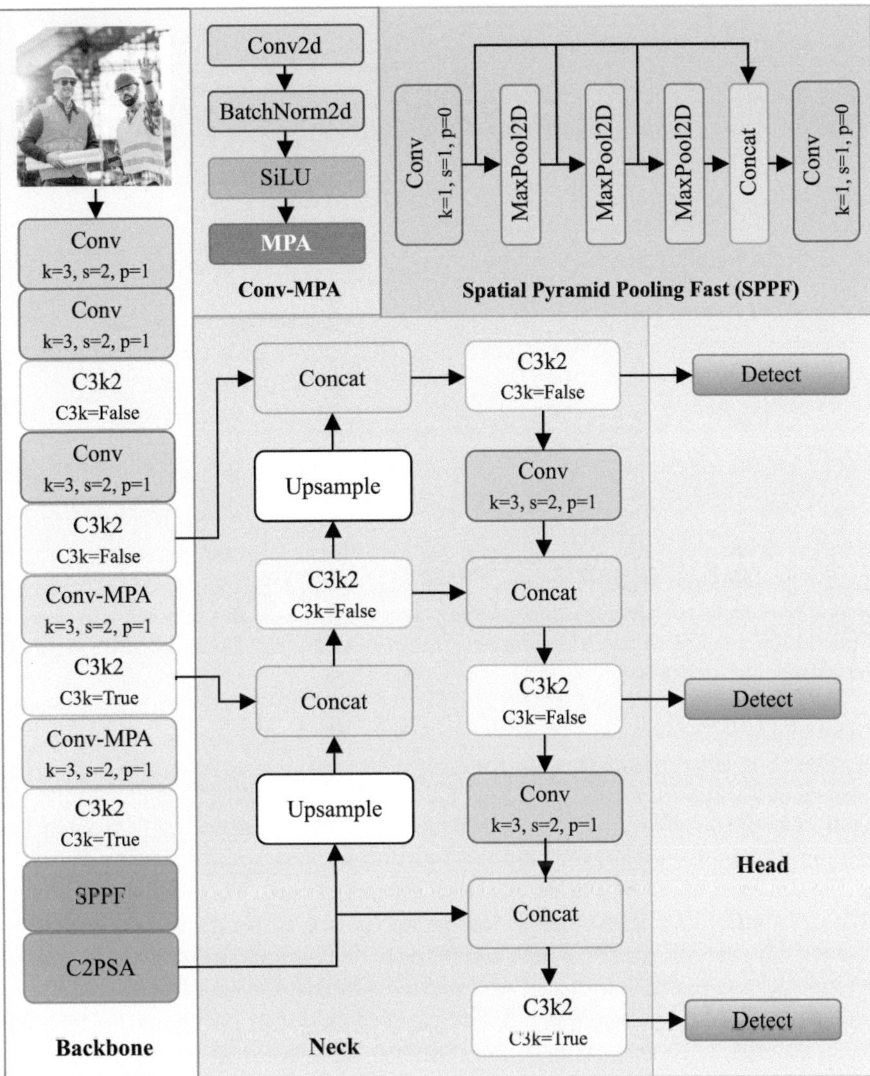

Fig. 1. The improved YOLO11-Nano using Multi-Perspective Attention inside the Conv-MPA blocks.

kernel (e.g., 3) to capture cross-channel interactions, followed by a sigmoid activation to create attention weights. These weights then recalibrate each channel in the original feature map, enabling the model to emphasize essential channels efficiently with minimal parameters.

MPA further enhances it by integrating the MPSA module that considers multi-perspectives. Rather than only employing Average Pooling and Max Pooling across Channel (APC and MPC) as two perspectives, it adds one more per-

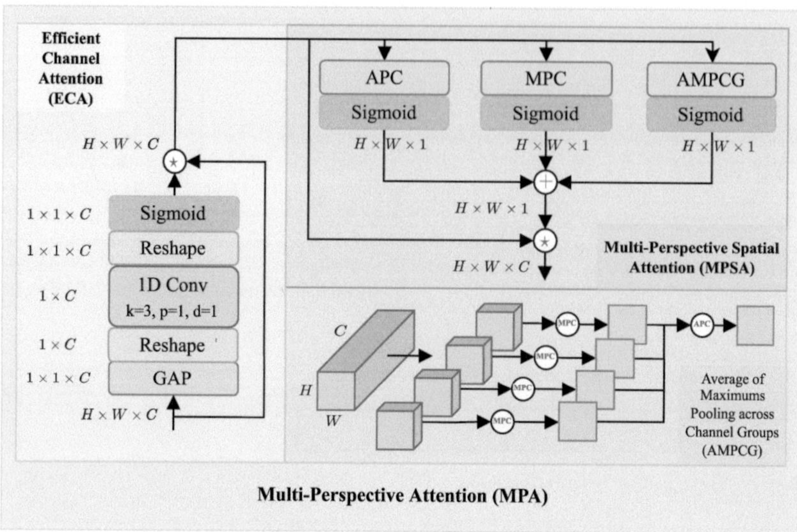

Fig. 2. The proposed Multi-Perspective Attention. APC, MPC, and AMPCG are average pooling across the channel, max pooling operations across the channel, and average of maximum pooling across the channel group, respectively. GAP indicates a global average pooling operation.

spective. The third perspective of the proposed spatial attention is based on the Average of Maximum Pooling across Channel Groups (AMPCG). This approach calculates spatial attention by grouping channels in a feature map, finding the maximum response within each spatial location for each group, and then averaging these maximum values to generate an attention map. This technique aims to highlight spatial locations of the feature map that consistently show high activations within channel groups, which can help the network focus on essential spatial regions without being dominated by specific channels. Given a feature map with dimensions $H \times W \times C$ where C is the number of channels, partition the channels into G groups, each containing C/G channels. For each spatial location in the feature map (H, W) within a group, compute the maximum activation across the channels within that group. It results in a map of maximum values for each spatial location in every group, emphasizing the strongest response across each group of channels. For each spatial location (H, W), it computes the average of the maximum values from all groups and applies Sigmoid activation. It produces a single attention map as the third perspective that emphasizes important spatial locations based on group responses. By grouping channels and focusing on the highest activations in each group, this method identifies consistent patterns across different types of feature responses, helping the model focus on relevant spatial areas without relying on specific channels alone.

Moreover, MPA performs Sigmoid activation for each perspective (APC, MPC, and AMPCG) and combines them with a summarization operation. This approach allows the resulting attention map to range from 0 to 3, which effectively increases the maximum possible attention score, which could allow for a stronger emphasis on highly attended regions. It provides greater flexibility in the range of attention values, potentially giving more weight to prominent features. The proposed MPA equation is defined as follows:

$$\mathrm{ECA}(\mathbf{X}) = \mathbf{X} * \sigma(\mathrm{C1}(\mathrm{GAP}(\mathbf{X}))), \tag{1}$$

$$\mathrm{MPSA}(\mathbf{X}') = \mathbf{X}' * (\sigma(\mathrm{APC}(\mathbf{X}')) + \sigma(\mathrm{MPC}(\mathbf{X}')) + \sigma(\mathrm{AMPCG}(\mathbf{X}'))), \tag{2}$$

$$\mathrm{MPA}(\mathbf{X}) = \mathrm{MPSA}(\mathrm{ECA}(\mathbf{X})), \tag{3}$$

where C1 and GAP are a 1D convolution operation with kernel size 1 and a global average pooling operation, respectively. APC, MPC, and AMPCG are average pooling across the channel, max pooling operations across the channel, and average of maximum pooling across the channel group, respectively. σ indicates a sigmoid activation function. In summary, the proposed spatial attention has three perspectives as follows:

1. Average Pooling across Channels (APC): Produces a more balanced attention map but may underrepresent important high-signal areas where high values are meaningful.
2. Maximum Pooling across Channels (MPC): Results in an attention map that highlights the extreme values from a particular channel, potentially leading to the essential information or may also indicate a noise.
3. Average of Maximum Pooling across Channel Groups (AMPCG): Provides a compromise by reducing sensitivity to noise while still capturing prominent features from multiple channel groups, leading to a more stable yet responsive attention map. It makes the attention map less sensitive to noise or outliers from individual channels, leading to more stable attention signals.

3.2 The Overall Architecture

YOLO11 builds upon its predecessors, YOLOv8, by introducing architectural enhancements in its backbone and neck, making it more efficient and accurate across various computer vision tasks. The backbone and neck in YOLO11 replace the C2f module from YOLOv8 with the C3k2 module, as shown in Fig. 3, a more adaptable feature extraction block. C3k2 toggles between using a standard bottleneck or C3k module (with two times the standard bottleneck inside) depending on a configurable parameter C3k. C3k is a Cross Stage Partial (CSP) bottleneck module consisting of three 1×1 convolutions and n times the standard bottleneck with customizable kernel sizes in which it applies 3×3 kernel size as the default setting. When C3k is assigned to False, the C3k2 behaves like the original C2f module with standard bottlenecks, but when set to True, it adopts the C3k module, enhancing feature fusion for better contextual understanding.

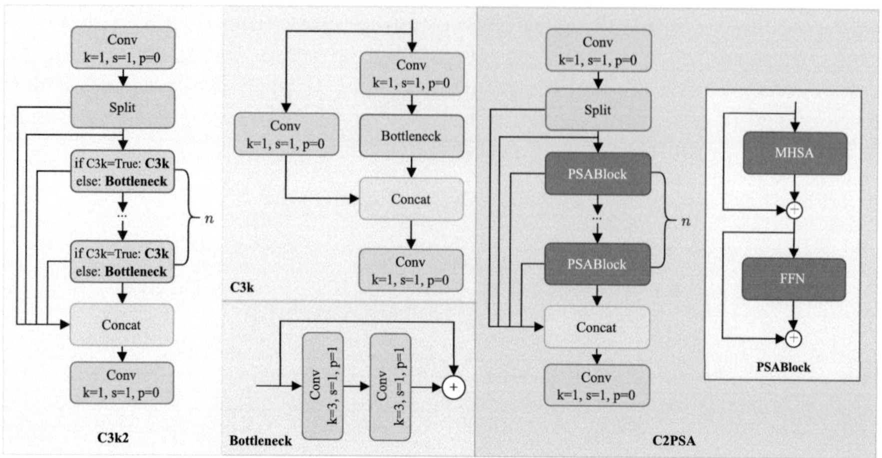

Fig. 3. The C3k2 and C2PSA blocks of YOLO11. PSA, MHSA, and FFN are Position-Sensitive Attention, a multi-head self-attention, and a feed-forward network, respectively.

In the last two C3k2 layers of the backbone and the final C3k2 layer of the neck, C3k is set to True, while the remaining layers have C3k set to False. In the first two C3k2 layers of the backbone, the channels are split into 75% and 25%, with the bottleneck operation applied to the 25% portion. For the remaining C3k2, it splits into the same portion (50% and 50%).

YOLO11 introduces the C2PSA module, as shown in Fig. 3, an advanced layer extending the functionality of the C2f by integrating a Position-Sensitive Attention (PSA) block. PSA block consists of a multi-head self-attention module (MHSA) and a feed-forward network (FFN) layers with shortcut connections. This shortcut enables residual connections, facilitating better gradient flow and improving model training stability. The FFN layer projects features and allows the model to capture more complex non-linear relationships and enrich feature representation.

The head of YOLO11 continues the trend set by YOLOv8 by employing an anchor-free, decoupled structure, independently handling objectness, classification, and regression tasks. For bounding-box loss, YOLO11 also employs CIoU loss [26] and Distribution Focal Loss (DFL) [11], in addition to binary cross-entropy for the classification loss (Cls). The complete loss function is outlined as follows:

$$L = \lambda_{CIoU} L_{CIoU} + \lambda_{DFL} L_{DFL} + \lambda_{Cls} L_{Cls}, \tag{4}$$

where λ is a balance parameter for each loss.

4 Implementation Settings

All experiments in this work are trained using the PyTorch and YOLO11 framework on an NVIDIA Tesla V100 32 GB GPU. This work trains the model over 300 epochs with a batch size of 128, utilizing Stochastic Gradient Descent (SGD) as the optimizer, an initial learning rate of 10^{-2}, and a momentum of 0.937. Following default settings, the balance parameters for box, class, and DFL loss weights are set to 7.5, 0.5, and 1.5, respectively. It uses 640×640 as the input dimension, with confidence and IoU thresholds for prediction fixed at 0.25 and 0.7, respectively. For real-time scenario evaluations, an Intel Core i7-9750H CPU @ 2.60GHz with 20GB RAM and NVIDIA Jetson Orin Nano with 8GB GPU memory are used to execute the model, measuring runtime performance in FPS.

Table 1. Experimental Result Comparison on PPE Detection (PPED) [14] and Color Helmet and Vest (CHV) [22] datasets.

Architectures	Params (M)	GFLOPs	Runtime (FPS)		mAP on PPED (%)		mAP on CHV (%)	
			CPU	JON	0.5	0.5:0.95	0.5	0.5:0.95
YOLOv3-tiny [16]	9.52	14.3	13.78	38.04	88.3	51.8	79.2	46.2
YOLOv5n [8]	2.18	5.8	25.47	34.11	90.4	55.8	85.0	49.3
YOLOv6n [10]	4.16	11.5	22.00	37.73	91.6	56.5	84.3	49.7
YOLOv8n [9]	2.69	6.8	23.06	35.91	90.8	56.9	85.4	49.6
YOLOv10n [19]	2.70	8.2	17.27	27.25	90.9	56.1	83.9	49.0
YOLO11n [9]	2.58	6.3	20.15	29.60	91.0	57.1	85.3	49.9
YOLO11n [9] + **MPA**	**2.58**	**6.3**	**19.94**	**28.09**	**92.3**	**59.6**	**85.5**	**50.5**

CPU and JON mean the runtime on an Intel Core i7-9750H CPU @ 2.60GHz and NVIDIA Jetson Orin Nano with 8GB GPU memory, respectively.

5 Experiments and Results

5.1 Evaluation on Datasets

PPE Detection (PPED). PPE Detection dataset [14] contains 9,733 images with 41,700 annotations and is sourced from the Roboflow website. It is divided into three subsets: 8,726 images for training, 507 for validation, and 500 for testing. The dataset includes five classes: helmet, no-helmet, no-vest, person, and vest. The improved YOLO11n model with MPA demonstrates superior performance over the baseline YOLO11n and other methods. Table 1 shows that it achieves 92.3% mAP@0.5 and 59.6% mAP@0.5:0.95, marking an increase of 1.3% in mAP@0.5 and 2.5% in mAP@0.5:0.95 compared to the baseline YOLO11n.

Color Helmet and Vest (CHV). CHV dataset [22] contains 1,330 images with 9,209 annotations and is sourced from the Roboflow website. It is split into three subsets: 1,064 images for training, 133 for validation, and 133 for testing.

The dataset has five classes: person, vest, blue helmet, red, white, and yellow helmet. The improved YOLO11n model with MPA also presents superior performance over the baseline YOLO11n and other methods. Table 1 displays that it achieves 85.5% mAP@0.5 and 50.5% mAP@0.5:0.95, marking an increase of 0.2% in mAP@0.5 and 0.6% in mAP@0.5:0.95 compared to the baseline YOLO11n.

5.2 Ablation Study

This subsection evaluates the impact of each component of the proposed MPA through an ablation analysis conducted on the PPED dataset [14]. The MPA module comprises ECA [23] and MPSA. Using only ECA [23] with the YOLO11n network achieves an mAP@0.5 of 91.4% and an mAP@0.5:0.95 of 58.6%, as shown in Table 2. Similarly, applying only the proposed MPSA with the YOLO11n network achieves 92.1% in mAP@0.5 and 58.3% in mAP@0.5:0.95. Combining ECA [23] and the proposed MPSA as the MPA module yields the best results, with an mAP@0.5 of 92.3% and an mAP@0.5:0.95 of 59.6%.

Table 2. Ablation Study of the proposed MPA on PPE Detection (PPED) [14] dataset.

Component	Params	GFLOPs	mAP on PPED (%)	
			0.5	0.5:0.95
ECA [23]	2,583,517	6.3	91.4	58.6
MPSA (Our)	2,583,511	6.3	92.1	58.3
ECA [23] + MPSA as MPA (Our)	2,583,517	6.3	92.3	59.6

Table 3. MPA Modules Analysis on PPE Detection (PPED) [14] dataset.

Settings	Params	GFLOPs	mAP on PPED (%)	
			0.5	0.5:0.95
APC	2,583,517	6.3	91.7	58.4
APC + MPC	2,583,517	6.3	91.7	58.6
APC + AMPCG	2,583,517	6.3	92.5	59.0
APC + MPC + AMPCG	2,583,517	6.3	92.3	59.6
$G = 8$	2,583,517	6.3	91.7	58.7
$G = 4$	2,583,517	6.3	92.3	59.6
$G = 2$	2,583,517	6.3	92.4	59.1
Summarization before Sigmoid	2,583,517	6.3	91.0	58.5
Summarization after Sigmoid	2,583,517	6.3	92.3	59.6

5.3 MPA Module Analysis

This work proposes the MPA module, which incorporates three perspectives (APC, MPC, and AMPCG) in the spatial attention component. Table 3 shows that combining these three perspectives achieves the highest mAP, outperforming the use of only one or two perspectives. This table also indicates that setting the number of groups in the AMPCG perspective to 4 ($G = 4$) yields the best mAP compared to using 8 ($G = 8$) or 2 ($G = 2$) groups. Additionally, the proposed MPA applies Sigmoid activation to each perspective individually, followed by a summarization operation ("Summarization after Sigmoid"), which delivers better mAP than performing summarization before Sigmoid activation ("Summarization before Sigmoid"), as demonstrated in Table 3.

Table 4. Attention Modules Comparison inside the last two Conv block of YOLO11n's backbone on PPE Detection (PPED) [14] dataset.

Attention Modules	Params	GFLOPs	mAP on PPED (%)	
			0.5	0.5:0.95
CBAM [23]	2,666,011	6.4	91.8	58.1
SE [6]	2,593,751	6.3	91.6	58.1
DGA [15]	2,648,407	6.4	90.8	58.6
ECA [20]	2,583,517	6.3	91.4	58.6
GCB [4]	2,625,529	6.4	90.3	58.9
CA [5]	2,593,543	6.3	92.1	59.0
MPA (Ours)	**2,583,517**	**6.3**	**92.3**	**59.6**

5.4 Attention Module Comparison

MPA is introduced as an attention module, applied on Conv-MPA blocks YOLO11n's backbone to enhance the performance. This section evaluates the effectiveness of MPA by comparing its performance against other attention modules, including Convolutional Block Attention Module (CBAM) [23], Squeeze and Excitation (SE) [6], Depth-wise Global Attention (DGA) [15], Efficient Channel Attention (ECA) [20], Global Context Block (GCB) [4] and Coordinate Attention [5] with the same setting. In this case, the proposed MPA utilizes on YOLO11n outperforms other attention modules and achieves 92.3% mAP@0.5 and 59.6% mAP@0.5:0.95 on PPED [14] dataset as demonstrated in Table 4.

5.5 Runtime Efficiency

The YOLO11n network, improved with the MPA module, operates in real-time on an Intel Core i7-9750H CPU and NVIDIA Jetson Orin Nano GPU devices, achieving an average of 19.94 and 28.09 FPS, respectively, as shown in Table 1. While it operates slightly slower than the baseline YOLO11n by 0.21 and 1.51 FPS on the respective device, the improved YOLO11n demonstrates higher mAP, increasing 1.3% and 2.5% on mAP@0.5 and mAP@0.5:0.95, respectively, on the PPED dataset [14]. Additionally, it shows mAP@0.5 and mAP@0.5:0.95 gains of 0.2% and 0.6%, respectively, on the CHV dataset [22]. Compared to the other methods, the improved YOLO11n ranks fifth. However, it achieves top performance based on mAP@0.5 and mAP@0.5:0.95 across both benchmark datasets.

5.6 Precision, Efficiency, and Speed Trade-Offs

The integration of the proposed MPA module into YOLO11n results in a significant improvement in detection performance, as reflected by a mAP@0.5 increase of 1.3% on the PPED dataset and 0.2% on the CHV dataset, along with an even more notable boost in mAP@0.5:0.95 by 2.5% and 0.6%, respectively. These gains highlight the module's ability to enhance detection precision. As the essential perspective, the MPA module achieves this without adding significant computational or memory overhead, as evidenced by the similar GFLOPs (6.3) and parameter count (2.58M). However, there is a slight trade-off in runtime efficiency, with a reduction of 1.04 FPS on the Intel Core i7-9750H CPU and 1.51 FPS on the NVIDIA Jetson Orin Nano GPU devices. This minor drop in speed may be acceptable in applications prioritizing accuracy over speed, particularly for resource-constrained environments where the constant computational and memory costs make the improved YOLO11n highly practical. Overall, the MPA module strikes a favorable balance, providing substantial precision improvements with minimal impact on speed.

5.7 Qualitative Result

This section presents a qualitative result, comparing the improved YOLO11n utilizing the proposed MPA module to YOLO11n as the baseline. The proposed model demonstrates better detection performance, as shown in Fig. 4. It detects a person without a vest, while the baseline YOLO11n fails to detect it, as displayed in the first column. In the second and third columns, the improved YOLO11n detects a person without a vest and a person with a helmet, respectively, which the baseline YOLO11n misses. Moreover, the improved YOLO11n generally shows a higher confidence score for detected objects than the baseline, as exhibited in the fourth and fifth columns. However, both networks still encounter challenges in scenarios involving small objects, where they struggle to detect people without vests, as noticed in the second and third columns.

Fig. 4. Qualitative Result Comparison between the YOLO11n as the baseline and the improved YOLO11n with MPA trained on PPED [14] dataset.

6 Conclusion

This work introduces a Multi-Perspective Attention (MPA) module as the novelty to enhance the YOLO11n model for PPE detection. The MPA module helps the feature extractors on the YOLO11n model to concentrate on essential features based on channel-specific details while also considering spatial-specific detail based on multi-perspectives in the feature map. Applied inside the Conv-MPA blocks in YOLO11n's backbone, MPA improves detection performance. The enhanced YOLO11n achieves 92.3% mAP@0.5, 59.6% mAP@0.5:0.95, and 85.5% mAP@0.5, 50.5% mAP@0.5:0.95 on PPED and CHV datasets, respectively, outperforming the other methods. Additionally, it operates at 19.94 and 28.09 FPS in real-time on an Intel Core i7-9750H CPU and NVIDIA Jetson Orin Nano GPU devices, respectively, delivering superior mAP. Future research may aim to train and evaluate the proposed network on additional benchmark datasets, particularly those with more variations in PPE types and complex environments, such as occlusions, lighting changes, and crowded scenes.

Acknowledgment. This result was supported by "Regional Innovation Strategy (RIS)" through the National Research Foundation of Korea(NRF) funded by the Ministry of Education(MOE)(2021RIS-003).

References

1. An, J., Putro, M.D., Priadana, A., Jo, K.H.: Improved yolov5 network with cbam for object detection vision drone. In: 2023 IEEE International Conference on Industrial Technology (ICIT). pp. 1–6 (2023). https://doi.org/10.1109/ICIT58465.2023.10143118
2. An, J., Putro, M.D., Priadana, A., Lee, Y., Kim, J., Jo, K.H.: Yolov5 with combination of coordinate attention and cbam for object detection on drone. In: IECON 2023- 49th Annual Conference of the IEEE Industrial Electronics Society. pp. 1–6 (2023). https://doi.org/10.1109/IECON51785.2023.10312634
3. Barlybayev, A., et al.: Personal protective equipment detection using yolov8 architecture on object detection benchmark datasets: a comparative study. Cogent Eng. **11**(1), 2333209 (2024)
4. Cao, Y., Xu, J., Lin, S., Wei, F., Hu, H.: Global context networks. IEEE Trans. Pattern Anal. Mach. Intell. **45**(6), 6881–6895 (2023). https://doi.org/10.1109/TPAMI.2020.3047209
5. Hou, Q., Zhou, D., Feng, J.: Coordinate attention for efficient mobile network design. In: 2021 IEEE/CVF Conference on Computer Vision and Pattern Recognition (CVPR). pp. 13708–13717 (2021). https://doi.org/10.1109/CVPR46437.2021.01350
6. Hu, J., Shen, L., Albanie, S., Sun, G., Wu, E.: Squeeze-and-excitation networks. IEEE Trans. Pattern Anal. Mach. Intell. **42**(8), 2011–2023 (2020). https://doi.org/10.1109/TPAMI.2019.2913372
7. Ji, X., Gong, F., Yuan, X., Wang, N.: A high-performance framework for personal protective equipment detection on the offshore drilling platform. Complex & Intell. Syst. **9**(5), 5637–5652 (2023)

8. Jocher, G.: YOLOv5 by Ultralytics (2020). https://doi.org/10.5281/zenodo.3908559, https://github.com/ultralytics/yolov5
9. Jocher, G., Qiu, J., Chaurasia, A.: Ultralytics YOLO (2023). https://github.com/ultralytics/ultralytics
10. Li, C., et al.: Yolov6: A single-stage object detection framework for industrial applications. arXiv preprint arXiv:2209.02976 (2022)
11. Li, X., et al.: Generalized focal loss: learning qualified and distributed bounding boxes for dense object detection. Adv. Neural. Inf. Process. Syst. **33**, 21002–21012 (2020)
12. Mohona, R.T., Nawer, S., Sakib, M.S.I., Uddin, M.N.: A yolov8 approach for personal protective equipment (ppe) detection to ensure workers' safety. In: 2024 3rd International Conference on Advancement in Electrical and Electronic Engineering (ICAEEE). pp. 1–6 (2024). https://doi.org/10.1109/ICAEEE62219.2024.10561752
13. Othman, U., Yang, E.: Human-robot collaborations in smart manufacturing environments: review and outlook. Sensors **23**(12), 5663 (2023)
14. PPEDETECTION: Ppe detection dataset. https://universe.roboflow.com/ppedetection-bxhrx/ppe-detection-obefe (2024). https://universe.roboflow.com/ppedetection-bxhrx/ppe-detection-obefe, Visited on 04 Nov 2024
15. Priadana, A., Putro, M.D., Vo, X.T., Jo, K.H.: An efficient face-based age group detector on a cpu using two perspective convolution with attention modules. In: 2022 International Conference on Multimedia Analysis and Pattern Recognition (MAPR). pp. 1–6. IEEE (2022)
16. Redmon, J., Farhadi, A.: Yolov3: An incremental improvement. arXiv preprint arXiv:1804.02767 (2018)
17. Samma, H., Al-Azani, S., Luqman, H., Alfarraj, M.: Contrastive-based yolov7 for personal protective equipment detection. Neural Comput. Appl. **36**(5), 2445–2457 (2024)
18. Tsamados, A., Floridi, L., Taddeo, M.: Human control of ai systems: from supervision to teaming. AI and Ethics pp. 1–14 (2024)
19. Wang, A., et al.: Yolov10: Real-time end-to-end object detection. arXiv preprint arXiv:2405.14458 (2024)
20. Wang, Q., Wu, B., Zhu, P., Li, P., Zuo, W., Hu, Q.: Eca-net: Efficient channel attention for deep convolutional neural networks. In: 2020 IEEE/CVF Conference on Computer Vision and Pattern Recognition (CVPR). pp. 11531–11539. IEEE (2020)
21. Wang, Z., Zhu, Y., Ji, Z., Liu, S., Zhang, Y.: An efficient yolov8-based model with cross-level path aggregation enabling personal protective equipment detection. IEEE Transactions on Industrial Informatics pp. 1–12 (2024). https://doi.org/10.1109/TII.2024.3431045
22. Wang, Z., Wu, Y., Yang, L., Thirunavukarasu, A., Evison, C., Zhao, Y.: Fast personal protective equipment detection for real construction sites using deep learning approaches. Sensors **21**(10), 3478 (2021)
23. Woo, S., Park, J., Lee, J.-Y., Kweon, I.S.: CBAM: Convolutional Block Attention Module. In: Ferrari, V., Hebert, M., Sminchisescu, C., Weiss, Y. (eds.) ECCV 2018. LNCS, vol. 11211, pp. 3–19. Springer, Cham (2018). https://doi.org/10.1007/978-3-030-01234-2_1
24. Xian, W., Yu, K., Han, F., Fang, L., He, D., Han, Q.L.: Advanced manufacturing in industry 5.0: A survey of key enabling technologies and future trends. IEEE Transactions on Industrial Informatics pp. 1–15 (2023). https://doi.org/10.1109/TII.2023.3274224

25. Yousif, I., Samaha, J., Ryu, J., Harik, R.: Safety 4.0: harnessing computer vision for advanced industrial protection. Manuf. Lett. **41**, 1342–1356 (2024)
26. Zheng, Z., Wang, P., Liu, W., Li, J., Ye, R., Ren, D.: Distance-iou loss: faster and better learning for bounding box regression. In: Proceedings of the AAAI conference on artificial intelligence. vol. 34, pp. 12993–13000 (2020)

Preliminary Experiments for Behavior Log Generation Considering Spatial Relationship Between Actions and Objects

Masae Yokota[1(✉)], Sarthak Pathak[2], Mihoko Niitsuma[2], and Kazunori Umeda[2]

[1] Precision Engineering Course, Graduate School of Science and Engineering, Chuo University, 1-13-27 Kasuga, Bunkyo-ku, Tokyo, Japan
yokota@sensor.mech.chuo-u.ac.jp

[2] Department of Precision Mechanics, Faculty of Science and Engineering, Chuo University, 1-13-27 Kasuga, Bunkyo-ku, Tokyo, Japan
{pathak,niitsuma,umeda}@mech.chuo-u.ac.jp

Abstract. This paper describes a method for creating human action sentences from video information, which aims to infer the purpose of human actions from video information. To develop a flexible human-robot communication method that enables robots to infer their own roles from the appearance of people, it is necessary to observe and convert human behavior into data. Therefore, we have created sentences describing human behavior by combining an action recognition model and an object detection algorithm, and we have organized the spatial relationships between objects and people. In Verification 1, a simple one-sentence explanation of the behavior was provided based on the distance between the two-dimensional (2D) coordinates of the person and the object taking the action from the video image information. Through the verification, we have identified issues in the generation of behavioral sentences. In Verification 2, we spatially organized their relationship based on the change in the three-dimensional (3D) coordinates of the object and the person. Through this validation, we were able to obtain spatial information on human behavior and object access records. In the future, by integrating these methods, we aim to generate an in-spatial action log that links human behavior and spatial information.

Keywords: Human-object Intention · Intelligent Room · Action recognition

1 Introduction

In recent years, flexible human-robot communication methods have been studied to improve the efficiency of human-robot communication and reduce the burden on humans [1–3]. In human-robot collaborative work, a person naturally understands the division of roles by observing the behavior and actions of the other person. However, in human-robot collaborative work, people often give explicit instructions to the robot, which

B. Kim (Ed.): IW-FCV 2025, CCIS 2769, pp. 273–283, 2026.
https://doi.org/10.1007/978-981-95-4578-0_23

increases the burden on the person during the work and prevents flexible communication. Therefore, methods to help robots understand the intent of human actions by observing and contextually interpreting records of human actions and access to objects have been studied [4]. In this paper, we attempted to generate action logs from spatial information of human actions and accessed objects in the observation space in order to make robots understand the potential purpose of human behaviors and to generate human action sentences from video image information. In Verification 1, the distance between the bounding boxes of detected actions and objects was observed, and the method of identifying the object that is the target of the action was discussed. In Validation 2, we organized the location of people and objects in the overhead view. From these results, we discuss and identify issues for the integration of the method and the automatic generation of human action sentences.

2 Related Works

Research is being conducted with the aim of improving the effectiveness of human-robot collaboration by building natural and intuitive communication methods using image information [5]. Among these methods, research is being conducted to understand human intention by observing human behavior, and robots are actively acting to assist human tasks [6]. In our study, based on the seven-step action model proposed by Norman [7], we believe that clear intentions are latent in a person's sequence of actions. For example, when the intention to go shopping is formed, a person plans and performs detailed actions such as "picking up a bag," "putting a purse in a bag," "putting on a jacket," "going to the entrance," "putting on shoes," and "opening the door." By contextually inferring a person's intentions from the history of the multiple actions performed, it is possible to predict the actions that will be performed after the inferred point in time. Thus, it is necessary to represent actions as data in order to understand and infer people's intentions, which is the ultimate goal of this research. Here, it is important to consider time series and context in order to understand the intention of a person's movement from the observation results of the person's behavior. Research is also being conducted to generate explanatory text from images, taking into account the interaction between people and objects [8].

However, it is difficult to construct a model from scratch that explains the meaning of each action and each accessed object, because it requires a huge amount of data sets and time. Therefore, this paper aims to organize human-object interaction from video information and represent it as data, and conducted the following two types of verification.

– Verification 1: Verification of a Method for Searching Objects for Action by 2D Distance Relationship between Action Detection Bounding Box and Object Detection Bounding Box
– Verification 2: Verification to identify the conditions necessary to identify the target object for action by observing the 3D position of a person and the 3D position of an object

3 Preliminary Verifications

3.1 Overview

Two types of elemental validation were performed to generate human action sentences from video image information. Both validations used MMAction2 [9] as the action detection algorithm and YOLO [10] as the object detection algorithm. A single video recorded in the environment shown in Fig. 1a was used for verification. The path of movement of the person is shown in Fig. 1b. The combined image taken from camera 1 to 4 is shown in Fig. 2a. The image taken from camera 5 is shown in Fig. 2b. The "chair" indicated by the purple triangle in Fig. 1b is the chair in Fig. 2a and Fig. 2b. The images were recorded at the same time. First, a person with a cup and a kettle approaches the dining table from the far left of the screen and sets them down, then goes to the far right to retrieve a book, returns to the dining table, sits on the chair, and finally drinks a drink while reading the book. In Verification 1, we used videos taken as shown in Fig. 2b. We verified the possible to extract the object of the action from the 2D distance between the center of the bounding box acquired when the action was detected and the center of the bounding box acquired when the object was detected. Then, in Verification 2, we used the video acquired in Fig. 2a. The location of the objects accessed by the person and the path of the person's movement were organized in an overhead view and compared to the timing at which the action occurred.

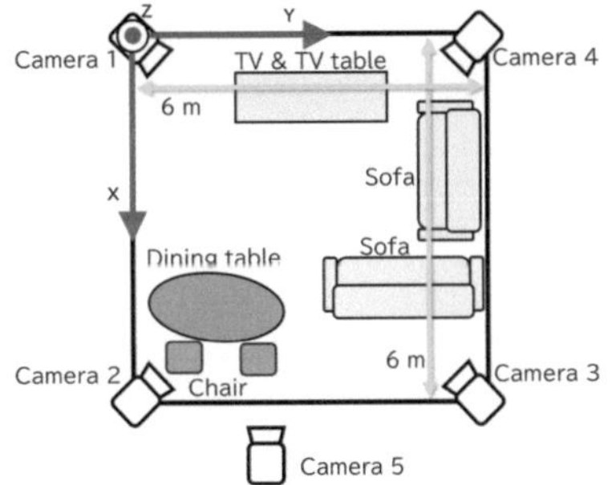

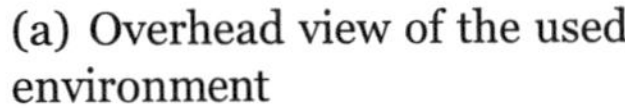
(a) Overhead view of the used environment

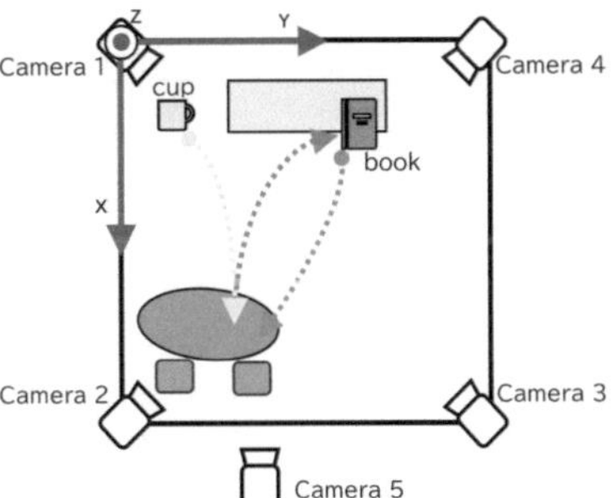

(b) Overhead view of a simplified representation of the behavior in the video used for verification

Fig. 1. Environment under which the video used for verification was recorded

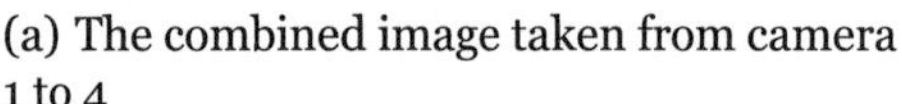
(a) The combined image taken from camera 1 to 4

(b) The image taken from camera 5

Fig. 2. The video images

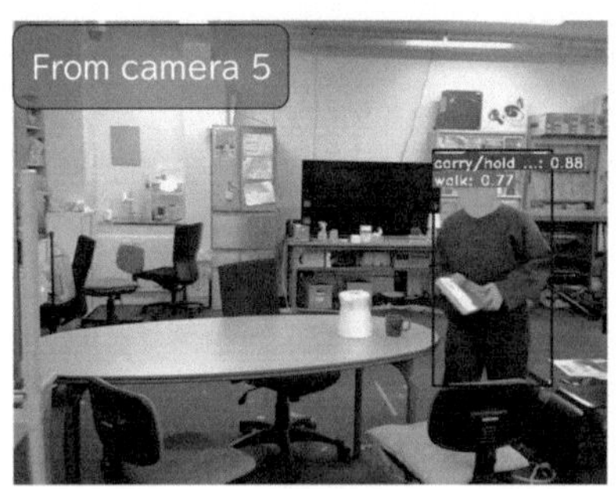

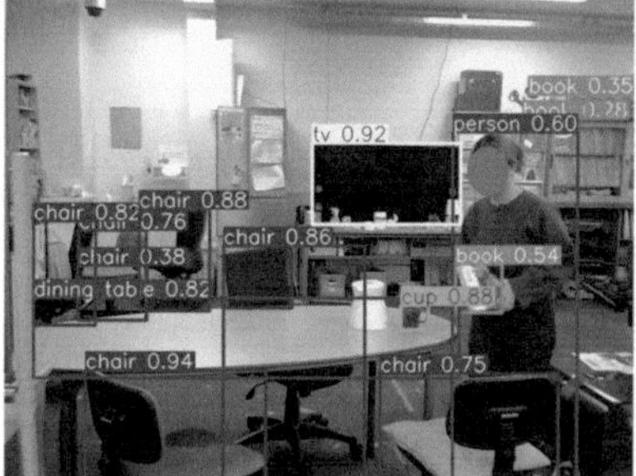

(a) The action detection result in camera 5

(b) The object detection result in camera 5

Fig. 3. The detection results

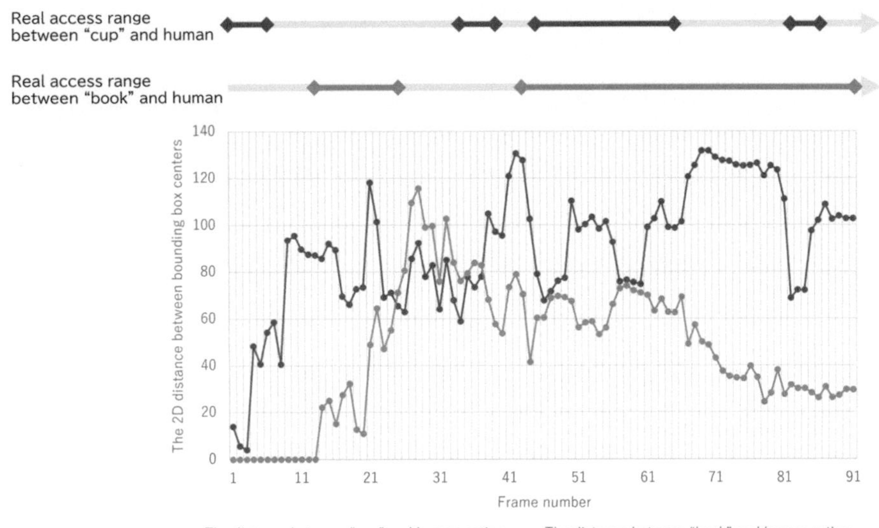

Fig. 4. The graph: Real access range and distance between the bounding box centers of each object and human action

3.2 Verification 1: Identification of Objects for Action Based on the Two-Dimensional Distance Between the Action and the Object's Bounding Box Center

In this verification, we aimed at automatic generation of action statements and identified objects to be acted upon by integrating the results of action detection and object detection. Using video images as shown in Fig. 2b, taken at the positions shown in Fig. 1, the results of action detection and object detection were integrated to identify the object to be acted upon. MMAction2 [9] developed by OpenMMlab was used for action detection. This detected the actions of a person in the video every 8 frames, as shown in Fig. 3a, and saved the action label name and the center coordinates of the bounding box at the time of action detection. YOLOv8 [10] was used for object detection, and the object name and the center coordinates of the bounding box detected in each frame were saved as shown in Fig. 3b.

The 2D distance between the bounding box centers of the detected action and the detected object was calculated. We focused only on the action "carry/hold (an object)" and assumed that the two possible objects for this behavior are "cup" and "book". The distance between the bounding box center in each frame and the true or false of the real access as a combination of actual actions and objects are shown in Fig. 4. The graphs are divided by attention to each object in Fig. 5.

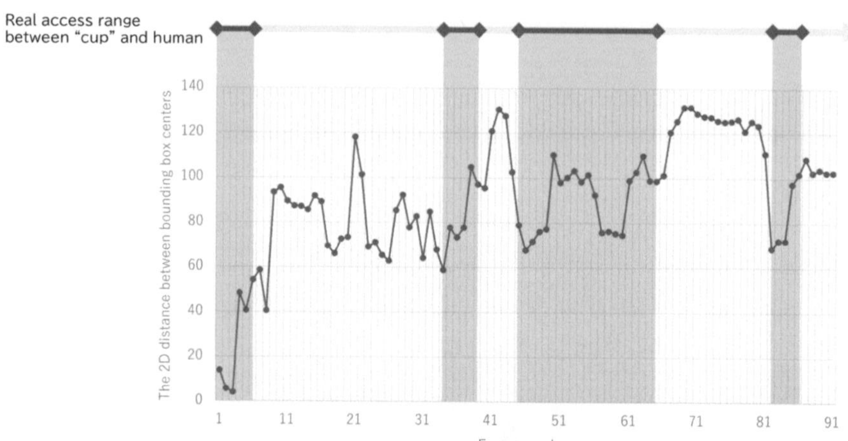

(a) The graph: Real access range and distance between the bounding box centers of "cup" and human action

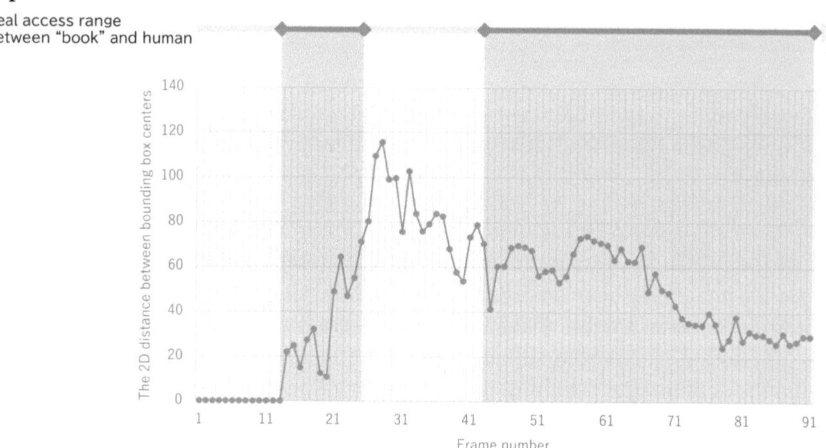

(b) The graph: Real access range and distance between the bounding box centers of "book" and human action

Fig. 5. The divided graph

The straight line above the line graph indicates the extent of actual contact between the object and the person. The gray arrows indicate the time series, and the blue line indicates the time between actual accesses between the "cup" and the person. The orange line indicates the time between the actual accesses between "book" and the person. Here, the cases when the object is being grasped and when it is being let go are excluded. The line graphs show the distance between the human action bounding box center and the respective object bounding box center at each frame point. In the initial frames, the bounding box center of the "book" could not be measured due to occlusion, so the distance is shown as 0.

3.3 Verification 2: Observation of Three-Dimensional Positional Relationships Between Objects and People for Clarification of Conditions for Identification of Objects to be Acted Upon

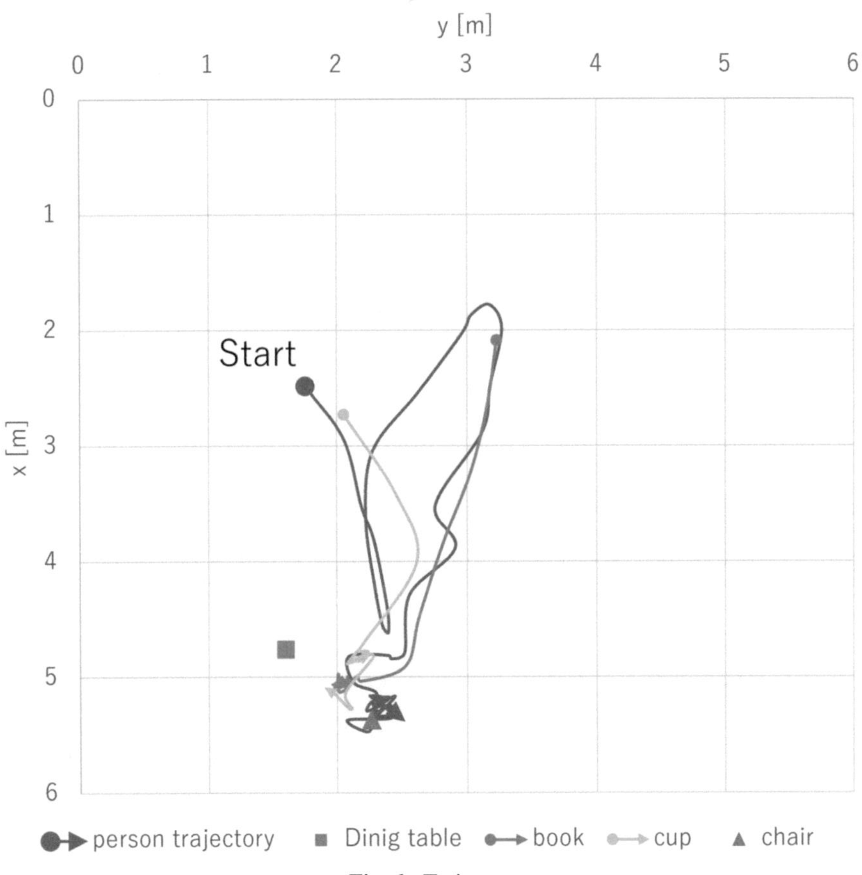

Fig. 6. Trajectory

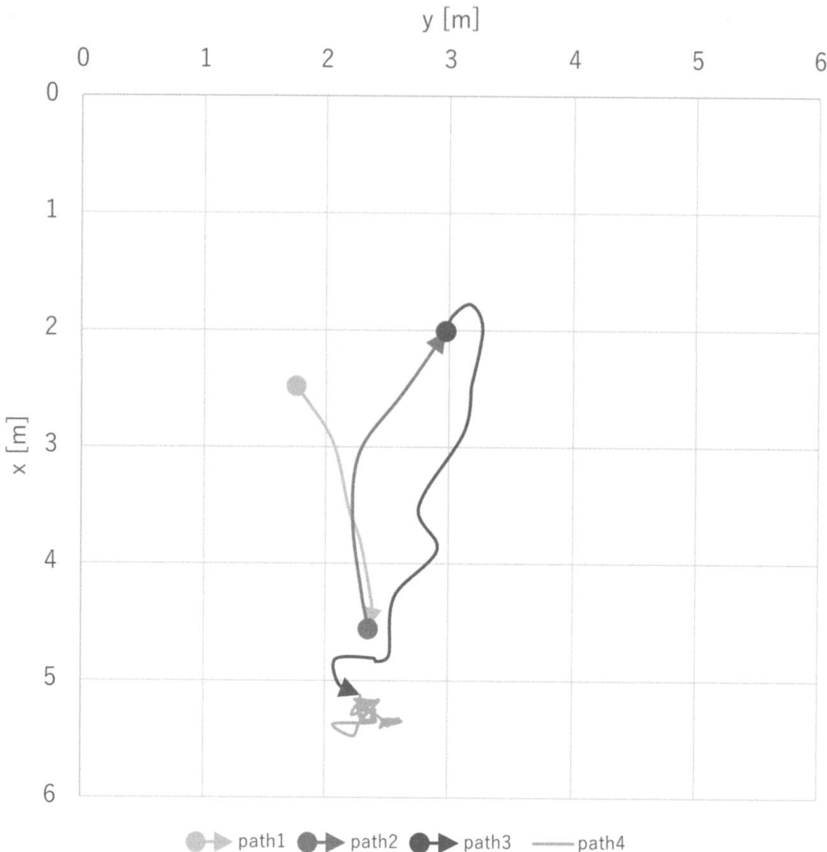

Fig. 7. The divided trajectory

In this verification, the spatial relationship between objects and people was organized using video images recorded from different angles of the video images used in Verification 1. Images obtained from 1 to 4 cameras in the environment shown in Fig. 1a were combined as shown in Fig. 2a, and object detection using YOLO was performed on these moving images to organize the relationship between the trajectory of the person and the position of the object. In this process, since the same point cannot be observed stably at the bounding box center of a person's whole body, we focused on the head, which can be approximated as a sphere, and used the path of the bounding box center of the head as the person's movement path.

As in Verification 1, we focused only on "carry/hold (an object)" when considering access to objects, and "cup" and "book" as objects that could cause this action. The movement paths of people and the changes in the positions of "cup" and "book" are plotted in Fig. 6. The positions of the dining table and chairs are also plotted to improve visibility as movement paths. The color-coded pathways based on the model diagram in Fig. 1b are shown in Fig. 7. Path1 is to walk up to "dining table" with "cup" and place it there. Path2 is to walk up to "dining table" and place it there. Path2 shows the path from "dining table" to "book." Path3 is the path from picking up "book" to walking to "dining table" and setting it down. After that, the position where the user is sitting on "chair" reading a book is path4.

4 Discussion

4.1 Discussion from verification 1

In Verification 1, we tried to identify objects by the distance between bounding box centers. Initially, we considered identifying which object a person is holding by determining the distance between the bounding box centers by a threshold value. A plot of the distance between the bounding box center of "cup" and "book" and the bounding box center of the human action is shown in Fig. 4. For each object, Fig. 5 shows the range of frames in which the person is actually holding the object and the distance between the action bounding box center and the object bounding box center in each frame.

From Fig. 5, it can be seen that in many cases the 2D distance is less than 100 when the object is actually held. Initially, we considered identifying which object a person is holding by judging the distance between bounding box centers by a threshold value. However, it is difficult to identify the target of the action by the threshold value because there are cases where the distance is greater than 100 even though the person is actually holding an object, and there are cases where the distance is less than 100 even when the person is not actually holding an object. This may be due to the fact that the size of each bounding box is not taken into account. In addition, it was difficult to distinguish the difference between what a person was touching and what was behind the person because of only 2D image. Therefore, we considered it necessary to consider the following situations in order to identify the target of a person's behavior.

- Taking into account the 3D distance between a person and an object
- Threshold setting considering the size of each bounding box of human actions and object bounding boxes

4.2 Discussion from Verification 2

Comparing the actual human path in Fig. 7 with the path model in Fig. 1b, it can be said that we were able to record human movements almost accurately. Looking at the paths of "cup" and "book," respectively, we can see that they follow the human motion. On the other hand, the trajectory of "cup" deviates significantly from the human's trajectory in the middle. This is thought to be due to the bending and stretching of the person's arms. Therefore, it is necessary to take into account the size of the person's body and the length of the arms and legs in order to recognize this kind of behavior. However, while trajectories are easy to observe when a person is moving with an object, changes in the 3D position of an object when a person is sitting in a chair are more minute than when moving.

Therefore, in order to observe the interaction between a person and an object when the person is stationary, it is necessary to consider the object to be focused on for each action, rather than only the coordinate change.

4.3 Discussion for the Future Work

Through these verifications and discussions, the following three points can be identified as future issues to be addressed in order to automatically generate human action sentences, focusing also on the object to be acted upon.

- Consideration of the respective sizes of the human behavior bounding box and object bounding box
- Identification of the target object of the action considering the nature of the action and the meaning of the object
- Changes in sentence expression depending on the combination of actions and objects

First, the search for an object to be acted upon should be performed by considering human behavior and the size of the object's bounding box. Even if the distance between the bounding box centers is large, the situation may be that the person is holding an object with arms extended. In the future, increasing the number of behaviors to be observed will improve the accuracy of the retrieval of objects to be acted upon, taking the size of the bounding box into consideration.

Next, it is necessary to consider the nature of the action and the meaning of the object. For example, in the case of "carry/hold," only objects that can be held in the hand may be the target of the action. For example, in the case of "carry/hold", only objects that can be carried by hand may be the target of the action, and in the case of "sit", a chair or sofa may be the target. By calculating the likelihood of each object in a person's surroundings being the target of each of these types of actions, it is possible to identify the target object of the action in combination with location information.

Finally, after identifying the target object, it is important to consider the combination of action expressions and objects in order to generate action sentences as natural expressions. For example, when combining "sit" with an object name to generate an action sentence, "on" is expected to be added in front of the object name. On the other hand, when multiple actions are being performed simultaneously, it is difficult to identify the target object and automatically generate natural sentences. In the future, we will observe various types of multiple actions being performed at the same time and search for a method to fuse location information with the results of action detection.

5 Conclusion

In this paper, we conducted a series of validations to fuse the results of action detection and object detection for the purpose of automatic generation of human action sentences. In Verification 1, the 2D distance between the center of the action detection bounding box and the center of the object detection bounding box was calculated, and the difference in distance was observed when the actual object was being accessed and when it was not. In Verification 2, we observed the 3D position coordinates of the person and the object in an overhead view to confirm the positional relationship in the video with the person holding the object in his/her hand. Through these verifications, we clarified issues for automatic generation of human action sentences by fusing the results of action and object detection. In the future, we aim to automatically generate human action sentences with the following points in mind, and to estimate a person's action intention based on the action history sentences.

- Search for objects for action considering the size of the action detection bounding box and object detection bounding box
- Identification of objects subject to action based on the nature of the action and the meaning of the object and adjustment of the expression of the behavior sequence

References

1. Mukherjee, D., Gupta, K., Chang, L.H., Najjaran, H.: A survey of robot learning strategies for human-robot collaboration in industrial settings. Robot. Comput.-Integr. Manuf. **73**, 102231 (2022)
2. Wei, D., Chen, L., Zhao, L., Zhou, H., Huang, B.: A vision-based measure of environmental effects on inferring human intention during human robot interaction. IEEE Sens. J. **22**(5), 4246–4256 (2022)
3. Zhang, Y., Doyle, T.: Integrating intention-based systems in human-robot interaction: a scoping review of sensors, algorithms, and trust. Front. Robot. AI **10** (2023)
4. Qiu, Y., Nagasaki, Y., Hara, K., Kataoka, H., Suzuki, R., Iwata, K.: VirtualHome action genome: a simulated spatio-temporal scene graph dataset with consistent relationship labels. In: 2023 IEEE/CVF Winter Conference on Applications of Computer Vision (WACV), pp. 3340–3349, USA (2023)
5. Nicole, R., Brendan, T., Dylan, C., Dana, K., Peter, C.: Robotic vision for human-robot interaction and collaboration: a survey and systematic review. ACM Trans. Hum.-Rob. Interact. **12**(1), 1–66 (2023)
6. Mazcaro, E.V., Sliwowski, D., Lee, D.: HOI4ABOT: human-object interaction anticipation for human intention reading collaborative roBOTs. In: 7th Conference on Robot Learning, pp. 1111–1130. PMLR (2023)
7. Norman, D.: The Design of Everyday Things (Revised and Expanded Edition). Cambridge, London (2013)
8. Zhang, H., Zhang, W., Qu, H., Liu, T.: Enhancing human-centered dynamic scene understanding via multiple LLMs collaborated reasoning. arXiv:2403.10107 (2024)
9. MMAction2 Contributors: OpenMMLab's Next Generation Video Understanding Toolbox and Benchmark (2020). https://github.com/open-mmlab/mmaction2
10. Terven, J.R., Córdova-Esparza, D.M.: A comprehensive review of YOLO architectures in computer vision: from YOLOv1 to YOLOv8 and YOLO-NAS. Mach. Learn. Knowl. Extract. **5**(4), 1680–1716 (2023)

Author Index

B. Kim (Ed.): IW-FCV 2025, CCIS 2769, pp. 285–286, 2026.
https://doi.org/10.1007/978-981-95-4578-0

MIX
Papier aus verantwortungsvollen Quellen
Paper from responsible sources
FSC® C105338

If you have any concerns about our products, you can contact us on
ProductSafety@springernature.com

In case Publisher is established outside the EU, the EU authorized representative is:
Springer Nature Customer Service Center GmbH
Europaplatz 3, 69115 Heidelberg, Germany

Printed by Libri Plureos GmbH
in Hamburg, Germany